Changing World Economic Order in the Post-Pandemic Period

Sushanta Kumar Mahapatra
The ICFAI Foundation for Higher Education (IFHE) (Deemed), Hyderabad, India

Vishal Sarin
Lovely Professional University, India

A volume in the Advances in Finance, Accounting, and Economics (AFAE) Book Series

IGI Global
PUBLISHER of TIMELY KNOWLEDGE

Published in the United States of America by
IGI Global
Business Science Reference (an imprint of IGI Global)
701 E. Chocolate Avenue
Hershey PA, USA 17033
Tel: 717-533-8845
Fax: 717-533-8661
E-mail: cust@igi-global.com
Web site: http://www.igi-global.com

Library of Congress Cataloging-in-Publication Data

Names: Sarin, Vishal, editor.
Title: Changing world economic order in the post-pandemic period / Vishal Sarin and Sushanta Kumar Mahapatra editors.
Description: Hershey, PA : Business Science Reference, [2021] | Includes bibliographical references and index. | Summary: "This book analyzes the impact of Covid-19 on the global economy and evaluates the performance of various countries during the pandemic and post-pandemic period"-- Provided by publisher.
Identifiers: LCCN 2020042229 (print) | LCCN 2020042230 (ebook) | ISBN 9781799868965 (hardcover) | ISBN 9781799868972 (softcover) | ISBN 9781799868989 (ebook)
Subjects: LCSH: International trade. | COVID-19 (Disease)--Economic aspects. | Economic history--21st century.
Classification: LCC HF1379 .H3648 2021 (print) | LCC HF1379 (ebook) | DDC 330.9--dc23
LC record available at https://lccn.loc.gov/2020042229
LC ebook record available at https://lccn.loc.gov/2020042230

This book is published in the IGI Global book series Advances in Finance, Accounting, and Economics (AFAE) (ISSN: 2327-5677; eISSN: 2327-5685)

British Cataloguing in Publication Data
A Cataloguing in Publication record for this book is available from the British Library.

For electronic access to this publication, please contact: eresources@igi-global.com.

Advances in Finance, Accounting, and Economics (AFAE) Book Series

Ahmed Driouchi
Al Akhawayn University, Morocco

ISSN:2327-5677
EISSN:2327-5685

Mission

In our changing economic and business environment, it is important to consider the financial changes occurring internationally as well as within individual organizations and business environments. Understanding these changes as well as the factors that influence them is crucial in preparing for our financial future and ensuring economic sustainability and growth.

The **Advances in Finance, Accounting, and Economics (AFAE)** book series aims to publish comprehensive and informative titles in all areas of economics and economic theory, finance, and accounting to assist in advancing the available knowledge and providing for further research development in these dynamic fields.

Coverage

- Labor Economics
- Interest Rates and Annuities
- International Economics
- Applied Finance
- Economics of Migration and Spatial Mobility
- Stock Market
- Corporate Finance
- Microfinance
- Wages and Employment
- E-Accounting

IGI Global is currently accepting manuscripts for publication within this series. To submit a proposal for a volume in this series, please contact our Acquisition Editors at Acquisitions@igi-global.com or visit: http://www.igi-global.com/publish/.

The Advances in Finance, Accounting, and Economics (AFAE) Book Series (ISSN 2327-5677) is published by IGI Global, 701 E. Chocolate Avenue, Hershey, PA 17033-1240, USA, www.igi-global.com. This series is composed of titles available for purchase individually; each title is edited to be contextually exclusive from any other title within the series. For pricing and ordering information please visit http://www.igi-global.com/book-series/advances-finance-accounting-economics/73685. Postmaster: Send all address changes to above address.

Titles in this Series

For a list of additional titles in this series, please visit: www.igi-global.com/book-series

Perspectives on Blockchain Technology and Responsible Investing
Sonal Trivedi (Chitkara Business School, Chitkara University, India) Rashmi Aggarwal (Chitkara Business School, Chitkara University, India) and Gurmeet Singh (The University of the South Pacific,Fiji)
Business Science Reference • © 2023 • 317pp • H/C (ISBN: 9781668483619) • US $250.00

Mainstreaming Cryptocurrency and the Future of Digital Finance
Hamed Taherdoost (University Canada West, Cnada)
Business Science Reference • © 2023 • 330pp • H/C (ISBN: 9781668483688) • US $250.00

Handbook of Research on Designing Sustainable Supply Chains to Achieve a Circular Economy
Yanamandra Ramakrishna (Skyline University College, UAE) and Siti Norida Wahab (Universiti Teknologi MARA, Malaysia)
Business Science Reference • © 2023 • 697pp • H/C (ISBN: 9781668476642) • US $295.00

Emerging Insights on the Relationship Between Cryptocurrencies and Decentralized Economic Models
Dhanapal Kesavan (SRM Institute of Science and Technology, India) and N. Mari Anand (Department of Business Studies, University of Technology and Applied Sciences, Salalah, Oman)
Business Science Reference • © 2023 • 256pp • H/C (ISBN: 9781668456910) • US $250.00

Exploring Business Ecosystems and Innovation Capacity Building in Global Economics
Mihir Joshi (Banasthali Vidyapith University, India) Mohsen Brahmi (University of Sfax, Tunisia) Luigi Aldieri (University of Salerno, Italy) and Concetto Paolo Vinci (University of Salerno, Italy)
Business Science Reference • © 2023 • 393pp • H/C (ISBN: 9781668467664) • US $250.00

Accounting and Financial Reporting Challenges for Government, Non-Profits, and the Private Sector
Fábio Albuquerque (Instituto Politécnico de Lisboa, Portugal) and Paula Gomes dos Santos (Instituto Politécnico de Lisboa, Portugal)
Business Science Reference • © 2023 • 320pp • H/C (ISBN: 9781668472934) • US $240.00

Concepts, Cases, and Regulations in Financial Fraud and Corruption
Abdul Rafay (University of Management and Technology, Pakistan)
Business Science Reference • © 2023 • 419pp • H/C (ISBN: 9781668450079) • US $250.00

IGI Global
PUBLISHER of TIMELY KNOWLEDGE

701 East Chocolate Avenue, Hershey, PA 17033, USA
Tel: 717-533-8845 x100 • Fax: 717-533-8661
E-Mail: cust@igi-global.com • www.igi-global.com

Table of Contents

Foreword xv

Preface xvi

Acknowledgment xix

Introduction xx

Chapter 1
Surviving Pandemics in the Long Run: Need for Sustainability in a COVID-19 World Economy 1
Shreyansh Budhia, The George Washington University, USA
Sushanta Kumar Mahapatra, The ICFAI Foundation for Higher Education (IFHE) (Deemed), Hyderabad, India

Chapter 2
Customer Behavioral Intention Towards Internet Banking During COVID-19: Empirical Evidence From Nepal 18
Roshan Adhikari, Quest International College, Pokhara University, Nepal
Niranjan Devkota, Kathmandu Model College, Tribhuvan University, Nepal
Krishna Dhakal, Quest International College, Pokhara University, Nepal
Surendra Mahato, Nepal Commerce Campus, Tribhuvan University, Nepal
Udaya Raj Paudel, Quest International College, Pokhara University, Nepal
Shila Mishra, National Planning Commission, Government of Nepal, Nepal

Chapter 3
Job Satisfaction and Work Productivity During the COVID-19 Pandemic: Involuntary Work From Home of Higher Education in Indonesia 39
Ida Nyoman Basmantra, Universitas Pendidikan Nasional, Indonesia
Aprilia Kusumaningtyas, Bina Nusantara University, Indonesia
Mochammad Firmansyah, Bina Nusantara University, Indonesia
Sevenpri Candra, Bina Nusantara University, Indonesia

Chapter 4
Post-COVID-19 World and Trajectories of a Crumbling World Order 63
Keshab Chandra Ratha, Gangadhar Meher University, India
Sushanta Kumar Mahapatra, The ICFAI Foundation for Higher Education (IFHE) (Deemed), Hyderabad, India

Chapter 5
Nutritional Security of Marginalised Groups in the Context of COVID-19: A Discourse 77
Sridevi Gummadi, University of Hyderabad, India
Balaji Patturi, University of Hyderabad, India
Priya Shanmugam, Mount Carmel College, India

Chapter 6
A Systematic Review on Indian Food Security Systems and Food Assistance Programmes (FAPs) in the Context of the COVID-19 Pandemic 89
Sugandh Arora, Sharda University, India
Tawheed Nabi, Lovely Professional University, India
Vishal Sarin, Lovely Professional University, India

Chapter 7
Curbing Seasonal Migration and Debt Bondage Post COVID-19 Pandemic in Western Odisha, India 107
Lopamudra Mishra, Sambalpur University, India

Chapter 8
Developing Strategies for Restoring the Affected Labor Force in the Post-COVID-19 Period in Rwanda 124
Eric Ruvuna, Kibogora Polytechnic, Rwanda
Celestin Pierre Rutayisire, Volgograd State University, Russia
Innocent Gahamanyi, Christian University of Rwanda, Rwanda
Fidele Tubanambazi Mweruli, Kibogora Polytechnic, Rwanda

Chapter 9
Digital Education During COVID-19 in Odisha: Challenges and Prospects 147
Minati Sahoo, Central University of Odisha, India
Karishma Rana, Central University of Odisha, India

Chapter 10
Impact of COVID-19 on the Fiscal Health of India: A Sub-National Analysis From Odisha State .. 166
Sushanta Kumar Mahapatra, The ICFAI Foundation for Higher Education (IFHE) (Deemed), Hyderabad, India
Pareswar Sahu, Barpali College, Barpali of Sambalpur University, India

Chapter 11
Indian Agriculture During COVID-19: Prospectus and Challenges ... 183
Rajender S. Godara, Lovely Professional University, India
Durafshan Jaihon Fetrat, Department of Business and Administration, Economics Faculty, Takhar University, Takhar, Afghanistan
Azatullah Nazari, Department of Business Administration and Economics Faculty, Takhar University, Takhar, Afghanistan

Chapter 12
Inter-Relationship of Health, Communication, and Commerce: A Study of the Healthcare Sector in Odisha, India ... 201
Sourav Gupta, Central University of Odisha, India
Minati Sahoo, Central University of Odisha, India

Chapter 13
New Normal Manufacturing Industry Post-Pandemic 2020 ... 220
Muskaan Arora, Thapar School of Liberal Arts and Sciences, Thapar University, Patiala, India
Archana Goel, Chitkara University, India

Chapter 14
The Socio-Economic Impact of the Pandemic on the Micro-, Small-, and Medium-Scale Enterprises ... 233
Ca Shilpa Vasant Bhide, Department of Management Sciences, Savitribai Phule Pune University, India

Chapter 15
Weavers' Livelihoods and the COVID-19 Pandemic: An Analysis of Sambalpuri Handloom, Odisha, India ... 248
Tushar Kanti Das, Sambalpur University, India

Compilation of References ... 265

About the Contributors ... 296

Index ... 303

Detailed Table of Contents

Foreword xv

Preface xvi

Acknowledgment xix

Introduction xx

Chapter 1
Surviving Pandemics in the Long Run: Need for Sustainability in a COVID-19 World Economy 1
Shreyansh Budhia, The George Washington University, USA
Sushanta Kumar Mahapatra, The ICFAI Foundation for Higher Education (IFHE) (Deemed), Hyderabad, India

In this chapter, the authors suggest that the world economy, under its current state of things, cannot function if it decides not to bring about a change in its key areas of operation. Based on this finding, the authors argue for a need to mainstream environmental, social, and governance (ESG)-related environmental metrices for goods and services developed by private and public institutions. They emphasize the need for the inclusion of an environmental clause in international trade agreements to account for sustainability. The chapter describes some areas of the gross domestic product (GDP) where sustainability can be included to account for our modern-day environmental problems. It stresses the need for implementation of carbon taxes and carbon tariffs to account for global emissions. The authors critically analyse the Paris Agreement and argue why it is not enough. They introduce the concept of climate restoration and brief on the scope of business opportunities carbon negative investments can provide investors with.

Chapter 2
Customer Behavioral Intention Towards Internet Banking During COVID-19: Empirical Evidence From Nepal 18
Roshan Adhikari, Quest International College, Pokhara University, Nepal
Niranjan Devkota, Kathmandu Model College, Tribhuvan University, Nepal
Krishna Dhakal, Quest International College, Pokhara University, Nepal
Surendra Mahato, Nepal Commerce Campus, Tribhuvan University, Nepal
Udaya Raj Paudel, Quest International College, Pokhara University, Nepal
Shila Mishra, National Planning Commission, Government of Nepal, Nepal

Providing banking services through digital platforms is an emerging channel of service delivery by commercial banks to their customers. especially in a developing country such as Nepal. However, this study aims to determine the customers' behavioral intention towards internet banking usage during COVID-19 in Kathmandu Valley. Data were evaluated quantitatively by using both descriptive and inferential statistics where questionnaire was deigned to collect the data and were entered in a KOBO Toolbox. SEM was used to analyze the relationships from 279 responses from Kathmandu Valley. Findings revealed perceived ease of use and perceived usefulness play a significant role in the behavioral intention towards internet banking during COVID-19, which fits TAM theory. Customers must experience better use of internet banking services without any interruptions, and a revolution in internet services is required in the Nepalese banking industry.

Chapter 3
Job Satisfaction and Work Productivity During the COVID-19 Pandemic: Involuntary Work From Home of Higher Education in Indonesia 39
Ida Nyoman Basmantra, Universitas Pendidikan Nasional, Indonesia
Aprilia Kusumaningtyas, Bina Nusantara University, Indonesia
Mochammad Firmansyah, Bina Nusantara University, Indonesia
Sevenpri Candra, Bina Nusantara University, Indonesia

The COVID-19 pandemic disrupted the nature of work. Involuntary work from home (IWFH), another form of telework, is increasingly promoted in sectors as a means to ensure continuity of operations in an emergency situation like a pandemic. This study includes the exploration of the relationship between involuntary work from home, communication functions, work-life balance, and its effect on work productivity and employee job satisfaction during this COVID-19 pandemic outbreak in the work situation of 100 employees at the higher educational institutions in Indonesia. The collected data of questionnaires were processed using the SEM method using the SmartPLS program. This study finds some critical factors shaping the experiences and outcomes of IWFH in pandemic situations. The success of work management depends on the communication function between employees to job satisfaction for work productivity.

Chapter 4
Post-COVID-19 World and Trajectories of a Crumbling World Order 63
Keshab Chandra Ratha, Gangadhar Meher University, India
Sushanta Kumar Mahapatra, The ICFAI Foundation for Higher Education (IFHE) (Deemed), Hyderabad, India

The pandemic poses the severest jolt to the U.S.-led international order, including the retraction of the United States from previously held global leadership. The extraordinary economic and medical response in the developed and opulent countries is simply not at hand for many developing countries. With COVID-19, international and multilateral bodies are not anywhere on the scene. Regional institutions such as the AU (African Union) and South Asian Association for Regional Cooperation (SAARC) are often treated as weak, lacking the habit of cooperation and under-resourced to address the pandemic. Globally, societies could turn into more self-seeking and inward-looking eventuating in further pushback against liberal policies in respect of migration and refugees. Absence of basic resources, lack of well-functioning and efficient healthcare systems, and the dearth of well-organised communication channels indicate inefficiency in the war against COVID-19. A concerted effort across each and every sector and discipline responsible for health is urgently called for in this grim hour.

Chapter 5
Nutritional Security of Marginalised Groups in the Context of COVID-19: A Discourse................... 77
Sridevi Gummadi, University of Hyderabad, India
Balaji Patturi, University of Hyderabad, India
Priya Shanmugam, Mount Carmel College, India

Malnutrition in all its forms has become the leading cause of poor health and death worldwide. The 2020 Global Nutrition Report stresses that the need to address malnutrition in all its forms by tackling injustices in food and health systems is now more urgent than ever. Over 820 million people went to bed hungry even before the COVID-19 pandemic, of which 110 million people were living in acute food insecurity. According to the World Food Programme, 135 million suffer from acute hunger largely due to man-made conflicts, climate change, and economic downturns. The COVID-19 pandemic could now double that number, putting an additional 130 million (total 265 million) people at risk of suffering acute hunger by the end of 2020. India is ranked 102 out of 117 countries the lowest in South Asia. Surprisingly Bangladesh, Nepal, and Pakistan are performing better in terms of GHI. In this chapter, the authors analyse the nutritional security of marginalised groups in Andhra Pradesh and Telangna State.

Chapter 6
A Systematic Review on Indian Food Security Systems and Food Assistance Programmes (FAPs) in the Context of the COVID-19 Pandemic 89
Sugandh Arora, Sharda University, India
Tawheed Nabi, Lovely Professional University, India
Vishal Sarin, Lovely Professional University, India

The COVID-19 pandemic has shaken the global economy, where India is the most affected economy. The crisis has an insignificant impact on the 2nd Sustainable Development Goal (SDG) to get rid of desire by 2030. The most deprived society may have a significant threat of poor health and malnutrition as a society cannot access nutritious and sustainable diets. Thus, pandemic generates an income shock projected to increase unemployment, poverty, and household food insecurity. Consequently, the purpose of this study is to acquire the relevant evidence from literature about food security and food assistance programmes. A systematic review was conducted across Academia, EBSCO, Google Scholar, JSTORE, Pub Med, Springer, and Scopus, and a search was performed between March-August 2020 for the accretion. Food security systems and FAPs would be analyzed more comprehensively and suggests the prerequisite for the central and state government to carefully utilize both non-governmental and administrative interventions to drop the hunger rate and improve the food security status.

Chapter 7
Curbing Seasonal Migration and Debt Bondage Post COVID-19 Pandemic in Western Odisha, India 107
Lopamudra Mishra, Sambalpur University, India

The COVID-19 pandemic has delivered a global economic shock of enormous magnitude. Provision of livelihoods to the retuned migrants is the important challenge faced by various state governments in India. Western Odisha continues to depict a picture of chronic underdevelopment. In this region, the type of migration that dominates is seasonal or circular migration. The aim of the present analysis is to investigate the factors responsible for the seasonal migration of debt bondage (Dadan) from the Western Odisha. The specific objectives of the study are to know the factors responsible for distress migration and to explore how debt-bondage is operating in the economic system. The present study has observed that seasonal migrants of Western Odisha are more likely to be from those households who are poor, socially disadvantaged, less educated, indebted, and landless.

Chapter 8
Developing Strategies for Restoring the Affected Labor Force in the Post-COVID-19 Period in Rwanda........ 124
Eric Ruvuna, Kibogora Polytechnic, Rwanda
Celestin Pierre Rutayisire, Volgograd State University, Russia
Innocent Gahamanyi, Christian University of Rwanda, Rwanda
Fidele Tubanambazi Mweruli, Kibogora Polytechnic, Rwanda

This study assessed the impact of the COVID-19 pandemic on labor force and advocated the main strategies to be implemented to restore the affected areas of labor force in Rwanda. The study was guided by three objectives: to explore the status of labor force trends before and during COVID-19 in Rwanda and its implications to the Rwandan economy, to assess the factors that led to reduction in labor force in Rwanda, and thirdly, to determine the strategies to recommend the Government of Rwanda (GoR) to restore the affected labor force sub-sector in the post-COVID-19 period. The trend analyses of the labor force before and during COVID-19 pandemic were drawn and revealed that there were changes in labor force before and during COVID-19 pandemic. Statistics were employed to the data set from National Institute of Statistics of Rwanda (NISR). The multiple regression model was used to express the GDP as a function of employment rate and unemployment rate reveals that the unemployment rate has governed the period of COVID-19 pandemic, and it was statistically significant in contributing negatively to GDP.

Chapter 9
Digital Education During COVID-19 in Odisha: Challenges and Prospects..................................... 147
Minati Sahoo, Central University of Odisha, India
Karishma Rana, Central University of Odisha, India

One of the worsts hit by the COVID-19 pandemic has been the education sector, which has led to the closure of all educational institutions. Hence, an effort has been made in this study to examine various issues and challenges of digital education in Odisha. The study found that most of the educational institutions in Odisha have gone for online teaching. Additionally, to promote e-learning, various digital platforms have been provided by the state and central governments. But digital education in Odisha is facing many challenges like uneven access of internet and digital gadgets, low tele density, lack of support structures, low computer literacy, and less competency. Additionally, power cut, financial constraints, lack of parent's involvement in the process are some of the issues that are adding woes to the effectiveness of digital education in teaching and learning process. Hence, there is need to evolve a judicious mix of normal and digital education with revised curricular post-COVID-19 to provide more learning opportunities for the all-around development of the students.

Chapter 10
Impact of COVID-19 on the Fiscal Health of India: A Sub-National Analysis From Odisha State .. 166
Sushanta Kumar Mahapatra, The ICFAI Foundation for Higher Education (IFHE) (Deemed), Hyderabad, India
Pareswar Sahu, Barpali College, Barpali of Sambalpur University, India

With the emergence of COVID-19 within Odisha, preventive measures like partial or total lockdown of the state have been undertaken by the government to control its spread despite the provision of health-related infrastructure. Among the 14 major states of India, Odisha is a poor state. However, the spread of the pandemic has become massive. In this context, this chapter attempts to examine the fiscal health of India at the sub-national level from the state of Odisha. The revenue generation capacity declines to a larger extent while expenditure responsibilities in terms of health expenditures expand tremendously. Consequently, the state has to face serious difficulties in sustaining its fiscal balance. This chapter observes that the fiscal health of the state deteriorated to a larger extent during the lockdown period than the pre-lockdown period. In such a critical situation, the state needs to plan effective strategies to raise the level of income through fiscal policy allowing economic activities compromising the sanitization measures of the pandemic.

Chapter 11
Indian Agriculture During COVID-19: Prospectus and Challenges.. 183
Rajender S. Godara, Lovely Professional University, India
Durafshan Jaihon Fetrat, Department of Business and Administration, Economics Faculty, Takhar University, Takhar, Afghanistan
Azatullah Nazari, Department of Business Administration and Economics Faculty, Takhar University, Takhar, Afghanistan

The purpose of this chapter is to summarize the initial evidence based on various research articles and sources. The results show that the effects of the agricultural epidemic can be categorized into supply, demand, labor, food security, food safety, and trade. COVID-19 by affecting the supply chain, demand and liquidity, firms, and by affecting the supply of labor, consumption of goods, and services and especially by reducing the income of consumers and producers of agricultural products in the short- and long-term affects the household economy as well as influences the economy of the agricultural sector. The market for some products in other countries has also been weakened, and part of the export of agricultural products has been affected both directly and indirectly. This chapter examines the impact of the Corona crisis on India's agricultural sector. The effect of the shock caused by the corona crisis on the supply chain of agricultural products, including consumption, production, distribution, and trade, as well as other economic effects are examined.

Chapter 12
Inter-Relationship of Health, Communication, and Commerce: A Study of the Healthcare Sector in Odisha, India 201
Sourav Gupta, Central University of Odisha, India
Minati Sahoo, Central University of Odisha, India

The Covid-19 has given a new dimension to the healthcare industry of India. The pandemic has exposed the limited health capacity of the states including Odisha. Hence an attempt has been made to evaluate the performance of healthcare services in Odisha. Further, it will also analyze the content of the advertising campaign used to popularize the health packages. It will critically study the communication approach, design and angles of the campaign and find out how they have been prepared to influence the people with pre-conceived desired aims. The study will be based on the secondary sources. The study infers that the performance of the government health sector is not up to the mark and the private hospitals have manipulated with the guidelines to attract the people through their campaign. Hence, measures to be taken to improve healthcare sector and to regulate manipulations by the private sector.

Chapter 13
New Normal Manufacturing Industry Post-Pandemic 2020 220
Muskaan Arora, Thapar School of Liberal Arts and Sciences, Thapar University, Patiala, India
Archana Goel, Chitkara University, India

Manufacturing industry plays a paramount role in the world economy, accounting for almost 16% of the global GDP in 2018. Manufacturing has been identified as the key driver of dynamic growth and development of the country. The COVID-19 pandemic has caused immense devastation around the world. Due to the downturn in the manufacturing industry along with the factory blackout, the Coronavirus epidemic reduced the global FDI by 5 per cent -15 per cent. The aim of this chapter is to highlight the need to understate the vital role of manufacturing industry in the Indian context. It will further discuss and elaborate on the impact of the 2020 pandemic on the manufacturing industry and would suggest a framework to manufacturing industry how it can come back in a new normal position post-COVID-19 scenario. Manufacturers who acknowledge this new standard discussed in the present chapter and will operate on it will have enough growth opportunities and can have long-term sustainable success.

Chapter 14
The Socio-Economic Impact of the Pandemic on the Micro-, Small-, and Medium-Scale Enterprises 233
Ca Shilpa Vasant Bhide, Department of Management Sciences, Savitribai Phule Pune University, India

The micro small and medium scale industry in India is an important sector, as it has contributed tremendously to the economic as well as social development. It has not only encouraged entrepreneurship but has also been instrumental in generating employment. The sector supports large-scale industries as it offers a wide range of products and services. The Covid 19 pandemic is having an impact on the sector such as loss of profit and revenue, loss of employment, and working capital problems. The chapter covers the impact in three stages: pre-pandemic, during the lock down, post-lock down and post-pandemic. It studies the remedial measures undertaken to revive and sustain the sector. It traces the risks, challenges, and opportunities for the sector. The chapter focuses on the journey of the MSMEs Sector from before the pandemic to the current situation and tries to analyse what lies ahead.

Chapter 15
Weavers' Livelihoods and the COVID-19 Pandemic: An Analysis of Sambalpuri Handloom, Odisha, India 248
Tushar Kanti Das, Sambalpur University, India

Sambalpuri Handloom weavers of Western Odisha are known for their rich skill, creativity, and innovative designs. Steady decline in the earnings has resulted in the migration of weavers both professionally and geographically. Economic crisis is forcing these weavers to face livelihood crisis. The weavers who have created history and brought glory by their rich artistry are being forced to change their livelihood. The present study has been undertaken in sixteen clusters of four districts of Western Odisha. It has been observed that the role played by the businessman (middleman) is quite important. Though the price of the product is quite high, the weavers are not satisfied with the emoluments amounts that they receive. The actual benefits from marketing of this handloom are accruing to the middlemen rather than the weavers. The COVID -19 pandemic and economic shutdown has broken the supply chain of both the backward and forward linkage of the Sambalpuri handloom industry. Necessary policy should be made both by the central and state governments to rescue these handloom weavers.

Compilation of References 265

About the Contributors 296

Index 303

Foreword

World Economic Order in the Post-Pandemic Period edited by Prof. Sushanta Kumar Mahapatra and Prof. Vishal Sarin is a resourceful compilation of articles that discuss impact of the COVID-19 on the global and regional economy using a variety of research methods.

The authors of the chapters emphasize on the most recent challenges of the COVID-19 outbreak covering different issues relating to changing world economic order in the post-pandemic period. With the world economy facing a roller-coaster ride during the pandemic and even after that, the confusion that still lurks in various sectors regarding the present and future situations needs to be clearly analysed along with facts. The authors have reflected on different dimensions of the society that have practically impacted the life of everyone across the globe. The topics have touched almost every aspect starting from common people to the global political and economic arena.

The editors and authors look at various policies and practices that have been put in place, and could be put in place such as globalisation, fiscal health, sustainability, healthcare, digital education, nutritional security, food security, the micro, small and medium enterprises, labour, migration, livelihood, and other related issues.

I highly recommend this book to those in government and academia who work in the area of international trade and development strategies. The editors should be complimented in drawing together the large number of authors from various regions, representing respected institutions, universities, and organizations, who made this book possible. The variety of talent, expertise, and experience on wide scope of topics, make this book a unique collection of information and analysis, and a valuable resource for anyone studying global economy and development.

To sum it up, this book is a handy collection of study material to see the global changes from a better perspective.

S. Mahendra Dev
The ICFAI Foundation for Higher Education (IFHE) (Deemed), Hyderabad, India & Institute for Development Studies, Visakhapatnam, India

Preface

Post COVID-19, the world shall never be the same as it used to be. Pandemic not only shattered many assumptions pertaining to Governance, global R&D expenditure and its orientation, self-professed economic developments and growth but also challenged our preparedness to any untoward challenge faced by human civilization in the most recent era where science and technology reached zenith. On the economic front, irrespective of the nature of the economy, the world stands still and the word "Lockdown" brought humans to a "new normal." To suppress the spread of COVID-19, many countries resorted to partially or full closure of their borders and restricted the movement of people. These restrictions put the world on "mandatory quarantine" mode. Mandatory quarantine restricts labor mobility, and workplace closure which later converted into supply shocks in the economy as these measures impaired the economy's production capacity, disrupting supplies. This later spilled over to the demand side as people were locked down in their homes and workers were laid off and lost income. Lowered tourist arrivals, receipts and lower goods trade also jeopardized global trade. This uncalled-for disruption posed many new challenges for policy makers to formulate appropriate macroeconomic policy response and also provide them the opportunity to ponder upon the preparedness of countries in terms of health facilities; appropriately compensating human resource; how to cushion immediate and severe economic shocks and to still maintain the livelihood of the society as a whole. Ever since, 30th January 2020, the day World Health Organization (WHO) declared the coronavirus outbreak, the governments across the world adopted an array of fiscal and monetary stimulus packages which included (a) provide cash handouts to keep jobs or provide goods and services; (b) support businesses via tax cuts, provision of credit and services; and (c) provide market liquidity support through various market instruments. In this context, Asian Development Bank (ADB) identified five types of stabilization or stimulus policies which governments can follow to minimize the economic impact of Covid -19. These policy measures include (a) support for the normal functioning of money market and short-term finance; (b) encouraging private credit creation; (c) direct lending to the non-financial sector including businesses, households, and local governments; (d) equity claims on the private sector; (e) direct support to income and/or revenue.

As per Asian Development Outlook (ADO) 2020's COVID-19 impact assessment report, COVID-19 will impact global GDP from \$5.8 trillion to \$8.8 trillion, i.e., 6.4% to 9.7% of global GDP. But on factoring in the policy response from the government—including direct intervention and revenue—the COVID-19 impact could be reduced to \$3.4 trillion to \$5.4 trillion under a long-term containment scenario. As per ADO, without policy response, output losses could reach \$8.8 trillion, job losses 242 million, and forgone labor income \$1.8 trillion. These will be difficult to recoup. Moreover, under the prevailing circumstances one cannot ignore the possibility of financial crisis, if the pandemic could not be contained in time.

Policymakers across the world are facing many dilemmas to face the unprecedented twin challenges of saving the health of the nation while maintaining the wealth of the nation. Raising productivity growth, enhancing businesses while maintaining health related instructions would be a herculean task which every government across the world would face. Upcoming era would seek a higher use of information and communication technology (ICT) in work engagements, delivery of health services, delivery of education and training, payment systems, trade and global supply chain. Compliance of social distancing policies and minimum disruption to economic activities would be a new mantra. Every activity which prompts economic growth like labor migration, health delivery system, imparting education to a wide spectrum of strata with varied challenges needs innovative solutions. The issue of social inclusion will become more prominent. Pandemic COVID-19 not only disrupted the economic activities, but it also bracketed out millions of children who were attaining education at subsidized pricing from government backed educational institutions but unable to afford ICT for bridging the gap in their education owing to the pandemic.

In Chapter 1, "Surviving Pandemics in the Long Run: Need for Sustainability in a COVID-19 World Economy," Shreyansh Budhia and Sushanta Kumar Mahapatra describe some areas of the Gross Domestic Product (GDP) where sustainability can be included to account for our modern-day environmental problems. It stresses the need for implementation of carbon taxes and carbon tariffs to account for global emissions. The authors critically analyse the Paris Agreement and argues on why it is not enough. They introduce the concept of climate restoration and give a brief on the scope of business opportunities carbon negative investments can provide investors with. In Chapter 2 on "Customers' Behavioral Intention Towards Internet Banking During COVID-19: Empirical Evidence From Nepal" Roshan Adhikari, Niranjan Devkota, Krishna Dhakal, Surendra Mahato, Udaya Raj Paudel, and Shila Mishra discussed the banking services through digital platforms is an emerging channel of service delivery by commercial banks to their customers especially, in a developing country such as Nepal. Their findings indicate that internet connection and heavy network traffic for operating internet banking are major challenges to internet banking.

In Chapter 3, "Job Satisfaction and Work Productivity During the COVID-19 Pandemic: Involuntary Work From Home of Higher Education in Indonesia," Ida Nyoman Basmantra, Aprilia Kusumaningtyas, Mochammad Firmansyah, and Sevenpri Candra discussed the exploration of the relationship between involuntary work from home, communication functions, work life balance, and its effect on work productivity and employee job satisfaction during this COVID-19 pandemic outbreak in the work situation of 100 employees at the higher educational institutions in Indonesia. In Chapter 4, "Post-Corona World and Trajectories of Crumbling World Order," Keshab Ratha and Sushanta Kumar Mahapatra emphasized that absence of basic resources, lack of well-functioning, and efficient healthcare system and the dearth of well-organised communication channels indicate inefficiency in the war against COVID-19.

In Chapter 5, "Nutritional Security of Marginalised Groups in the Context of COVID-19: A Discourse," Sridevi Gummadi, Balaji Patturi, and Priya Shanmugam analyse the nutritional security of marginalised groups in Andhra Pradesh and Telangna State of India. In Chapter 6, "A Systematic Review on Indian Food Security System and Food Assistance Programmes (FAPs) in the Context of the COVID-19 Pandemic," Sugandh Arora, Tawheed Nabi, and Vishal Sarin did a systematic review on Food security systems, FAPs and analyzed more comprehensively the prerequisite for the central and state government to carefully utilize both non-governmental and administrative interventions to drop the hunger rate and improve the food security status. In Chapter 7 on "Curbing Seasonal Migration and Debt Bondage Post COVID-19 Pandemic in Western Odisha, India" Lopamudra Mishra observed that seasonal migrants of western Odisha are more likely to be from those households who are poor, socially disadvantaged, less educated, indebted, and landless.

In Chapter 8, “Developing Strategies for Restoring the Affected Labor Force in the Post-COVID-19 Period in Rwanda,” Ruvuna Eric, Celestin Rutayisire, Innocent Gahamanyi and Fidele Mweruli assessed the impact of COVID-19 pandemic on labor force and advocate main strategies to be implemented to restore the affected areas of labor force in Rwanda. In Chapter 9, titled “Digital Education During COVID-19 in Odisha: Challenges and Prospects,” Minati Sahoo and Karishma Rana examine various issues and challenges of digital education in Odisha. Chapter 10, “Impact of COVID-19 in the Fiscal Health of India: A Sub-National Analysis From Odisha State,” has Sushanta Kumar Mahapatra and Pareswar Sahu examine the fiscal health of India at the sub-national level from the state of Odisha. This paper observes that the fiscal health of the state deteriorated to a larger extent during the lockdown period than the pre-lockdown period. In such a critical situation, the state needs to plan effective strategies to raise the level of income through fiscal policy allowing economic activities compromising the sanitization measures of the pandemic.

“Indian Agriculture During COVID-19: Prospectus and Challenges” is Chapter 11, and Rajender Singh, Durafshan Fetrat, and Azatullah Nazari examine the impact of the Corona crisis on India’s agricultural sector, focusing on the effect of the shock caused by the corona crisis on the supply chain of agricultural products, including consumption, production, distribution, and trade, as well as other economic effects are examined. Chapter 12 is “Inter-Relationship of Health, Communication, and Commerce: A Study of the Healthcare Sector in Odisha.” It analyzed the content of the advertising campaign used to popularize the health packages. Chapter 13 is “New Normal Manufacturing Industry Post Pandemic 2020: New Normal Manufacturing,” and Dr. Muskaan Arora and Archana Goel highlighted the vital role of the manufacturing industry in the Indian context and discussed the impact of Pandemic 2020 on the manufacturing industry by suggesting a framework how it can come back in a new normal position post COVID-19 scenario.

In Chapter 14, “The Socio-Economic Impact of the Pandemic on the Micro, Small, and Medium Scale Enterprises,” Ca Shilpa Bhide covers the impact in three stages: pre-pandemic, during the lock down, post lockdown and post pandemic. In Chapter 15, “Weavers’ Livelihoods and the COVID-19 Pandemic: An Analysis of Sambalpuri Handloom, Odisha, India,” Tushar Das emphasized that the COVID-19 pandemic and economic shutdown has broken the supply chain of both the backward and forward linkage of the Sambalpuri handloom industry.

In view of this, the present book provides scientific knowledge to the readers with a comprehensive overview of the impact of the COVID-19 on the global and regional economy. Hopefully this work will provide some tangible solutions and attainable perspectives to policymakers to fight a long battle with pandemic while keeping the morale of the people and economy high. This pandemic has put the idea of Globalization to test as nations are decoupling from globalization to serve their best interests. The editors believe that this publication will prove to be much sought in the institutions of higher learning, not only in developing countries but also in various parts of the world.

Sushanta Kumar Mahapatra
The ICFAI Foundation for Higher Education (IFHE) (Deemed), Hyderabad, India

Vishal Sarin
Lovely Professional University, India

Acknowledgment

The editors would like to acknowledge the help of all the people involved in this project and, more specifically, to the authors and reviewers that took part in the review process. Without their support, this book would not have become a reality. First, the editors would like to thank each one of the authors for their contributions. Our sincere gratitude goes to the chapter's authors who contributed their time and expertise to this book. Second, the editors wish to acknowledge the valuable contributions of the reviewers regarding the improvement of quality, coherence, and content presentation of chapters. Most of the authors also served as referees; we highly appreciate their double task. The editors are especially thankful to Dr. Chakravarthy Rangarajan for writing few words about the book and to Prof. S. Mahendra Dev for forwarding. The editors are grateful to Badri Narayanan Gopalakrishnan, Tanima Dutta, Angelina Olivas, Assistant Development Editor, Jocelynn Hessler, Senior Development Editor, Melissa Wagner, Lindsay Wertman and other editorial team at IGI-Global, for publishing these chapters in *Changing World Economic Order in the Post-Pandemic Period*. We are also grateful to the anonymous reviewers for their comments which led to substantial improvements and reorganizations of these chapters. We express our gratitude to the faculty, staff and management of Department of Economics, ICFAI School of Social Sciences, ICFAI Business School (IBS) Hyderabad, The ICFAI Foundation for Higher Education (IFHE), Deemed University, its constituent and Mittal School of Business, Lovely Professional University, India for extending all possible support and cooperation in carrying out this study. We thank them all.

Sushanta Kumar Mahapatra
The ICFAI Foundation for Higher Education (IFHE) (Deemed), Hyderabad, India

Vishal Sarin
Lovely Professional University, India

ABOUT THE BOOK

It is my pleasure to write about the book *Changing World Economic Order in the Post-Pandemic Period,* edited by Prof. Sushanta Kumar Mahapatra and Prof. Vishal Sarin. The editors and authors have discussed various issues and challenges relating to globalisation, fiscal health, sustainability, healthcare, digital education, nutritional security, food security, the micro, small and medium enterprises, labour, migration, livelihood and other related issues. The pandemic had an enormous impact on the economy. The human tragedy was high exposing the weaknesses of our health systems. Thus, the pandemic has several lessons to teach. All these issues and more are covered extensively by the authors of various chapters.

This book is recommended for use by university students, researchers, policymakers, economic actors, economists, government officials, academicians, and anyone interested in the impact of a pandemic on the global and regional economies and how to deal with such issues in the future. I complement the editors in bringing together such a large number of authors drawn from various universities and organizations. I hope that the diverse topics covered in the book will be of interest to scholars of institutions of higher learning not only from the developing countries but also the developed which has also suffered equally.

Chakravarthi Rangarajan
Madras School of Economics, India

Chapter 1
Surviving Pandemics in the Long Run:
Need for Sustainability in a COVID-19 World Economy

Shreyansh Budhia
The George Washington University, USA

Sushanta Kumar Mahapatra
https://orcid.org/0000-0002-0831-3621
The ICFAI Foundation for Higher Education (IFHE) (Deemed), Hyderabad, India

ABSTRACT

In this chapter, the authors suggest that the world economy, under its current state of things, cannot function if it decides not to bring about a change in its key areas of operation. Based on this finding, the authors argue for a need to mainstream environmental, social, and governance (ESG)-related environmental metrices for goods and services developed by private and public institutions. They emphasize the need for the inclusion of an environmental clause in international trade agreements to account for sustainability. The chapter describes some areas of the gross domestic product (GDP) where sustainability can be included to account for our modern-day environmental problems. It stresses the need for implementation of carbon taxes and carbon tariffs to account for global emissions. The authors critically analyse the Paris Agreement and argue why it is not enough. They introduce the concept of climate restoration and brief on the scope of business opportunities carbon negative investments can provide investors with.

DOI: 10.4018/978-1-7998-6896-5.ch001

INTRODUCTION

On November 17th 2019, a 55-year old man with a case of pneumonia allegedly came to doctors' attention in China's Wuhan (World Health Organization, 2020). The etiology, or the cause, perplexed them. One to five more similar cases popped up each day since then. And by December 20th, there were 60 confirmed cases of a pneumonia with an unknown cause (World Health Organization, 2020). Ten days later, the Wuhan Municipal Health Commission reported a cluster of cases of pneumonia. Eventually, by the end of the first week of January 2020, WHO reported that Chinese authorities had determined that the outbreak was caused by a novel coronavirus (World Health Organization, 2020).

Ever since then, the coronavirus outbreak has claimed 6.7 million lives worldwide as of February 7th 2023 (Worldometer, 2020). In countries like India and Brazil, total deaths have exceeded 500,000 people (Worldometer, 2020). The United States has seen more than 1.1 million casualties (Worldometer, 2020). Many European countries like Italy, Germany, Greece, and the UK have already experienced a third wave as of April 2021 (Worldometer, 2020).

The pandemic has also had a net negative impact on the global economy. The IMF, in early 2020, predicted that the global economy might witness a cumulative loss of over $12 trillion from Covid19 over the years 2020 and 2021 (Rebucci et al., 2020). The World Bank predicted that while emerging markets and developing economies might contract by 2.5% - their weakest growth rate in at least sixty years - advanced economies, counterintuitively, might shrink by 7 percent (Rebucci et al., 2020). Every major economic region in the world was projected to contract significantly. Many reports predicted that places like South Asia, and Sub Saharan Africa might contract by 2.7%, and 2.8% simultaneously (International Monetary Fund, 2020). Europe, Central Asia, and Latin America, however, were projected to contract by a larger value of 4.7% (International Monetary Fund, 2020). In fact, it is only East Asia and the Pacific that was predicted to register a net positive GDP expansion with a meagre growth rate of 0.5% (International Monetary Fund, 2020). And while GDP contractions from different economic regions might already ring bells of apprehension for most, reports predicted that independent nations might register even more severe economic consequences. OECD predicted that real GDP growth rates might contract for countries like Mexico, Italy, India, and the UK by more than 10%. For countries like Argentina and South Africa, this value was projected to be greater than 11% (International Monetary Fund, 2020). According to the World Bank, industries globally, ranging from energy and utilities, to healthcare, tourism, and commodities have gravely suffered as a consequence of the pandemic (McKinsey & Company, 2022). All these numbers were mostly proven later on in terms of severe economic recession in most listed economies. And while the world in 2020 and 2021 continued on betting for a vaccine, it had entirely managed to not care enough about the root cause of the problem.

Covid19 is one of several long-term consequences of running our modern economy in an unsustainable manner. The disease that spread due to unregulated trade in endangered wildlife and destruction of ecologically sensitive habitats is just one of several pandemics that have had similar environmental and zoonotic origins. According to Gebreyes et al, about 75% of emerging infectious diseases are zoonotic in nature accounting for billions of illnesses. These diseases, that usually originate from destruction of the environment or trading different species of wildlife, often have significant impact on lives of people and the health of different economies. A Scientific American article reports that zoonotic epidemics alone account for millions of deaths annually all across the globe. HIV, for example originated from Chimps in Central Africa, likely jumped to humans through consumption of bushmeat, or meat from wildlife, and continues to affect millions annually (Ashe, 2020). According to the Global HIV & AIDS statistics from the UN, in 2019, 1.7 million people became newly infected with HIV, 25.4 million were accessing antiretroviral therapy, 38 million were globally living with the virus, and 690,000 died from AIDS-related illnesses (Ashe, 2020). Since the start of the epidemic, 75.7 million people have become infected with the virus and 32.7 million have been declared dead. Ebola, another bushmeat born pandemic, has consistently shown a death rate ranging from 22% to 88% with an average case fatality rate of 50% since its first outbreak in the Democratic Republic of Congo in 1996 (Ashe, 2020).

Similar to the novel Covid19, the SARS outbreak originated in China from a civet (a small mammal), MERS from a camel in the middle east, Nipah from unsustainable use of pig farms, and Zika from an unsustainable use of Zika forests in Uganda (Ashe, 2020). According to the US Centres for Disease Control and Prevention (CDC), three quarters of new or emerging diseases that infect humans originate from pathogens found in different fauna. These pathogens come under close interaction with humans when their habitats are unsustainably depleted for industrial processes. According to a 2017 study, Ebola outbreaks are more likely to occur in places in Central and West Africa that have experienced recent unsustainable deforestation (Olivero et al, 2017). When Belgian colonists in Congo built the railways and cities through unsustainable destruction of the environment, lentiviruses from local macaques made their way into humans later compounding on the HIV epidemic (Ashe, 2020). And when British Colonialists in Bangladesh cut down the Sunderban wetlands for rice farms, bacteria now known as cholera travelled throughout the world and made it to its corners as far reaching as Haiti where a recent 2010 outbreak killed some 9,000 Haitians. Cholera had 7 outbreaks since it first jumped on humans, while HIV continues to kill people throughout the world on an annual basis (Ashe, 2020).

And while covid19 might make us point at global pandemics as the biggest of all possible environmental catastrophes, they aren't the only ecological shock predicted for our future global economies. Climate change, according to most economic estimates, overshadows the economic and livelihood related losses ever caused by pandemics. According to various estimates, if temperature rose by the currently accepted 2C target, the global GDP would fall by 15%. If temperatures, however, rose to 3C, global GDP would permanently fall by 25% (Martinich & Crimmins, 2019). In contrast, for a scenario where nothing is done to curb emissions, global GDP would see a decline by more than 30% permanently by 2050 (Martinich & Crimmins, 2019). According to Morgan Stanley, climate change already has caused whole of North America $415 billion in the last three years, much of that due to wildfires and hurricanes. Temperature increase globally has already been contributing to sea level rise, extinction of glaciers, wildfires, and droughts.

According to the Hindukush Himalaya assessment report, if humans fail to reach the 2C target, 70 percent of all Himalayan and Hindukush glaciers feeding major rivers in eight Asian countries might go extinct endangering food security for 2/3rds of the entire human population (Wester et al, 2019). Countries like China, India, Vietnam, and Pakistan might be severely impacted. According to a 2019 report published in the magazine *Nature*, if global temperatures rose 2.8C from pre industrial levels by 2100, it would cost the United States at least $296 billion each year (Martinich & Crimmins, 2019). However, if they increased by 4.5C a large net negative impact on 22 business and economic sectors could actually cost the American economy at least $520 billion each year (Martinich & Crimmins, 2019). As unrealistic as those values might seem, according to Ricke et al, these numbers aren't the highest. In fact, their paper suggests that India might actually have to pay a heavier price under both the scenarios and might be more adversely affected in comparison to the United States.

The World Bank predicts that India could experience severe droughts, flash floods, highly unpredictable rainfall patterns, and depleting groundwater resources. Melting glaciers in the Himalayas could threaten glacier fed north Indian rivers like the Ganges, Indus, and Brahmaputra thereby impacting irrigation and food security for at least 749 million people. Sea level rise, on the other hand, might lead to saltwater intrusion in the coastal areas consequently impacting agriculture, degrading groundwater quality, contaminating drinking water, and possibly causing a rise in cholera outbreaks and diarrhea cases. The World Bank reports that cities like Kolkata and Mumbai are particularly vulnerable to the impacts of sea level rise, flooding of rivers, and climate caused tropical cyclones.

Climate consequences in India, however, are not just limited to agriculture, irrigation, or livelihoods. According to a report commissioned by the National Intelligence Council, climate change might lead to a refugee crisis tempting people from neighbouring flood-stricken Bangladesh to migrate to India. This in turn may exacerbate tensions between the two countries and put a strain on relations between the Indian central government and its various state governments. Similarly, India might also register an abrupt increase in inequality, a crisis in energy supply meeting its demand, and a spike in cases of communicable diseases. And while India and the US might seem to be the two most climate impacted regions in the world, other places might register equally devastating impacts.

West Africa, for instance, has been identified by the UN IPCC as a climate change hotspot projected to observe abrupt decrease in crop yields and production. Under the worst climate change scenario, most climate models predict that a mean yield of 13% in major cereal crops is predicted to reduce in central and western Africa by 2050. Similarly, Northern Africa might register a 11% reduction, and East and Southern Africa 8%. According to the African Climate Policy Centre, for scenarios ranging from an increase in global temperatures from 1C to 4C in comparison to pre industrial levels, overall GDP for the continent is expected to shrink by 2.5% t0 12.12%. This however, can be even worse for western Africa where a 4C temperature rise might shrink the GDP by 22.09%.

Figure 1. Long-term impacts of climate change on Africa's GDP (% change/year) according to four global temperature increase scenarios for the five subregions and for the whole of Africa

Subregions	GDP (% Change/Year)			
	1° C	2° C	3° C	4° C
North (n = 7)	−0.76 ± 0.16	−1.63 ± 0.36	−2.72 ± 0.61	−4.11 ± 0.97
West (n = 15)	−4.46 ± 0.63	−9.79 ± 1.35	−15.62 ± 2.08	−22.09 ± 2.78
Central (n = 9)	−1.17 ± 0.45	−2.82 ± 1.10	−5.53 ± 1.56	−9.13 ± 2.16
East (n = 14)	−2.01 ± 0.20	−4.51 ± 0.34	−7.55 ± 0.63	−11.16 ± 0.85
Southern (n = 10)	−1.18 ±0.64	−2.68 ± 1.54	−4.40 ± 2.56	−6.49 ± 3.75
Whole of Africa (n = 55)	−2.25 ± 1.52	−5.01 ± 3.30	−8.28 ± 5.12	−12.12 ± 7.04

Places in the developed world might be climate impacted too. Australia, for instance, has recently seen a surge in climate driven bushfires. According to an analysis carried out by the World Weather Attribution consortium, the 2019-2020 Australian Bushfires that burned 37,500 square miles of land, cost $5 billion to the economy, and possibly reduced economic growth by 0.5%, was likely caused and made worse by climate change. The study suggests that global warming increased the risk of hot, dry weather that's likely to cause bushfires by at least 30%. However, this research also suggests that the actual numbers might be higher. To put things in the context, the size of the land area burned by these fires is bigger than present day Portugal. And while independent nations might be adversely impacted by climate change, multinational companies might altogether experience a similar brunt.

In 2018, the Carbon Disclosure Project asked more than 7,000 companies worldwide to assess their financial risks due to global warming. After gathering the data, the project discovered that 215 of the world's 500 biggest companies, valued at $17 trillion collectively, could lose at least $1 trillion due to climate change by 2023. Most of these costs came from dealing with disruptions in their operations, net losses in assets lost to climate catastrophes, and prices paid as a result of changing climate policies. According to a blog by Columbia University's Earth Institute, companies like Alphabet (Google's parent company) will likely have to deal with rising cooling costs for its data centres, while suppliers for Hitachi Ltd. In Southeast Asia could be disrupted by flooding. And while these events might impact companies in the future, some firms have already braced the brunt of climate change in the present. General Electric cost its investors $193 billion because it overestimated the demand for natural gas and underestimated that for renewable energy. After California's Paradise wildfire, PG&E became liable for fire damages and had to file for bankruptcy. Similarly, Western Digital Technologies, a hard disk manufacturer, suffered huge losses in 2011 after flooding in Thailand disrupted production.

And while pandemics and climate change might seem two distinct environmental catastrophes on the economy, they actually are closely linked. According to an article published by the Harvard TH Chan School of Public Health, climate change alters our relationship with other species on Earth. And it is precisely this alteration that increases our chances of infection and negatively affects our health. To be more specific, a heating planet expands habitats of several animal species that move up from tropics closer towards the poles. A consequence of this is the fact that species that earlier living in different habitats come in close contact with each other. This proximity facilitates the transfer of pathogens to new hosts. According to the same article, several root causes of climate change also increase the likelihood and the risk of pandemics. Deforestation for example, which impacts the climate and occurs mostly for agricultural purposes, is one of the largest causes of habitat loss worldwide. It forces animals out of their ecosystems, makes them migrate to distant places and potentially contact humans or other forms of wildlife. It is often this contact that transfers potentially dangerous microbes creating outbreaks of lethal epidemics. Unsurprisingly, however, deforestation is also one of the several causes of anthropogenic climate change. Destroying forests not only releases stored carbon, but it also permanently dismantles ecosystems that could have acted as carbon sinks had they survived destruction.

To sum up the arguments made above, destruction of the environment can have negative consequences on the economy. These economic effects, termed as externalities, often have a long-term impact that is not accounted for in our cost benefit analysis models. Since the onset of industrial revolution, we have had telltale signs of impending environmental catastrophes as a consequence of our reckless industrial processes. Over the years, climate caused natural catastrophes such as wildfires, floods, and droughts, pollution caused spike in respiratory diseases and death rates, extinction caused extirpation of life sustaining ecosystems and diverse gene pools, and wildlife trade caused epidemics have already shown us the economic consequences of exploiting the natural world in an unsustainable manner. And scientific projections confirm that these events will continue to haunt our global economy and livelihoods even more if we resist action and fail to bring about a change. Covid19 was a wakeup call. It showed the world what an unsustainable pathway to development can do to our modern society. Therefore, it entirely rests upon us as individual citizens, professionals, consumers, voters, and policymakers to listen to that wake-up call and steer our global economies accordingly.

Making Gross Domestic Product (GDP) Green

Economics as a discipline seems to have revolved around the idea of developing indicators that measure overall economic growth of a society. These indicators, that measure gains in real income levels, unemployment, inflation, or investment, are often synonymized with the idea of welfare. The higher the real GDP growth rate for example, the higher a society's state of overall wellbeing. Consider the case of nominal GDP for instance. According to Aitken (2019), GDP is often treated as shorthand for national economic wellbeing even though it was never intended to be. A country's nominal GDP (Y) for instance, is expressed as a sum of its consumption (C), investment (I), government expenditure (G), and net export (NX). Higher a nation's overall level of consumption, higher is its overall GDP, and therefore higher the wellbeing. This idea has a couple of disadvantages that limit its scope.

First, the concept of GDP does not take into account what resources make consumption possible. This failure to explicitly account for a country's inventory stock fails to give any info about the rate of depletion and replenishment of a country's resources. Since these resources make production of consumable goods and therefore consumption possible, a lack of info about the potential availability of such resources in the future gives us no idea about how much consumption is possible in the future. And second, GDP as a variable lacks a temporal component. There is no distinction between short term and long term. It says a lot about where we stand now and fails to say anything about where we would be in the future if we continue to do things the way we have been doing. This promotes the idea of unchecked, limitless, and unsustainable expansion therefore putting countries delusional to reality.

These two shortcomings unfortunately have positioned countries into expansionist models that have often called for unchecked growth and development without regards to future consequences. And these shortcomings mostly escaped required attention until the 70s when the negative environmental consequences of unchecked growth and expansion started to become obvious. Economists like William Nordhaus and James Tobin were amongst the first to entertain the idea of incorporating an environmental component into widely accepted macroeconomic variables. In 1972, the duo introduced a model that would adjust GDP to include the value of environmental damages, unpaid work, and leisure time. This variable, that they called Measure of Economic Welfare or MEW, was supposed to be weighted against and include the cost of degradation of the environment. Later on, Yusuf Ahmad, Salah El Serafy, and Ernst Lutz worked on a report titled "Economic Accounting for Sustainable Development" and compiled several papers in order to explore various methods that could help them account for the environment within the central idea of income. One of the authors of this report went on to propose that at least part of the sale of natural capital should not be included in the calculation of the GDP. Similarly, John Hartwick from the economics department of Canada based Queen's University tried to account for the depletion of natural resource stock within the calculation of Net National Product, a metric similar to the GDP.

These efforts however, continued for a long time. In 1993, the US Bureau of Economic Analysis began working on redesigning GDP as a metric to account for other factors such as environmental degradation. Consequently, when the results were released in 1994, they showed that actual GDP numbers were inflated and were exaggerating the value added by mining activities to the economy. Corporate politics, however, caught up leading to a House Representative from West Virginia lobbying for termination of GDP recalculation. Consequently, the program was canceled in the United States.

In early 2004, China began its efforts to account for the environment using its own green GDP. However, when the final set of values was reported in 2007, it became clear to the country's government that a GDP weighted against the environment produced values that were unacceptable politically. The program, consequently, was terminated. Similarly, India's environment minister mentioned that a Green GDP program was being worked on in the year 2009 and that India's GDP numbers might be adjusted to the environment by 2015. However, that never happened and as of 2018, the program allegedly has been lost in oblivion.

As observed in the cases above, politics is often at the core of decision-making for policies and usually gets to overrule verdicts issued by rigorous analytics. Under such cases, it often falls within the domain of private individuals, international nonprofits, and alternative analytical agencies to derive values for such indicators. As of now, while there are several international organizations developing metrices of sustainability, there might not be many agencies exploring development of Green GDP. Consequently, while the concept can potentially add real assessment and value to the discipline of sustainability, it sits in rut waiting to be rediscovered and recalculated.

Need for Carbon Taxes and Carbon Tariffs

A carbon tax is a carbon pricing scheme levied as a tax on the carbon content of a fuel. The primary motive of such a tax is to disincentivize polluters from emitting greenhouse gases into the atmosphere. A carbon tax, therefore, is used as a policy tool, meant to direct free market to look into ways processes of production could be made lesser carbon intense. Carbon taxes today are favored across many countries. In fact, countries like Sweden, and Finland have been amongst the first to implement a carbon tax. Sweden, for instance, enacted the tax on carbon emissions in 1991, while Finland did so in the year 1990. According to the Tax Foundation, Sweden's carbon tax has helped the country cut down its carbon emissions while maintaining a sustained and continuous GDP growth. The organization reports that contrary to popular belief, Sweden actually reported a per capita increase in real GDP by more than 50% between 1990 and 2019. In fact, within the same time period, the Scandinavian nation also reduced its emissions by 27%. This reduction was facilitated by decrease in emissions from the industrial sector, and the domestic transport industry.

Similarly, carbon tax enacted in Canada's British Columbia sharply reduced the province's emissions, help it cut back on its gasoline consumption, and dropped overall natural gas usage. According to the University of British Columbia's professor Kathryn Harrison, it also encouraged a greater uptake of fuel-efficient vehicles.

However, while carbon taxes have previously shown net positive benefits, they are not void of criticism. According to various sources, carbon taxes are amongst the most regressive forms of taxation. They tax the poorest by a marginally higher proportion than they tax the richest. Some sources also suggest that a carbon tax promotes leakage – a phenomenon where firms shift their production processes to neighboring jurisdictions to avoid being taxed and then import back the finished good for sale at a lower price. Leakage, at least theoretically, can be a tool for industries to avoid carbon taxation and can also encourage dumping. Some researchers also suggest that carbon taxes are distortionary and can lead to tax interaction effect.

While these arguments pose challenge to the cause of a carbon tax, through efficient and better planned policies, they can be overcome. According to Budhia (2020), if the economy could be divided into multiple stages depending on the steps of production and consumption, there would be three unique stages. The first or the fundamental step would primarily include extraction of raw materials like coal and petroleum or import of such fuels that are later used for production of other things. The second or intermediary step would include use of such raw materials to produce intermediary goods such as power, plastics, and different petrochemical products. The third or the final step would include production of saleable commodities that enter supermarkets, grocery stores, and other consumer friendly outlets. According to Budhia (2020), imposing a carbon tax on this third stage widens the tax base for a carbon tax consequently reducing its regressive nature, and decreasing distortions in the economy. As far as leakages are concerned, Budhia (2020) suggests for a carbon tariff levied that takes socioeconomic equity and protectionist concerns into account simultaneously to deliver results that least violate WTO regulations while also catering to domestic protectionist concerns.

Carbon tariffs, coincidently, might actually be about to be a reality in EU. As of October 2020, according to various sources, the EU had been planning to leavy carbon tariffs on carbon rich imports from every major trading partner.

Mainstreaming ESG Metrices

The ESG criteria is a long-held investment tool that asks investors to incorporate environmental, social, and governance factors into decision making before investing on any firm or corporation. It is also a tool that helps companies assess their environmental and social impact, and the relationship between their different employees, stake holders, and managers. Growing concerns of sustainability issues such as climate change and corporate social responsibility have added to the pressure of firms aligning their performances with the one dictated as closer to being sustainable by the ESG metric. Research has shown that ESG might be a good indicator of overall growth and performance of a firm. The better a firm performs in terms of ESG, the higher long term returns it might guarantee. In fact, according to James Purcell, Global Head of Sustainable and Impact Investment at UBS Wealth Management CIO, "sustainable investing has moved out of the shadows into the mainstream. Clients want to know where their money is invested and, increasingly, what the impact is." Consequently, there has been a trend of ESG integrating among mainstream investors. In 2006, when the UN Principle for Responsible Investment (UN PRI) was launched, 63 investment firms managing $6.5 trillion worth of assets signed a commitment to incorporate ESG into their investment decisions. However, according to a Harvard Business Review article, this number had increased to 2450 firms representing $82 trillion worth of assets by June 2019. This trend however, is not limited to corporate asset managers. A Harvard Business Review article reports that 78% of asset owners consider ESG management a key issue when looking for an asset manager. In fact, the same article also says that in a 2018 UBS Investor Watch global survey, 81 percent of people wished for an allegiance between their consumption spending patterns and their values, 86 percent of respondents said sustainable investment strategies encouraged companies to engage in better busines practices, and 82% thought sustainable companies were a good investment idea because of their forward thinking and better management. Also, a whooping 58% majority believes that ESG will be the new normal in a decade.

While ESG might seem to be a coherent investment ideology across all criteria of demographics, it seems as if people from different global economic regions might express different degrees of allegiance with the metric. According to a 2019 UBS survey, Europe seems to have the highest percentage of asset owners who invest actively in ESG. 82 percent of respondents from Europe said they made ESG their everyday investment activity. These respondents also reported that in the next five years, factors like biodiversity loss and climate change might become more relevant to their investment decisions than financial factors. In Americas however, this proportion was comparatively less with 70% of respondents saying they made ESG their everyday investment activity.

But is ESG enough? According to Felix Preston, the director of Sustainability Insights at the Generation Investment Management, ESG puts spotlight on what is available rather than what is most important. In other words, it puts an emphasis on the short term over the long term and fails to provide a roadmap to long term sustainability. ESG today is a scheme that rates companies on how sustainable they are. It compares companies against each other and suggests which companies are more sustainable than the others. However, it does not lay out a plan on what level of sustainability is required to reach specific environmental targets beneficial for the economy. Therefore, according to Felix Preston from Generation Investment Management, ESG data will have to undergo a transformation if it has to help guide transformations in economy.

ESG also measures sustainability not only in terms of the environment, but also in terms of society, the 'S,' and governance, the 'G.' This non exclusivity of the index towards the environment can put firms with higher performing social and governance indicators and low performing environmental indicator well above a firm that performs well in terms of the environment but demonstrates a low performance in social and governance indicators. This non exclusivity can deem firms sustainable even when they are not so in terms of the environment. Therefore, ESG is definitely a good starting point. However, to bring about a sustainable change for the economy, we need to develop roadmaps for firms to help them better align with and reach long term sustainability related goals.

Need for a Socially Responsible Consumer

Modern society in the face of upcoming social challenges has already introduced the concept of Corporate Social Responsibility (CSR). The need for multinationals and big firms to become sustainable and be responsible has been well recognized by the society. However, Consumer Social Responsibility (CnSR), or the need for consumers to make conscious consumption choices has unfortunately not gained an equal amount of attention. And while CSR and CnSR might seem distinct to some individuals, the two are closely interconnected in reality. In fact, Consumer Social Responsibility is often a driving force that creates a need for CSR.

Take electric cars as an example, for instance. According to Vitell (2014), if a company offers more fuel-efficient cars, or even electric cars in order to participate in being socially responsible, it will only survive the marketplace if there exists an actual demand for those electric cars. Therefore, it is the marketplace, and the desirability of socially responsible behavior in the marketplace, that creates a demand for corporate social responsibility. This desirability of socially responsible behavior is termed as consumer social responsibility. For purposes of sustainability therefore, it is important to create a demand within consumers for socially responsible corporate behavior. And in order to create that demand, net set of non-profit agencies, firms, and the government need to enter the marketplace.

This is exactly the trend in the market that has been observed in the last couple of years. Third party firms like the Rainforest Action Network, Rainforest Alliance, and the Roundtable on Sustainable Palm Oil become agencies that rate consumer products on sustainability scales and certify whether or nor products meet their sustainability criteria. Take the Forest Steward Council, or the FSC, for instance. The FSC provides certification and accreditation services for firms, organizations, and different communities interested in responsible forestry. Certified products can be identified in supermarket shelves by consumers using an ecolabel put on their packaging. A consequence of this branding is the fact that practices, such as these, spread awareness within consumers about the need for sustainability, make consumers choose sustainable products and services over their unsustainable market competitors, and therefore compel other firms to comply to sustainability standards and get certified to avoid losing market share and revenue. Using such a sustainability certification, there can be a real market impact. According to Erica Di Girolami and Bas Arts from Wageningen University, the Forest Stewardship Council for instance, has had a net positive impact on its certified forests in terms of ecosystem services offered, conservation of different species of fauna, and preservation of flora. In terms of conservation of fauna, forests certified by the FSC registered a net positive impact in almost all examined sample sites when compared to non-certified conventionally logged forests. All studies included in the research demonstrated a net positive impact on wild fauna and their conservation. These species, however, also included one listed as endangered by the International Union of Conservation of Nature (IUCN).

Success of some of these environment certification and ecolabel services indicates that we might need more of these in the future. Considering the consequences of environmental destruction, pandemics, and climate change, we might need more third-party agencies, with no chance of monopoly, to independently examine economic processes and certify companies on their sustainability performances. This way, a conscious environment promoting consumer social responsibility and, consequently, corporate social responsibility might be attainable to a greater degree.

Why Paris Agreement is not Enough

Climate change, as previously discussed, is a global emergency that crosses national borders and endangers water, food, environmental, and national security for many countries. In order to combat climate change and its negative impacts, 197 countries, on December 12th 2015, adopted the Paris Agreement at the 21st Conference of Parties (COP21) in Paris. A year later, the agreement entered into force and aimed at reducing greenhouse gas emissions and limiting global temperature increase to 2C.

According to the Untied Nations, the Paris Agreement provides a framework to guide nations over the coming decades in combatting climate change. It provides a pathway to developed countries to better coordinate in their fight against climate change and assist developing countries in mitigating and adapting to the changing climate.

The Paris Agreement formally entered into force on November 4th 2016 with the United States leaving the agreement, 195 parties signing it and 189 ratifying later. Over the last five years, this treaty has been deemed the single most important climate treaty in the world. With election of Joe Biden as the president elect in 2020 elections, there are chances that the US might rejoin the Paris Climate accord. Countries globally have already developed their pathways into cutting their emissions or being carbon neutral by set dates in the future. Many have already made set targets and enacted policies that might help them achieve those goals.

Paris agreement, however, might just not be enough. Limiting the planet's warming to a 2C target or a 1.5C target already makes several extreme weather events observed today the norm of the future. According to Hare et al. (2016), in a world that is 2C warmer than pre industrial levels, average length of a warm spell would increase by 26 days, and 11 days than what it is today across places like northern parts of Australia, and central and Southern territories respectively. Under a scenario with 1.5C degree warming however, the warm spell duration will still increase by 14 days in Northern Australia and by 6 days in Southern Australia. According to Carbon Brief's interactive climate map, a 2C scenario would increase annual maximum daily temperature by 2.6C, and a 1.5C scenario would increase it by 1.7C. Under the former, the number of hot days around the globe will increase by 25% with average global warm spell duration increasing by 35 days. And under the latter, the increase in hot days would be a spike by 16% and growth in warm spell duration by 17 days. The same interactive map also suggests that the proportion of population facing at least one severe heatwave every two years in a 2C scenario would be 70%. While for a 1.5C scenario, this would be 50%. Drought lengths in a 2C scenario would increase by 4 months. While in a 1.5C scenario they would increase by 2 months.

Similarly, in a 2C scenario, global population flooded in coastal areas would be around 30 million per year by 2055. For a 1.5C scenario however, this would be 28 million people per year by 2055. These numbers, according to the interactive map would increase astronomically by 2095 when 60 million people, and 72 million people would be flooded in coastal areas per year in a 1.5C, and a 2C scenario respectively. For the economy, under a 1.5C scenario, the global per capita GDP might shrink by 8% by 2100. This figure, under a 2C scenario however, would be as large as 13%. In fact annual flood damage losses from sea level rise would be around \$10.21 trillion in a 1.5C world, and around \$11.7 trillion in a 2C world. Diseases like Malaria might see a surge in favorable land for transmission by 19% in a 1.5C world. In a 2C world however, this number might be around 27%.

More statistical data can be demonstrated here to show the impact of a 1.5C and a 2C warming, but the point needed to be made is already clear. Neither a 1.5C world, nor a 2C world is habitable as demonstrated by the analytically derived numbers above. And while the Paris Agreement has had countries agreeing to limit warming by either of these two targets, it doesn't end people's miseries due to climate change. Put in other words, the Paris targets and the Paris Agreement is just not enough. In order to actually avoid the climate catastrophe entirely, perhaps limiting carbon emissions or being carbon neutral might not be enough. Countries might have to restore climate and carbon, and become carbon negative. Such goals might require greater investment in R&D and a greater investment in businesses and industries that restore the climate and make carbon intensive ways of production carbon neutral or possibly carbon negative. The next section of this chapter will explore this topic in greater detail.

The second drawback of the Paris Climate Accord is its nonbinding nature. There is absolutely no mechanism to make sure countries stick to their goals. Under such a scenario, everything, from countries randomly quitting to the free rider problem is entirely possible. In fact, its nonbinding nature was one of the reasons the Trump administration could quit it without having to face consequences. And while the 2020 president elect has promised to reenter the accord, there still exists no mechanism to check future exits. Added on to that, countries under the currently agreed to Paris Accord can get away with failure to meet their climate pledges without having to face any consequences. There exists absolutely no mechanism of checks and balances to make countries accountable. And under such conditions, while the Paris Accord is a good first step, it definitely is not the answer.

Restoration of the Climate?

An emerging thought in the sphere of climate policies has been proposing for the need to invest in already existing R&D technology that sequester greenhouse gases from the atmosphere and convert them into raw materials and consumer products. This ideology, widely referred to as climate restoration has been gaining traction recently considering its potential capacity to sequester emissions, create business opportunities, and help carbon intensive businesses become carbon neutral or even carbon negative in some cases.

According to the Arizona State University's professor Sanjeev Khagram, global climate restoration could provide trillions of dollars' worth of economic opportunities while simultaneously benefiting the environment and the society. His paper published by the Thunderbird School of Management suggests that if the world could make right choices over the next 2-3 years, we could unlock benefits worth $26 trillion from now until 2030. This could also potentially help our world economy create 65 million new low carbon jobs, and avoid at least 700,000 premature deaths from air pollution related health hazards.

According to Khagram, the financial value of market opportunities in climate restoration could range between at least $1 trillion to $3 trillion per year by 2030. However, the broader economic, social, and environmental benefits of climate restoration might actually be around $3 trillion - $5 trillion per year by 2030.

In fact, this issue has gained enough traction to have its first two Annual Global Climate Restoration Forums held at the United Nations. The idea largely is to use existing technologies to bring carbon levels in the atmosphere back to pre-industrial levels. Synthetic limestone for instance is one such technology that adherents of climate restoration policy talk about as a carbon negative business. The narrative, as it goes, suggests that the process of manufacturing limestone synthetically absorbs carbon dioxide from the atmosphere. Therefore, the resulting limestone manufactured synthetically is made from absorption of carbon dioxide and is carbon negative. This limestone, when used in manufacturing of cement, can either help make the manufacturing process carbon neutral, or in some specific cases, create a carbon negative cement. If, however, this could be done in a larger scale, the impact could be much more significant. According to various estimates, cement manufacturing is one of the biggest carbon polluters. A 2018 BBC article reports that cement might be the source of about 8% of the world's carbon emissions. If, hypothetically, that entire sector could be made carbon neutral or carbon negative, the net effect of this on the environment could bring about some substantial benefit.

A California based firm, for example, has already started manufacturing carbon neutral cement. This cement, which the firm often succeeds in making carbon negative, has been used as an industrial grade construction component for various infrastructure projects around the San Francisco bay area.

Other methods of climate restoration that have been touted by people like Khagram and the California based Foundation for Climate Restoration include ocean iron fertilization, reclamation of degraded land, afforestation, manufacturing of carbon fiber, graphene, and carbon composites. Likewise, switching electric grids to solar, wind, and other renewable sources, while simultaneously exploring other sources of renewable energy are often touted as ways towards the future too.

Reforming the CITES Agreement

As discussed earlier in this chapter, covid19 has zoonotic origins. It came from trading in endangered wildlife. And while it wasn't the only zoonotic pandemic that occurred in the history of humanity, it was definitely one amongst the worst to impact our livelihoods and our economies. With the surfacing of covid19 however, it has come to obvious attention of many policymakers that in order for our world economies to avoid future pandemics, it is also a must to curb or severely regulate trade in wildlife, and conserve their habitats. Much attention has come to the need to reform the Convention on International Trade in Endangered Species of Wild Fauna and Flora (CITES). So, what is CITES?

CITES, according to the definition provided by the treaty's website, is an international agreement between governments that aims to ensure that international trade in specimens of wild animals and plants does not threaten their survival. According to a Scientific American article, it is a binding agreement whose decisions carry the weight of law in its 182 member countries, including the United States, and any other nation that wishes to engage in trade with those countries. The Scientific American article reports that since 1975, this treaty has provided a legal framework, and an enforceable regulatory regime for international trade in wildlife. Consequently, CITES prohibits commercial trade in over 1,000 species and strictly regulates it in more than 35,000 others. The treaty also has formal relations with the UN Food and Agriculture Organization (FAO), and the World Organization for Animal Health (OIE).

To this date CITES has enforced itself across countries through compliance procedures. It requires countries to have their own regulations that confirm to CITES requirements. If countries fail to oblige to its terms of trade, they are banned from trade. According to its ex secretary general John E Scanlon, "CITES is unique among international environmental agreements because it makes decisions that are legally binding on its members, supported by transparent compliance process."

However, CITES unfortunately hasn't taken public health or epidemic related issues into account for its decision-making process. According to Scanlon, considering the expertise of the treaty in already dealing with trade in wildlife, and considering the zoonotic and wildlife trade related origin of pandemics, it makes more sense to broaden the scope of CITES and include health risks and pandemics within its jurisdiction. This, of course, he believes, would be a more efficient idea than to have other international organizations craft a new pandemic and wildlife trade related treaty from scratch.

CONCLUSION

Throughout this paper we explored the intersection of different environmental catastrophes and their consequences on livelihoods of people and the economy. We discovered the zoonotic origins of Covid19 and briefly discussed the reasons why it is important to regulate destruction of wildlife habitats and trade in endangered wildlife. We explored climate change and its projected consequences if nothing is done. We analyzed the limits of our modern economic indicators and briefly studied the history of concepts like the Green GDP. We briefly examined the needs, limits, and benefits of carbon taxes and carbon tariffs. We studied what private individuals can do to combat the climate crisis and the role of individual investors, investment firms, citizens, and independent consumers. This paper also examined the need for implementation of ESG metrics and analyzed why they might not be enough. It established the relationship between Consumer Social Responsibility and Corporate Social Responsibility and learned how one influences the other. It briefed us about the importance of environmental certification services and ecolabels in being independent forces that direct free markets towards sustainability. Through this paper, we explored why Paris Agreement might not be enough and why its nonbinding nature might be a true hindrance towards its promised goals and objectives. We also discovered the field of climate restoration and its promises for society. And ultimately, we looked into the CITES agreement and how it can be expanded to prevent future pandemics.

Through all the topics covered in this paper, a coherent narrative on a need for sustainability was clear. All different metrics explored pointed at the urgency of our global environmental collapse and its impact on the economy. And all treaties described seemed to show the limits of our present day narrative in solving some of our economic and environmental problems. Throughout the paper, it became clear that in order for our economies to survive, we need to bring about a change. It became obvious that there is a need for sustainability in a post covid19 world economy. For if, there were to be none, our world as we know today might not remain the same.

REFERENCES

Adoption of the Paris Agreement. (n.d.). Retrieved November 28, 2020, from https://unfccc.int/files/essential_background/convention/application/pdf/english_paris_agreement.pdf

Aitken, A. (n.d.). *Measuring Welfare Beyond GDP*. Retrieved November 28, 2020, from https://journals.sagepub.com/doi/full/10.1177/002795011924900110

Al Jazeera. (2020, September 29). *'Agonising milestone': One million people dead from COVID-19*. Retrieved November 28, 2020, from https://www.aljazeera.com/news/2020/9/29/global-death-toll-from-covid-19-exceeds-one-million-people

Ashe, D. (2020, June 15). *A Crucial Step Toward Preventing Wildlife-Related Pandemics*. Retrieved November 28, 2020, from https://www.scientificamerican.com/article/a-crucial-step-toward-preventing-wildlife-related-pandemics/

Carbon Pricing. (n.d.a). *CDP Disclosure Best Practice*. Retrieved November 28, 2020, from http://b8f65cb373b1b7b15feb-c70d8ead6ced550b4d987d7c03fcdd1d.r81.cf3.rackcdn.com/cms/guidance_docs/pdfs/000/001/567/original/CDP-technical-note-carbon-pricing.pdf?1523952114

Carbon Pricing. (n.d.b). Retrieved November 28, 2020, from https://www.cdp.net/en/climate/carbon-pricing

Climate damages and adaptation potential across. (n.d.). *Nature*. Retrieved November 28, 2020, from https://www.nature.com/articles/s41558-019-0444-6.epdf?no_publisher_access=1&r3_referer=nature

Climate Restoration. (n.d.). Retrieved November 28, 2020, from https://foundationforclimaterestoration.org/wp-content/uploads/2020/03/20200306c_f4cr4_white-paper.pdf

Climatechange 27 07 03. (n.d.). WHO. Retrieved November 28, 2020, from https://www.who.int/globalchange/climate/en/chapter6.pdf

Coronavirus and Climate Change. (2020, July 6). Retrieved November 28, 2020, from https://www.hsph.harvard.edu/c-change/subtopics/coronavirus-and-climate-change/

Coronavirus cases: Worldometer. (2023, February 7). Retrieved February 7, 2023, from https://www.worldometers.info/coronavirus/

Coronavirus disease (COVID-19). (n.d.). Retrieved November 28, 2020, from https://www.who.int/emergencies/diseases/novel-coronavirus-2019

COVID-19. Implications for business. (2020, November 25). Retrieved November 28, 2020, from https://www.mckinsey.com/business-functions/risk/our-insights/covid-19-implications-for-business

COVID-19 to slash global economic output by $8.5 trillion over next two years. (n.d.). UN DESA Department of Economic and Social Affairs. Retrieved November 28, 2020, from https://www.un.org/development/desa/en/news/policy/wesp-mid-2020-report.html

Documents & Reports - All Documents. (n.d.). The World Bank. Retrieved November 28, 2020, from https://documents.worldbank.org/curated/en/156521468767069279/pdf/multi-page.pdf

Economic consequences of Covid-19: A multi-country analysis. (n.d.). Retrieved November 28, 2020, from https://voxeu.org/article/economic-consequences-covid-19-multi-country-analysis

Economically Sustainable Carbon Capture. (n.d.). Retrieved November 28, 2020, from https://www.blueplanet-ltd.com/

ESG. Do you or Don't you? (n.d.). UBS Global - Asset Management. Retrieved November 28, 2020, from https://www.ubs.com/global/en/asset-management/insights/sustainable-and-impact-investing/2019/esg-do-you-or-don-t-you.html

ESG in the Mainstream: The Role for Companies and. (n.d.). BSR. Retrieved November 28, 2020, from https://www.bsr.org/reports/BSR_ESG_Integration_Report__Sept_2009_final.pdf

First Covid-19 case happened in November, China government records show - report. (2020, March 13). Retrieved November 28, 2020, from https://www.theguardian.com/world/2020/mar/13/first-covid-19-case-happened-in-november-china-government-records-show-report

Forest and Nature Policy Group. (n.d.). Retrieved November 28, 2020, from https://www.wur.nl/upload_mm/6/e/6/998c6e88-c6e2-4a38-92e3-c883ea847cee_20181010_Environmental_impacts_forest_certifications.pdf

Global Climate Restoration for. (n.d.). Retrieved November 28, 2020, from https://thunderbird.asu.edu/sites/default/files/global_climate_restoration_report_2020.pdf

Global warming: Severe consequences for Africa. (n.d.). Africa Renewal. Retrieved November 28, 2020, from https://www.un.org/africarenewal/magazine/december-2018-march-2019/global-warming-severe-consequences-africa

Gopinath, C. (n.d.). *IMF: New predictions suggest a deeper recession and a slower recovery*. Retrieved November 28, 2020, from https://www.weforum.org/agenda/2020/06/imf-lockdown-recession-covid19-coronavirus-economics-recession/

How Africa will be affected by climate change. (2019, December 15). Retrieved November 28, 2020, from https://www.bbc.com/news/world-africa-50726701

Implications of the 1.5°C limit in the Paris Agreement for. (n.d.). Retrieved November 28, 2020, from https://climateanalytics.org/media/1p5_australia_report_ci.pdf

Insights: System Positive. (n.d.). Retrieved November 28, 2020, from https://www.generationim.com/research-centre/insights/system-positive/

Is Europe's far-right using coronavirus as a new avenue of agitation? (2020, November 26). Retrieved November 28, 2020, from https://www.euronews.com/2020/11/26/is-europe-s-far-right-using-covid-restrictions-as-a-new-avenue-of-agitation

Is Sustainable Investing Moving Into the Mainstream? (2019, December 2). Sponsor Content From UBS. Retrieved November 28, 2020, from https://hbr.org/sponsored/2019/11/is-sustainable-investing-moving-into-the-mainstream

Listings of WHO's response to COVID-19. (n.d.). Retrieved November 28, 2020, from https://www.who.int/news/item/29-06-2020-covidtimeline

Olivero, J., Real, R., & FA, J. E. (n.d.). *Recent loss of closed forests is associated with ebola virus disease outbreaks*. Scientific reports. https://pubmed.ncbi.nlm.nih.gov/29085050/

Pneumonia of unknown cause – China. (2020, January 30). Retrieved November 28, 2020, from https://www.who.int/csr/don/05-january-2020-pneumonia-of-unkown-cause-china/en/

The Future of ESG Data. (n.d.). Retrieved November 28, 2020, from https://www.generationim.com/research-centre/insights/the-future-of-esg-data/

The Paris Agreement. (n.d.). Retrieved November 28, 2020, from https://www.un.org/en/climatechange/paris-agreement

This paper does not represent US Government views. (n.d.). dni.gov. Retrieved November 28, 2020, from https://www.dni.gov/files/documents/climate2030_india.pdf

What are the impacts of climate change? (n.d.). Retrieved November 28, 2020, from https://www.science.org.au/learning/general-audience/science-climate-change/7-what-are-impacts-of-climate-change

What is CITES? (n.d.). Retrieved November 28, 2020, from https://cites.org/eng/disc/what.php

World Economic Outlook Update. June 2020: A Crisis Like No Other, An Uncertain Recovery. (2020, June 1). Retrieved November 28, 2020, from https://www.imf.org/en/Publications/WEO/Issues/2020/06/24/WEOUpdateJune2020

World's biggest companies face $1 trillion in climate change risks. (n.d.). Retrieved November 28, 2020, from https://www.cdp.net/en/articles/media/worlds-biggest-companies-face-1-trillion-in-climate-change-risks

ADDITIONAL READING

Brown, A. (2018, June 29). Mapping photosynthesis. Retrieved November 28, 2020, from https://www.nature.com/articles/s41558-018-0221-y

Elflein, J. (2020, November 26). Coronavirus deaths worldwide by country. Retrieved November 28, 2020, from https://www.statista.com/statistics/1093256/novel-coronavirus-2019ncov-deaths-worldwide-by-country/

Ghosh, P. (2020, March 04). Climate change boosted Australia bushfire risk by at least 30%. Retrieved November 28, 2020, from https://www.bbc.com/news/science-environment-51742646

Jonsson, S., Ydstedt, A., & Asen, E. (2020, November 09). Looking Back on 30 Years of Carbon Taxes in Sweden. Retrieved November 28, 2020, from https://taxfoundation.org/sweden-carbon-tax-revenue-greenhouse-gas-emissions/

Kahn, J., & Yardley, J. (2007, August 26). As China Roars, Pollution Reaches Deadly Extremes. Retrieved November 28, 2020, from https://www.nytimes.com/2007/08/26/world/asia/26china.html

Lempert, R., Marangoni, G., Keller, K., & Duke, J. (2018, April 06). Is Climate Restoration an Appropriate Policy Goal? Retrieved November 28, 2020, from https://www.rand.org/pubs/research_reports/RR2442.html

Pearce, R. (n.d.). The impacts of climate change at 1.5C, 2C and beyond. Retrieved November 28, 2020, from https://interactive.carbonbrief.org/impacts-climate-change-one-point-five-degrees-two-degrees/

Piven, B. (2019, September 18). Climate restoration: Environmental coalition launches 2050 push. Retrieved November 28, 2020, from https://www.aljazeera.com/ajimpact/climate-restoration-environmental-coalition-launches-2050-push-190917222918962.html

Simon, M. (n.d.). The Terrible Consequences of Australia's Uber-Bushfires. Retrieved November 28, 2020, from https://www.wired.com/story/the-terrible-consequences-of-australias-uber-bushfires/

Surabhi, A. (2018, January 15). 'Green GDP' plans gathering dust in government corridors. Retrieved November 28, 2020, from https://www.thehindubusinessline.com/economy/green-gdp-plans-gathering-dust-in-government-corridors/article9345806.ece

Chapter 2
Customer Behavioral Intention Towards Internet Banking During COVID-19:
Empirical Evidence From Nepal

Roshan Adhikari
Quest International College, Pokhara University, Nepal

Niranjan Devkota
https://orcid.org/0000-0001-9989-0397
Kathmandu Model College, Tribhuvan University, Nepal

Krishna Dhakal
https://orcid.org/0000-0002-6668-9707
Quest International College, Pokhara University, Nepal

Surendra Mahato
Nepal Commerce Campus, Tribhuvan University, Nepal

Udaya Raj Paudel
Quest International College, Pokhara University, Nepal

Shila Mishra
National Planning Commission, Government of Nepal, Nepal

ABSTRACT

Providing banking services through digital platforms is an emerging channel of service delivery by commercial banks to their customers. especially in a developing country such as Nepal. However, this study aims to determine the customers' behavioral intention towards internet banking usage during COVID-19 in Kathmandu Valley. Data were evaluated quantitatively by using both descriptive and inferential statistics where questionnaire was deigned to collect the data and were entered in a KOBO Toolbox. SEM was used to analyze the relationships from 279 responses from Kathmandu Valley. Findings revealed perceived ease of use and perceived usefulness play a significant role in the behavioral intention towards internet banking during COVID-19, which fits TAM theory. Customers must experience better use of internet banking services without any interruptions, and a revolution in internet services is required in the Nepalese banking industry.

DOI: 10.4018/978-1-7998-6896-5.ch002

INTRODUCTION

The internet is one of the most recent developments in communication, with the first email being delivered in a fraction of a second in 1972. This technology enables the transmission of almost endless amounts of data around the world (Poster, 2011). As a result of the use of information and communication technology, most organizations' methods of conducting commercial transactions and responding to client requests have changed (Apulu & Latham, 2011). ICTs have facilitated the development of more business-oriented information systems that support management tasks such as planning, controlling, and coordination, as well as the introduction of new products and service market opportunities (Matos et al., 2009). In the banking sector, BFIs are attempting to increase their competitiveness, expand their customer base, lower transaction costs, improve response quality and timeliness, expand advertising and branding opportunities, enable self-service and service customization (Mohammed & Ward, 2006).

Many financial institutions have noticed that one of the competitive marketing techniques is the distribution channel (Mols, 1999). Nowadays, a bank can use a variety of new channels to serve customers and differentiate itself from competitors, such as telephone banking and Internet banking (Calisir & Gumussoy, 2008) where internet technologies have fundamentally altered how banks deliver services and how customers perform their banking transactions. However, internet banking is one of these technologies that is gradually becoming a preferred distribution route for both service providers and clients (Haque, 2009). The use of the internet as a remote delivery channel for banking services is characterized as internet banking, and an internet bank is defined as a bank that provides (web-based) transactional services (Gopalakrishnan et al., 2003) where customers can utilize internet banking to perform all of their normal banking tasks, such as online bill payments, balance inquiries, and fund transfers to other accounts, without having to visit a bank branch (Sandhu & Arora, 2020; González et al., 2008; Adhikari, 2019).

In developing countries like Nepal, providing banking services via digital platforms is an emerging route for commercial banks to deliver services to its consumers, particularly in developing countries like Nepal (Dasgupta et.al, 2011). Customers' behavior is influenced by the various factors in adopting the banking services. Nepal's E-Participation Index has soared to 55th place in the world in 2018, up from 89th place in 2016. From 0.5085 in 2016 to 0.7809 in 2018, the E-Participation Index (EPI) score has improved. This demonstrated that the country's e-Participation has gradually expanded and thus Nepal is improving in terms of technology deployment and application (UN, 2020). Nepal's banking industry has been making tremendous progress in terms of technological innovation and aggressive integration of information technology into bank operations (Banstola, 2008) which results a great opportunity to increase internet banking users in Nepal. Moreover, Nepal Rastra Bank is focused on developing and upgrading payment infrastructures, formulating and executing legal and regulatory frameworks, supporting innovation, and boosting digital payment awareness (NRB, 2020). Internet Banking users in one survey in Nepal made by Tan et al., (2020) revealed that it had a positive view and experience with internet banking services. In all situations, the acceptance showed that more than half of the population saw perceived utility, perceived danger, and perceived usability of internet banking services as good. So, due to the extensive usability and usefulness of internet banking in Nepal and in the global context this concern has become popular.

Moreover, the cashless system has been emerging widely not only in Nepal but all around the globe. But despite of all the positive sides, in Nepal internet banking is almost being replaced by the mobile banking users due to the extensive use of mobile phones in Nepal. According to the FY 2076/77 the number of mobile banking users are 1,13,06,797 whereas the number of internet banking users are only

10,31,227 in Nepal (Mastran, 2021). Additionally, adoption of internet banking is complicated by factors such as bank location, demographics, quality service, privacy risk, security issues, and so on (Jha, 2020). In Nepal, the banking sector is rapidly expanding; however online banking is still in its infancy compared to other countries. Banks have spent a lot of money on technology and have only had success with ATMs, but they haven't marketed internet banking sufficiently. If banks recognize the potential of internet banking, they will be able to provide significant assistance to society while also profiting handsomely (Ansari, 2019; Banstola, 2008). The current condition of online banking which also includes internet banking in Nepal appears to be devoid of technological and physical aspects, based on the introduction of online banking and its prospects (Adhikari, 2019).

The most prevalent perspectives on internet banking are that the internet has a broad significance, but it is unable to reach a huge client base owing to a lack of awareness, advertising, and expertise. As a result, it's vital for marketers to emphasize the advantages of using internet banking in their advertising and marketing so that customers see the worth of doing so (Chauhan et al., 2019). However, according to certain studies, people avoid utilizing internet banking services due to security and trust concerns (Patel & Patel, 2018).

In the context of Nepal, research on topics such as internet banking malfunctions, digital fraud, data reliability, online and open connection security, and their influence on customers is needed to be explored further which can be considered as challenges (Tan et al., 2020). Other elements such as perceived ease of use, perceived usefulness, social influence and their impact, according to the findings in the Nepalese context, have still to be investigated. Newly integrated models and theories can also be applied to understand the relationship between the components in further studies. Studies linking COVID-19 with internet banking is also not done in Nepal. It can be studied further. Still several questions were unanswered in the context of internet banking which still needed to be addressed they are: What are the behavioral intentions towards internet banking usage during COVID-19 in Kathmandu Valley? What are the challenges of internet banking during COVID-19 in Kathmandu Valley? What is the managerial solution for the challenges of internet banking in Kathmandu Valley during COVID-19? The major objective of this study is to measure the customers' behavioral intention towards internet banking usage during COVID-19 in Kathmandu Valley addressing customers' behavioral intention towards internet banking during COVID-19, knowing the challenges of internet banking by providing the challenges of internet banking in Kathmandu valley during COVID-19.

This study is structured into five different sections: Section 2 deals with a literature review followed by research methods in Section 3. Section 4 shows and examines the parameters acquired. Last but not the least, Section 5 gives findings of this study.

Research Methods

Several theories such as technological acceptance, Technology Continuance Theory, Theory of Planned Behavior, E-SERVQUAL Model, Technology Acceptance Model (TAM), and Expectation-Confirmation Theory were reviewed in this study. However, the researcher opted to utilize TAM, as significant number of research investigations were conducted in addition to the core question of the nature and conceptualization of internet banking (Ahmad, 2018). Similarly, the technology acceptance model is one of the most often used models for studying information system acceptability. However, customers' perceptions of internet banking are heavily influenced by its perceived usefulness and simplicity of use, hence using a technological acceptance model to research consumer acceptance of online banking is beneficial

(Alshurideh et al., 2021). In addition, the model stated that online banking acceptance may be modeled using TAM variables (PU and PEOU) as well as four additional factors relating to perceived enjoyment (PE), security and privacy, and Internet connection quality (Davis, 1986). Besides, the degree to which a user thinks that their initial expectations are being confirmed during real use is referred to as confirmation. Similarly, perceived usefulness is proven to be a constant variable in examining user behavior at both the early and late stages of adoption (McLean et al., 2020). However, expectation confirmation has been shown to have a considerable impact on perceived utility and pleasure; users will be satisfied if the internet banking service meets their expectations for the service (Rahi & Ghani, 2019).

The researcher established the following conceptual framework based on TAM and existing literature on Internet Banking where perceived usefulness, perceived ease of use, perceived security and social influence are independent variables and behavioral intention to use internet banking is dependent variable as shown in Figure 1.

Figure 1. Conceptual framework
Source: Modified and adapted from Patel and Patel (2018)

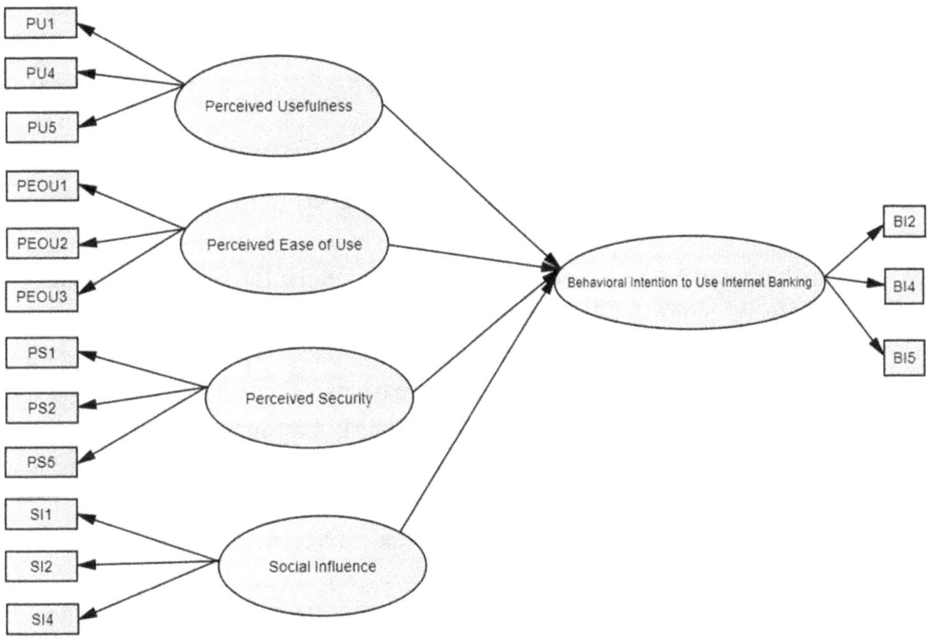

Perceived Usefulness and Behavioral Intention to Use Internet Banking

Hassan and Wood (2020) depict that consumers' perceptions of the experience's outcome are referred to as perceived utility. The term "perceived usefulness" alludes to someone's conviction that a specific tactic would enable them to perform better at work. In addition, Moslehpour et al. (2018) indicates that another factor that contributes to the perceived utility is the ease with which one virtual store may be compared to another virtual store. Therefore, customers' behavior is determined by how useful the technology is and how the new technology will improve or accelerate his or her performance. So, there is a very important relation between perceived usefulness and behavior towards technology.

H1: Perceived usefulness has a significant positive impact on customers' behavioral intentions to use internet banking services.

Perceived Ease of Use and Behavioral Intention to Use Internet Banking

Internet services using behavior is related with how customers can adopt the technology. Mutahar et al. (2018) depict that to prevent the "under-used" helpful system problem, mobile banking and internet banking systems must be simple to understand and operate. In addition, clients will be less hesitant to adopt IT applications if they are simple to use. However, customers will likely to show their behavior if technology is not complex to use. Similarly, Namahoot and Laohavichien (2018) indicated perceived behavioral control is a factor that helps people understand how they feel about utilizing technology. Study of Featherman et al. (2010) indicates that e-service providers should think about the advantages of designing more user-friendly platforms and training customers on how to use them so that risks are reduced and intentions to use the e-service grow.

H2: Perceived Ease of Use has a significant positive impact on customers' behavioral intentions to use internet banking services.

Perceived Security and Behavioral Intention to Use Internet Banking

Electronic services are hindered by the possibility of losing personal information or transactions (Nguyen, 2020). However, consumers' judgment or perception of whether a system or service given by a corporation is secure enough for them to perform a transaction is interpreted as perceived security (Wilson et al., 2021). Likewise, Rahi and Ghani (2018) in order to increase users' confidence in using internet banking, banks should focus on new features and perceived security measures. Besides, Janahi (2021) says individuals' willingness to apply for online services may be reduced due to security concerns ranging from personal information disclosure to money loss. Therefore, customers tend to have a better trust in internet banking if higher level of security is believed to exist (Normalini et al., 2019).

H3: Perceived security has a significant positive impact on customers' behavioral intentions to use internet banking services.

Social Influence and Behavioral Intention to Use Internet Banking

When it comes to adopting new technology, people tend to consult their social network, and they are impacted by the perceived social pressure from important ones (Matsuo et al., 2018) which also impacts on behavioral intention to use the internet services (Fedorko & Bačik, 2021). Similarly, Rahi and Ngah (2018) revealed individuals who believe that others think highly of their use of new items or services are more likely to employ these products or technology services. Users' decisions to use online banking are influenced by peer and family pressure in the sphere of Internet banking (lrfan Bashir, 2015).

H4: Social influence has a significant positive impact on customers' behavioral intentions to use internet banking services.

Behavioral intention to Use Internet Banking

Client satisfaction and service quality must be a prerequisite for customer behavior intentions (Iqbal et al., 2018). However, customers' attitudes toward the use of new technology are often thought to have an impact on their behavioral intentions where users' behavioral intents to make mobile payments are influenced by characteristics such as self-efficacy, risk, trust, security, and attitude (Chao, 2019). Users' adoption of information technology systems, according to TAM, is influenced by their intention to use the systems, which is influenced by their views about the system. The perceived usefulness (PU) and perceived ease of use (PE) of information technology systems influence users' views about them (Davis, 1980). Social influence and perceived security are the two additional variables that have impacts upon the behavioral intention towards internet banking usage.

Empirical Framework

Davis (1980) introduced the technology acceptance model (TAM) with two main objectives. First, by providing new theoretical insights into successful information system design and execution, it should help us better understand user acceptance processes. Second, TAM should lay the theoretical groundwork for a practical "user acceptability testing" technique, which allows system designers and implementers to assess proposed new systems prior to implementation. Potential users would be given system prototypes and their motivation to adopt alternative systems would be monitored in order to implement the proposed model in user acceptance testing (Davis, 1980). Structural equation modeling paradigm will be used to test the TAM model in my research. The equations defining the proposed model are given below:

$$\text{EOU} = \beta 1 \text{ System} + e$$

$$\text{USEF} = \beta 1 \text{ System} + \beta 2 \text{ EOU} + e$$

$$\text{ATT} = \beta 1 \text{ EOU} + \beta 2 \text{ USEF} + e$$

$$\text{USE} = \beta 1 \text{ ATT} + e$$

where,

EOU = Perceived Ease of Use

USEF = Perceived Usefulness

ATT = Attitude towards using

USE = Actual System Use

β = Specified Parameters

e = Error

Variable and Its Definition

This section discusses the variables used in the analysis as well as the hypothesis that was developed. The variables that will be used in the research have already described and established and present in Table 2.

Table 1. Variables with its definitions

Construct	Indicators	Variables	Details
Perceived Ease of Use (PEOU)	**PEOU1**	User- Friendly	Internet banking services clear and understandable
	PEOU2	Easy to Operate	Overall function easy to conduct
	PEOU3	Skillful	Easy to become skillful at the use of the Internet Banking services
Perceived Usefulness (PU)	**PU1**	Quickness	Enable users to accomplish the task more quickly than traditional banking(Cheng et al., 2006)
	PU4	Convenient	Enables users to complete the banking activities conveniently
	PU5	Advantageous	Overall using internet banking services is advantageous
Perceived Security (PS)	**PS1**	Privacy	Using internet banking services wouldn't reveal personal information
	PS2	Trustworthy	Users trust the technology
	PS5	Verification	Bank has the ability to verify users' identity for security purpose
Social Influence (SI)	**SI1**	Importance of People	Important people think of the use of Internet banking
	SI2	Influence of People	People influencing in use of the platform
	SI4	Image	Using internet banking services enhances the image in the society
Behavioral Intention (BI)	**BI2**	Recommendation	Strongly recommend others to use internet banking
	BI4	Frequency	Frequently use internet banking in the future
	BI5	Prediction	Given the access there is the prediction of the usage of the platform

Notes: PEOU4, PEOU5, PU2, PU3, PS3, PS4, SI3, SI5, BI1 and BI3 were dropped after performing Confirmatory and Exploratory Factor Analysis and these items value remain below 0.5.

Study Area, Sampling, and Population

Kathmandu, Lalitpur and Bhaktapur are three districts of Kathmandu valley- located between 27°32'13" and 27°49'10" north latitudes and 85°11'31" and 85°31'38" east longitudes, at a height of 1,300 meters above sea level (Maharjan et al., 2022; Adhikari et al., 2022). Since, Kathmandu is Nepal's capital and one of the few places with a dense population and a hub for a variety of important enterprises and banks, conducting an internet banking research would produce more accurate and dependable results.

Additionally, online activity is centered in Kathmandu and a half-dozen other towns, with very limited web penetration in rural areas, Kathmandu valley (see Figure 2) is chosen as study area for this study. However, target population is the internet banking users of Kathmandu Valley. As per Nepal Rastra Bank (2021), Mobile banking, ATMs, and online banking are used by 32.03 percent, 20.35 percent, and 3.86 percent of account holders, respectively (Kutu et al., 2023). Besides, internet banking users are in the minority compared to ATM card and mobile banking users.

Figure 2. Study area
Source: ArcGIS, Study Area

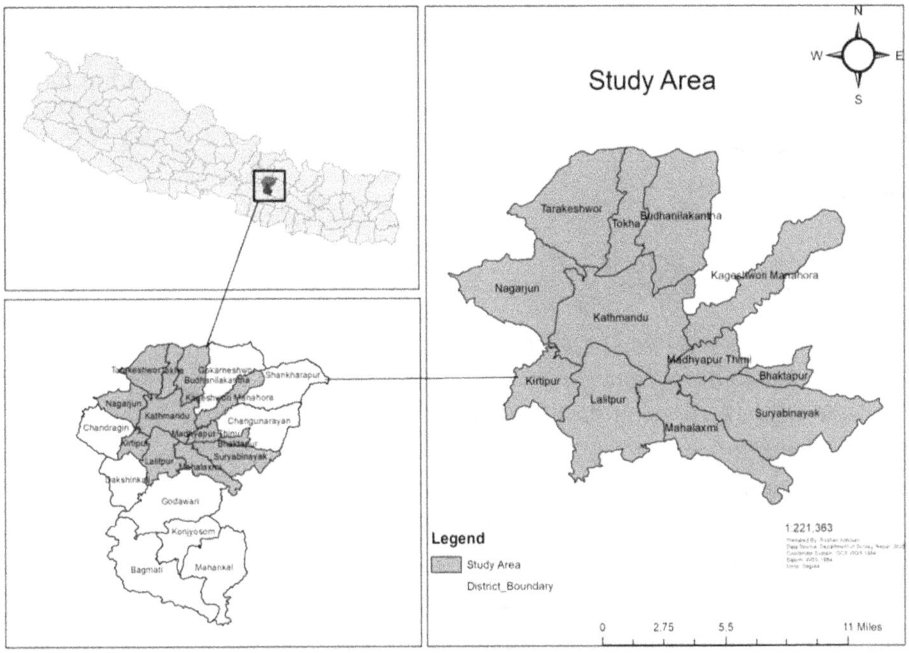

As the numbers of respondents or customers who use the internet banking services are unknown under the periphery of Kathmandu Valley, there is no defined sample frame for the collection of data; the researcher opted to choose the non-probability sampling. Specifically, convenience sampling (Etikan 2016) was chosen it is gives time effectiveness and is least expensive, more data can be collected within a short period of time. Besides, sample were taken from the potential internet banking users who are aware of internet banking services who also use it. For populations that are large, Cochran developed the equation to yield a representative sample for proportions which is also suitable for non-probability sampling technique.

$n_0 = z^2pq/e^2$ (Naing, 2003) (i)

Where, n_0= sample size required for study

Standard tabulated value for 5% level of significance (z)= 1.96

p= prevalence or proportion of an event 50%
Allowable error that can be tolerated (e)= 6%.
Thus, the final sample size required for this study is 280.

Research Instruments and Data Analysis Technique

During data collection, a standardized questionnaire was devised and established to perform a study on customers' behavioral intentions regarding internet banking usage during COVID. Internet banking customers were invited to participate in the survey. The primary data was gathered using checklist in KOBO Toolbox which were designed in straightforward and simple language to describe their objective and address the study's difficulty. Data were collected from February 2022 to March 2022 through face-to-face encounters with some respondents, as well as phone conversations. Besides, the data was analyzed with descriptive and inferential approaches, including structural equation modeling. KOBO Toolbox, Microsoft Excel, and SPSS AMOS were used for data analysis.

Results and Discussion

Socio-Demographic Characteristics

Socio-demographic data usually contains the respondents' personal characteristics. Age, gender, education level, occupation, and monthly income were all considered in this study. However, result indicates that 62.72% of the customers who uses internet banking were male; 49.82% of them are ranging from 20-30 having master's and above degree (57.71%). It also indicates that majority of the customers who uses internet banking are students (34.05%). However, 41.58% indicates that they earn below NRs. 20,000 per months (see Figure 2) which indicates that internet banking activities are mostly conducted by the middle-class people whose income level is average. Several studies like Correa and Montero (2013), Amin (2016) and Jayasiri et al. (2016) indicates that young male respondents are more influenced by the advantages of IB and they are expected to be the prevailing when using IB and appears that having a higher degree of academic understanding improves the adoption and implementation of internet banking activities, respectively. In addition, internet banking activities are also influenced by the profession of the people. In nutshell, Danurdoro and Wulandari (2016) revealed students and banks are increasingly offering internet banking services, allowing students to complete banking transactions online. Likewise, of Aboagye et al. (2016) states middle-class customers do not exclusively use online banking services.

Factors Influencing the Behavioral Intention Towards Internet Banking Usage

The impact of numerous factors during COVID on behavioral intention to use online banking is described in depth in the following sections, with each variable being discussed separately. Each construct is followed by a set of questions in which respondents are asked to indicate whether they strongly disagree (1), disagree (2), neutral (3), agree (4), or strongly agree (5) with the assertion.

Table 2. Socio-demographic characteristics

Variables	In Numbers	In Percentage
Sex		
Male	175	62.72%
Female	104	37.28%
Age		
Below 20	4	1.43%
20-30	139	49.82%
31-40	60	21.51%
41-50	40	15.77%
Above 50	32	11.47%
Education Level		
Intermediate	27	9.68%
Bachelor's Level	91	32.62%
Master's and Above	121	57.71%
Profession		
Student	95	34.05%
Banker	79	28.32%
Teacher	39	12.9%
Businessman	11	3.94%
Others	58	20.9%
Income Level		
Below 20,000	116	41.58%
20,001-40,000	64	22.94%
40,001-60,000	61	21.86%
60,001-80,000	15	5.38%
80,000 and Above	23	8.24%

Source: Survey

Perceived Ease of Use contains the explanatory variables such as user-friendly, easy to operate and skillful. Result indicates that internet banking services are clear and understandable and are user friendly. A crucial driver of usability is the user friendliness of domain names, as well as the navigation tools provided on websites (Singhal & Padhmanabhan, 2009). It also indicates that IB is easy to operate and customers agree the fact that it is easy to become skillful in the usage of internet banking. Likewise, quickness, convenient and advantageous are explanatory variables under *perceived usefulness* where customers agree that internet banking enables users to accomplish the tasks more quickly, the internet banking activities are convenient or effortless and are advantageous to use. Besides, Singhal and Padhmanabhan (2009) also stated that internet banking is convenient however, traditional banking channels do not offer many of the benefits that online banking does (Lee, 2009). Finally, the vast majority of customers consider internet banking to be extremely beneficial in every manner.

Likewise, *Perceived Security* contains the privacy, trustworthy and verification as explanatory variables. Result depict that using internet banking services would not reveal their personal information while negligible proportion of users declares that internet banking will disclose their privacy. In addition, internet banking is trustworthy in all aspects and has its ability to verify users' identity for security purpose. One study made in Nepal by Khatri & Upadhyaya-Dhungel, (2013) also supports that internet banking has aided people in completing banking duties more quickly and feeling more secure in their financial transactions. They have faith in their bank's internet banking website. Similarly, *social influence* contains importance of people, influence of people and image. Result revealed that it is not that much importance of people to use internet banking and there is disgrace that important people think that he/she should use internet banking and disagree with the fact that using the internet banking services improves the image in the society. In addition, Safeena et al. (2014) believes that customers are attracted to internet banking due to perceived benefits rather than societal pressure. Lastly, *behavioral intention* to use internet banking has an explanatory variable such as recommendation, frequency and prediction. However, results revealed that customers who are enthusiastic about making payments over the Internet will enthusiastically recommend it to others and will frequently use the internet banking services in future. In addition, customers who are more likely to embrace and support new technologies are more likely to become adopters and evangelists (Rahi & Ngah, 2018).

Figure 3. Variables discussion

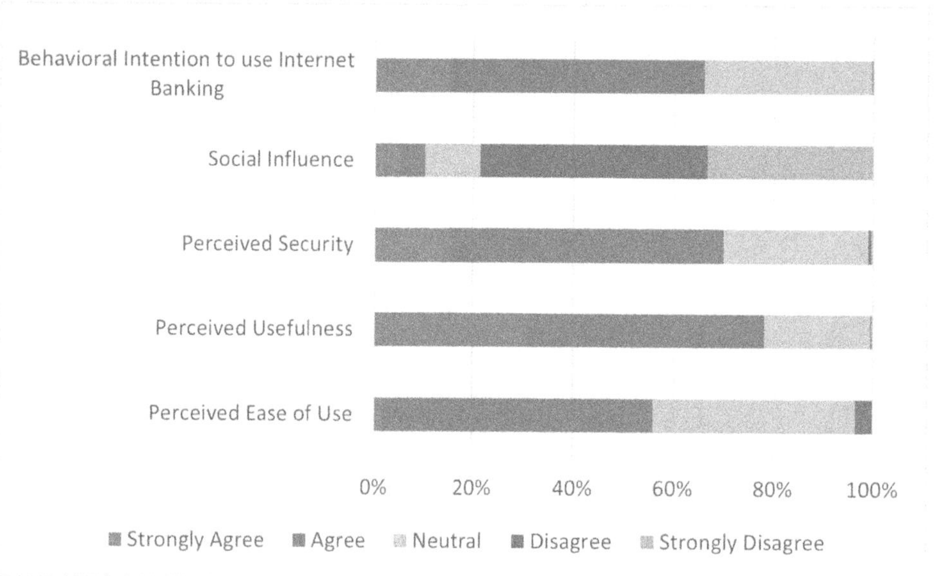

Prospects of Internet Banking During COVID-19

Despite the advantages of internet banking, the people face a variety of issues and hurdles. This study indicates that there are issues and challenges while adopting internet banking and revealed that major challenges of internet banking during COVID 19 are poor internet speed (78.92%) and heavy network traffic (77.27%), whereas other challenges are the fear of the viruses to the system (23.55%), whereas 19.83% feel fear of losing social relationship with bankers, internet sites malfunction (12.40%), fear of hackers (12.80%) and privacy issue (8.67%) (see Table 3). Similarly, respondents were asked from whom such challenges had come. Respondents believed that Organization Policy (91.42%), Government Policy (80.36%), Customers (53.12%), IT Officers (41.36%), Stakeholders (15.14%), BOD (5.31%), and competitors were the major entities responsible for the successful adoption of Internet Banking during COVID (3.54%) whereas, the study of Lukovic (2021) concludes that banks are not liable if their consumers do not have access to the internet.

Table 3. Challenges of internet banking during COVID-19

Factors	Number of Respondents	Percentage
Poor internet Speed	191	78.92%
Heavy Network Traffic	187	77.27%
Fear of Viruses to the system	57	23.55%
Losing social relationship with the bankers	48	19.83%
Fear of hackers	31	12.80%
Internet sites malfunction	30	12.40%
Privacy concerns	21	8.68%

Source: Field Study

Table 4 shows the managerial solutions for the challenges of internet banking. Therefore, this study indicates that flawless connectivity of the internet (52.43%), Upgradation of the system (43.07%), Technical problems Resolution (35.20%) making system secured (32.58%) are major managerial solutions for the challenges of internet banking and directed to organization to solve them.

Table 4. Managerial solutions for the challenges of internet banking

Factors	Number of Respondents	Percentage
Strong Internet Connection	140	52.43%
Upgradation of the system	115	43.07%
Technical problems Resolution	94	35.20%
Make Secured	87	32.58%

Source: Field Study

Inferential Analysis

Summary Statistics and EFA

Descriptive statistics shows the responses' mean and standard deviation lies from 3.5341 to 4.1720 and 0.56509 to 0.75636, respectively, indicating minimal dispersion. However, this study indicate the skewness of each variable lies between -1 and below +1 denoting negative skewness of data which suggest that the tail on the left side is longer (Blanca et al., 2013). Similarly, all kurtosis values range between -2 to +2 which denotes that the distribution is not excessively raised which indicates that data is free from normality. In this study, the KMO value is 0.718 and it satisfies the 0.60 criterion. In the same way, the p-value (significance threshold) is 0.000, indicating that the data is significant and less than 0.05. Likewise, for common bias it is found that the cumulative value of the common bias is 21.087% which is less than 50% which is a good outcome and free from common method bias.

Confirmatory Factor Analysis and Measurement Model

The fitness indices CMN/DF, RMR, RMSEA, GFI, IFT, TLI, and CFI are used to determine if the model fit is excellent or not. Therefore, in this study, the CMN/DF default value is 1.875<5, RMR value is 0.036< 0.08, RMSEA value is 0.056<0.08, GFI value is 0.934, IFI value is 0.968, TLI value is 0.9588 and CFI value is 0.968 which is >0.90 indicating for excellent fit indices. Similarly, to analyze the measurement instruments in this study, only two validity approaches will be used: convergent validity and discriminant validity. They were used to verify the data's reliability and validity as indicated in Tables 5 and 6. In order to confirm the requirement of the convergence validity the data must satisfy the condition that the CR must be greater than 0.7. Similarly, AVE must be greater than 0.5. While, to fulfil the condition of discriminant validity AVE must be greater than MSV and the square root of AVE should be greater than the correlation. Since the result of my analysis meets the entire above criterion it can be said that there are no issues of both convergence and discriminant validity.

Table 5. Reliability and validity

Construct	Indicators	Factor Loading	Cronbach's Alpha	CR	AVE	MSV
Perceived Ease of Use	PEOU1	0.942	0.943	0.817	0.599	0.056
	PEOU2	0.949				
	PEOU3	0.943				
Perceived Usefulness	PU1	0.870	0.845	0.847	0.649	0.056
	PU4	0.836				
	PU5	0.882				
Perceived Security	PS1	0.889	0.843	0.944	0.849	0.015
	PS2	0.864				
	PS5	0.853				
Social Influence	SI1	0.892	0.825	0.845	0.646	0.016
	SI2	0.874				
	SI4	0.804				
Behavioral Intention to Use Internet Banking	BI2	0.870	0.817	0.836	0.632	0.046
	BI4	0.833				
	BI5	0.840				

Source: Field Survey

Table 6. Latest construct correlation

	BI	PU	PEOU	PS	SI
BI	**0.774**				
PU	0.236	**0.805**			
PEOU	-0.120	0.122	**0.921**		
PS	0.097	0.078	0.043	**0.804**	
SI	0.133	0.214	-0.053	0.127	**0.795**

Source: Field Survey

Test of Hypothesis

In Table 7, H1 and H2 are accepted which implies that there is significant relationship. In contrast, H3 and H4 are rejected that leads to the conclusion that there is insignificant relationship between the variable in the respective hypothesis. SEM is utilized in the inferential phase of the inquiry to look at regression analysis, variable analysis, and the normality pattern. Five factors are investigated when latent variables are compared to observable variables. The model's fitness criteria show the fitness. The result shows that the value obtained from X^2/df (CMIN/DF) is 1.875 which is less than 3. The p value suggesting a meaningful association between latent variables and observable variables is less than 0.1, according to the data. Because the meaning level of all hypotheses (p-value) is less than 0.1, the hypotheses in this study are broadly accepted. As a result, all of the study's independent variables have a significant impact on all contingent factor hypotheses.

Figure 4. Structural model

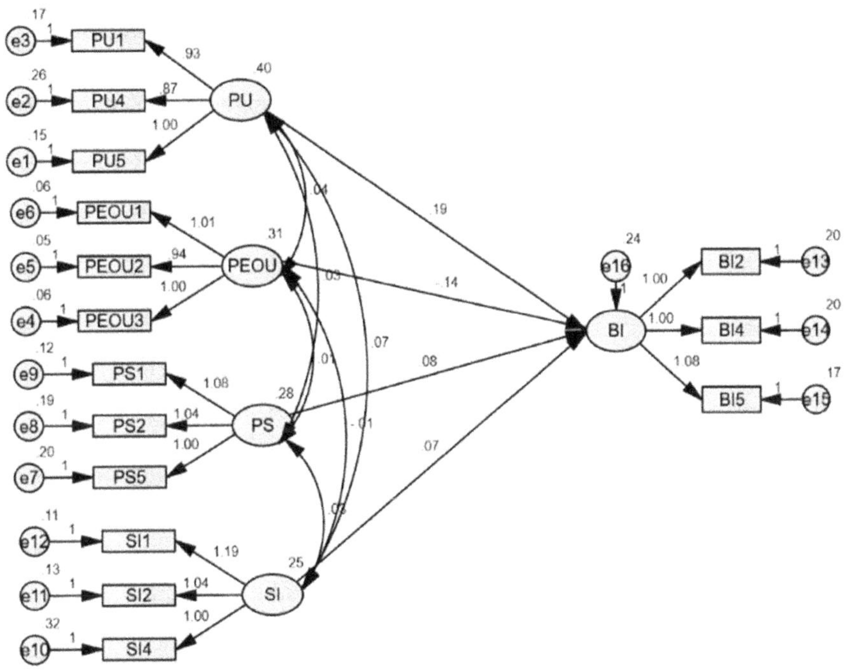

Table 7. Path estimates for structural model

Hypothesis	Estimate	S.E.	C.R.	P	Hypothesis Result
H1: Perceived Usefulness → Behavioral Intention to Use Internet Banking	.191	.061	3.157	.002	Significant
H2: Perceived Ease of Use → Behavioral Intention to Use Internet Banking	-.139	.063	-2.200	.028	Significant
H3: Perceived Security → Behavioral Intention to Use Internet Banking	.075	.069	1.095	.273	Insignificant
H4: Social Influence → Behavioral Intention to Use Internet Banking	.067	.074	.908	.364	Insignificant

Discussion and Conclusion

The reliability test and multiple linear correlations were used to build and test the link between the variables in this investigation. Table 7 shows that two out of four hypotheses are significant. Perceived Usefulness and Perceived Ease of Use of use have a positive impact on behavioral intention to use internet banking, according to supported hypothesis 1 and 2. The study of Patel and Patel (2018) also provided the same consequences. According to the hypothesis 1, people who believed that the tasks like bill payments, fund transfer, viewing the statements and so on can be done more quickly and conveniently have the substantial effect on the behavioral intention to use internet banking. To avoid becoming infected with the Corona virus during the COVID-19 pandemic, people work and study from home and limit their external interactions. As a result of the condition, the community's lifestyle must alter, and internet outlets are preferred (Iriani & Andjarwati, 2020). Customers who visit branches during the COVID phase believe that doing so will force them to stand in line for a long time and enhance their chances of receiving COVID-19, therefore they believe that starting internet banking is preferable (Naeem & Ozuem, 2021). One study made by (Guriting & Oly Ndubisi, 2006) also says that there is significant impact of Perceived Usefulness on online banking adoption intention.

User friendly interface, easy to become skilled in operating the system, easiness in all the functions of the internet banking comes under the Perceived Ease of Use. The study made by (Guriting & Oly Ndubisi, 2006; Giovanis et al., 2012) also says that there is significant impact of Perceived Ease of Use and intention towards the use of internet banking. Customers can access their accounts at any time of day or night via internet banking. Internet banking also eliminates the anxiety associated with handling actual currency, lowers transaction costs, saves time, and provides for immediate access from any location also comes under the Perceived Ease of Use (Maqbool, 2018).

The hypothesis 3 says that the perceived security has insignificant impact on the behavioral intention towards internet banking. Security concerns might not totally affect the internet banking behavior of the people (Khatri & Upadhyaya-Dhungel, 2013). During pandemic internet banking is only the option since physical travel was risky. People find the internet banking trustworthy and secured. One study of (Damghanian et al., 2016) also concludes in his study that customers' adoption of internet banking was not influenced by their perception of security. The rejected hypothesis 4 states that the social influence has insignificant impact on the behavioral intention towards internet banking usage. This hypothesis supports the findings made by (William Lewis, 2003) which also supports the fact that there were no discernible effects from a variety of social forces on internet banking adoption.

The authors went to great attempts to increase the sample size and go deeper into the variables. Regardless, there are several faults in the research. Because it had to be completed in a short amount of time to achieve a degree requirement, the study was limited to a particular topic. More research is needed on this topic in various parts of the country to gain a better grasp of how local people feel about it. This study solely employed a questionnaire survey approach; however, in addition to these surveys, a few in-depth interviews or focused group discussions could have aided in determining the underlying cause of perceived good and negative impacts, satisfaction, and participation in internet banking activities. Studies should focus on the multiple implications on the country as a whole in order to better grasp the extent of internet banking. COVID-19 had a detrimental impact on the banking industry from 2020 to 2022. Because this study focuses on the COVID period, it's important to consider how internet banking users react in terms of perceived impacts, support for internet banking intentions to use, platform trust, and people's involvement in internet banking in the post-COVID-19 era.

The primary goal of this study is to assess customers' behavioral intentions regarding internet banking during COVID-19 in Kathmandu Valley. The research also has specific goals, including analyzing the obstacles of internet banking among internet banking customers in Kathmandu Valley during COVID, and then analyzing the managerial solutions to the challenges of internet banking in Kathmandu Valley during COVID-19. Besides, a theoretical review reveals that numerous ideas coming from the field of internet banking, as well as consumers' behavioral intentions to use it, have been related to the notion of Internet Banking to give solid theoretical knowledge. Because of rising financial worries, technical challenges, and digital inclusiveness, many countries are paying attention to Internet Banking practices. This empirical research has given us valuable insights on how to grasp internet banking during COVID in various parts of the country. Concerns have been raised about the function of internet banking during pandemics and its impact on human behavior, according to the studies. My study looked at the impact of various factors on Internet Banking behavior by examining the conceptual relationships between independent variables (Perceived Usefulness, Perceived Ease of Use, Perceived Security, and Social Influence) and the dependent variable (Behavioral Intention to Use Internet Banking). Convenience Data was acquired from online banking customers in the Kathmandu Valley using a sampling method, while primary data was collected using a structured questionnaire and interviews. In addition, a variety of analytical methodologies were used to thoroughly inspect and analyze the study data, including descriptive and inferential analysis using the Structured Equation Model (SEM).

The findings of the study can be used to develop a variety of solutions, particularly for internet banking practices in Nepal. Effective government and organization policies can be the strategy to improve the experience of internet banking. It will eventually lead to long-term technological progress while also assisting in the reduction of errors in the internet banking system. Improvements in Internet Banking also assist banks in achieving successful results, such as gaining a first mover advantage. Many banks can also get a competitive advantage by building a brand image and growing customer numbers. Since internet banking is not as popular as mobile banking, increasing public awareness of the importance of internet banking may lead to a rise in the number of internet banking users. Internet banking is becoming increasingly important in many banks and among IT workers. IT specialists, as intellectual experts in technology components, can help improve the efficiency of internet banking. However, further change is required before individuals and banks can make the huge leap toward ensuring online banking efficiency in all of their activities.

Funding

There is no funding support for this study

Conflict of Interest

The authors declare no conflict of interest

Ethical Approval

Ethical approval for the study has granted from Quest Research Management Cell, Quest International College. This paper is the part of MBA research.

Informed Consent

Informed consent was granted with the respondents before proceed the survey with them.

REFERENCES

Aboagye, E., Ansong, M., & Dagadu, J. (2016). E-Banking Preferences and Middle Class Values in Ghana. *Journal of Computing*, *4*(2), 35–46. doi:10.12691/jcsa-4-2-2

Adhikari, B., Devkota, N., Parajuli, S., Paudel, U. R., Upretee, S., Mahato, S., . . . Dhakal, K. (2023). Teachers' Perceptions on Adoption of Education 4.0 in Schools in Nepal: Evidence From Structural Equation Modelling. In Handbook of Research on Education Institutions, Skills, and Jobs in the Digital Era (pp. 341-358). IGI Global.

Adhikari, K. P. (2019). Determinants of E-Banking in Nepal. *Management Dynamics*, *22*(2), 89–94. doi:10.3126/md.v22i2.30241

Ahasanul Haque, A. (2009). *Issues of E-Banking Transaction: An Empirical Investigation on Malaysian Customers Perception*. Academic Press.

Ahmad, M. (2018). *Review of The Technology Acceptance Model (TAM) in Internet banking and Mobile banking*. Academic Press.

Alshurideh, M. T., Al Kurdi, B., & Salloum, S. A. (2021). The moderation effect of gender on accepting electronic payment technology: a study on United Arab Emirates consumers. *Review of International Business and Strategy*.

Apulu, I., & Latham, A. (2011). Drivers for Information and Communication Technology Adoption: A Case Study of Nigerian Small and Medium Sized Enterprises. *International Journal of Business and Management*, *6*(5). Advance online publication. doi:10.5539/ijbm.v6n5p51

Blanca, M. J., Arnau, J., López-Montiel, D., Bono, R., & Bendayan, R. (2013). Skewness and kurtosis in real data samples. *Methodology: European Journal of Research Methods for the Behavioral and Social Sciences*, *9*(2), 78–84. doi:10.1027/1614-2241/a000057

Calisir, F., & Gumussoy, C. A. (2008). Internet banking versus other banking channels: Young consumers' view. *International Journal of Information Management*, *28*(3), 215–221. doi:10.1016/j.ijinfomgt.2008.02.009

Camarinha-Matos, L. M., Afsarmanesh, H., Galeano, N., & Molina, A. (2009). Collaborative networked organizations - Concepts and practice in manufacturing enterprises. *Computers & Industrial Engineering*, *57*(1), 46–60. doi:10.1016/j.cie.2008.11.024

Chao, C. M. (2019). Factors determining the behavioral intention to use mobile learning: An application and extension of the UTAUT model. *Frontiers in Psychology*, *10*(1), 1–14. doi:10.3389/fpsyg.2019.01652 PMID:31379679

Chauhan, V., Yadav, R., & Choudhary, V. (2019). Analyzing the impact of consumer innovativeness and perceived risk in internet banking adoption: A study of Indian consumers. *International Journal of Bank Marketing*, *37*(1), 323–339. doi:10.1108/IJBM-02-2018-0028

Cheng, T. C. E., Lam, D. Y. C., & Yeung, A. C. L. (2006). Adoption of internet banking: An empirical study in Hong Kong. *Decision Support Systems*, *42*(3), 1558–1572. doi:10.1016/j.dss.2006.01.002

Damghanian, H., Zarei, A., & Siahsarani Kojuri, M. A. (2016). Impact of Perceived Security on Trust, Perceived Risk, and Acceptance of Online Banking in Iran. *Journal of Internet Commerce*, *15*(3), 214–238. doi:10.1080/15332861.2016.1191052

Danurdoro, K., & Wulandari, D. (2016). The Impact of Perceived Usefulness, Perceived Ease of Use, Subjective Norm, and Experience Toward Student's Intention to Use Internet Banking. *Jurnal Ekonomi Dan Ekonomi Studi Pembangunan*, *8*(1), 17–22. doi:10.17977/um002v8i12016p017

Dasgupta, S., Paul, R., & Fuloria, S. (2011). An Empirical Study to Understand the Different Antecedents of Relationship Quality in the Indian Context with Reference to the Mobile Telecommunication Sector. *Romanian Journal of Marketing*, *6*(1), 1–117.

Etikan, I. (2016). Comparison of Convenience Sampling and Purposive Sampling. *American Journal of Theoretical and Applied Statistics*, *5*(1), 1. doi:10.11648/j.ajtas.20160501.11

Featherman, M. S., Miyazaki, A. D., & Sprott, D. E. (2010). Reducing online privacy risk to facilitate e-service adoption: The influence of perceived ease of use and corporate credibility. *Journal of Services Marketing*, *24*(3), 219–229. doi:10.1108/08876041011040622

Fedorko, I., & Bačik, R. (2021). *Performance expectancy using electronic banking: Effort expectancy and social influence factors as main determinants of performance expectancy using electronic banking*. doi:10.21511/bbs.16(2).2021.03

Fred, D., & Davis, J. (1980). *A technology acceptance model for empirically testing new end-user information systems: theory and results*. doi:10.1126/science.146.3652.1648

Giovanis, A. N., Binioris, S., & Polychronopoulos, G. (2012). An extension of TAM model with IDT and security/privacy risk in the adoption of internet banking services in Greece. *EuroMed Journal of Business*, *7*(1), 24–53. doi:10.1108/14502191211225365

González, M. E., Mueller, R. D., & Mack, R. W. (2008). An Alternative Approach in Service Quality: An e-Banking Case Study. *The Quality Management Journal*, *15*(1), 41–58. doi:10.1080/10686967.2008.11918055

Gopalakrishnan, S., Wischnevsky, J. D., & Damanpour, F. (2003). A multilevel analysis of factors influencing the adoption of internet banking. *IEEE Transactions on Engineering Management*, *50*(4), 413–426. doi:10.1109/TEM.2003.819648

Guriting, P., & Oly Ndubisi, N. (2006). Borneo online banking: Evaluating customer perceptions and behavioural intention. *Management Research News*, *29*(January), 6–15. doi:10.1108/01409170610645402

Hassan, H. E., & Wood, V. R. (2020). Does country culture influence consumers' perceptions toward mobile banking? A comparison between Egypt and the United States. *Telematics and Informatics*, *46*, 101312. doi:10.1016/j.tele.2019.101312

Iriani, S. S., & Andjarwati, A. L. (2020). Analysis of perceived usefulness, perceived ease of use, and perceived risk toward online shopping in the era of Covid-19 pandemic. *Systematic Reviews in Pharmacy*, *11*(12), 313–320. doi:10.31838rp.2020.12.50

Janahi, Y. (2021). *The Impact of Internet Banking Adoption in The Kingdom of Bahrain - Overcoming Barriers to Adoption Through the Use of Biometrics*. Academic Press.

Jha, R. (2020). Challenges of adoption of internet banking service in cooperative banks in India. *UGC Care Group I Journal*, *10*(7), 178–194. doi:10.1108/IJBM-01-2013-0001

Jiyaul Hak Ansari, H. A. A. K. (2019). Course code : BE309E Name / Candidate no.: Jiyaul Hak Ansari Hafiz Abrar Anwar Khan Total number of pages. Academic Press.

Khatri, J. R., & Upadhyaya-Dhungel, K. (2013). Internet Banking in Nepal: Use and Challenges. *Banking Journal*, *3*(2), 57–77. doi:10.3126/bj.v3i2.8544

Kutu, S., Devkota, N., Upretee, S., Paudel, U. R., & Dhakal, K. (2023). Commercial Bank Readiness for Adoption of Marketing 4.0: Evidence From Nepal. In Marketing and Advertising in the Online-to-Offline (O2O) World (pp. 247-266). IGI Global.

Lai, V. S., & Li, H. (2005). *Technology acceptance model for internet banking : An invariance analysis*. doi:10.1016/j.im.2004.01.007

Lee, M. C. (2009). Factors influencing the adoption of internet banking: An integration of TAM and TPB with perceived risk and perceived benefit. *Electronic Commerce Research and Applications*, *8*(3), 130–141. doi:10.1016/j.elerap.2008.11.006

Lrfan Bashir, C. M. (2015). *Trust, Social Influence, Self-Efficacy, Perceived Risk and Internet Banking Acceptance: An Extension of Technology Acceptance Model in Indian Context*. Academic Press.

Lukovic, V. (2021). *Online Banking and Information Technology During the Covid-19 Pandemic: Between the Need and the Ability*. Academic Press.

Maharjan, P., Devkota, N., Mahapatra, S., Padda, I. U. H., Dhakal, K., & Mahato, S., ... Bhattarai, U. (2022, Summer). FinTech Adoption among Online Grocery Buyers during COVID-19 Lockdowns in Nepal. *Journal of Private Enterprise*, *37*, 57–89.

Maqbool, A. (2018). Review of the technology acceptance model (TAM) in internet banking and mobile banking. *International Journal of Information Communication Technology and Digital Convergence*, *3*(1), 23–41.

Mastran, S. (2021). Opportunities and Challenges of Online Banking in Nepal. *The Batuk*, *7*(2), 37–51. doi:10.3126/batuk.v7i2.39498

Matsuo, M., Minami, C., & Matsuyama, T. (2018). Social influence on innovation resistance in internet banking services. *Journal of Retailing and Consumer Services, 45*(August), 42–51. doi:10.1016/j.jretconser.2018.08.005

McLean, G., Osei-Frimpong, K., Al-Nabhani, K., & Marriott, H. (2020). Examining consumer attitudes towards retailers' m-commerce mobile applications–An initial adoption vs. continuous use perspective. *Journal of Business Research, 106*, 139–157. doi:10.1016/j.jbusres.2019.08.032

Mohammed, A. H., & Ward, T. (2006). The effect of automated service quality on Australian banks' financial performance and the mediating role of customer satisfaction. *Marketing Intelligence & Planning, 24*(2), 127–147. doi:10.1108/02634500610653991

Mols, N. P. (1999). The Internet and the banks' strategic distribution channel decisions. *International Journal of Bank Marketing, 17*(6), 295–300. doi:10.1108/02652329910300341

Moslehpour, M., Pham, V. K., Wong, W. K., & Bilgiçli, I. (2018). e-purchase intention of Taiwanese consumers: Sustainable mediation of perceived usefulness and perceived ease of use. *Sustainability (Basel), 10*(1), 234. Advance online publication. doi:10.3390u10010234

Mutahar, A. M., Daud, N. M., Thurasamy, R., Isaac, O., & Abdulsalam, R. (2018). The Mediating of Perceived Usefulness and Perceived Ease of Use. *International Journal of Technology Diffusion, 9*(2), 21–40. doi:10.4018/IJTD.2018040102

Naeem, M., & Ozuem, W. (2021). The role of social media in internet banking transition during COVID-19 pandemic: Using multiple methods and sources in qualitative research. *Journal of Retailing and Consumer Services, 60*(October), 102483. doi:10.1016/j.jretconser.2021.102483

Naing, N. N. (2003). Determination of sample size. *The Malaysian Journal of Medical Sciences : MJMS, 10*(2), 84–86. PMID:23386802

Namahoot, K. S., & Laohavichien, T. (2018). Assessing the intentions to use internet banking: The role of perceived risk and trust as mediating factors. *International Journal of Bank Marketing, 36*(2), 256–276. doi:10.1108/IJBM-11-2016-0159

Nepal Rastra Bank. (2021). Financial Access in Nepal. Academic Press.

Nguyen, O. T. (2020). Factors affecting the intention to use digital banking in Vietnam. *Journal of Asian Finance. Economics and Business, 7*(3), 303–310. doi:10.13106/jafeb.2020.vol7.no3.303

NRB. (2020). *Payment System Oversight report.* NRB.

Patel, K. J., & Patel, H. J. (2018). Adoption of internet banking services in Gujarat. *International Journal of Bank Marketing, 36*(1), 147–169. doi:10.1108/IJBM-08-2016-0104

Rahi, S., & Abd. Ghani, M. (2018). The role of UTAUT, DOI, perceived technology security and game elements in internet banking adoption. *World Journal of Science. Technology and Sustainable Development, 15*(4), 338–356. doi:10.1108/WJSTSD-05-2018-0040

Rahi, S., & Ngah, A. H. (2018). *A structural equation model for evaluating user's intention to adopt internet banking and intention to recommend technology.* https://doi.org/ doi:10.5267/j.ac.2018.03.002

Sandhu, S., & Arora, S. (2020). Customers' usage behaviour of e-banking services: Interplay of electronic banking and traditional banking. *International Journal of Finance and Economics,* 1–13. doi:10.1002/ijfe.2266

Shahid Iqbal, M., Ul Hassan, M., & Habibah, U. (2018). Impact of self-service technology (SST) service quality on customer loyalty and behavioral intention: The mediating role of customer satisfaction. *Cogent Business and Management*, *5*(1), 1. Advance online publication. doi:10.1080/23311975.2018.1423770

Singhal, D., & Padhmanabhan, V. (2009). A Study on Customer Perception Towards Internet Banking: Identifying Major Contributing Factors. *Journal of Nepalese Business Studies*, *5*(1), 101–111. doi:10.3126/jnbs.v5i1.2088

Tan, W., Rajkarnikar, N., Jeong, S. R., Shrestha, D., & Wenan, T. (2020). *Consumers attitude towards Internet banking services in an underdeveloped country: A case of Pokhara. Journal of Internet Services and Applications, 21*(5), 75–85

William Lewis, R. A. (2003). Sources of influence on beliefs about information technology use: An empirical study of knowledge workers1 By. *Management Information Systems Quarterly*, *27*(4), 657–678. doi:10.2307/30036552

Wilson, N., Alvita, M., & Wibisono, J. (2021). the Effect of Perceived Ease of Use and Perceived Security Toward Satisfaction and Repurchase Intention. *Jurnal Muara Ilmu Ekonomi Dan Bisnis*, *5*(1), 145. doi:10.24912/jmieb.v5i1.10489

Chapter 3
Job Satisfaction and Work Productivity During the COVID-19 Pandemic:
Involuntary Work From Home of Higher Education in Indonesia

Ida Nyoman Basmantra
Universitas Pendidikan Nasional, Indonesia

Aprilia Kusumaningtyas
Bina Nusantara University, Indonesia

Mochammad Firmansyah
Bina Nusantara University, Indonesia

Sevenpri Candra
https://orcid.org/0000-0002-3604-4748
Bina Nusantara University, Indonesia

ABSTRACT

The COVID-19 pandemic disrupted the nature of work. Involuntary work from home (IWFH), another form of telework, is increasingly promoted in sectors as a means to ensure continuity of operations in an emergency situation like a pandemic. This study includes the exploration of the relationship between involuntary work from home, communication functions, work-life balance, and its effect on work productivity and employee job satisfaction during this COVID-19 pandemic outbreak in the work situation of 100 employees at the higher educational institutions in Indonesia. The collected data of questionnaires were processed using the SEM method using the SmartPLS program. This study finds some critical factors shaping the experiences and outcomes of IWFH in pandemic situations. The success of work management depends on the communication function between employees to job satisfaction for work productivity.

DOI: 10.4018/978-1-7998-6896-5.ch003

INTRODUCTION

The corona virus outbreak (COVID-19) has threatened the health of the entire world community. According to the World Health Organization (WHO), COVID-19 is now officially categorized as a pandemic whose spread is getting faster. In addition, this pandemic also occurs not only targeting one region or country but also simultaneously (Sebayang, 2020). Pandemic can literally be defined as a virus with a scale of disease spread that occurs globally throughout the world and has a higher level than the epidemic (WHO, 2020). In this situation, WHO is warning all countries in the world to increase preparedness in preventing and managing the pandemic. This of course requires the state to make policies especially for all sectors. This policy aims to limit all activities both economically, socially, educationally, and everything that requires an interaction to break the chain of spread of this virus. One visible impact is the company. Companies are required to carry out involuntary work from home (IWFH) which means that all employees work at home. This of course triggered forcibly so that the company can adjust this situation as quickly as possible with an adequate digital platform. For many small companies and organizations, the situation tends to be very different, remote work may be limited to e-mail and other non-operational systems (Felstead and Henseke, 2017). Breaking organizations down into individuals who work at home with different requirements and meeting the needs of each individual is not a simple approach, but may be important, regarding the urgency in some cases, especially in Covid19 crisis situation.

In a crisis situation, clear policies are urgently needed for formal regulation of involuntary work from home (IWFH) institutionalized by the government, so that the expectations of work become clear in an uncertain disaster situation (Golden and Pyora, 2011). This illustrates a situation that changes forcefully, where and how people work in a pandemic raises significant employment problems. Particularly, being able to eliminate the voluntary nature of work because it requires employees to work from home in a disaster situation to change a working condition. As in the midst of the outbreak of Covid-19, many companies in Indonesia have begun to implement work from home (WFH) policies. The current work from home is a follow-up in Indonesia to minimize the spread of Covid-19, people are asked to work, study and worship from home, one of which is to create a system of working from home. This appeal, in particular having a serious impact on the national education situation, has been followed up by the Minister of Education and Culture in efforts to prevent Covid-19 in the educational environment. Literally, learning activities can work at home/residence, but it is ensured that all office operational management activities are also carried out online. In particular for higher education, the prohibition applies to all face-to-face activities where many participants have to be postponed or canceled. In the case of higher education institutions, internal compliance is needed suddenly in forming a unit that is tasked with monitoring the implementation of internal control in each of its duties and functions. In the event of an unusual policy like work from home, of course, a certain strategy is needed in terms of monitoring the implementation of control over the implementation of organizational duties and functions in education, especially higher education institutions, namely universities. Involuntary work from home which is fully carried out, does occur simultaneously in educational institutions, especially universities which have employees who are forced to work from home to run remote working. Particularly in the situation of organizations in higher education institutions, the enactment of this matter is regulated by the Minister of Education Circular Letter No.19/Year 2020 concerning the adjustment of the work system of the state civil apparatus in an effort to prevent the spread of Covid19 in the environment of government agencies. Data from the Minister of Education and Culture of Indonesia (2020) reports that about 1104 public and private institutions (as of March 19, 2020) have eliminated activities in the education unit. This said that if students study at home or each other's residence, educators, and employees can also work from home by maximizing the digital platform or information system. So that the involuntary Work from Home process is one type of telecommuting/tele working/remote working which is a work model where employees get the flexibility to work in terms of place and time of work with the help of technology (Smith et al., 2015). In order for telecommuting to work properly, it is necessary to maximize the communication function in a good organization, which is based and aimed at results, not the detailed observations of each employee individually (Hoeven and Zoonen, 2020). Surprisingly, very little research has focused on involuntary work from home based on a pandemic context, and limited research has been conducted on employee job satisfaction which has an effect on employees' productivity during Covid-19 situation, especially on operational scope of higher educational institution office staff.

The Covid-19 outbreak is an opportunity for companies to re-analyze the relationship between companies and their employees, and enhance corporate culture that is mutually beneficial to both parties (Lu, 2020). Implementation of the IWFH policy has several advantages and also at the same time enables problems that may arise. The benefits of work from home can be felt both by the tertiary institution and by the lecturers and staff themselves. Benefits for employees include: cost savings, time effectiveness, balance between work and personal life, etc. As for institutions, the benefits can be in the form of operational cost efficiency, time flexibility, increasing productivity, etc. But in addition to the positive side, this policy certainly has a negative impact that can be caused such as: the absence of direct supervision that is beneficial to the company and for the employees themselves, the loss of social interaction between employees, from the institutional side will be felt loss of control and trust towards employees who teleworking as a form of media work from home. In addition, the expansion of work to the home individually, raises significant work problems around the balance of employee privacy and the right to safety and security of organizational data.

Disease on pandemic situations, natural disasters, and other causes that occur outside of what has been planned by the institution/organization, changing where and how people work after a disaster raises significant work fears. In particular, removing the voluntary nature of the context of work from home to involuntary work from home by 'requiring' staff to work from home in a disaster situation changes the nature of work (Donnelly and Thomson, 2015). From these conditions, bringing individual work to home raises significant legal and labor issues around the balance of worker privacy and the right to safety with the security of organizational data good job satisfaction from the workers. Work life balance (WLB) and job satisfaction may have an impact on productivity at work (Mušura et al., 2013). Chimote and Srivastava (2013) concluded that reducing absenteeism, increasing productivity, and ensuring loyalty and retention are WLB benefits from an organizational perspective, while employee perspectives highlight job satisfaction, job security, autonomy, stress reduction and improve health as WLB benefits. Many organizations explore various alternative work arrangements to take advantage of the benefits of WLB in this situation. The fact of working from home due to a coercion of an unredictable situation makes administration more difficult, because communication in the media used when working at home is inefficient and many employees are absent from work due to personal matters (Lu-Hai, 2020). One of the perceived impacts on the implementation of work from home is the loss of communication and control functions for employees as examined by ter Hoeven and Zoonen (2020). For this reason, it is necessary to establish communication and performance relationships between employees during work from home, namely by monitoring communications, providing feedback, and communication climate (Tsai and Chuang, 2009).

Furthermore, analysis from Rupiettaa et al., (2017), shows that working from home has a statistically significant positive effect on work effort. In addition, they found that employees who work from home are also more productive. Thus, implementing a work from home system becomes a useful strategy for the organization. In addition, employees have the highest intrinsic motivation if they are not only responsible for their work but also get regular feedback about their performance. This means that organizations need to ensure that they provide appropriate feedback. The more often employees work from home, the higher the work effort they provide. For this reason, in practice work from home also requires support from companies / organizations and support from fellow workers. This will affect the welfare of workers (performance, engagement, and retention) as well as job satisfaction (Bentley et al., 2016).

Work-life balance plays an important role in job satisfaction (compared to subjective work productivity experiences) and has an impact on job satisfaction through subjective experience of productivity (compared to subjective productivity experience through job satisfaction). Therefore work-life balance is able to overcome low levels of job satisfaction and subjective experience in work productivity (Jackson and Fransman, 2018). Research by prioritizing employee satisfaction by referring to the level of productivity and to obtain a comprehensive picture, also examines the alternative relationship between job satisfaction and work productivity during pandemic throught work from home in higher educational isntsitution. More specifically, this study investigates the effect of work productivity and job satisfaction in the relationship between involuntary work from home, work-life balance, and communication functions on the other hand. This research is important in the realm of educational institution to break the chain of Covid-19 spread, and it is hoped that the implementation of work from home will not reduce the achievement of the performance targets mandated by the organization. Thus this policy can still function optimally in monitoring the line of defense at the management level who is fully responsible for carrying out all organizational policies by carrying out internal control continuously in all stages of learning activities, especially higher education.

The problem identification of this research covers the relationship between involuntary work from home, communication functions, work life balance, and its effect on work productivity and employee job satisfaction amid this covid-19 pandemic outbreak in the work situation of employees at the higher educational institutions.

The objectives of this research are to determine whether or not there are relationships or effects between involuntary work from home, communication functions, work life balance, and its effect on work productivity and employee job satisfaction amid this covid-19 pandemic outbreak in the work situation of employees at the higher educational institutions.

The scope of this research is to explain the extent to which the research area were explored in its implementation and determine the parameters in the research operated. The scope of this study includes the exploration of the relationship between involuntary work from home, communication functions, work life balance, and its effect on work productivity and employee job satisfaction amid this covid-19 pandemic outbreak in the work situation of employees at the higher educational institutions.

LITERATURE REVIEW

Involuntary Work From Home

According to Crosbie and Moore (2004), work from home is one type of telecommuting / tele working / remote working which is a work model where employees get the flexibility to work in terms of place and time of work with the help of technology. Meanwhile, involuntary work from home is driven by urgent conditions such as disasters or pandemics, which disrupt work and shape a culture of ambiguity by shifting priorities for individuals, organizations and the wider community. In this compelling situation, a company or organization operates in an uncertain environment that encourages a reassessment of workspace configuration and adoption of new ways of working (Drabek and McEntire, 2003). According to Golden (2009), in this case telework has the ability to mobilize a very large workforce, this is important for the survival of the organization. For this reason, in order for telecommuting to work properly, a good management style is needed, which is based and aimed at results, not the detailed observation of each employee individually. This refers to management based on objectives (management by objectives) as opposed to observation-based management (management by observation).

The term telecommuting and telework itself began to develop in 1973, the originator was named Jack Niles. According to Crosbie and Moore (2004), Work from home / work from home means paid work done mainly from home (at least 20 hours per week). Working from home will provide flexible time for workers to provide life balance for employees. On the other hand, it also provides benefits for the company. Work from home is one element of a work life balance strategy or work life balance that has a positive relationship in increasing work productivity (Andrade, Maureen Snow, et.al. 2019). It was found that higher productivity, lower turnover, reduced organizational costs, increased company stability, and even reduced environmental impact due to reduced travel distances as a result of flexible and effective work arrangements were anticipated as a result of human resource practices.

According to Donnelly and Thomson (2015), in circumstances that force involuntary work from home, there are some special challenges namely the uncertain external environment outside the control of the organization or employees, the level of individual autonomy and the availability of individual work processes for employees to manage volatility in home. In addition, in this case the leader must prepare and support the implementation of involuntary work from home, in relation to work allocation, work management, and work schedules. In his research, it shows that in a highly volatile environment, individual flexibility in managing work flow, time and speed can ensure the efficiency and productivity of employees in the organization.

The effectiveness of this work from home policy needs to be measured as well as possible, from a number of studies conducted it has been concluded that work from home can provide savings both in terms of the company and for employees, but still the outcome needs to be measured as discussed in the research literature conducted by Arso, et al., (2018). Bloom et al., (2015) argues, sometimes a policy that is taken does not work as expected including this work from home policy, a question that is often asked whether working from this house really runs as it should. One of the perceived impacts on the implementation of work from home is the loss of communication and control functions for employees as examined by Hoeven and Zoonen (2020). For this reason, it is necessary to establish communication and performance relationships between employees during work from home, namely by supervising communication, providing feedback, and communication functions (Tsai and Chuang, 2009).

Communication Functions

According to Greenberg (2011), communication can be interpreted as a process in which a person, group, or organization (sender) sends one type of information (message) to another person, group, or organization (recipient). Communication within the organization is important to create a shared understanding of the information conveyed to each other so as to achieve organizational goals. In practice, there are of course communication controls that are carried out to increase effectiveness in the workplace, for example facilitating work coordination with colleagues in geographical distances (Mazmanian, 2013). Thus, the use of communication technology is needed in the context of working remotely because each individual has control over their communication practices (Mazmanian, 2013; Piszczek, 2017).

In its application, communication is one of the key factors in work from home during this pandemic. The biggest contributor to communication and performance relationships between employees is the oversight of communication, feedback, and the communication climate (Tsai and Chuang, 2009). Hoeven, et al. (2020) argue that the communication control function in work from home increases the sense of freedom for employees to use communication technology and can increase productivity, effectiveness at work, and improve coordination with colleagues. Online communication is carried out during work from home using various platforms. Stephanie, et al. (2018) suggested the use of communication channels such as video and telephone has a positive impact on the level of satisfaction of communicating someone. Video communication channels are considered to have the closest face-to-face communication experience, while telephone communication can be done because talking on the telephone can provide variety and offer more nonverbal cues than e-mail or messages. In work from home, according to Jackson and Fransman (2018), of course there will be disturbances caused by family members at home, therefore the role of communication is important so that workers can communicate work schedules when working from home with family members to reduce disruption in work . In another research, Bentley et al. (2015) argues that work from home can generate feelings of social alienation from some individuals, therefore it is important to communicate between employees or workers to reduce their sense of social alienation. Communication when working from home can be done through several platforms provided by the company. In addition, the communication function can also play a role in balancing work life and family life (work life balance) of workers to improve employee satisfaction on their job responsibility (Jackson and Fransman, 2018).

Work-Life Balance

Work-life balance is a condition where the individual is able to manage and share work responsibilities, family life and other responsibilities so that there is no conflict between family life and work careers as well as an increase in motivation, productivity and loyalty to work (Singh and Khanna, 2011). Work from home is one element of a work life balance strategy that has a positive relationship in increasing work productivity (Andrade et al., 2019). Work-life balance is generally related to work time, flexibility, welfare, family, demographics, migration, leisure and so on. Work-life balance is essential because not achieving work-life balance results in low job satisfaction, low happiness, work-life conflict, and burnout for employees.

According to Frame and Hartog (2003), work-life balance means employees can freely use flexible work hours to balance their work or work with other commitments such as family, hobbies, arts, studies, and not just focus on their work. In addition, one important aspect that can determine whether or not there is a conflict between work and personal life. For example, role conflict and role ambiguity in the family can affect work-life balance. The trend towards flexible work patterns is also designed by current technological developments where business can be done away from the office environment and supported by much cheaper financial factors, making work easier to do (Jeanne and Trace, 2004). Therefore, it is important to see, there are positive benefits to be gained by assessing work balance in the application of the home itself (Andrade et al., 2019). This means that, there are improvements in work and life patterns to more effectively do work from home and the work is not related to aspects of life, related to spatial or conceptual.

As Jeanne and Trace (2004) conclude, many companies are considering adopting homework policies, but there are a number of considerations to create a balance between work and home life which is certainly a goal worth doing. There are many difficulties remaining in employment for minimum wages for workers who carry out this work situation on the basis of an undesirable condition. Research conducted by Felstead and Henseke (2017), shows that one of the challenges in working at home is the difficulty of quitting work, even though working hours are over. In addition, it can also have an impact having difficulty in maintaining focus in the midst of work. This is due to the many distractions from the personal life of the employee.

As an effect of involuntary work from home, one of the related variables is the existence of work and life balance which is explained by Jyothi and Jyothi (2012) as the need to achieve a balance between the demands of employees' family lives and their work life/activities. Satisfaction with work life balance is defined by Valcour (2007) as 'the overall level of satisfaction that results from assessing one's level of success in meeting work demands and family roles' (Fransman, 2015). Utilizing flexible work hours allows employees to manage priorities under their direct control, whether family or personal needs or organizational needs. (Fransman, 2015).

Work Productivity

Work productivity is the ability to obtain maximum benefits from the facilities and infrastructure available by producing optimal output. The definition shows that work productivity is a mental attitude that always has the view that the quality of life today must be better than yesterday, and tomorrow must be better than today. Work productivity in the company can be achieved if the following three factors are met, namely: a. Time productivity, in this case related to the determination of work schedules according to the percentage of time used. b. Human resource productivity is determined by habits that have been embedded in employees so that they can support effective work or vice versa. c. Productivity associated with work facilities and infrastructure is concerned with conditions, climate, and a good working atmosphere. One aspect of work productivity is the physical condition of the workplace atmosphere, explained that the pleasant physical condition of the workplace is needed and makes a real contribution in increasing work productivity.

A study in 2019 survey by Larson et al. said that working from home (WFH) not only benefits employees by eliminating their daily trips, but also increases their work productivity and leads to a healthier lifestyle. Study results from Jackson, et al. (2018), also concluded that by working from home, worker productivity increased by an average of 13%, due to a reduction in rest and sick days combined with comfort in the work environment. These findings state that employees in work from homework designs can benefit from increased work productivity. Furthermore, an analysis by Caramela (2020) states that in employee performance assessments can be demonstrated by the correlation between working from home and increasing productivity that is relatively consistently positive. Also supported by the results of the analysis of Rupiettaa et al., (2017), shows that working from home has a statistically significant positive effect on work productivity. Thus, implementing a work from home system is a useful strategy for the organization because more productive employees have high intrinsic motivation if they also get regular feedback about their performance.

Job Satisfaction

Job satisfaction is defined as an affective relationship with one's work that is a function of several factors including the nature of the job, elements of human resources, and organizational environment (Boswell, et al., 2009). McShane, et al. (2010) described job satisfaction as an evaluation of a person's work and work context. The level of job satisfaction is associated with a high level of commitment and improvement in productivity. In addition, everyone with a high level of satisfaction will show a positive attitude towards his career (Pirbasti, et al., 2014). In relation to work from home, according to Fransman (2015) remote work has a positive effect on employee job satisfaction.

Based on research from Jackson and Fransman (2018), work from home provides benefits for employees and the company and has a significant impact on employee job satisfaction. In the same research, it was stated that work from home does not always increase job satisfaction, because there are several disturbances that occur at home that can be caused by family members. In addition, there are several factors that can increase employee job satisfaction when working from home, including support from the company itself and fellow colleagues. Bentley, et al., (2015) in his research proved that support from the company and support from fellow colleagues will have a positive impact with job satisfaction. Support from companies and coworkers can reduce individual feelings of social alienation because they rarely interact with colleagues directly. So, companies that want to get positive benefits from work from home must pay attention to and be able to support their workers and this must be reflected in the policies and practices of work from home.

Involuntary Work From Home and Job Satisfaction

Through work home during the pandemic, it could increase job satisfaction of the employee (Bhattarai, 2020). The study stated that 64.58% adult workers and 33.42% young workers are satisfied with the work from home (involuntary work from home). It stated that work from home has different situation and different working condition from the normal situation, involuntary work from home that caused by the pandemic forced the employee to work from home based on the government regulation. The effect of involuntary work from home to the job satisfaction is proven by the research that working condition and working environment also significantly associated with job satisfaction (Viotti et al., 2020).

Hypothesis 1: There is relationship between involuntary work from home and job satisfaction.

Communication Functions and Job Satisfaction

Based on Ibrahim et al. (2018) findings, communication function has a positive impact on job satisfaction. From this study, communication becomes one of the determinant factors to job satisfaction through interpersonal relationship among employees. In this case, social skills, which consists of communication, give an impact on job satisfaction of an employee (Ibrahim et al., 2018). Another finding from Jacobs et al. (2015), stated that there is a positive impact of communication function towards job satisfaction. An effective communication is essential in communicating objectives and goals to employees (Jacobs et al., 2010). Clear and efficient communication will help employees to focus on the important goals and duties, and their work responsibilities will be easy to accomplish (Jacobs et al., 2015). A study from Smith et al. (2015), also found that there is a significant relationship between communication function and job satisfaction. This study specifically explains about the communication channel of e-mail, video, and phone communication towards job satisfaction. The results of the study show that an organization could encourage a wide variety of communication channels for communication in order to maximize the access to meet employees' needs (Smith et al., 2015). Therefore, it will increase the job satisfaction.

Hypothesis 2: There is a relationship between communication function and job satisfaction.

Work-Life Balance and Job Satisfaction

The findings show that work life balance has a deep impact on individual / employee job satisfaction in the organization. If the level of work-life balance of an employee is high, the commitment to their work will also high and the job satisfaction is also higher (Pathak, 2019). From this study, it stated on aggregate domain in which past literature suggests that work-life balance has a direct impact on employee job satisfaction. Work-life balance is partly the responsibility of the employer and the responsibility of the individual, so that it can measure the level of job satisfaction of both parties (Pathak, 2019). On the other hand, another research showed that work-life balance has a significant effect on job satisfaction, but work-life balance does not have a significant effect on organizational commitment and work motivation. Research by Mas-Machuca, et al. (2016) shows the work-life balance of employees is positively related to organizational pride and job satisfaction. High WLB levels are more positively related to work and life satisfaction for individuals in work culture (Haara, et al., 2014). It means high WLB levels are more positively related to work and life satisfaction. Harra et.al (2014) found strong support for WLB which is beneficial for employees from any job situation to increase job satisfaction. WLB is positively associated with work and life satisfaction.

Hypothesis 3: There is a relationship between work life balance and job satisfaction.

Involuntary Work From Home and Work Productivity

Involuntary work from home can make the employee more productive (Golden and Veiga, 2008; Martinez-Sanchez et al., 2008; Tremblay and Genin, 2007), teleworkers can be more productive because they can work during their most productive time and be less distracted by co-workers. Involuntary work from home is another form of teleworking, the effect of teleworking to work productivity also increases labor productivity Kazekami (2019). As we know, according to Crosbie and Moore (2004), work from home is one type of telecommuting/tele working and the study by Kazekami (2018) show that the effect of performing telework between teleworkers and no teleworkers, the discretion to work partially increases labor productivity. From the above empirical studies, the IWFH is significantly positive to work productivity in the pandemic situation.

Hypothesis 4: There is a relationship between involuntary work from home and work productivity.

Communication Function and Work Productivity

According to a study from Kang et al. (2017), there was a positive and strong relationship between communication function and work productivity. Based on this study, communication function has an important role in employee perception and assessment of a quality relationship of employee with organization and reinforces the importance of transparent and two-way communication towards employee relations. Also found that a good communication function in an organization will contribute to a higher level of work productivity of employee (Kang et al., 2017).

Another finding from Karanges et al. (2014), also stated that here was a positive and significant relationship between communication function and work productivity. Communication function such as support from other employees and supervisor will give a significant part in developing and maintaining an optimal work productivity of employee. In an organization, the communication function also important in facilitating supervisor-employee relationship, employee to employee relations, as a tool to express values and goals, so it will result in a favorable organization-employee relationship (Karanges et al., 2014).

Hypothesis 5: There is a relationship between communication function and work productivity.

Work-Life Balance and Work Productivity

Work-life balance has indeed been found to be a major factor in increasing employee productivity and this has a positive impact on organizational performance in general (Semlali and Hassi, 2016). Organizations need to implement effective work-life balance policies, namely policies that allow employees to remain socially connected to society while costs and turnover are controlled, and productivity is increased (Helmle et al., 2014). Leitão et al. (2019) revealed the importance of subjective and behavioral components of the quality of work life and their effect on forming individual collaborators' desire to contribute for strengthening organizational productivity. In the initial stage, the relationship between the qualities of work life in WLB is obtained which positively affects individual work productivity, then becomes the benchmark for improving organizational performance. In relation to this pandemic situation, a study conducted by Torres and Edwards (2020) stated that 45 percent of respondents admitted that working from home was as productive as working in an office. There were 22 percent even claimed to be more productive when IWFH was in the midst of this pandemic and felt that work-life balance had also improved. Thus, it can be concluded that work life balance can affect employee work productivity. If the work-life balance is good, it will increase work productivity in this pandemic situation.

Hypothesis 6: There is a relationship between work life balance and work productivity.

Job Satisfaction and Work Productivity

Job satisfaction has a positive impact to work productivity (Abdulwahab, 2015). Based on the study, job satisfaction will result on the enhancement employees' performance and they will contribute more to the overall success of an organizations. The research also suggests that it is important for an organization by focusing on the improvement of satisfaction and performance, so it will helps foster the work productivity of employees (Abdulwahab, 2015). According to Jackson et al. (2018), job satisfaction has significant role to the work productivity. This study explained that employees who are satisfy with their jobs be more productive, also performing a job well could lead to job satisfaction (Jackson et al., 2018). Employees are true asset for any organization; therefore, it is important to keep high level of job satisfaction for employees. The increase in job satisfaction among employees will lead to an increase in work productivity, because satisfied employees will work harder and work with full devotion, which is will increase the organizational productivity (Imran et al., 2015).

Hypothesis 7: There is a relationship between job satisfaction and work productivity.

Involuntary Work From Home and Work-Life Balance

Work from home is one element of a work life balance strategy that has a positive relationship in increasing work productivity (Andrade et al., 2019). It was found that higher productivity, lower turnover, reduced organizational costs, increased company stability, and even reduced environmental impact due to reduced travel distance as a result of flexible work arrangements had been anticipated as a result of human resource practices. According to Jackson and Fransman (2018), work-life balance is a strong predictor of job satisfaction for employees. Larson (2020) founds that many demands of work that must be completed sometimes force some people to lose the balance between the world of work and personal life. However, with the work from home policy, it is easier for someone to share their roles. There are times when he focuses on office work hours and there are also times when he can carry out his personal life without a burden. So that there is a positive influence in the application of work from home to a person's work life balance.

Hypothesis 8: There is a relationship between involuntary work from home and work life balance.

Involuntary Work From Home and Communication Function

One of the perceived impacts on the implementation of work from home is the loss of communication and control functions for employees as examined by Hoeven and Zoonen (2020). For this reason, it is necessary to establish communication and performance relationships between employees during work from home, namely by monitoring communications, providing feedback, and communication climate (Tsai and Chuang, 2009). Virtual communication function which means that office work can be carried out in any geographic location as long as the workplace is connected to a fixed company location through an electronic communication system based on information and technology. This work from home policy has significant consequences on the condition of the communication function related to the readiness of work equipment and the availability of adequate information technology equipment. The communication channels that can be used, according to Smith et al. (2015), is through video and telephone communication. The implementation of work from home has positively impact through virtual communication, video, and telephone channels as the media on the communication functions.

Hypothesis 9: There is a relationship between involuntary work from home and communication function.

Figure 1. Research model

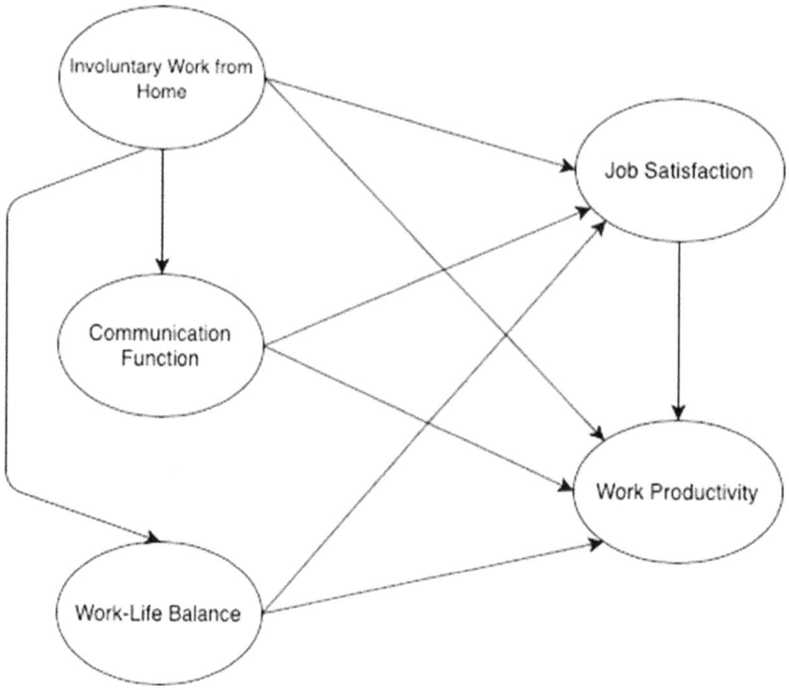

RESEARCH METHODS

The purpose of this study is to investigate the correlation between the role of the application of involuntary work from home (IWFH) by employees in educational institutions during the Covid-19 pandemic, to their work productivity, work life balance, and job satisfaction, with mediating variables, namely the communication function. Determination of the sample using probability techniques with a simple random sampling method. The target of this research population was the employees who work in a higher educational institution (University, Institute, Collage) in Regional Higher Educational Institution VIII (LLDIKTI VIII) in Bali Province, who do work from home by involuntary as a result of government policy in anticipating the spread of the Covid-19 outbreak. The reason why this research conducted on higher educational institutions as a sample population was because of educational institutions as companies that were still operating or still running during this pandemic of Covid-19 even though the teaching patterns change from the system traditionally become online learning and all of its employees apply the involuntary work from home (IWFH) system. The reason choosing the location of LLDIKTI VIII-Bali was that comparing with NTB and NTT, Bali has the highest population of universities, tourism destination, and as province of Covid-19 deployment rate in East of Indonesia so local governments and central government provide policies to apply IWFH to all educational institutions.

Data collection in this research used an online-based questionnaire method in the form of Google forms. Through this questionnaire, it was expected to know someone's opinion or response to a problem, it could be distributed to large numbers of respondents in a relatively short time, could capture information on a broad scale with a fast time, and keep the confidentiality of respondents to answer in accordance with his personal opinion. The questionnaire that was used is closed questions using a four-point

Likert format ranging from strongly disagree (1) to strongly agree (4). Furthermore, this questionnaire was accompanied by a cover letter or letter of introduction from the author explaining the purpose and objectives of the study, ensuring the anonymity of respondents, and the voluntary nature of the study and the contacts of the researchers. To collect data, the questionnaire was distributed by each researcher to their colleagues and distributed online in the form either through WhatsApp or social media such as Instagram, Facebook, or LinkedIn.

DATA ANALYSIS AND DISCUSSIONS

This research was conducted by collected 100 respondent data that met the criteria of this study; the organization applies work from home and the respondent works in the province of Bali. From 100 respondents, there are 70 women and 30 men respondents. Based on the educational background, there are 20 respondents with Senior High School/Equal level, 4 respondents with D1/D2/D3/D4 level, 68 respondents with Bachelor level, 6 respondents with Magister level, and 2 respondents with Doctoral level. As for the employment status of the respondents are 57 permanent employees and 43 employees on contract/honorarium. Meanwhile, the job level or employment level of the respondent are 52 staffs, 6 seniors, 34 middle level, and 8 executives. The collected data is then processed using the SEM method using the SmartPLS program. All of the variables are valid and reliable with Average Variance Extracted (AVE) is more than 0.50 and Composite Reliability more than 0.70 (Haire et al., 1998).

Table 1. Validity and reliability test

Variable	Composite Reliability	Average Variance Extracted (AVE)
Involuntary Work from Home	0.915	0.651
Communication Function	0.868	0.524
Work Life Balance	0.915	0.579
Job Satisfaction	0.933	0.634
Work Productivity	0.933	0.700

Table 2. Outer Loadings

	Variable	Outer Loadings
Involuntary Work from Home		
	Work from home (WFH) policy gives me more time to get work done	0.699
	Flexibility in work duration during work from home (WFH) makes me effective in getting my work done	0.791
	During work from home (WFH), working hours to complete office work are set according to working hours while in the office	0.653
	During work from home (WFH), I have the freedom to decide when to start and end work	0.682
	The place where I work at home is a comfortable place to do my work	0.707
	The workplace atmosphere and facilities at home make me more effective at work	0.789

continues on following page

Table 2. Continued

Variable	Outer Loadings
Communication Function	
During work from home (WFH), the instructions or job information I receive can be understood well	0.783
I have no problem in understanding the instructions or job information from my supervisor	0.483
The flow of decision-making in the organization is clear and can be implemented properly	0.903
Communication between employees and supervisors goes well in decision making	0.873
Communication with supervisors is effective in completing every job	0.882
During work from home (WFH), interactions with colleagues are effective in completing work	0.864
Work Life Balance	
I am still excited to do other things I want even though I have to finish my office work in this pandemic situation from home	0.704
I do not miss personal activities even though I have a lot of time occupied by my job when working from home	0.762
All office work is still enjoyable even though I have a lot of personal activities to do at home	0.862
I remain excited to work more effectively in pandemic situation despite various problems in my personal life	0.789
In pandemic situation, my work is better to be done at home	0.788
The implementation of work from home (WFH) has actually helped me to deal with personal problems	0.831
My personal life gives me the strength or encouragement to work from home	0.792
My personal life helps me feel ready to work from home (WFH) for the next day	0.860
Work Productivity	
During work from home (WFH), I can complete my office tasks on time	0.897
During work from home (WFH), I am always disciplined to report my work on an ongoing basis	0.842
During work from home (WFH), I can work on work instructions properly and optimally	0.859
With the work from home (WFH) policy I am able to create new, creative ideas to support my work	0.800
During work from home (WFH), the results of my work performance can be achieved above the set standard	0.780
When I work from home (WFH), the work facilities and infrastructure that I use can support the completion of my work.	0.838
Job Satisfaction	
During work from home (WFH), the work I do has varied activities	0.795
The organization where I work gives the authority to work independently, both in concept and in the method used	0.836
During work from home (WFH), the leader always supervises the work of each employee	0.696
Leaders are willing to help provide solutions to the problems faced	0.843
In working relationships in pandemic situation, colleagues can still apply the principle of openness to me	0.809
Colleagues are always ready to help with my work even though we are in work from home (WFH) situation	0.864
The income I received is still appropriate and not reduced compared to the income before the work from home (WFH) was done	0.548
The income I receive is in accordance with my current workload	0.634

By using path coefficients, it shows the p-values for each hypothesis. We accepted all hypothesis with p-value < 0.05, the results can be seen in Table 3.

Table 3. Hypothesis result

Hypothesis	P-Values	Note
H1. Involuntary work from home is related to job satisfaction.	0.000	Accepted
H2. Communication functions is related to job satisfaction.	0.004	Accepted
H3. Work life balance is related to job satisfaction.	0.000	Accepted
H4. Involuntary work from home is not related to work productivity.	0.340	Rejected
H5. Communication functions is not related to work productivity.	0.166	Rejected
H6. Work life balance is related to work productivity.	0.000	Accepted
H7. Job satisfaction has the relationship with work productivity.	0.029	Accepted
H8. Involuntary work from home has relationship with work life balance.	0.000	Accepted
H9. Involuntary work from home has relationship with communication function	0.000	Accepted

Based on the data analysis, this research confirms that involuntary work from home has a significant and positive relationship to the job satisfaction. This research also confirms a study by Bhattarai (2020), which explained that there are several factors that influencing the job satisfaction during work from home. First is financial factors, this is related to the salary that they earn during work from home is not reduced or in accordance with the workload. Besides that, work from home has positive and sinificant effect to job satisfaction because there is an opportunity of cost-saving and reduce expenses, such as transportation or gas expenses and eating out cost (Bhattarai, 2020), since since the government has urged people to reduce the intensity of their activities outside home and it is advisable to shop for 1-2 weeks supplies. Second, the social/factors that influenced job satisfaction during work from home. A sense of leadership and/or teamwork needs to be fulfilled during work from home (Bhattarai, 2020), even though there are differences in leadership and teamwork style, our research shown that the organization where the respondent works has good leadership or is in accordance with the work pattern before working from home, and has good teamwork that supports each other's work. Besides, involuntary work from home could decrease stress levels making job satisfaction increase. When they are able to complete work better and faster, of course this will increase job satisfaction so that employees become loyal to the company (Lu, 2020). Involuntary work from home makes their job satisfaction increases. This happens and impact to work stress decreases so that job satisfaction increase and influce their work productivity too. At work, work from home is more flexible, especially when they are tired of working, they can move from the desk to the living room, terrace, garden, room or other room in the house that is comfortable for working. In addition to being flexible about the problem of the workplace, in terms of involuntary work from home time it can also be adjusted flexibly. Most importantly, when working from home, employees can be responsible for their work.

There is relationship between involuntary work from home and communication function. Involuntary work from home has a significant and positive impact on communication function. While working from home, there will be an increase in virtual communication activities via email, video and telephone channels, so that work can be completed even if it is done not face to face with other employees. Through these channels, it will give impact to the employees' on the level of satisfaction of communicating someone (Stephanie et al., 2015). Besides that, as stated by previous study by Hoeven et al. (2020), through IWFH the employees will have the freedom in choosing which communication technology that suitable for them to have an effective interaction with co-workers to complete their work.

In terms of communication functions, there is a relationship by significant and positive effect on job satisfaction. During work, of course, the employees will socialize directly, but there is a different pattern during work from home where the socialization is done virtually. It is shown that there is an effect on job satisfaction, because the organization, leaders, and with other employees have good communication, so it is easier to support and complete their work. The organization in which the respondent works can provide clear directions for the job, and can assist employees in completing their duties (Jacobs, 2010; Jacobs et al., 2015). Besides that, respondents are also accustomed to using technology such as e-mail, video, and phone communication, and organizations can encourage various communication channels to maximize access that can meet employee needs (Smith et al., 2015). In today's life, work from office sometimes takes a long time to travel and road conditions are uncertain. But working from home can save travel time and people may have extra time for their friends and family, which can increased the job satisfaction through the communication function (Bhattarai, 2020).

On the other hand, involuntary work from home and communication function has no relationship to the work productivity. This is in contrast to several studies conducted before, where there are significant and positive effects between involuntary work from home to productivity as well as the communication function to work productivity. Previous studies stated that involuntary work from home has a positive effect on work productivity, where employees can manage their working hours when they are productive, concentrate more and also have no interference from colleagues (Golden and Veiga, 2008; Martinez-Sanchez et al., 2008; Tremblay and Genin, 2007). Also, communication function including support from other colleague and supervisor as well as leaders' communication ability will give impact to the employees work productivity (Karanges et al., 2014; Ferinia, 2015). In this case, there is a difference in the practice of work as usual and involuntary work from home. During this pandemic, most of the time was spent at home with family, of course there were some disruptions in its implementation that can interfere employees' work productivity. Most of our respondents do not experience problems with facilities and infrastructure that can support the completion of work and there are no obstacles in communication infrastructure. But there are several obstacles that can affect the communication function of work productivity, such as situations at home that are not conducive to work and other disturbances. So it can give impact on the completion of work that is not on time, unable to be disciplined in reporting work, and inhibition of new creative ideas that support employees' work.

The advantage of implementing the first work from home is that office operating costs have decreased, there is no need to provide computers, workplaces, internet, electricity and lunch for workers (Jackson et al. 2018). Those particular factors are related to support communication function for office operations. Unfortunately those facilities could not be provided in employee's house while they have to do their work. It such an important factor for employees in coordinating and finishing their jobs. Thus decrease their communication functions and work productivity. Besides, according to Jackson, Leon and Fransman, Edwina (2018), work-life balance is a strong predictor of job satisfaction for employees. But in his findings it is said that work from home does not always increase productivity and job satisfaction, because there are disturbances caused by families when working at home. In this Covid19 pandemic situation19, the implementation of IWFH which is a sudden coercion situation, not only affects work productivity but employees often feel pressured, mentally and physically, and now they are trying to find ways to balance life with work (Lu, 2020). Therefore, a work schedule is needed when working from home and communicated with family members to minimize distractions. To monitor workers when doing work from home is more difficult than when working in an office directly. A good system is needed to monitor every worker and not too rigid in terms of regulations, so that this does not become a big problem. In addition, there must be a good productivity measurement tool to coordinate and communicate with managers and colleagues, as well as good coordination for communication function to enable remote work.

This research also found that IWFH has relationship of significantly positive influence on work life balance, also work life balance has significant and positive influence to the job satisfaction. The organization should recognize the work life balance of its employees in order to retain the employees and increase their job satisfaction, because employees have family and other responsibilities and personal interests (Pathak, 2019). Work life balance also has significant and positive effect to work productivity. According to Torres and Edwards (2020), employees are tending to be more productive during work from home implementation during this pandemic. Employees that are supported and appreciated by the organization and cooperative working environment will increase the productivity of the employees (Leitão et al., 2019). With the implementation of work from home during this pandemic, it can help employees to complete work well even though there are some problems in their personal life. This is because problems can be resolved quickly as employees work from home. In addition, employees also feel better by working from home during pandemic, because they can protect their families at home from the virus compared to working from the office. Working from home directly will be closer to the family, especially for those who have small children who need attention from parents (Lu, 2020). With support from family or home environment and good support from the organization, this can increase job satisfaction and work productivity of employees. Work life balance is a balance between work and daily life (Larson, 2020). By working from home it will give a good or positive impact to the employees' work life balance. As stated by previous research, Krasulja et al. (2015) there is flexibility in managing time during the day, the possibility of taking care of children and family while working from home. Employees can be closer to their families and the environment so that life balance is fulfilled. Even though the employees are working in their working hours, but there is a different atmosphere or environment, because they are surrounded by their family. This balance between work and life can be achieved when he has good work productivity so that he can allocate time according to his respective portions. During the pandemic, the employees will feel safe to work from home so they can protect their own health and families health.

Job satisfaction has the relationship with work productivity, this is in line with previous studies. Job satisfaction represents employee welfare and employee retention, high levels of employee job satisfaction are associated with high commitment and increased work productivity. On this circumstance, often there are coworkers in one office who are toxic, annoy or often create problems. People like this are very annoying in terms of work productivity. Not to mention other distractions in the office that affect a lot in terms of work mood and productivity. It is different from when working from home where the atmosphere is more comfortable, calm and conducive so that you focus more on work. Some things that can increase job satisfaction in work from home are that workers can arrange work schedules and salaries that in accordance with their work (Jacobs et al., 2018), all of these factors can increase employee productivity. The results emphasized job satisfaction has significant role to the work productivity. It explained that higher educational employees who are satisfy with their jobs be more productive, also performing a job well could lead to job satisfaction. Literally, employees are true asset for any organization; therefore, it is important to keep high level of job satisfaction for employees. The increase in job satisfaction among employees will lead to an increase in work productivity, because satisfied employees will work harder and work with full devotion, which is will increase the organizational productivity (Imran et al., 2015).

Referring to forced work from home in this pandemic situation, based on the results above, it also shows a negative impact on work productivity and communication function. Due to involuntary work from home, not all work can be done from home (Larson, 2020). From all of the strengths and weaknesses above, the problem that often occurs in implementing involuntary work from home is the problem of supervising and monitoring the work of each employee. Emerging the role of quality assurance in its function as internal control is to ensure that the work is carried out in accordance with applicable regulations.

The implementation of forced labor from home in a pandemic situation in LLDIKTI VIII Bali is becoming more important given the need for regular evaluation of the implementation of work from home, especially since this policy is the first time this has been implemented. Given the emergence of a new cluster that spreads the Covid19 virus, IWFH is still being enforced in various work units, especially at universities. In addition, there are certain jobs that cannot be done online, they must be done in person (Kang et al., 2017).

This is necessary that work from home remains productive, is able to communicate clearly with superiors and ensure that they understand what the leadership expects (Lu, 2020). As much communication as possible either by voice (telephone), short messages, or face to face or virtual such as video calls, Skype, Zoom. Superiors must provide direction in the form of clear communication and maintain subordinate morale. Not having a complete workspace at home when starting to work remotely can cause productivity to temporarily decrease, so it requires support from higher education facilities.

CONCLUSION AND IMPLICATIONS

Working from home or work from home is the system chosen by the government to reduce the spread of the new type of corona virus (SARS-CoV-2) which causes Covid-19. Working from home is expected to maintain social distancing, namely reducing the mobility of people, maintaining physical distance, and reducing crowds. The research was a development study of the work from home method during the Covid-19 pandemic. The working from home method was carried out by a pandemic situation on the basis of government policies, WFH working method is called Involuntary work from home. This study includes the exploration of the relationship between involuntary work from home, communication functions, work life balance, and its effect on work productivity and employee job satisfaction during this Covid-19 pandemic outbreak in the work situation of employees at the higher educational institutions in LLDIKTI VIII Bali.

The results show that involuntary work from home is significantly positively related to job satisfaction, which explained that there are several factors that influencing the job satisfaction during work from home including working environment. There is a significantly positively effect of communication function on job satisfaction. The success of work management also depends on the communication function between employees through job satisfaction. Formal work done from home will certainly affect work life balance, in this study examined the balance between personal life and work carried out by IWFH where the results of this study found that in IWFH conditions, work life balance is significantly positively related to job satisfaction.

The results indicate the involuntary work from home has no significantly positively related to work productivity. The hypothesis was rejected. The Communication functions has also no significant positively related to work productivity which assumed is rejected. This shows that in IWFH conditions work productivity and communication functions are reduced.

Work life balance has significantly positively effect on work productivity. This hypothesis is accepted, assumed that employees who are supported and appreciated by the organization and cooperative working environment will increase the productivity of the employees. Finally, there is a significant positively effect between job satisfaction in the relationship with work productivity. Job satisfaction represents employee welfare and employee retention, high levels of employee job satisfaction are associated with high commitment and increased work productivity.

Involuntary work from home has a significant and positive impact on communication function. While working from home, there will be an increase in virtual communication activities via email, video and telephone channels, so that work can be completed even if it is done not face to face with other employees. Through this research also found that IWFH has significantly positive influence on work life balance, also work life balance has significant and positive influence to the job satisfaction. By working from home it will give a good or positive impact to the employees' work life balance. Due to there is flexibility in managing time during the day, the possibility of taking care of children and family while working from home. During the pandemic, the employees will feel safe to work from home so they can protect their own health and families health.

It can be ascertained that the results of this study have positive implications for the various parties involved in this research. From the various kinds of problems raised in this research, it has been revealed that the results of the research have had a direct impact on the parties concerned. especially for workers in the field of higher education, especially LLDIKTI VIII Bali. The implementation of IWFH has a positive impact on employee job satisfaction, but not for work productivity and communication functions. The communication function is the biggest challenge when doing work from home, especially in the realm of higher education. For this reason, it must always be online and easy to contact, so that when there is a discussion or coordination, no information is missed. The frequency of communication must also be done as often as possible to keep communication between teams running smoothly and without miscommunication.

It is suggested that future research should include other variables and other sectors, which use more involuntary work from home to firmly establish the impact of IWFH on job satisfaction and the experience of work productivity. The use of bigger sample and the inclusion of staff from other sectors could increase the generalizability of the findings on this study.

REFERENCES

Alvaro, M., de Assisand, G., & Fernando, L. (2011). Lessons Learned from September 11th: Telework As an Organizational Resource to the Business Continuity Planning. *The Japanese Journal of Telework*, *9*(1), 46–51.

Andrade, M. S., Westover, J. H., & Kupka, B. A. (2019). The Role of Work-Life Balance and Worker Scheduling Flexibility in Predicting Global Comparative Job Satisfaction. *International Journal of Human Resource Studies*, *9*(2), 80. doi:10.5296/ijhrs.v9i2.14375

Arso, S. S., Sfenrianto, S., & Wahyudi, M. (2018). Employee Performance Measurement in Teleworking Using Balanced Scorecard. *Iranian Journal of Electrical and Computer Engineering*, *8*(6), 5178. doi:10.11591/ijece.v8i6.pp5178-5184

Bailey, D. E., & Kurland, N. B. (2002). A Review of Telework Research: Findings, New Directions, and Lessons for the Study of Modern Work. *Journal of Organizational Behavior*, *23*(4), 383–400. doi:10.1002/job.144

Bentley, T., Teo, S., Mcleod, L., Tan, F., Bosua, R., & Gloet, M. (2016). The role of organisational support in teleworker wellbeing: A socio-technical systems approach. *Applied Ergonomics*, *52*, 207–215. doi:10.1016/j.apergo.2015.07.019 PMID:26360212

Bhattarai, M. (2020). Working from Home and Job Satisfaction During the Pandemic Times. doi:10.13140/RG.2.2.21515.11046

Bloom, N., Liang, J., Roberts, J., & Ying, Z. J. (2015). Does Working from Home Work? Evidence from a Chinese Experiment. *The Quarterly Journal of Economics*, *130*(1), 165–218. doi:10.1093/qje/qju032

Boswell, W. R., Shipp, A. J., Payne, S. C., & Culbertson, S. S. (2009). Changes in newcomer job satisfaction over time: Examining the pattern of honeymoons and hangovers. *The Journal of Applied Psychology*, *94*(4), 844–858. doi:10.1037/a0014975 PMID:19594229

Brough, P., Holt, J., Bauld, R., & Biggs, A. (2008). The Ability of Work-Life Balance Policies to Inñuence Key Social/Organizational Issues. *Asia Pacific Journal of Human Resources*, *46*(3), 261–274.

Caba. (2020). *What financial wellbeing*. Retrieved at https://www.caba.org.uk/help-and-guides/information/what-financial-wellbeing

Caramela, S. (2020). *Working from Home Increases Productivity.* https://www.businessnewsdaily.com/15259-working-from-home-more-productive.html

Crosbie & Moore. (2004). Work–life Balance and Working from Home. *Social Policy & Society, 3*(3), 223–233 doi:10.1017/S1474746404001733

Donnelly, N., & Proctor-Thomson, S. B. (2015). Disrupted work: Home-based teleworking (HbTW) in the aftermath of a natural disaster. *New Technology, Work and Employment*, *30*(1), 47–61. doi:10.1111/ntwe.12040

Drabek, T. E., & McEntire, D. A. (2003). Emergent Phenomena and the Sociology of Disaster: Lessons, Trends and Opportunities from the Research Literature. *Disaster Prevention and Management*, *12*(2), 97–112. doi:10.1108/09653560310474214

Felstead, A., & Henseke, G. (2017). Assessing the growth of remote working and its consequences for effort, well-being and work-life balance. *New Technology, Work and Employment*, *32*(3), 195–212. doi:10.1111/ntwe.12097

Felstead, A., Jewson, N., & Walters, S. (2003). Managerial Control of Employees Working at Home. *British Journal of Industrial Relations*, *41*(2), 241–264. doi:10.1111/1467-8543.00271

Ferinia, R. (2015). Contribution of Knowledge Leader and Communication toward Employee Productivity at West Java Conference Office. *International Journal of Basic and Applied Sciences*, *4*(2), 193. doi:10.14419/ijbas.v4i2.4176

Golden, T. (2009). Applying Technology to Work: Toward a Better Understanding of Telework. *Organizational Management Journal*, *6*(4), 241–250. doi:10.1057/omj.2009.33

Greenberg, J. (2011). *Behavior in Organizations* (8th ed.). Pearson Education.

Harker Martin, B., & MacDonnell, R. (2012). Is Telework Effective for Organizations? A Meta-Analysis of Empirical Research on Perceptions of Telework and Organizational Outcomes. *Management Research Review*, *35*(7), 602–616. doi:10.1108/01409171211238820

Hartog, M., & Frame, P. (2003). *From Rhetoric to Reality into The Swap of Ethical Practice: Implementing Work-Life Balance*. Blackwell Publishing Ltd.

Hoeven, C. L. T., & Zoonen, W. V. (2020). Helping Others and Feeling Engaged in the Context of Workplace Flexibility: The Importance of Communication Control. *International Journal of Business Communication*. Advance online publication. doi:10.1177/2329488419898799

Ibrahim, M., Abdullah, Z., Md Syed, M., & Yatim, M. (2018). *Supervisory Communication and Employees' Job Satisfaction in the Small and Medium-Sized Enterprises (SMEs)*. Jurnal Komunikasi. *Malaysian Journal of Communication*, *34*(4), 285–302. doi:10.17576/JKMJC-2018-3404-17

Imran, R., Majeed, M., & Ayub, A. (2015). Impact of Organizational Justice, Job Security and Job satisfaction on Organizational Productivity. *Journal of Economics, Business and Management, 3*(9). doi: .2015.v3.295 doi:10.7763/joebm

Jackson, K., & Kallaste, E. (2010). Beyond Flexibility: Reallocation of Responsibilities in the Case of Telework. *New Technology, Work and Employment*, *25*(3), 196–209. doi:10.1111/j.1468-005X.2010.00248.x

Jackson, L. T., & Fransman, E. I. (2018). Flexi work, financial well-being, work–life balance and their effects on subjective experiences of productivity and job satisfaction of females in an institution of higher learning. *Suid-Afrikaanse Tydskrif vir Ekonomiese en Bestuurswetenskappe*, *21*(1). Advance online publication. doi:10.4102ajems.v21i1.1487

Jacobs, M., Yu, W., & Chavez, R. (2016). The effect of internal communication and employee satisfaction on supply chain integration. *International Journal of Production Economics*, *171*, 60–70. doi:10.1016/j.ijpe.2015.10.015

Jarrod, M. (2014, December). Outcomes of work–life balance on job satisfaction, life satisfaction and mental health: A study across seven cultures. *Journal of Vocational Behavior*, *85*(3), 361–363. doi:10.1016/j.jvb.2014.08.010

Jeanne, C. (2004). Social Work in a Multicultural Society. *Social Work*, *49*(1), 5–6. doi:10.1093w/49.1.5 PMID:14964513

Kaduk, A., Genadek, K., Kelly, E. L., & Moen, P. E. (2019). Involuntary vs. voluntary flexible work: Insights for scholars and stakeholders. *Community Work & Family*, *22*(4), 412–442. doi:10.1080/13668803.2019.1616532 PMID:36090310

Kang, M., & Sung, M. (2017). How symmetrical employee communication leads to employee engagement and positive employee communication behaviors. *Journal of Communication Management (London), 21*(1), 82–102. doi:10.1108/JCOM-04-2016-0026

Karanges, E., Johnston, K., Beatson, A., & Lings, I. (2015). The influence of internal communication on employee engagement: A pilot study. *Public Relations Review, 41*(1), 129–131. doi:10.1016/j.pubrev.2014.12.003

Kazekami, S. (2019). Mechanisms to improve labor productivity by performing telework. *Telecommunications Policy, 101868.* Advance online publication. doi:10.1016/j.telpol.2019.101868

Khaled, A. B. (2019). Impact of Work-Life Balance, Happiness at Work, on Employee Performance. *International Business Research, 12*(2). doi:10.5539/ibr.v12n2p99

Larson, B. (2020). *Companies Can Help Employees Working Remotely During the Covid-19 Pandemic.* Northeastern University Boston.

Larson, B. Z. (2019). It Time to Let Employees Work from Anywhere? *Harvard Business Review.* Retrieved at https://hbr.org/2019/08/is-it-time-to-let-employees-work-from-anywhere

Leitão, J., Pereira, D., & Gonçalves, Â. (2019). Quality of Work Life and Organizational Performance: Workers' Feelings of Contributing, or Not, to the Organization's Productivity. *International Journal of Environmental Research and Public Health, 16*(20), 3803. doi:10.3390/ijerph16203803 PMID:31658595

Lu-Hai, L. (2020). *How Covid-19 led to a nationwide work-from-home experiment.* Retrieved at https://www.bbc.com/worklife/article/20200309-coronavirus-covid-19-advice-chinas-work-at-home-experiment

Mahbob, M., & Wan Sulaiman, W. (2015). Kepentingan Kecerdasan Emosi dalam Komunikasi Keorganisasian dan Pengaruhnya Terhadap Kepuasan Kerja [The Importance of Emotional Intelligence in Organizational Communication and Its Influence on Job Satisfaction]. *Journal of Communication, 31*(2), 533–546. doi:10.17576/JKMJC-2015-3102-30

Mahler, J. (2012). The Telework Divide: Managerial and Personnel Challenges of Telework. *Review of Public Personnel Administration, 32*(4), 407–418. doi:10.1177/0734371X12458127

Maruyama, T., & Tietze, S. (2012). From Anxiety to Assurance: Concerns and Outcomes of Telework. *Personnel Review, 41*(4), 450–469. doi:10.1108/00483481211229375

Mas-Machuca, M., Berbegal-Mirabent, J., & Alegre, I. (2016). Work-life balance and its relationship with organizational pride and job satisfaction. *Journal of Managerial Psychology, 31*(2), 586–602. doi:10.1108/JMP-09-2014-0272

Mazmanian, M. (2013). *Avoiding the Trap of Constant Connectivity: When Congruent Frames Allow for Heterogeneous* Practices. *Academy of Management Journal, 56*(5), 1225–1250. doi:10.5465/amj.2010.0787

Monica, T., & Edwards-Levy, A. (2020). *Many Workers Would Prefer to Keep Working from Home at Least Some of the Time-Most People Working from Home Due to The Coronavirus Wouldn't Be Disappointed If the Change Were Permanent, A New HuffPost/YouGov Survey Finds.* You Gov & Huffing Post. Retrieved at https://www.huffpost.com/entry/work-from-home-permanent-survey_l_5ecd34d6c5b67f9b9befbc86

Nilles, J. M. (1998). *Managing Telework: Strategies for Managing the Virtual Workforce*. John Wiley & Sons.

Nilles, J. M., Carlson, F. R., Gray, P., & Hanneman, G. (1976). *The Telecommunications— Transportation Tradeoff, Options for Tomorrow*. John Wiley & Sons.

Paripurna, D., & Gede, I. (2013). Pengaruh Kepemimpinan, Lingkungan Kerja dan Komunikasi terhadap Kepuasan Kerja Karyawan. *E-Jurnal Manajemen-Universitas Udayana*, *2*(5), 58–67.

Pathak, A. (2019). Work Life Balance & Job Satisfaction: A Literature Review. *International Journal of Computer Sciences and Engineering*. Retrieved at https://www.researchgate.net/publication/332112828_Work_Life_Balance_Job_Satisfaction_A_Literature_Review

Pirbasti, M. F., Bashar, H. P., Ramezani, A., Moradi, M., & Tabatabai, S. (2014). The relationship between job satisfaction and organizational commitment. *Advances in Environmental Biology*, *8*(10), 318–323.

Piszczek, M. M. (2016). Boundary control and controlled boundaries: Organizational expectations for technology use at the work-family interface. *Journal of Organizational Behavior*, *38*(4), 592–611. doi:10.1002/job.2153

Pyöriä, P. (2011). Managing Telework: Risks, Fears and Rules. *Management Research Review*, *34*(4), 386–399. doi:10.1108/01409171111117843

Riadi, M. (2019). *Produktivitas Kerja - Pengertian, Aspek dan Pengukuran*. Retrieved at https://www.kajianpustaka.com/2019/11/produktivitas-kerja-pengertian-aspek-pengukuran-dan-faktor-yang-mempengaruhi.html

Rupietta, K., & Beckmann, M. (2017). Working from Home – What is the Effect on Employees' Effort? *Schmalenbach Business Review*, *70*(1), 25–55. doi:10.100741464-017-0043-x

Shmailan, A. (2015). The relationship between job satisfaction, job performance and employee engagement: An explorative study. *Issues in Business Management and Economics*, *4*(1), 1–8. doi:10.15739/IBME.16.001

Siagian, S. P. (2014). *Manajemen Sumber Daya Manusia*. Bumi Aksara.

Singh, P., & Khanna, P. (2011). Work-Life Balance a Tool for Increased Employee Productivity and Retention. *Lachoo Management Journal*.

Smith, S. A., Patmos, A., & Pitts, M. J. (2015). Communication and Teleworking: A Study of Communication Channel Satisfaction, Personality, and Job Satisfaction for Teleworking Employees. *International Journal of Business Communication*, *55*(1), 44–68. doi:10.1177/2329488415589101

Tsai, M.-T., Chuang, S.-S., & Hsieh, W.-P. (2009). An integrated process model of communication satisfaction and organizational outcomes. *Social Behavior and Personality*, *37*(6), 825–834. doi:10.2224bp.2009.37.6.825

Viotti, S., Sottimano, I., Converso, D., & Guidetti, G. (2020). The relationship between psychosocial characteristics of the work environment and job satisfaction in an Italian public ECE service: A cross-lagged study. *Early Childhood Research Quarterly*, *53*, 464–475. doi:10.1016/j.ecresq.2020.06.002

Winarso, W. (2018). Organizational communication; a conceptual framework. INA-Rxiv. Retrieved at doi:10.31227/osf.io/g9ubc

ADDITIONAL READING

Bhattarai, M. (2020). Working from Home and Job Satisfaction During the Pandemic Times. doi:10.13140/RG.2.2.21515.11046

Silvermann, B. (2020, July 15). *Are Employees More Productive Working From Home?* Retrieved from https://www.business.com/articles/are-employees-more-productive-working-from-home/

Chapter 4
Post-COVID-19 World and Trajectories of a Crumbling World Order

Keshab Chandra Ratha
Gangadhar Meher University, India

Sushanta Kumar Mahapatra
https://orcid.org/0000-0002-0831-3621
The ICFAI Foundation for Higher Education (IFHE) (Deemed), Hyderabad, India

ABSTRACT

The pandemic poses the severest jolt to the U.S.-led international order, including the retraction of the United States from previously held global leadership. The extraordinary economic and medical response in the developed and opulent countries is simply not at hand for many developing countries. With COVID-19, international and multilateral bodies are not anywhere on the scene. Regional institutions such as the AU (African Union) and South Asian Association for Regional Cooperation (SAARC) are often treated as weak, lacking the habit of cooperation and under-resourced to address the pandemic. Globally, societies could turn into more self-seeking and inward-looking eventuating in further pushback against liberal policies in respect of migration and refugees. Absence of basic resources, lack of well-functioning and efficient healthcare systems, and the dearth of well-organised communication channels indicate inefficiency in the war against COVID-19. A concerted effort across each and every sector and discipline responsible for health is urgently called for in this grim hour.

INTRODUCTION

COVID-19 pandemic is actually a world-changing event. The pandemic is a potential threat to humanity after the Second World War that has affected all countries and sectors of economy. As the COVID-19 crisis continues to become more intense, the significant post-pandemic effects on health and economy is injurious for the most developed nations as well as the poorer, weaker and more vulnerable communities of developing countries alongside with the risks of rising inequality. The challenges are bigger in size

DOI: 10.4018/978-1-7998-6896-5.ch004

sensational in Africa, Latin America and South Asia, where health systems of governments are noticeably feeble to respond (Ian Goldin and Robert Muggah,2020). The pandemic poses a severest jolt to the U.S.-led international order, including the retraction of the United States from previously held global leadership. The pandemic has culminated in weakening order by putting pressure on governments, splitting up societies, aggravating societal disparities, intensifying differences between the United States and China, and showcasing the vast deviation between global issues and the world's capacity to tackle them through existing international institutions (Haass,2020). COVID-19 has caused severe disturbance all over the world. The extraordinary economic and medical approach to handle the pandemic in the rich countries is simply not at hand for many developing countries. The extraordinary economic and medical approach to handle the pandemic in the rich countries is simply not at hand for many developing countries. The dreadful implication is that the results are going to be far more severe and far reaching to poorer countries. Significant improvement in development and democracy in many Latin American, African, and Asian societies has turned backward in direction. The severity of the impacts depends on duration of the pandemic and reaction of governments to the national and international issues. COVID-19 has larger and unequal impact within and across the countries. (Prassi et al., 2020). In a strongly integrated world, the impacts of the disease beyond mortality and morbidity has become clearly visible since the outbreak.

MAJOR RESEARCH QUESTIONS AND METHOD OF STUDY

1. How did international bodies and regional institutions play a weak role in mitigating the pandemic?
2. How corona virus is responsible for abrupt increase of deep-seated racism?
3. How will coronavirus impact on globalization?
4. How COVID 19 is evolving and reshaping the global economy?
5. What is the way forward?
6. What is the way out?

The method of study employed for the project is normative, historical analytical, descriptive and comparative. The study had made exhaustive collections both from the primary as well as secondary sources. In the primary sources, the researcher has consulted reports, documents, treaties, parliamentary debates etc. for the primary sources. And for the secondary sources, the researcher has taken views from the books, journals, articles, newspapers and internet sites. In fact, some of the discussions and comments from the outstanding personalities had proved to be quite helpful to the scholar in developing a real insight into the crisis.

FADING ORGANIZATIONS

Global problems call for global responses. Many international as well as multilateral bodies are not anywhere on the scene when it comes to deal with hardships of fighting Covid-19. The pandemic has also eaten away the integrity of organizations like the WHO. During the pandemic WHO remained under scathing attack from numerous countries and experts, in view of its importance. Its early acts of supporting the Chinese efforts has put it in a defensive state as the U.S. blames the outbreak of the disease on a Chinese biotech lab and accuses Beijing for withholding vital information regarding the disease. The brute reality is that these institutions have been played in the hands of big power politics (Sood, 2020). The global institutional framework is misleading; operated by the great powers, facing the paucity of funds. The global institutional architecture of the 1940s cannot contribute the humanity to meet the challenges of the 2020s.

The 75th anniversary of UN's existence as an international body has come with acute pain, grief, agony and sadness. The body stands currently under threat. International economy is looking towards a historical collapse, and to make the situations worse, no viable Covid-19 vaccine has been discovered up till now. The UN as an institution bereft of any expertise in dealing with such a threat for the reason that it primarily deals with matters in respect of cordial relations between nation-states. The global order has basically changed in the last 100 years, and today's world runs on global economic trade and cooperation, which is a distinguishing symbol of globalization and modernity. Covid-19 poses a danger to undo all this, if its act of spreading is not kept in bay at the earliest possible movement. The longer this pandemic continues to exist, the longer would be the damage to the health of global economy, given that most countries affected are following the principle of 'to each his own'. The UN is afraid of both an economic crisis as well as a larger humanitarian crisis. It is established by history that any humanitarian crisis acts upon the poor the most, amounting to loss of livelihood and even death. The UN could not do much in holding up the spread of the coronavirus and preventing deaths (Jha, 2020).

It has been estimated that every year US$3.4 billion is required to fund "global functions" of WHO pandemic preparedness programmes. However, the funds for global pandemic preparedness of the WHO are not enough to meet the target. Government of wealthy countries have been opposing the redistributive demands put forth by developing countries and hence, the WHO was left chronically funded. Western governments desire to give a high priority to health sector loans through the World Bank. The WHO has never been bestowed with requisite independence, powers or resources by the Countries required to fulfill its mission to ensure "the attainment by all peoples of the highest possible level of health". The WHO is literally helpless to force critical information-sharing or enforce pandemic preparedness. The WHO finds itself prepared for battle at the mercy of member states that are obstructive and consequently the organization is burdened with decreasing resources. It is simply empowered witha small number of tools to directly supervise outbreaks of infectious diseases, coordinate pandemic planning, allocate resources to needy countries, or ensure effective execution of preparedness measures at country-level. The WHO needs to serve a central global function, palliating against the danger of states becoming overwhelmed. Eventually, it could reduce the hazardous impact that unmanaged economic globalization has had on public healthcare systems, many of which have not been ready to deal with the seriousness of COVID-19 (Pegram, 2020). The system that has been designed to provide a global response to pandemic has terribly failed. Covid-19 has already affected the globe, closing down many countries for months. Governments, and even sub-national governments, are competing intensely to deal with limited medical stocks, while crucial supply chains have been interrupted following many restrictions. . The World Health Organization, the centerpiece of global health governance, has been kicked downstairs, with US President Donald Trump moving to draw back all American funding to the WHO on 14 April 2020 (Hameiri, 2020).

Two key elements of global health governance system have to lead the failure during the Covid-19 outbreak. First is the inefficiency of the WHO in the field of surveillance of the disease and response coordination. Experts are of the view that the WHO was simply not suitable for this purpose. This arises from its submissiveness to major funding states.

Although the Declaration was signed by developed countries, there was aconcern regarding potential redistribution of demands. As a result, the WHO was largely withdrawn financial support from its main funders, i.e. Western European countries and the Unites States. A large share of health aid for developing countries was channeled through the World Bank, which became part of the Bank's agenda in increasing structural adjustment. The operational budget of the was reduced to meager levels, and contributing states moving to voluntary and project-based funding ensuring that the WHO follow their preferred objectives. By the 2000s, the budget was regulated around 80% and today, the total annual budget of the WHO is around $5.6 billion. Compared to that the Australian federal health budget for 2019-20 was $120 billion, and even bigger if the states' budget is included. This has had the effect of restricting the WHO's capacity, consequently making it highly responsive to its main funding states, thereby jeopardizing its independence. The structure of the WHO's primary donors has changed since 1978 as China is at present the third-biggest provider of compulsory, "assessed", contributions to the WHO. It is more likely to become the second-biggest donor after US decision to stop funding. Another crucial aspect of global health governance before the Covid-19 outbreak was its operation through domestic institutions (Hameiri, 2020). Although the assumptions were clear about the infections spreading across the world rapidly, because of the poor governance systems and limited financial support in developing countries, that are subjected to constant surveillance by the WHO, it was difficult to curb the spread. Funded by the developed countries, that are dealing with the pandemic in their own countries, the WHO failed provide necessary support to the developing countries which lead to failure of global health governance system since the emergence of Covid-19.

Soon after the outbreak of the pandemic in China, the WHO was criticized for being silent on China's trick to hide the initial outbreak. Again, China's denial in mid-January 2020 about the human-to-human transmission in Wuhan which was endorsed by the WHO was widely criticized. According to many, the WHO was obvious to genuflect to one of its main funders. However, when the disease started spreading to the developed countries, that were used to financing and showing limited involvement, their governments started focusing on addressing the situation in their countries reducing their contribution to the global issues.

Before Covid-19, the global system for addressing outbreaks of infectious disease was clearly not in shape for purpose. However, regardless of the avert from global governance in recent years, there is a dire need to develop more efficient, durable, equitable and better funded structures of cross-border cooperation to cater to the ubiquitous threat of pandemics (Hameiri, 2020). There are more unfavorable days waiting for the WTO. Different trade rules have worked best as long as the global economy was very lively and profitable and runs without meeting a crisis. Since the last major discussion was held at WTO in 2008, many issues have remained unaddressed. It's seeming to get worse if countries need to bring their domestic industries flipside, because they would need space for policy malleability. And WTO will be superfluous in such cases. For instance, on the matter of subsidies for small industries, countries may not be like to take advice of the WTO. The subsidies issue for agriculture is going to be cast aside. If the rules of WTO are cast away, then it's a free-for-all situation where lies the problem. However, the impact on global governance systems needs to be understood properly.

FAILURE OF REGIONAL INSTITUTIONS

The outputs of regional institutions are not satisfactory at all. The SAARC initiative taken by India's Prime Minister Narendra Modi, lasted only for a short time. The EU, the most developed and wee-organized post-national regional arrangement, stood helpless when the spread of the virus became uncontrolled in Europe. Its member states preferred to turn inward for solutions as their first instinct was self-help, not regional coordination...

The Southeast Asian regional bloc initially proved deficient to come up with a collective food security and also refused to notice the impacts of the pandemic on migrant workers. In the same way, the Association of Southeast Asian Nations (ASEAN) has come under fierce condemnation for utter failure to build a "concerted ASEAN response" to fight the virus. The Southeast Asian regional bloc in the beginning was unsuccessful to come up with a collective food security and also refused to pay attention to the impacts of the pandemic on migrant workers. In mid-April, ASEAN leaders validated their commitment to ensuring food security at the special ASEAN plus three (China, Japan and South Korea) video conference summit on coronavirus disease, though that needs to be to translated on the ground.

On the other hand, regional institutions such as the AU and South Asian Association for Regional Cooperation (SAARC) that are often treated as weak, lacking the habit of cooperation and under-resourced, emerged as key platforms for initiating collective response among member-states. These regional bodies continue to suffer from long-standing political issues of trust deficit among member-states such as India-Pakistan relations within the SAARC framework. These regional dimensions of the global response to the coronavirus pandemic are present in different geographies and involve regional institutions both in developed and developing regions. Assessing the impact of the role of regional institutions on the pandemic will require more comparative study of regional bodies as well as how major players view and frame their approach towards regions/sub region. Even so, it may not be erroneous to suggest that the factors driving the regional dimensions in recent developments are likely to shape the emerging global governance system (Yhome, 2020).

DEEP-SEATED RACISM

Another unwanted outcome of the pandemic is abrupt increase of discrimination in various forms of. Across the globe, societies are more likely to turn into inward-looking and self-seeking eventuating in further repulse against liberal policies in respect of migration and refugees. Questions concerning the source of goods are likely to be asked. Advanced states will like to impose strict phytosanitary measures on products imported from the less developed countries. Lockdowns and travel restrictions could the new normal across the globe. The irony of the situation is, political globalisation can be an answer to many questions, but COVID-19 might further limit it.

According to Puritan, the associated declarations based on birth and class about hygiene could become sharper. Such practices would get deeper with the virus growing persistence of the virus. (Jacob, 2020). The COVID-19 pandemic has exposed social and political loop-holes existing within communities, which include radicalized and discriminatory responses to fear, affecting marginalised groups unreasonably, etc. Policies of COVID-19 have affected people disproportionately considering many factors. Migrants and people who are over-represented in lower socioeconomic groups, have limited health-care access, or have to work in precarious jobs. Because of lack of space to live, self-isolation is often not possible, resulting in higher risk of viral spread. Ethnic minority groups are found at greater risk because of the occurrence of more than one illness-for example, high rates of hypertension in Black populations and diabetes in south Asians. Often, migrants, particularly those without documents, avoid hospitals to escape identification and reporting, ultimately caring threats of spread of the infection. Discrimination within social, political, and historical contexts is still there in many parts of the world. Political leaders have dishonestly appropriated the COVID-19 crisis to strengthen racial discrimination. Matteo Salvini, former Deputy Prime Minister of Italy, called for border closure wrongly linking COVID-19 to African asylum seekers. Similarly, President Donald Trump has referred severe respiratory syndrome of coronavirus 2 as the Chinese virus, at the same time linked the health threat to foreign policy and trade negotiations (Devakumar, 2020).

It is a human tendency to support the attributes of the groups that we belong to but that depletes the strength of other groups. This process could eventuate to perceptions regarding the other groups as lacking appropriate culture, rationality, morality, or self-restraint. Such prejudice towards others is often inflamed by uncertainty and fear as the mankind is facing in the current situation.

REVERSING THE TREND OF GLOBALIZATION

COVID-19 brings a change imbalance of power across the globe, the future of globalization and traditional concept of national security. The uncontrolled spread of COVID-19 is also an indication towards the failure of the contemporary order of the world and many of its institutions. COVID-19 has made visible the worst reestablishment of native cultural traits of the global leadership confronted with a major crisis. Also, United Nations Security Council taking so long to meet and discuss the pandemic bears a testimony to the UN's irrelevance. The true face of humanity is getting exposed with awful combination of a world that is interconnected and the deadly virus that the world is yet to deal with. After the lockdown is completely finished, the entire humanity needs to be mentally disposed to come up against new political and social realities. Globalization is facing a major threat as governments decided to limit global trade and travelling of people to reduce exposure to the virus. The COVID-19 pandemic added extra fear and uncertainty to people's confusion, giving rise to new behaviors and beliefs. The economic interdependence which is the prime feature of recent globalization is becoming deglutinated and with it affecting the policy assumptions of governments of many countries and the livelihoods of billions of people (Labonte et al., 2020).

Capitalism and technological advancements, two pillars of globalization, are the prime reasons for which mankind is currently facing the crisis ofCOVID-19 pandemic. Covid-19 turned into a pandemic easily with the hyperactive universal transportation system through the mobilization and communication of masses. The preventive and protective measures designed and adopted by most states to control the virus badly affected the international trade and globalization. The United States sealed the US-Canada border and the border that US shares with Mexico to regulate non-essential travel. Similarly, China brought to a stop entry of foreigners, and ceased moving all international flights. Similarly, the European Union imposed a 30-day ban on nonessential travel. Bans and restrictions of various types were imposed by many other states. The current state of isolated solutions will continue for some times. Many states realized that every other state is dealing with their own internal issues and it is difficult to find help from others. Globalization along with global cooperation lost its credibility and its most like to continue. Nationalism becomes stronger, and protectionists and populists find louder voice to express their views (Yacoub & Zomor, 2020).

As the term "slobalisation" rightly replaced the term globalisation, the global financial crisis has stooped the world trade from 10%growth to 1%-2%. With the WTO talks coming to a halt, the global economic interdependence has received a big jolt. Countries will have to reshape their economies and freshly strategize their import and export policies as the imminent dangers and difficulties of overdependence on foreign supplies become apparent. As the pandemic has hindered the growth of Neoliberal economic globalization, there is a increasing chance of recession. Although localization has become the new norm during the pandemic, the pre-existing loop-holes of the global orders along with the hazards of Covid-19 have added to the norm. Former National Security Adviser Shivshankar Menon rightly warns, "We are headed for a poorer, meaner, and smaller world."

Many people view it as a withdrawal from hyper globalization. However, the assumption that COVID-19 will direct towards a more inclusive and balanced form of economic and political globalization is perhaps put into a wrong place. Interventions of states in the matters of economy and protectionism are the means of dealing with the situation and that's what states will do after the crisis comes to an end. The state is not successful in its attempts to curb the pandemic in spite of its claims about preparedness on national security. However, the state has returned with more power, authenticity and observation methodologies. The state, which was losing its authority on global economic forces, has come up as the safe havenforthe people. With the severe jolt that globalization has faced, state-led models of globalization and economic development would gain preference over (big) corporates-led globalization. But, the involvement of the states to take in a big capital is the key concern. Considering the mutual dependence between the state and big capital, it can be found that the states have become accustomed to safe guard the interests of their corporations, in many cases at the cost of the general public.

IMPACT ON GLOBAL ECONOMY

The novel coronavirus (COVID-19) outbreak which was originated in December 2019 at Wuhan city in China has transmuted into an unparalleled economic blackout in the world. (Mishra et al., 2020). The delay came from the slow response in countries around the world. From denial to making little significance of the numbers, to wrong perception on the resistance to the spread of a contagious disease within a population and to logistical challenges to make virus testing in place, all in fact hindered the progress of policy responses in most of the West. The United States, in an election year, was particularly sluggish in its response at the federal level, led as it is by a president who seems more concerned that a potent reaction to the virus would move down "his" stock market numbers. As a result, precious time was whiled away.

The rest of the world fares worse than China. Low-income countries are predominantly at risk even if their growth rates are for now projected to remain positive. The virus is likely to hit them hard for numerous causes. First, their health systems are far less developed than that of OECD countries or those of China, and the rich East Asian economies currently affected. Second, a large part of the population works in the informal sector without any social security or health insurance. Thus they are far more susceptible to a speed downward trend than workers in the formal sector. One of the concerns in respect of the wide dispersion of the pandemic is that workers will fail to afford to self-isolate if they have the disease. (Baldwin & Mauroo, 2020) While informality has multiplied across the board and now affects some two thirds of the global labour force, it will strongly drop as income rises, as indicated by this ILO Report. Finally, unlike rich countries, the flight to safety increased interest rates for them and thus their governments will find it harder to spend the money needed to contain the virus and counter the economic impact (Hofman, 2020).

The world economic received its major blow after the great depression of 1930 in the form of Corona pandemic. However, the current pandemic is able to shake the base of highly globalized world that is strengthen with interconnected production network and financial market (Sahoo & Ashwani, 2020). Analysts are afraid of the fact that the global economy may head for another recession if spread of the virus is not checked in time. Everyone is unaware about duration for which the virus is going to remain powerful, to what extent the concerned authorities in different countries are capable of checking new cases and the resources they are going to use to treat old ones. The functionality, behavior and durability of the virus is surely unpredictable. On the other hand, according to Rabobank, as he briefed it to the media, the world is certainly going to face a global recession. As estimated by IMF, Global GDP growth, that was 2.9% the last year, was predicted to be 1.6% for 2020, Economists, all over the world, have same opinion about the global recession. Institute for International Finance had predicted in the early March this year that global economic growth could stoop to 1%. Stock markets touched a new low as the oil prices fall drastically. The UN's United Nations Conference on Trade and Development (UNCTAD), related the virus outbreak to global economy predicting it could cause the global economy to pay up to $2-trillion this year. Also, the pandemic could bring a recession in some countries making global economic growth go below 2.5% (Sood, 2020).

Businesses encounter the challenges in terms of production, following shutting down of factories provisionally, almost every industry, with a large section of the employees having to be in strict isolation. As India is dependent on China for supply of many products, a great share of India's market became unstable following China's industry sectors facing slowdown because of the pandemic. Industries of pharmaceutical and pesticide sectors largely depend on the raw material imported from China, while the jewelry industry of India has a big market in China. According to the annual Economic and Social Survey of UNESCAP, Covid-19, which was being visualized as an unseen crisis, has hit the economy in the form of shock. Many countries in Asia Pacific, whose economy is, to a large extent, dependent on Tourism and commodities trading, have become weaker. India is in better position as the government doesn't allow go through lower global prices. Still, disruption in work, especially those supporting manufacturing, trading and services need to be taken care of. This is a violent blow to the volatile world economy and definitely, many things will not remain same after we come out of the pandemic (Sood, 2020).

With the World Trade Organization (WTO) estimating the global trade to slope downwards as much as 32%, countries with large economies will first try to build up themselves. For example, 50% of India's trade is directly associated with small and medium enterprises and small economic sectors as many big players are also direct or indirectly associated with smaller producers. Most of the economies will try to develop from a point where they will find themselves in a few months while simultaneously thinking in terms of integrating themselves back with the rest of the world (Sood, 2020).

Energy politics is another major aspect of discussion considering the renewable and green energy technologies for which the US is emerging as a major player. But the impact will be on West Asian countries that are primarily dependent on the oil revenues for the economic depression and the depressed oil price will bring a world of difference in the trading. Rivalries in the many regions have often brought about local conflicts which can now turn into political instability in countries. Rise in nationalism and response to protectionist may lengthen the duration of the economic recession leading to depression, polarization and inequalities. In future, the unpredictability and turbulent times will grow higher (Sood, 2020).

The major economy of South Asia region, India was put under lockdown as a result of COVID-19's development. Because of the pandemic's lower income and broad shocks, the economy will remain stagnant. The initial GDP loss projected for fiscal year 2020/2021 (April to March) was 9.6%, however in the March 2021 update, this was reduced to 8.5 percent. The economy has been rocked by the pandemic's long-term effects, with revised projections in October 2019 estimating a reduction of 16.5 percentage points in 2020/2021 and 1.8 percentage points in 2021/2022. The January 2021 revised estimates, on the other hand, suggest a positive trend of 1.1 percent return into the green zone. The global recovery is expected to boost exports and resuscitate the export-led industrial network by late 2021 (Khan et al., 2022).

THE PERILOUS PATH

The negative outcome for the successful fight against COVID-19 is a result of lacking in well-functioning health care system, unavailability ob basic resources and scarcity of well-coordinated channels which is essential for effective communication. Both diagnosis and treatment have emerged as a global challenge for Covid-19. The pandemic, in particular, has caused an increase in mortality globally and bearing adversarial consequences in countries where the healthcare systems are underdeveloped. To add it further economic burden of the disease could be extensive and critical, which may include long-term lagging in economic growth and short-term financial jolts. It may result in negative impacts on economic growth, igniting the possibility of increase political conflicts and instability. Businesses will continue collapsing if the countries restrict the cross-border movement for longer. This will further add to the difficulties to fight against COVID 19 and as a consequence, people living in some of the developing nations may continue to suffer and die from other preventable diseases (Da'ar OB, Haji M, JradiH., 2020). Covid-19 is presenting humanity with unbelievable challenges to confront. The coronavirus pandemic has caused to shake the world and its long shadow will stay in the society for years together (Kolodco, 2020). Multilateral institutions are more likely to continue in a state of deterioration by multiple agents, unsolved issues and questions (FGV IIU International Intelligence Unit, 2020).

The foreign policy establishment in America seems to be more disconnected from the kitchens of power than ever. The future of America's global leadership and the so-called American-led liberal order has become imbalanced. Trump and Trumpism might produce irregularities (Kristensen, 2017). The post-coronavirus environment is most likely to provide fuel rather than neutralize U.S.-China geo-economic competition (Cronin, Doran & Rough, 2020). China techno-nationalism and protectionism will sharpen the global pandemic causing huge social, economic, and political consequences.

The global institutional architecture of the 1940s cannot extend a supporting hand for humanity to encounter the tough challenges of the 2020s. Hence, to maintain the future of society globally new ways of international system and social contract between states needs to be develops. It is a foregone conclusion that COVID-19 will hurl down the waning of globalization. Racism is extremely destructive; disparaging and it will not lend a hand for us to pass through the ongoing crisis. In the current scenario, the world calls for good science having useful function to carry out in action. Efficient leadership, along with solidarity, kindness and respect for all members of our community and those beyond our borders is the need of the hour. Science alone can introduce some new measures for health care providers so that they can rise to their fullest potential to prevent and treat this and future viral pandemics. In this connection, innovative technologies to deal with global emergencies are urgent necessities.

Currently, the necessary public-health measures such as closing educational institutions, maintaining social distancing and shutting factories are contributing to the economic slowdown. Cities, states regions and leaders have to face the challenges of protecting their people from the deadly virus while taking care of the financial and social development for the future. It seems that the virus has a major contribution to the economic and political turmoil other than disturbing the human health status globally. Even the U.S., cannot defeat the virus in a merely national effort. Ultimately, addressing the urgency of the time must be joined with a global collaborative vision and program. The corona virus has struck with extraordinary scale and ferocity. Testing is not enough to find out the extent of infection, while reversing its spread is a herculean task. Efficient and farsighted government is keenly required to triumph over globally spread unprecedented obstacles of the pandemic. Sustaining the public trust is key to social solidarity, to the relation of societies with each other, and to international peace and stability (Kissinger, 2020).

The exact shape of the upcoming order is still mysterious, even if it is going towards multi-polarity. This does not mean, however, that it will also bring about increased multilateralism. Indeed, global actors have the chance to choose between cooperative multi-polarity and competitive multi-polarity. The former is more worth having, since it is more stable and nonviolent. But the paradox of the global crisis is that while optimum solutions are multilateral and coordinated, the political reactions to the crisis tend to activate isolationism and protectionism, leading not towards cooperation, but towards competition. Countries can still choose for cooperation in the expectation of shaping a better world, but this will call for courageous decisions from global and emerging powers (Renard, 2009).

THE WAY OUT

Policies to deal with the worldwide untoward situation caused by COVID-19 must carry through the need of three criteria. First, they must direct towards the point to minimize the loss of life resulting from the disease. Second, there should be a fundamental approach to restore economic and social life at the earliest possible to avoid the devastating and long-term consequences, in the areas of education, health, food security and livelihood. The lockdowns have already cost immeasurable loss and will grow deeper if there is further delay in establishing strong health care systems, education, and stabilizing the businesses. Although the direct impact of COVID-19 on the health of non-elderly people is small, the indirect impact of lockdown in terms of mental and physical heath and overall well-being is precise, especially for the unprivileged people and in poorer countries. Third, they must aim at a developing a strategic wayto fight the crisis. The measure will be designed not merely to manage it for an indefinite period through, but for instance and periodic lockdowns.

There are three criteria that recommend the directions of policies. First, infections that doesn't result in lasting illness or fatalities must be treated as on balance desirable, while considering the suitable policies. So long as the disease is moving around and no medical productive insight has been succeeded in accomplishing the specific purpose. If the flow of people who get the infection is reduced to a considerable extent, there will be visible decline in people being exposed to the infection. Extensive testing and contact-tracing can contribute to restrict the spread of infections and diminish the threat to people particularly at risk, but this will have to continue for an undefined period. While calls for required infrastructure for public health have been neglected in many countries, the necessity to rebuild an efficient basic health system is underscored by some other countries who have succeeded in dealing with the outbreak, for instance Kerala and New Zealand (Reddy, 2020).

Testing on a mass scale and curbing the spread of the infection over the time lowering the death rate still a tough task even in developed countries who are the possessor of superior curative health infrastructure. Vital societal objectives like education, businesses and also health itself had to bear the cost of adopted means of delaying the spread such as lockdowns. As the circumstances differ for different countries, appropriate life saving strategies may also differ for the countries although the goal is same.

Second, policies must be developed to bridge the gap between restoring economic output and planning adequate investment in dealing with the disease. Costs of measures to stop the spreading of the disease, like mass testing and vaccine development, need to be regarded as restoring the social norms. Till now the contribution to develop a vaccine for the virusto the international fund is very low which clearly reveals the extent of mismatch between the losses that already have happened and is going to happen worldwide, and investments to limit those losses. The failure to sponsor vaccine development is an indication of lack of proper attention for the issue as the expected gains of individual countries would be more than paying for the required investment. Granting credentials to the interdependence involved in successfully fighting the disease, along with its economic and social outcomes, the UN must take the leadership position that has been neglected so far (Reddy, 2020).

Third, 'the most important design of policies should allow getting back of normal social and economic status. Such policies should be strategized and aimed at allowing the segments of the population at the low risk to go back to work places, while keeping safe the people who are potentially at higher-risk. Systematic collection of test results and other required data can be put into service in order to maintain restrictions. Large gatherings can be kept from happening, however younger persons can be allowed for unavoidable crowd. There should be financial or other types of compensation for elderly and vulnerable. Infrastructure should be developed for public who have no choice at home for self-isolation. Public actions must facilitate and lend support to desired behaviors. Technology can play a valuable role but cannot be taken as an alternative for voluntary choices and public understanding brought up by supportive public policies that do away with obstacles and develop benefits of the desirable behaviors. An effective approach to balance and achieve desired goal should be strategized. The aim must be to keep down risks while maintaining interdependence, instead of building walls around individuals, localities or countries (Reddy, 2020).

Smart and suitable policies can be formed to carry on contacts across nations. Keeping in mind the infection rates that have moved upwards all over the place, the benefit of isolation to bring down the proliferation of the disease is confined within certain limits, but its other costs are huge. To keep the disease under check in one's own society through positive acceptance of internal measures is more realistic than to guarantee its control in all places. Countries that have been successful in accomplishing control over the disease can start connecting to the world with their efforts, without waiting for the international contacts to be restored. The interest of each and the interests of all now come about at the same time, not only within nations but for entire humanity (Reddy, 2020). Coronavirus transmission speed is affected by a country's level of globalization, both in terms of initial arrival, infection rate, and fatality ratio. More globally integrated countries are damaged more rapidly and severely. As a result of travel and migration, there is more human interaction. The implication is that pandemics can be avoided by introducing early temporary inter-country isolation measures that focus on people mobility (Zimmermann et al., 2020).

There is a dire need for the global coalition to deal with the pandemic. This is an opportune moment to work together to defeat a common enemy that endangers the lives of all. The affinity between national and international entities is considered as the opposite solution for the question of cooperation in a pandemic. From an ethical globalance perspective, not a global government is the solution but beefing up global governance in terms of strong cooperative actions. The relation between international law and national law is crucial for national sovereignty and the weight of international commitments. National law regulates the rules within one nation while international law has to regulate the rules between nations in international relations and interactions. Globalance constitutes as balance between Sovereignty and Solidarity (Stückelberger, 2020). With an unparalleled quantity of shocks affecting the global economy adversely, developing economies and emerging markets are encountering extra challenges in view of their weaker healthcare systems, constrained macroeconomic policy space, often lack of diversified economies, and in some cases high risk of debt distress. They fail to ensure sufficient and much needed social protection through the crisis which is devoid of the support of the global and international communities. Joint action is of paramount significance for human solidarity, and to speed up the end of the pandemic and secure a healthy global economy more quickly (International Monetary Fund, 2020). A concerted effort across all sectors and disciplines responsible for health is urgently called for in the present hour. The World Health Organization (WHO), the UN Food and Agriculture Organization and the World Organization for Animal Health need to promote a collaborative "One-Health" approach, engaging physicians, veterinarians, epidemiologists, laboratory scientists, nurses, basic scientists and other health professionals to find out better solutions to keep at bay future outbreaks or, at least, trim down their impact. The pandemic will continue with its impact until the virus is contained in each country. This externality states the reason for the international community to join together in facilitating developing economies and emerging market to fight against the disease, carrying on research on vaccines and therapies, and sharing good practices that put a stop to new eruptions.

REFERENCES

Cronin, Doran, & Rough. (2020). *Geopolitical Implications of the Coronavirus*. Hudson Institute.

Da'ar, O. B., Haji, M., & Jradi, H. (2020). Potential implications for weak health systems and conflict zones in the Middle East and North Africa region. *The International Journal of Health Planning and Management*.

Devakumar, D., & Sunil, S. (2020). Racism and discrimination in COVID-19 responses. *Lancet*.

Dossier. (2020). Pandemic and the Crisis of Capitalism. *Rethinking Marxism*.

FGV IIU International Intelligence Unit Rio. (2020). *FGV IIU Flash Notes the World Corona Changed: Preliminary Thoughts on the Coming World Order*. Author.

Goldin, I., & Muggah, R. (2020). End of International Cooperation? How Corona virus Has Changed the World Permanently. *The National Interest*. https://nationalinterest.org/blog/buzz/end-international-cooperation-how-coronavirus-has-changed-world-permanently-139092

Haass, R. (2020). Foreword. In *The End of World Order and American Foreign Policy*. Council Special Report No. 86. https://cdn.cfr.org/sites/default/files/report_pdf/the-end-of-world-order-and-american-foreign-policy-csr.pdf

Hameiri, S. (2020). Covid-19: Why did global health governance fail? *The Interpreter Lowy Institute*. https://www.lowyinstitute.org/the-interpreter/covid-19-why-did-global-health-governance-fail

Hofman, B. (2020). Final, long-term risk is that the pandemic will feed protectionism around the world, The COVID-19 Pandemic. *EAI, 14*.

International Monetary Fund. (2020). *COVID-19-Impact and Policy Considerations*. G-20 Finance Ministers and Central Bank Governors' Virtual Meeting.

Jha, M. (2020). The Un Role in times of Corona Virus. *The Business Line*.

Khan, M. A., Naqvi, H. A., Hakeem, M. M., Din, G. M., & Iqbal, N. (2022). Economic and financial impact of the COVID-19 pandemic in South Asia. *Environmental Science and Pollution Research International, 29*(11), 15703–15712. doi:10.100711356-021-16894-9 PMID:34636009

Kissinger, H. A. (2020). The Corona Virus Pandemic will forever alter the World Order. *The Wall Street Journal*. https://www.wsj.com/articles/the-coronavirus-pandemic-will-forever-alter-the-world-order-11585953005

Kolodko, G. W. (2020a). After the Calamity: Economics and Politics in the Post-Pandemic World. *Sociological Review, 2*(210), 20. https://www.pte.pl/pliki/2/36/Kolodko.pdf

Kristensen, P. M. (2017). After Abdication: America Debates the Future of Global Leadership. *Chin. Polit. Sci. Rev, 2*(4), 550–566. doi:10.100741111-017-0078-7

Mishra, A. K., Rath, B. N., & Dash, A. K. (2020). *Does Indian Financial Market Nosedive by COVID-19 Outbreak in Comparison to Post-Implementation of Demonetisation and GST?* Asia Pacific Applied Economics Association Working Paper Series, WP/AP/2020-01.

Pegram, T. (2020). Coronavirus is a failure of global governance – now the world needs a radical transformation. *Conversation*.

Prassl, Boniva, Golin, & Rauh. (2020). *Inequality in the Impact of the Coronavirus Shock: Evidence from Real Time Surveys*. IZA institute of Labour Economics.

Reddy, S. (2020). A roadmap to tackle Covid-19. *The Hindu*.

Renard, T. (2009). The Coming Order: Strategic and Geopolitical Impacts of the Economic Crisis. *World Politics Review*.

Sahoo, Pravakar, & Ashwani. (2020). *Covid 19 and The Indian Economy: Impact on Growth, Manufacturing, Trade and MSME sector*. IEG Working Paper, 390.

Sanni, Y., Otu, A., & Labonté, R. (2020). Globalisation in the time of COVID-19: Repositioning Africa to meet the immediate and remote challenges. *Globalization and Health, 16*(1), 51. doi:10.118612992-020-00581-4 PMID:32580728

Sood, R. (2020). The trends shaping the post-COVID-19 world. *The Hindu*.

Stückelberger, C. (2020). *Post-Corona World: Balancing International Cooperation ad National Sovereignty*. MGIMO University. https://repository.globethics.net/bitstream/handle/20.500.12424/3958494/St%C3%BCckelberger%20%20Post_Corona_Virus_National_Sovereignty.pdf?sequence=1&isAllowed=y

YacoubA. R.ZomorM. E. (2020). Would COVID-19 be the turning point in history for the globalization era? The short-term and long-term impact of COVID-19 on Globalization. https://ssrn.com/abstract=3570142 orhttp://dx.doi.org/10.2139/ssrn.3570142 doi:10.2139/ssrn.3570142

Yhome, K. (2020). *Regional dimensions of global response to COVID-19*. Observer Research Foundation.

Zimmermann, K. F., Karabulut, G., Bilgin, M. H., & Doker, A. C. (2020). Inter-country distancing, globalisation and the coronavirus pandemic. *World Economy*, *43*(6), 1484–1498. doi:10.1111/twec.12969 PMID:32836720

Chapter 5
Nutritional Security of Marginalised Groups in the Context of COVID-19:
A Discourse

Sridevi Gummadi
University of Hyderabad, India

Balaji Patturi
University of Hyderabad, India

Priya Shanmugam
Mount Carmel College, India

ABSTRACT

Malnutrition in all its forms has become the leading cause of poor health and death worldwide. The 2020 Global Nutrition Report stresses that the need to address malnutrition in all its forms by tackling injustices in food and health systems is now more urgent than ever. Over 820 million people went to bed hungry even before the COVID-19 pandemic, of which 110 million people were living in acute food insecurity. According to the World Food Programme, 135 million suffer from acute hunger largely due to man-made conflicts, climate change, and economic downturns. The COVID-19 pandemic could now double that number, putting an additional 130 million (total 265 million) people at risk of suffering acute hunger by the end of 2020. India is ranked 102 out of 117 countries the lowest in South Asia. Surprisingly Bangladesh, Nepal, and Pakistan are performing better in terms of GHI. In this chapter, the authors analyse the nutritional security of marginalised groups in Andhra Pradesh and Telangna State.

DOI: 10.4018/978-1-7998-6896-5.ch005

INTRODUCTION

The food security has been an ongoing issue with every incumbent Indian government. Despite celebrated committees having given reports on this issue even before this unprecedented pandemic, the paradigm of leaving everything to market and declining role of centre and state in social sector expenditure and primary sector prevailed. The desertion and obliviousness of conditions of the migrant labour who are vastly marginalised, neglect of public health and welfare of the vulnerable sections of the people raising questions on the role of central and state governments. The entire country dismayed after the spread of covid-19 to the public but the pandemic induced hourly decisioned lockdown by the central government has made people especially vulnerable; migrant workers suffer into absolute immiseration, they have no bargaining power in a technological advanced country with abundant trade unions, they could have bargained for higher wages but that was not possible in India so they just suffered immiseration.

With the disruption of the food supply chains nationwide in the coming year, the non-availability of food coupled with the lack of purchasing power will lead to *extensive hunger*. Difficulty in maintaining food production, restrictions on trade and limitations on labour mobility can lead to lower farm incomes and food shortages, adding another layer of complexity to fight back against Covid-19. Across the country, huge number of workers who have been migrated, who are working locally, farmers, fishermen, sellers, ragpickers, and the deprived were facing extreme distress and also food shortage, because their livelihoods have been disrupted by the unprecedented lockdown. The exceptional hardship faced by migrant workers since the outbreak of virus might result in fear trauma. Starvation and hardship of migrant workers have created further an unprecedented humanitarian crisis, as millions of households with dwindling savings have no way to access food and other basic necessities in the near future.

India having huge population of marginalised community who are engaged in migrant working informal sector has not foreseen the consequences of their plight at a time like the current pandemic situation. In the light of aforementioned understanding, following sections in the paper details with non-nutritional facets of the marginalised groups in Telangana and Andhra Pradesh states, and covid-19's impact on their lives and also the vital issue of their food security.

CONTEXT

The Global Hunger Index 2022 ranked India at 107 out of 121 nations and it fared only better than Afghanistan at 109 whereas its neighboring countries improved better viz. Pakistan at 99, Nepal at 81, Bangladesh at 84 and Sri Lanka 64.It has been found that from 2016-20, 17.3% of children in India are wasted while 34.7% of children under five are stunted and from 2019 data, it suggests that 3.4% of children die before turning five years old. The report identified conflict, climate change, and COVID-19 as the reasons for any progress that has been made against hunger in recent years. Particularly covid-19 pandemic, which has shaken the world throughout for two years i.e., 2020 and 2021, has made us to learn how vulnerable we are to global disruption and the associated health and economic concerns (Chatterjee et. al.,2021).

On a national scale, high prevalence of poverty and inequality in access to nutritious food are found among particular communities in rural and urban areas, poverty and malnutrition rates are high and urban areas are among the new epicenters of poverty and hunger. While food production and the market are vital dimensions vastly debated in literature, there is mere understanding on how food reaches the plate and is scantier in terms of various pathways, negotiations, choices and cultures influencing who eats what and why. The constraints, states and institutions role aspects, economic access to food, employment, access to land, prices of food grains and food distribution and inadequate availability of food grains will have little relevance if people do not possess purchasing power to procure them for their consumption. Though there are several studies available at global, macro and meso levels, literature is scanty at household level in-depth analysis on marginalized groups.

India produced 291.95 million tonnes of food grains in 2019-20, yet 69% of deaths of children under the age of five have been attributed to malnutrition by UNICEF in its State of the World's Children report. The UNICEF study found that 8.8 lakh children in India below the age of five died prematurely in 2018. Of those, 69% died of malnutrition. Nearly 690 million people are undernourished, 144 million children suffer from stunting – a sign of chronic undernutrition. About 47 million children suffered from wasting in 2018, a sign of acute undernutrition, and 5.3 million children died before their fifth birthday, in many cases as a result of undernutrition (Jyotishi and Sridevi, 2021).

National Family Health Survey (NFHS) fifth round, though not yet out for all the states and Union Territories (UTs), tells a similar gloomy story. NFHS-5 factsheets for 22 states/ UTs show chronic undernutrition has increased in 13 states/UTs, whereas underweight has increased in 16 states/UTs. Around 51.4% of women in the reproductive age group (15-49 years) were anemic, according to NFHS-4 (2015-16) data. This figure has not improved during NFHS-5, based on the data available for many states and UTs (ibid.)

The pandemic has threatened India's food security landscape across all four indicators, viz. availability, access, utilisation and stability. It has in turn further intensified the existing problem of malnutrition among women and children. A group of volunteers maintained a database of deaths, unrelated to the virus, reported in the media for the period March-July 2020. The number of news reports is more than 700, listing more than 1,000 deaths across the country. The reasons include exhaustion, starvation, hunger, distress suicide, and so on. Several migrant labourers lost their lives on the road while walking back to their hometowns on empty stomachs during the first and very hastily implemented nation-wide lockdown. These incidents were well-documented in the media. The second wave of the pandemic and the resulting burdens of health expenditure as well as localised lockdowns have once again risked the livelihoods of many. Data from the Centre for Monitoring Indian Economy shows that nearly 17 million daily wage labourers and small traders, such as street vendors, lost employment in the month of May 2021 alone. (ibid.)

FOOD INSECURITY

Undernourishment and related health Issus have been one of the dreaded realities of India. Across the states the picture varies according to the intensity of poverty, literacy, low density of health infrastructure and state support policies. The total food grain production in India is estimated at a record of 308.65 million tones which is 11.15 million tonnes higher than in the year 2019-20 (Economic Survey, 2021-22).

Despite this huge production, parallelly 224.3 million people are undernourished, 20 million children under the age of five are affected by wasting, 36.1 million under the age of five are affected by stunting, 187.3 million adult women are affected by anemia (FAO, 2022), under-five mortality rate is 41.9 per cent (NHFS, 5). The GHI report points out "Idea's child wasting rate, at 19.3 percent, is the highest of any country in the world" (GHI, 2022).

Figure 1. Per capita output and net availability of food grains: India
Source: Directorate of Economics and Statistics, Department of Agriculture, Cooperation and Farmers Welfare, Ministry of Agriculture and Farmers Welfare.

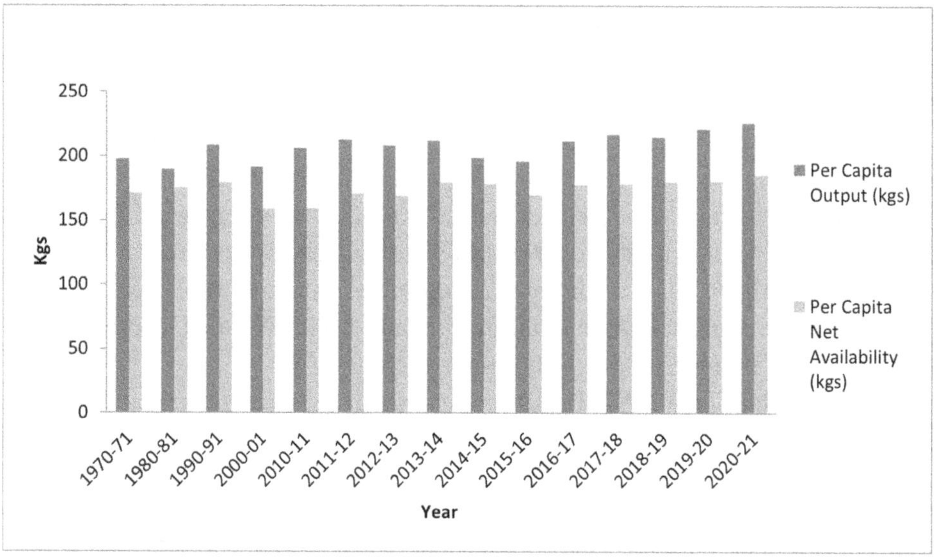

The Right to Food Campaign and the Centre for Equity Studies along with a group of organisations have conducted Hunger Watch Survey between December 2021 and January 2022across 14 states covering a total of 79 per cent of households and calculated "food insecurity" based on the Global Food Insecurity Experience Scale developed by FAO. The survey revealed that 25 per cent of the families had faced "severe food insecurity. Table 1 and Figure 2 gives the total number of respondents surveyed in 14 major states in India and the percentage of social composition of the respondents accordingly.

Majority of the respondents had faced food insecurity in the month preceding the survey and 31 per cent had reported slight food insecurity, 23 per cent had faced moderate food insecurity, and about 25 per cent had faced severe food insecurity. Approximately 60 per cent had concerned about not having adequate food and they were unable to consume healthy or nutritious food.

Appallingly, for about 45 per cent of the respondents had reported that their household haven't had any food besides at least one family member used to go to bed by skipping a meal in a day in the month prior to the survey period.

The survey has covered enough social groups viz. 31 per cent of the respondents belong to Scheduled Tribe (ST), 25 per cent belongs to Scheduled Caste (SC). The survey also covered a Particularly Vulnerable Tribal Groups community and they are amounting to 06 per cent. Additionally, the survey also covered religiously viz. 64 per cent of the respondents belong to Hindus whereas 18 per cent of the respondents belong to Muslims. The study highlights that 66 per cent of the respondents had their income decreased and 60 per cent of the respondents have received half wages when compared with the pre covid-19 phase. And 45 per cent of the households have been buried in debts. Interestingly, about 71 per cent of the respondents were women (Hunger Watch Survey, 2021).

Table 1. Number of respondents: State wise

S. No.	State	Total Number of Respondents
1	Andhra Pradesh	150
2	Bihar	178
3	Chhattisgarh	254
4	Delhi	280
5	Gujarat	549
6	Himachal Pradesh	260
7	Jharkhand	166
8	Karnataka	154
9	Madhya Pradesh	821
10	Maharashtra	1182
11	Rajasthan	105
12	Telangana	98
13	Uttar Pradesh	508
14	West Bengal	1992

Source: Hunger Watch Press Handouts. (https://phmovement.org/wp-content/uploads/2022/09/Feb-23-Hunger-Watch-Press-Handouts-1.pdf)

Figure 2. Social composition of the respondents: In percentage
Source: Hunger Watch Press Handouts (https://phmovement.org/wp-content/uploads/2022/09/Feb-23-Hunger-Watch-Press-Handouts-1.pdf)

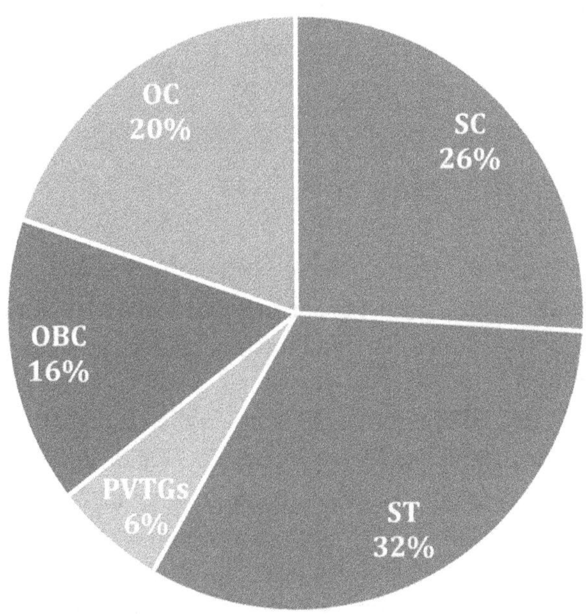

On the other hand, India has seen approximately 224 deaths related to starvation, hunger and economic distress in the pandemic period and 209 deaths due to accidents during walking when the mode of transport was cut down by the government (Aman et al. 2020). Below figure reveals the complete picture of non-virus deaths during the pandemic period.

Figure 3. Non-virus deaths by category
Source: Thejesh GN (https://thejeshgn.com/projects/covid19-india/non-virus-deaths/#Charts)

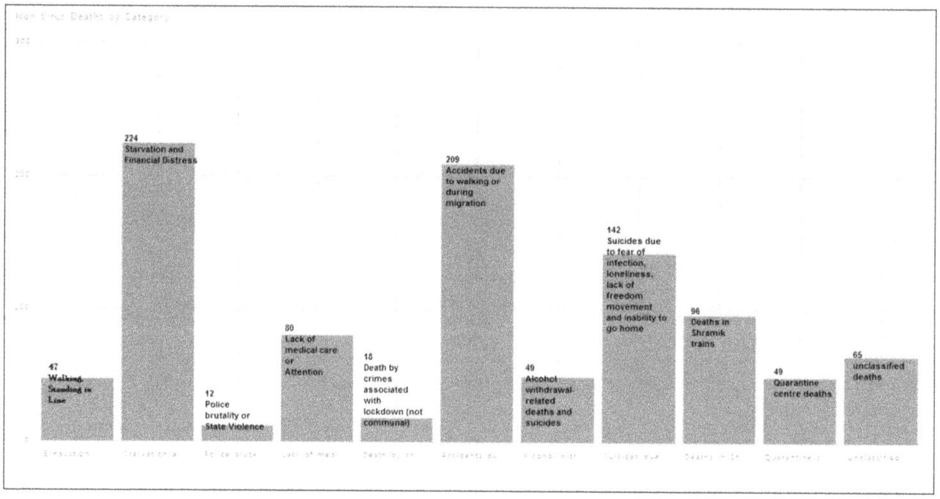

The category of deaths includes deaths due to starvation and financial distress, exhaustion, accidents during migration, lack or denial of medical care, suicides, police brutality, crimes, and alcohol-withdrawal, deaths in Shramik trains, Quarantine deaths, suicides due to the fear of infection. The 'unclassified' category refers to the data where the information isn't received substantially.

UNEMPLOYMENT RATE IN INDIA

In India, the unemployment is seen at an increasing phase steadily. The main reason could be attributed as most of the companies/employers do not wish to spend additional time and money to train their fresher. In the past years, in 2017, India had around 18.3 million unemployed people and 18.6 in 2018 and high in 2019 amounting to 18.9 million unemployed people (Singh, 2018) besides this, the rate of unemployment in 2018 is 3.5 per cent, in the year 2020 it is 8per cent and in the year 2021 it is 5.98 per cent (Figure 4).

To capture the post sudden Jantha Curfew in March 2020 and ongoing pandemic unemployment situation in India, Telangana and Andhra Pradesh, monthly data viz. April, May and June from CMIE has been borrowed. It is evident from Figure 5 that the pandemic has pushed many people to having joblessness condition in India, Telangana and Andhra Pradesh.

Figure 2 reveals that, post March 2020, the rate of unemployment in the months of April and May, it was 20.5 and 17.4 per cent in Andhra Pradesh. In Telangana, the rate of unemployment stood at 6.2 and 14.7 per cent and at the national level, the rate of unemployment stood at 23.5 and 21.7 per cent.

The highest was Puducherry (76 and 59 per cent) and Tamil Nadu (50 and 33) followed by Bihar (46 per cent) in both the months.

Figure 4. Unemployment rate: India – 1991-2021
Source: CMIE. Unemployment Rate Monthly time series (%): India

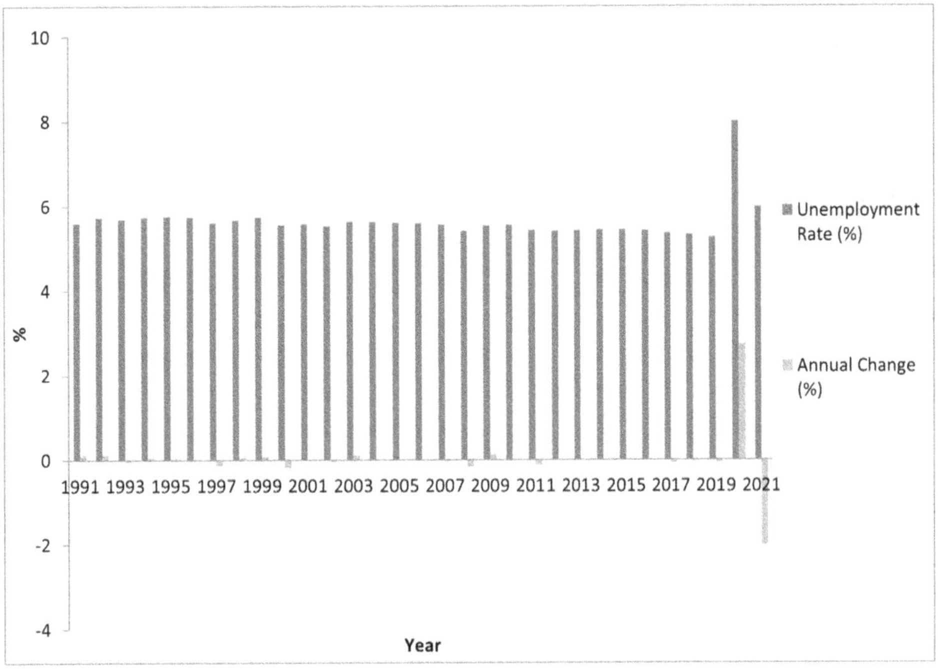

Figure 5. Monthly unemployment rate in Telugu States and India: 2016-2022
Source: CMIE. Unemployment Rate Monthly time series (%): India

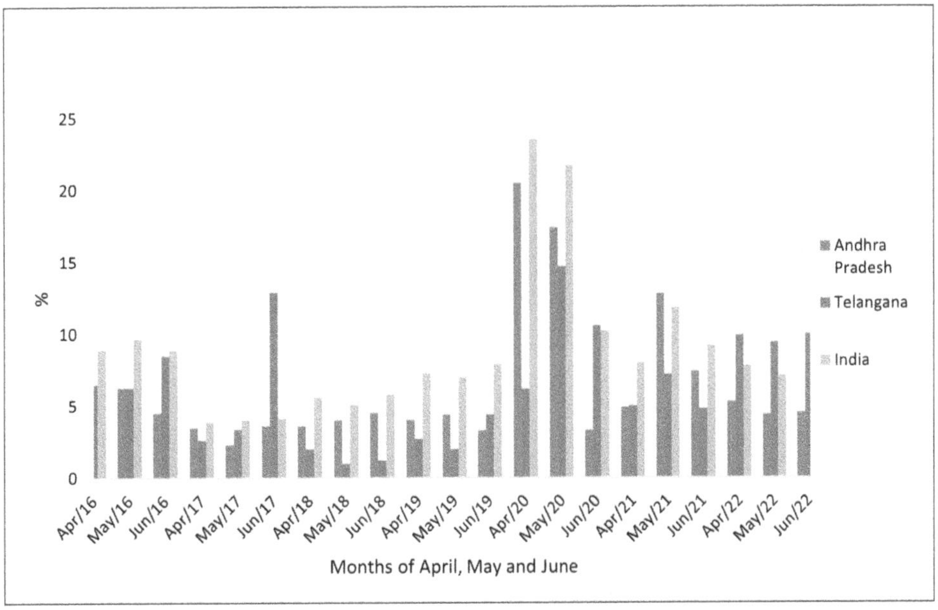

With the rising unemployment rate, The Hunger Watch Survey reported that approximately 70 per cent of the respondents had an income of less than Rs. 7,000 per month during the lockdown period and about 34 per cent of the respondents reported that their consumption of cereals in the last month was satisfactory. Scanty consumption of nutrient rich foods and a large proportion of households reported that they had consumed nutritious foods less than three times a month. And 28 per cent of the households reported that they had pulses very few times in a month.

Forty-one per cent of the respondents have said that the nutritional quality and quantity of food the household eats had deteriorated when compared to pre-pandemic period. And 67 per cent of the respondents could not afford cooking gas in the month prior to the survey period.

NUTRITIONAL SECURITY

NITI Aayog released report during June 2021 highlighting the fact that 11 states, including the most populous ones, scored less than 50 out of 100 in reaching zero hunger. Andhra Pradesh and Telangana scored less than 50 out of 100 in reaching Zero Hunger, but interestingly in overall performance of the state Andhra Pradesh is in third position. The pandemic has threatened India's food security landscape across all four indicators: availability, access, stability, and utilization. It could in turn further intensify the existing problem of malnutrition among women and children (Sridevi et al., 2021).

NFHS 5 fact sheets for 22 states/Union Territories (UT) shows, chronic undernutrition has increased in 13 states/UTs, whereas, underweight has increased in 16 states/UTs despite ambitious state support programs like *Poshan Abhiyaan*, malnutrition is still high.

Figure 6. Nutritional status of children: Social category – India

*Source: International Institute for Population Sciences (IIPS) and ICF. National Family Health Survey; 5 (2019-21). *Don't know: Percentage of the people who have not revealed their caste identity during survey.*

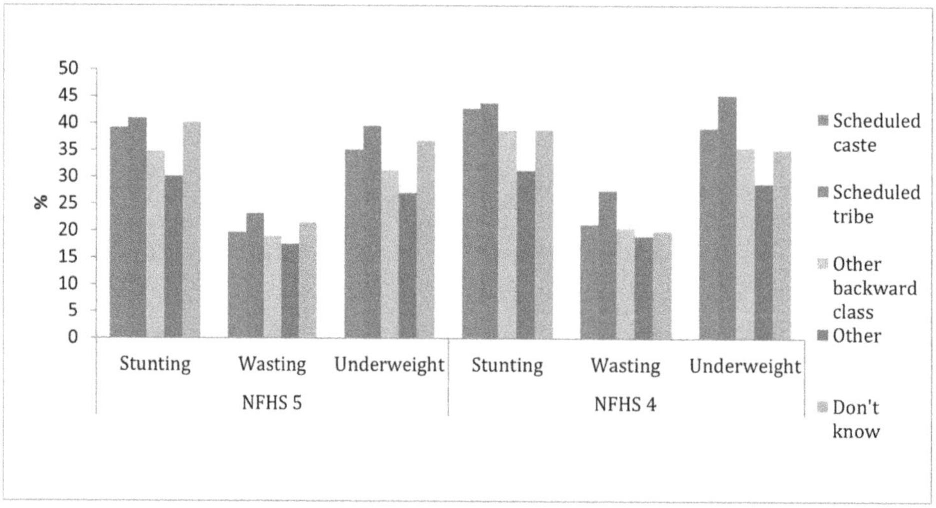

Figure 7. Nutritional status of children: Social category Andhra Pradesh
Source: International Institute for Population Sciences (IIPS) and ICF. National Family Health Survey; 5 (2019-21)

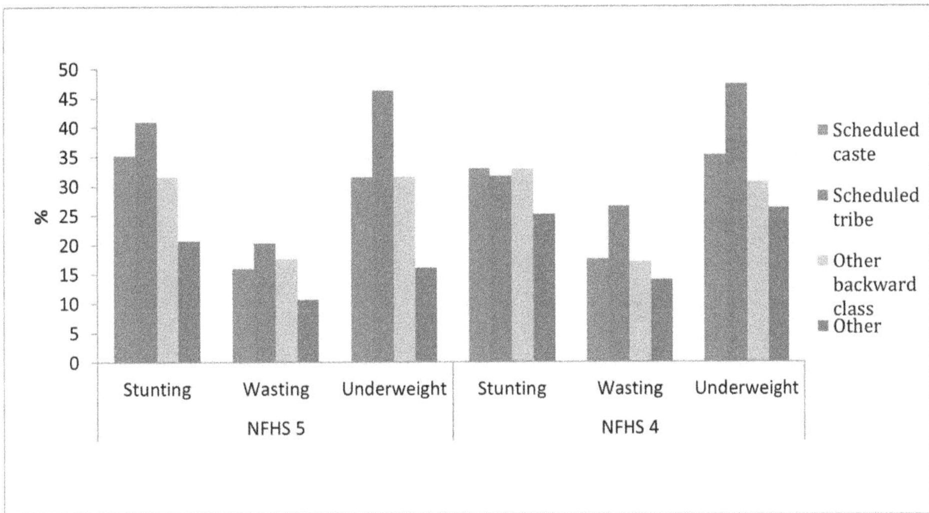

Figure 8. Nutritional status of children: Social category – Telangana
Source: International Institute for Population Sciences (IIPS) and ICF. National Family Health Survey; 5 (2019-21)

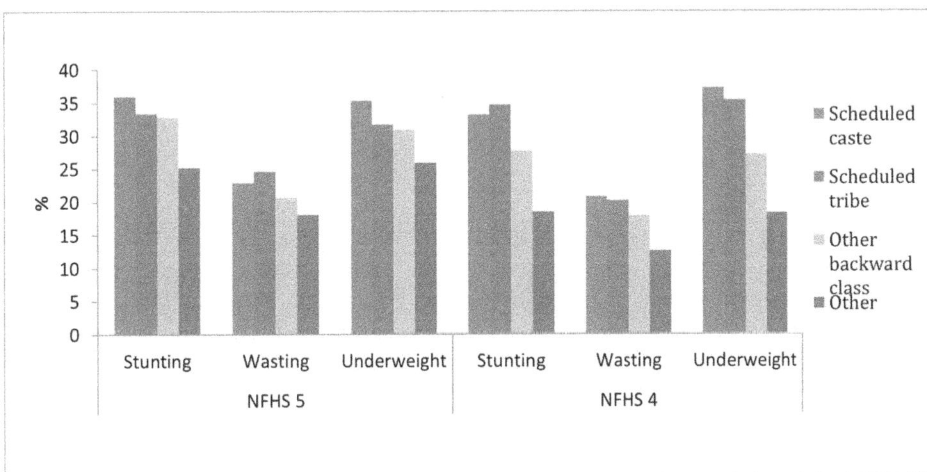

It evident from NFHS 4 and 5 that the nutritional indicators of children belonging to marginalized communities are deteriorating than non-vulnerable sections in India, Telangana and Andhra Pradesh. Interestingly, In India, people who haven't mentioned their caste identification are seen to have deterioration in their nourishment. In Andhra Pradesh, children belonging to ST community and in Telangana children belonging to SC and ST are prone to malnourished. In Telangana, according to NFHS 4 and 5, the proportion of the children below the five years in the urban region who are underweight have gone up from 22 per cent to 26 per cent; stunted children from 21 per cent to 28 per cent and children who are wasted have increased from 15 per cent to 20 per cent.

The BMI and Anemia of the women belonging to reproductive age group of between 15 and 49 is also a worrisome. Figure 9 and 10 have pictured that BMI of women in Telugu states and India is improving over the years but cannot be neglected by as the anemia is worsening the health of the women in every aspect.

Figure 9. BMI of women: AP and Telangana – Various rounds of NFHS
Source: International Institute for Population Sciences (IIPS) and ICF. National Family Health Survey; 5 (2019-21)

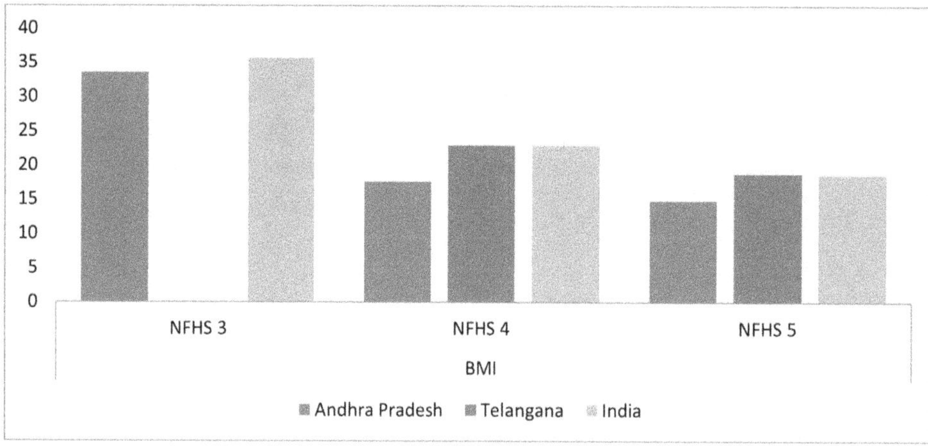

Figure 10. Anemia of women: AP and Telangana – Various rounds of NFHS
Source: International Institute for Population Sciences (IIPS) and ICF. National Family Health Survey; 5 (2019-21)

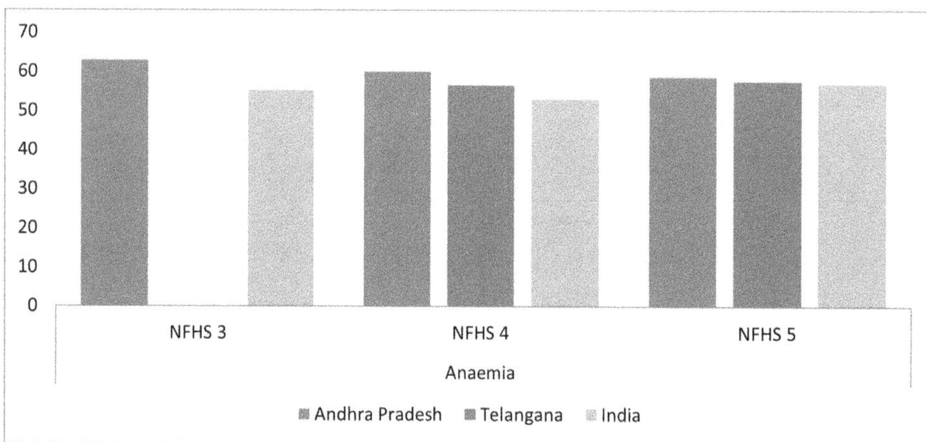

Around half of the women who are in the reproductive age group (15-49 years) are suffering from anemia and also interestingly the obesity is rising in urban females. Given the magnitude of the problem, there is a need to understand the food value chain, especially at the point of consumption and assess its availability, accessibility, utilisation and stability [the four critical dimensions of food and nutrition security (FNS)]. While food production and the market are critical dimensions generally well discussed in literature, there is little knowledge on how food reaches the plate. The knowledge base is further inadequate in terms of various pathways, negotiations, choices and cultures influencing who eats what and why. What are the constraints in availing and accessing nutritious food? What role do the state and other institutions play in addressing under-nutrition?

The main emphasis of the SDG is to reduce malnutrition and provide food security to all (Goal No.2 by 2030, zero hunger and all forms of malnutrition). 40 per cent of children in Telangana and Andhra Pradesh are malnourished majority belong to vulnerable groups. Among these groups, the prevalence of stunting is highest amongst children from STs (41.0 per cent), followed by SCs (35.2 per cent) and OBCs (31.6 per cent). Women whose BMI is below normal (<18.5 kg/m^2) is highest among ST (21.1 per cent) followed by OBC (16.1 per cent) and SC (15.0 per cent) anemia among children 6-59 months across social groups is very high based on NFHS 5 for Andhra Pradesh. For Telangana state these percentages are high. Apart from indirect interventions, there is a need to directly focus on nutritional deficiencies and address them in timely manner (Gummadi et al., 2021). A paradigm shift from caloric consumption to consumption of micronutrient and protein-rich food as well as the four pillars namely availability, accessibility, utilisation and stability through direct and indirect modes of targeting are crucial. While indirect means would include understanding bottlenecks and improving the production and value chain processes of nutrition-rich food products, the direct method would involve provisioning of adequate nutritious food to malnourished groups. Undernourishment and related health issues have been one of the one of the dreaded realities of India. Across the states the picture varies according to the intensity of poverty, literacy, low density of health infrastructure and state support policies.

CONCLUSION

The food security has been an ongoing issue with every incumbent Indian government. Despite celebrated committees having given reports on this issue even before this unprecedented pandemic, the paradigm of leaving everything to market and declining role of center and state in social sector expenditure and primary sector prevailed. With the disruption of the food supply chains nationwide in the coming year, the non-availability of food coupled with the lack of purchasing power will lead to *extensive hunger*. India having huge population of marginalised community who are engaged in migrant working informal sector has not foreseen the consequences of their plight at a time like the current pandemic situation. Based upon the Hunger Watch Survey, it is learnt that25 per cent of the families had faced “severe food insecurity” and for about 45 per cent of the respondents had reported that their household haven’t had any food. Appallingly, India has seen approximately 224 deaths related to starvation, hunger and economic distress in the pandemic period. India recorded highest unemployment rate at 23.5 and 21.7 per cent in the months of April and May, 2020. Having said this, Hunger Watch Survey revealed that approximately 70 per cent of the respondents had an income of less than Rs. 7,000 per month during the lockdown and about 34 per cent of the respondents reported that their consumption of cereals in the last month was satisfactory. Scanty consumption of nutrient rich foods and a large proportion of households reported that they had consumed nutritious foods less than three times a month. And 28 per cent of the households reported that they had pulses very few times in a month. Also, 67 per cent of the respondents could not afford cooking gas in the month prior to the survey period. The NFHS 4 and 5 rounds revealed that the nutritional indicators of children belonging to marginalized communities are deteriorating than non-vulnerable sections in India, Telangana and Andhra Pradesh. In Telangana, according to NFHS 4 and 5, the proportion of the children below the five years in the urban region who are underweight have gone up from 22 per cent to 26 per cent; stunted children from 21 per cent to 28 per cent and children who are wasted have increased from 15 per cent to 20 per cent. The BMI and Anemia of the women belonging to reproductive age group of between 15 and 49 is also a worrisome. Around half of the women who are in the reproductive age group (15-49 years) are suffering from anemia and also interestingly the obesity is rising in urban females. A paradigm shift from caloric consumption to consumption of micronutrient and protein-rich food as well as the four pillars namely availability, accessibility, utilisation and stability through direct and indirect modes of targeting are crucial.

ACKNOWLEDGMENT

This research was supported by Institute of Eminence -University of Hyderabad and project titled "Understanding and Addressing Food and Nutrition Security issues among Vulnerable Groups: An Interdisciplinary study in Andhra Pradesh and Telangana" (No. UoH/IoE/RC1/RC1-20-032).

The major portion of the study has been drawn from two published research papers of the first author, mentioned accordingly in the reference section.

REFERENCES

Aman, K. S., Krushna, R., & Thejesh, G. N. (2020). *India Non-Virus Deaths During lockdown (Version 20200730)* [Data set]. Zenodo., doi:10.5281/zenodo.4630198

Chatterji, S., McDougal, L., Johns, N., Ghule, M., Rao, N., & Raj, A. (2021). COVID-19-Related financial hardship, job loss, and mental health symptoms: Findings from a cross-sectional study in a rural agrarian community in India. *International Journal of Environmental Research and Public Health*, *18*(16), 8647. doi:10.3390/ijerph18168647 PMID:34444394

Gummadi, S., Jyotishi, A., & Prashanth, D. (2021). Malnutrition and Inequality among the Vulnerable Social Groups: A Study of Two Villages. *Journal of Development Policy Review*, *1*(4).

Jyotishi, A., & Sridevi, G. (2021). A hunger-free nation: How India can leverage existing institutions. *The News Minute*.

People's Health Movement. (2022). *Hunger Watch Press Handouts*. https://phmovement.org/wp-content/uploads/2022/09/Feb-23-Hunger-Watch-Press-Handouts-1.pdf

Singh, R. (2018). The cause of unemployment in current market scenario. *Vivechan International Journal of Research*, *9*(1), 81–86.

Upadhyay, R. P., & Palanivel, C. (2011). Challenges in achieving food security in India. *Iranian Journal of Public Health*, *40*(4), 31–36. PMID:23113100

von Grebmeret, K. (2022). *Global Hunger Index Food Systems Transformation And Local Governance*. Concern Worldwide and Welthungerhilfe. https://www.globalhungerindex.org/pdf/en/2022.pdf

Chapter 6
A Systematic Review on Indian Food Security Systems and Food Assistance Programmes (FAPs) in the Context of the COVID-19 Pandemic

Sugandh Arora
https://orcid.org/0000-0002-4740-5270
Sharda University, India

Tawheed Nabi
Lovely Professional University, India

Vishal Sarin
Lovely Professional University, India

ABSTRACT

The COVID-19 pandemic has shaken the global economy, where India is the most affected economy. The crisis has an insignificant impact on the 2nd Sustainable Development Goal (SDG) to get rid of desire by 2030. The most deprived society may have a significant threat of poor health and malnutrition as a society cannot access nutritious and sustainable diets. Thus, pandemic generates an income shock projected to increase unemployment, poverty, and household food insecurity. Consequently, the purpose of this study is to acquire the relevant evidence from literature about food security and food assistance programmes. A systematic review was conducted across Academia, EBSCO, Google Scholar, JSTORE, Pub Med, Springer, and Scopus, and a search was performed between March-August 2020 for the accretion. Food security systems and FAPs would be analyzed more comprehensively and suggests the prerequisite for the central and state government to carefully utilize both non-governmental and administrative interventions to drop the hunger rate and improve the food security status.

DOI: 10.4018/978-1-7998-6896-5.ch006

INTRODUCTION

Covid-19 pandemic, the primary cause of illness, death, and economic devastation, ultimately bent the food security system and supply chain. The effects of COVID-19 on the billions of individuals afflicted by the epidemic is not confined to the virus's direct health hazards. It impacts negatively on regional and national food supply chains and economy, compromising their food security. COVID-19 showed the flaws in regional and international systems, as well as the vulnerability of our food supply chains and how easily they may be disrupted. In summary, it gives light on the essential issue of food system resilience and its relationship to people's food and nutrition security. Globally, the epidemic has worsened food insecurity, resulting in adverse public health repercussions (Udmale et al., 2020; Singh et al., 2020). Food insecurity refers to a person or family's inability to obtain sufficient food consistently owing to a lack of financial or other resources (USDA, 2019).

To contain the spread of this pandemic, countries immediately commenced the lockdown, self-isolation and social distancing approach, given the rapid rise in the population of infected persons. These unanticipated restrictions in physical, social and economic activities interrupted the ability to earn a living and affected economic sectors at various levels, ranging from the primary sector to manufacturing and services; thereby threatening the attainment of the second Sustainable Development Goal (SDG) targeted at achieving food security, ending hunger and improved nutrition (Nicola et al., 2020; Niles et al., 2020).

The economic access and affordability posed a threat to food security in two ways: households lost income wholly or partially as a result of completely lockdowns (Laborde et al., 2020 and Bene et al., 2020), and food prices could rise as a result of supply shortages caused by transportation and travel restrictions (Laborde et al., 2020; Bene et al., 2020 and Devereux et al., 2020). As a result of the decline in incomes, foods such as vegetables, fruits and animal products became more expensive (Laborde et al., 2020). School closures may impact a more significant proportion of low-income households due to their inaccessibility (Laborde et al., 2020). Numerous problems arose due to mobility restrictions imposed by economic access barriers (Bene et al., 2020; Devereux et al., 2020; Workie et al., 2020; Naja and Hanadeh, 2020). When stockpiling food, a person's fear of losing physical access to food prompted some people to panic-buy, putting those who were unable to purchase in large quantities at a disadvantage (Workie et al., 2020 Naja and Hanadeh, 2020). A critical step toward resolving India's hunger and poverty has been taken. The country's national and state governments have cooperated to implement the distribution system. Public Distribution System (PDS) is also renowned for providing subsidized food and establishing a global distribution network following World War II (Kishore and Chakrabarti, 2015).

The Epidemic shocks and food security studies have previously been conducted in 35 developing countries across four continents, including Africa, Latin America, Oceania, and Asia. Inadequate healthcare, a lack of proper social safety nets, and malnutrition pose substantial global food security threats, particularly in nations with widespread poverty. Additionally, during a pandemic, four components of food security are harmed the most: availability and access to food, income, job position, savings and the family head's nutrition. The extreme and stringent lockdown has forecast substantial monetary damage, with several assessments envisaging unfavorable GDP progress (Ray, 2020). This prevailing condition adversely hit the most vulnerable section, with lower earnings, reduced employment opportunities, and supply chain disruption, threatening the economy's food security (Gettleman and Raj, 2020). The consequences on the food supply chain and security system are adversely impacted. Because of the widespread epidemic, offering free food, nutrition counseling, and e-marketing to food-insecure people, contributions, Flexible safety nets and food-based intervention programmes are critical components of ensuring adequate food security in times of disaster. Access to both official *viz.,* Food Assistance Programmes (FAPs) and informal like as food on credit, exchanging products for food for food assistance may both increase families' risk of food insecurity and mitigate its effects. India has created its measures and tactics to help the public learn from the COVID-19 pandemic. The central government facilitated the direct cash transfer and food security efforts among the 800 million deprived and vulnerable individuals and announced a $261 billion economic relief fund package (NSE India, 2020). As a result, the government should promptly increase monetary assistance and provide subsidized food to maintain food affordability. In the medium term, the government can establish relationships with NGOs and private agencies that work on food and nutrition safety, such as the Honduran government, which, in collaboration with the World Food Program, works with local school districts and staff to ensure that families and children receive the proper meal through the Mid-day Meal Scheme and ICDS programmes. Consequently, the current study purposes to acquire the relevant evidence from literature about food security and Food Assistance Programmes (FAPs).

Material and Methods

The literature was systematically reviewed using the *'Preferred Reporting Items for Systematic Reviews and Meta-Analyses (PRISMA)'* criteria (Moher et al., 2009). To increase the quality of systematic reviews, the article suggests a minimal set of standards and methods for authoring items. A search was launched in March 2020 to gather and review articles published between March 2020 and July 2021.

Search Strategy

A comprehensive review of literature on food security system and food assistance programs (FAPs) in India was carried out by following the "*Preferred Reporting Items for Systematic Reviews and Meta-Analysis (PRISMA) guidelines*" (Oberoi & Kansra, 2019 and Arora et al., 2021). An extensive literature search was conducted by searching several databases using prearranged keyword settings. All the publications such as articles, thesis, and reference articles were observed. Numerous databases were included for works of literature published between March 2020 and August 2020 indexed in Scopus, ProQuest, EBSCO, Grey literature (FAO, World Bank, IFPRI, UNSDG), and peer-reviewed journals. Comprehensive literature will address food security issues, nutrition, agriculture sustainability, safety net programs, resilience, policies, and programs focused on food security. In this comprehensive review, publications in electronic databases and libraries were reviewed.

Table 1. Keywords and search term

Keywords Search Criteria	
Covid-19	Coronavirus, Pandemic, Epidemic, Covid-19 and shocks
Food Assistance Programmes	Public distribution System, TPDS, Indian PDS, Revamped PDS, Storage and Distribution, Fair Price shops, ICDS (Integrated Child Development Programme, NFSA (National Food Security Act)
Food Security	Food accessibility, Food availability, Food utilization, Procurement, Distribution, Food Choice, Resilience of food system, Sustainability

Furthermore, the relevant international journal will be explored. Additional studies were analyzed by scrutinizing the references of including articles or backward referencing, which led to the expansion of the search articles list. The search terms were adjusted by the various databases to intensifier the possibility of retrieving material using words or phrases, *viz.* 'India', 'Coronavirus', 'Pandemic', 'Epidemic', 'Covid-19', 'Shocks', 'Public Distribution System (PDS)', 'Targeted Public Distribution System (TPDS)', 'Revamped Public Distribution System (RPDS)', 'Storage and Distribution', 'Fair Price Shops (FPSs)', 'Integrated Child Development Programme (ICDS)', 'National Food Security Act (NFSA), 'Food accessibility', 'Food availability, 'Food utilization', 'Procurement', 'Distribution', 'Food Choice', 'Resilience of food system', 'Sustainability' and 'Vulnerability' were utilized to attain the results. Using the desk search criteria, 365 studies were found, including duplicates. Later, it was discovered that 187 items were duplicates and were instantly removed.

Inclusion and Exclusion Criteria

The relevance of the remaining 178 studies was determined by accessing their title, abstract, and keywords. The articles that have been included are as follows: a) including all the publications, which have been conducted on the food security and based on the various assistance programs and policies using the policy models frameworks and provide guidelines as well as implications; b) covering Indian nation and its states; c) were conducted under the peer-reviewed publications; d) were published between March 2020 to July 2021; e) were indexed in ProQuest, ABCD, EBSCO. As a result, the screening procedure made it easier to select 27 articles. The majority of articles were excluded on the ground that they a) published in non-peer reviewed journals; b) not been published in the English languages; c) publications not available in the full text; d) presented the sustainable intensification and challenges; e) were conference articles and posters (Oberoi & Kansra, 2020).

Identification of Relevant Papers

The process of identification of relevant papers can be witnessed in Figure 1. Primarily screened the titles of all the searches; after the title was deemed, the abstracts were screened to identify potentially relevant articles and to assess the eligibility criteria for inclusion and exclusion criteria. Data were extracted, and only 27 articles met the eligibility criteria for this study.

Results

Prior studies highlighted the effects of the epidemic on food and nutritional security. A detailed examination of the preceding literature on food security and Food Assistance Programs (FAPs) was taken into consideration. A brief account of the work reported by the past researchers has been discussed according to constructs wise under the following heads.

Figure 1. PRISMA framework for detailed methods
Source: Authors compilation based on Moher et al. (2009) and Oberoi and Kansra (2019).

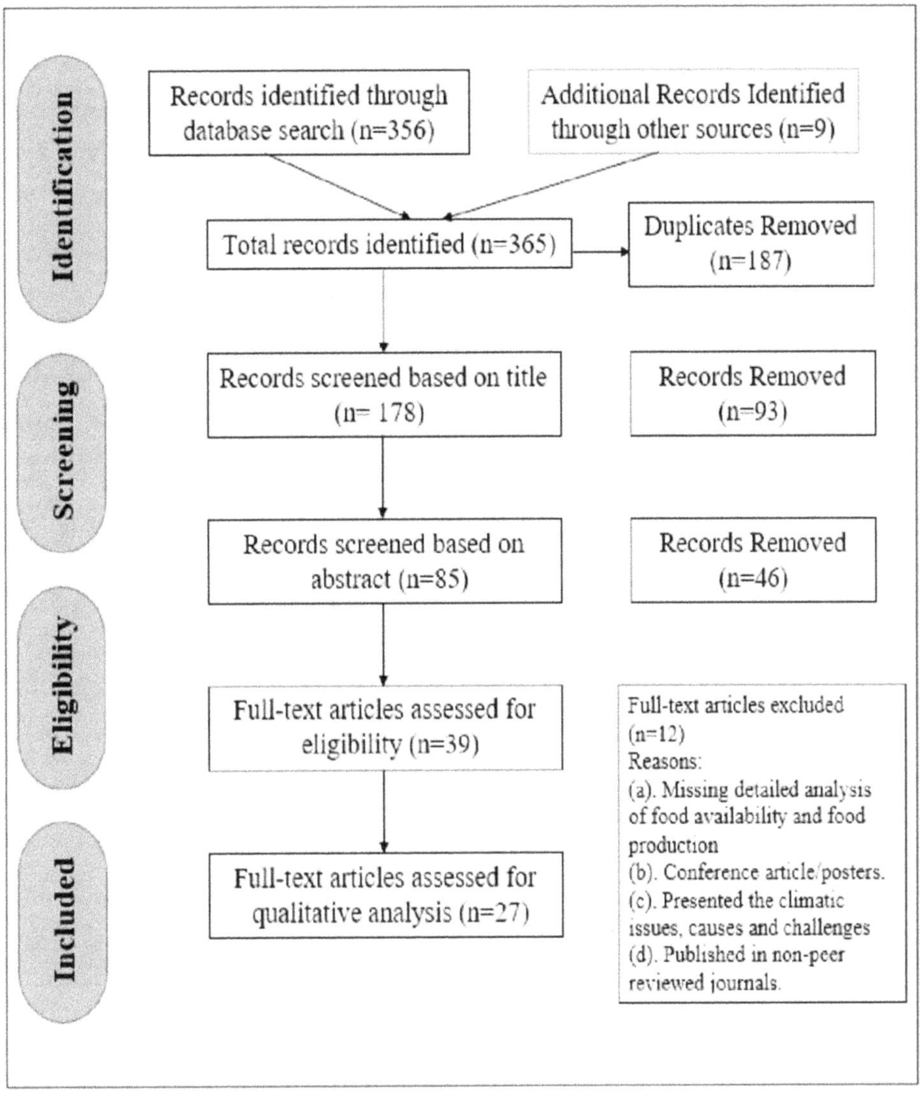

Table 2. Summary of food security and food assistance programs profile of review studies

Sr. No	Author	Year	Study Area	Major Findings
1.	Cariappa AGA et al.	August 2020	Developing Countries	The study accessed that consumer suffered from extreme and strange anxiety during the epidemic, as evidenced by the survey. The investigation resulted that 75.31percent of consumers experience a hike in the price of food, adversely impacting consumers' livelihood.
2.	Athnere S. et al.	August 2020	India	The study revealed that India is primarily based on agricultural activities. So, policymakers focused on planning farming and made the country self-reliant and sufficient.
3.	Singh S. et al.	July 2020	Tamil Nadu, India	The study employed a simulation model of the PDS network, which can aid in the development of a robust supply chain capable of meeting demand. Additionally, it assists in giving decision-making support for vehicle rerouting.

continues on following page

Table 2. Continued

Sr. No	Author	Year	Study Area	Major Findings
4.	Shirsath et al.,	September 2020	Northwest India (Punjab and Haryana)	The study has used ex-ante spatial modeling and revealed that productivity of rice losses under delay scenario would be very low compared to wheat production. Late rice transplantation can exacerbate winter air pollution, posing additional health hazards. So, to address these challenges, technological options and new policy approaches must have opted.
5.	Mishra, K., & Rampal, J	June 2020	India	The study highlighted the status of hunger and food security and discussed productivity, education, and wages. In the end, it underlined the need for government and non-government interventions.
6.	Dev, S. M., & Sengupta, R.	April 2020	India	The article discussed the epidemic's impact on several sectors of the Indian economy and assessed the central government's and RBI's initiatives designed to mitigate economic shocks.
7.	Chatterjee, R	April 2020	India	India's technical advancements and inventive techniques help bridge the gap between various shocks such as socioeconomic and health. Even automated machinery and ICT should be deployed to assist farmers during this critical period of workforce migration. As a result, both the federal and state governments must play a significant role in economic strengthening.
8.	Erokhin, V., & Gao, T	August 2020	45 developing Countries	The study sought to close the gap by examining the relationship between food security status, trade, food inflation, currency volatility, and coronavirus in 45 developing nations classified into three income groups. Additionally, discovered that the pandemic is more predictable in upper-middle-income individuals. Additionally, the study built a methodology framework to assist decision-makers in estimating economic factors.
9.	Pathak, P., Gope, T., & Bader, N	June 2020	India and its Various states	The review-based study provided a basic understanding of food security, the problem faced by old citizens, and vulnerable society. The study also analyzed the macro-level thinking to strengthen the Public Distribution System and discussed various policies allied with farmers, laborers, and migrant workers.
10.	Harris et al.,	July 2020	India, 4states (Jharkhand, Andhra Pradesh, Karnataka, and Assam (448 farmers)	The study investigated the production, prices, incomes, diet, and sales shocks of India's vegetable farmers, producers, and consumers and revealed that most household consumption fell almost 30 percent. Informed that the Indian government ensure the livelihoods of farmers by providing loans and tax relief
11.	Ghosh J.	July 2020	India	The study showed a considerable shift in macroeconomic strategy is required to enable the economy and livelihoods while increasing public health spending during the epidemic.
12.	Upadhyay	April 2020	India and some states (especially in Kerala)	The study focused on ICDS and Mid-day meal schemes that have been affected by the risk of child nutrition during coronavirus and suggested that govt. and NGOs must coordinate and scale up the nutritional services for children through the Public Distribution System and home food delivery.
13.	Ceballos et al.,	August 2020	India (Odisha and Haryana) (1515 respondents)	The study uncovered significant variability in how the pandemic affected farmers, revealing that consumers and farmers in Haryana encountered more significant disruptions than those in Odisha due to decreased food availability in marketplaces. Farmers in Odisha, too, have profited from different cropping patterns.
14.	Reardon	May 2020	India	The study resulted that high transaction costs and uncertainty due to the prevailing situation in the economy transformed the supply chain and put food security at risk.
15.	Brizi, A., & Biraglia	September, 2020	India and the United States of America	The study examined the effects of coronavirus on food stockpiling and its waste. Applying the sequential mediation model revealed how individuals in need of closure did not get enough food and wasted more. Genders and countries of residency demonstrated a moderate mediating influence of gender roles on stockpiling and the food waste process in both nations.
16.	Sukhwani et al.,	August 2020	India, Nagpur state	The study discussed the urban and rural supply chain, which was reported to break down. The study assessed perceived household food security, immediate concern, and critical information based on food, grocery, and government apps and websites.
17.	Mahajan, K., & Tomar, S	March 2020	India	The study examined how pandemics disrupt food supply chains, and the dataset revealed a 10% decrease in the availability of fruits, vegetables, and edible oil. Additionally, this pandemic wreaked havoc on the long-distance food supply system.

continues on following page

Table 2. Continued

Sr. No	Author	Year	Study Area	Major Findings
18.	Kharbikar et al.,	June 2020	India	The study examined the socioeconomic consequences of pandemics on the food and agriculture industries. The research recommended some safeguards, well-designed capacity-building initiatives, and the execution of government schemes.
19.	Naja, F., & Hamadeh, R.	April 2020	India	The study examined the nutritional and dietary intake at global, national, community, and household levels and revealed some recommendations based on each level to maintain the physical mental health of the individual as well as resilience between the various communities
20.	Gopalan, H. S., & Misra, A..	May 2020	India	The study concentrated on the utilization component of food security from a public health perspective. This study's review assisted in cascading the effects of a pandemic on economic decline and recommended healthcare and governmental control initiatives.
21.	Pérez-Escamilla et al.,	May 2020	India	The study concentrated on the need to safeguard children, pregnant women, and breastfeeding mothers from pandemics and to eliminate inadequate food systems, while also maintaining social protection and nutritional security, particularly for lactating mothers and children. .
22.	Ray, P et al.,	July 2020	India	The study projected future global concerns related to food security and malnutrition explored the numerous issues associated with farm instability, public-private partnerships, and ICAR institutions' methods for meeting future demands.
23.	Sukhwani et al.,	August 2020	Nagpur (Maharashtra), India	The study concentrated on Nagpur, a city in the Indian state of Maharashtra, where the urban-rural food supply systems appeared to have been disrupted, as were government actions to protect public health and food supply, based on a month-long chronology of the COVID-19 epidemic. Simultaneously, city inhabitants have isolated themselves to their homes and their ideas of household food security.
24.	Gupta et al.,	June 2021	India	The study analyses the pandemic's impact on non-staples vs. staples and on the diversity of women's diets in Uttar Pradesh's four economically challenged districts. The study found that household food expenditures and the diversity of women's diets decreased in May 2020 compared to May 2019. Despite PDS, direct benefit transfer, and Anganwadi rationing, 80%, 50%, and 30% of surveyed households, respectively. By June 2020, national and state spending had recovered to pre-lockdown levels, but district spending had not. The study emphasized the importance of gender-responsive safety nets. As a result, dietary inequities within households were reduced.
25.	Nguyen et al.,	April 2021	Uttar Pradesh, India	The study focused on the pandemic impact on Household Food Insecurity (HFI) and the consequences for child feeding patterns and coping mechanisms. In households with food poverty, children's diets were less diverse.
26.	Agarwal	January 2021	India	The study focused not only the direct consequences of livelihood loss due to pandemics on women's incomes, but also the indirect effects on intrahousehold dynamics and vulnerabilities. And this precarity and danger are experienced not only by women who have lost paid careers, but also by women who worked unpaid on damaged family businesses. Furthermore, women might be disproportionately affected not only by the erosion of their own livelihoods, but also by the loss of male occupations and return migration from cities to villages, which can result in occupational crowding, extended domestic duties, hunger, and even domestic violence.
27.	Kesar et al.,	March 2021	India	Almost 80% of households reduced food consumption, more than 60% ran out of money for a week's worth of needs, and a third took out a loan to cover pandemic-related expenses. While they emphasised the critical need for effective livelihood support and economic recovery, they also emphasised the importance of critically evaluating the current development trajectory, in which decades of rapid economic growth have failed to translate into more secure livelihoods for the vast majority of the workforce.

Food Security During COVID-19

The epidemic is intimidating all dimensions of food security, accessibility, exploitation, steadiness, and food consumption (Kumar, 2020). According to UNSDG (2020), "Thousands of the people are facing the food shortage issue as well as starvation pre-Covid-19, and if the instant corrective measures are not applied at the proper time, then the world has to face the food crisis". Recently, FAO and UN (2020) declared that an average of 83 to 132 million of the population faced food hunger severely due to this pandemic condition. The whole financial and farming sectors are at high risk in India, and the overall severity of every industry is adversely affected. According to CGIAR (2020), The prevalent condition adversely impacted rice production in which subsidized industrial farming is heavily used primarily in Punjab. Even the food availability does not show any significant results. In India, food availability in grain stock was about 58.4 million tons and lentils about 3 million tons till March 1, 2020. Other supplies such as vegetables, fruits, and poultry products comprise 78 percent of the total utilization. The food supply chain of fresh vegetables, fruits, and grains has been adversely affected during this pandemic (Ivanov and Dolgui, 2020).

Reduction of the demand and breakdown of the supply system had triggered the production, ultimately creating a considerable loss for the farmers, dealers, and customers (Kumar, 2020). Due to shutdown, unpredictable natural calamity, insects attack, and the clash between the countries ultimately intercept the food supply and decline the food safety in the various perspectives. Even FAO (2020), the survey stated the small marginal farmers' issues regarding the purchase of seeds and fertilizers due to the high cost, which results in a dire reduction in the domestic returns. Even the pandemic affects the procurement because the lockdown duration was when the harvest period was at peak and the maturity stage. Unavailability of labor and the migration of the work interrupted some harvesting events, predominately the Legumes and cereals in Northwest India (Dev,2020). About 60 percent of the farmers confronted a severe yield reduction (Seema,2020). In Northwest India, where the field activities are dependable on the contract of the farmers and laborers, due to the lockdown, there was the inadequacy of deliveries which affected crops harvesting, especially wheat production (Jhajhria et al., 2020). The wheat harvesting in northern India shambled due to labor and transportation facilities (Jhajhria et al., 2020 Brahmane et al., 2020). Shortfall in the production in northwest India profound the national and household food security ramifications since Punjab and Haryana contribute about 50 percent of staple food procured and distributed by GOI (DPFP, 2020 and Chauhan et al., 2012). During the Pandemic, India must choose between human loss, starvation, and malnutrition. The country's shutdown is expected to cause serious economic damage and a negative GDP (Ray, 2020). The current condition has harmed the most vulnerable members of society, resulting in job loss, reduction in salaries, and supply chain disruption, all of which threaten to deteriorate food security (Gettleman and Raj, 2020). Food scarcity is unavoidable in this complicated circumstance, where the majority of the logistics system has been shut down. Reduced wheat and rice output has a negative impact on the food and nutrition security of poor households in Northwest India (Singh et al., 2020). The supply chain disruption has had an effect on product prices, which is another form of food poverty (Dun. et al., 2020).

Food-Based Safety Net Programs

Both state and Central govt run the food-based safety net programs that support the millions of individuals/households to access food, cash, health facilities, and other supports. The government announced a 22.6-billion-dollar relief package and food components. The National Food Security Act (NFSA) was signed on July 5, 2013; it has been seen as one of India's most significant steps toward providing food security for its citizens. At Rs 3 per kilogram for rice, Rs 2 for wheat, and Rs1 for coarse grains, qualified households can purchase up to a five-kilogram-a-year supply for each member of their family. Agricultural producers in India are financially supported by the Indian government, which purchases agricultural grains at a minimum support price (MSP). the grain is transported to the Fair Price Shops (FPSs), where ration card holders can purchase subsidized food. The NFSA, one of the world's largest social security programmes, covers approximately 810 million Indians (Pillay and Kumar, 2019). The Act guarantees the right to food to 75% of India's rural population and 50% of its urban population. The National Food Security Act (NFSA), 2013, and the Public Distribution System (PDS) both play critical roles by distributing 5 kilograms of wheat or rice and 1 kilogram of selected pulses every month. Initially, the Government of India announced a relief fund of 1.74 lakh crore rupees and measures to increase food components available through the Targeted Public Distribution System (TPDS) for the first three months, doubling the number of food items available and providing free distribution of 5 kilograms of rice or wheat and 1 kilogram of pulses, as well as additional cash assistance to vulnerable families. This ration distribution scheme was prolonged for an additional two months through the use of another economic enticement.

Public Distribution System (PDS) and National Food Security Act (NFSA), 2013

In the current scenario, GOI has declared that India has surplus food grains, i.e., 272.19 lakh tons of rice and 162.79 lakhs tons of wheat. As of April, around 74.2 lakh tons of wheat and 135 lakh tons of rice were available, which resulted in the availability of food grains. As a result, the Indian government has proposed many measures to address the country's serious food security crisis caused by the shutdown. Under PMGKAY (Pradhan Mantri Garib Kalyan Ann Yojana), free distribution of an additional 5kg of food grains per person and 1kg legumes to 800 million people for the next three months under the NFSA, 2013 (DPFP, 2020) and also lifted the quota of subsidized food for the next six months. Due to the pandemic, the government has suspended the biometric authentication system, leading to leakage in the distribution system. Bihar government ordered to seal more than 50 depots (Fair price shops) for unproven rambling of black marketing of food grains during ongoing lockdown (Khan, 2020). The Public Distribution System depends on the harvest followed by the excellent procurement of food grains. The government has been facing an uphill task for procuring the wheat, and less procurement will create an issue in the availability and supply of food grains in the coming period.

Some states like the Government of Tamil Nadu had ordered to distribute 1000 rupees each to the cardholders and supply the tur dal, oil, sugar, and rice to all the entitled families through the Fair price shops in April 2020. Another token system has been adopted to avoid overcrowding at the depots (Pathak et al., 2020). In Gujarat, the state government has decided to distribute 3.5 kg of wheat and 1.5 kg rice (per person), 1kg pulse, sugar, and salt per family to all the ration cardholders. Antyodaya Anna Yojana (AAY) and Below Poverty Line (BPL), migrant workers from other states, also got the food grain kits under Annapurna Yojana Scheme from seventeen thousand fair price shops (FCI and Pathak et al., 2020). The government of Uttar Pradesh provided free ration to all the ration cardholders. Nearly 522 community kitchens had been set up to give a proper diet to needy people and ramped up to 26,298 mobile vans and manual carts to deliver vegetables and fruits at the doorstep. In Delhi, the government had decided to provide 1.5 times more rations to all the entitled families under the Public Distribution System and cooked meals twice a day to the homeless in the night shelter.

Feeding Programmes (Mid-Day Meals and Integrated Child Development Services)

According to a report by the United Nations Children's Fund (UNICEF), around 370 million individuals may lose access to a nutritious food as a result of a pandemic. To combat and manage the worst cases of hunger and malnutrition, the Ministry of Human Resource Development (MHRD) directed all Union Territories and states to continue providing mid-day meals, food security allowances, and cooking costs to meet the nutritional needs of all eligible children under this scheme. This chain is continued by around 33 states and 5 union territories. Union Minister of Human Resource Development (UMHRD) also announced an increased allocation of the Mid-Day Meal (MDM) with an additional expenditure of 1700 crore rupee; the cooking cost had enhanced to 8100 crores from 73 crores rupee for smoothening function. Anganwadi Services' Supplementary Nutrition Program (SNP) provides dry rations or hot cooked meals to 64 million children between six months and six years (Ministry of Women and Child Development, 2020). Mid-Day Meals provides one hot prepared meal every day to 115.9 million school-going children in grades I through VIII (Mid-Day Meal Portal). Anganwadi and schools were shut down by the lockdown imposed in March, disrupting both services. In anticipation of this disturbance, the Supreme Court ordered states to ensure healthy food for children in March (In re- MDMS, 2020). Dry rations for children have been sent to their homes in some states. However, there are several inconsistencies and inadequacies in implementing the plan (Jain, 2020). Both programs have been under-reported. A free noon meal was only offered to about 50 percent of rural and 21.4 percent of urban children before COVID-19 (NSO, 2019). Pregnant and lactating women received only 46 percent of the SNP's Take-Home Ration in 2019, while 10 crore school children, 17 percent of youngsters received a Hot-Cooked Meal, despite enrolment rates of 64 percent (PTI, 2019).

During the pandemic, the Integrated Child Development Services (ICDS) programme appeared to have sprung the trend. More youngsters enrolled and benefited from the programme than in the past. According to the Department of Women and Child Development (July 2020), the programme covered around 41.93 lakh children aged 6 months to 6 years and provided them with a free ration. According to the statistical data, this initiative covered 90.92 percent of the children targeted.

The Anganwadi system was also vital in conserving the ecosystem, not just for its fundamental functions, but also for averting pandemic problems in rural populations. The value chain of this technology was instantly repurposed to enable the continuation of services and the delivery of digital solutions and an extensive network of frontline workers. The State administration has launched a number of initiatives to aid health personnel who are assisting rural areas during this time of need. The Uttarakhand State Government gave a 4-lakh-rupee life insurance policy to Anganwadi employees, aides, and mini frontline workers (Hindustan times,2020). In Maharashtra, the Chief Minister offered 50 lakh rupees in health coverage for Anganwadi workers and helpers under the Yodha Kalyan Yojana (YKY). The Pradhan Mantri Garib Kalyan Yojana (PMGKY) of the Chief Government provides benefits to health, police, and other government employees. THR (take-home rations) have been delivered throughout this period by Anganwadi workers and assistants to children aged 0-3 years, malnourished children aged 3-6 years, and pregnant and nursing mothers (World Bank, 2020). Provision of additional sustenance becomes even more vital for underprivileged segments of society (GOI, 2020).

Role of NGOs

NGOs played a significant role in easing up the economy. NGOs step forward to assist migrant workers by identifying Covid-19 hotspots and providing critical services to the most vulnerable members of society, including transgender, disabled workers, homeless, and urban low-income families, by providing them with adequate food, water, medical care, and transportation (Mor, 2020). In Tamil Nadu, "Amma canteens," "Mukhyamantri Dal-Bhat Yojana" in Jharkhand, and "Aam Aadmi canteen" in Delhi, among others, provide subsidised food to the urban poor, engage thousands of volunteers, and serve as a pillar in addressing food security challenges. Women's self-help groups made a significant contribution to rural areas by giving nutritious food to millions of hungry and stranded labourers. Master Choa Kok Sui's (MCKS) cuisine, the Hungry Foundation Delhi, and work in Orissa, Jharkhand, and Delhi have been imbued with the ability to effect change in and around us and to have a visible impact on people's lives by providing meals for the hungry and equipping them with the tools necessary to transition from despair to hope. Khalsa Aid International also provides free food and oxygen concentrators to the underprivileged in Punjab, Chandigarh, and Delhi. By implementing the Mid-Day Meal Scheme in government-aided and government-run schools, the Akshaya Patra Foundation (APF) seeks to abolish classroom hunger.

Additionally, Akshaya Patra seeks to eliminate malnutrition and safeguard children's right to education who face socioeconomic adversity. Partnerships with the Government of India and various State Governments, as well as consistent funding from corporates, individual contributors, and well-wishers, have enabled them to grow from serving 1,500 children in five schools in 2000 to serving 1.8 million children today. They now operate the world's largest (non-profit) mid-day meal programme, providing nutritious meals to nearly 1.8 million children in 19,039 schools across 12 states and two union territories in India. The Khanna Chahine foundation was established in March 2020 as a citizen-led initiative to meet the acute food needs of Mumbai's homeless, migrant workers, daily wage labourers, and other disadvantaged communities. Civil society organizations (CSOs) responded to the evident misery of the vulnerable community, which found itself unexpectedly food and livelihood insecure. NGOs such as Goonj and Akshay Patra intensified their efforts to provide food, rations, daily necessities, and basic health safety goods such as masks and soaps.

DISCUSSION

COVID-19 has heightened household concerns about the food system's present capacity. However, during the epidemic, the cost was a significant factor in food security. In addition to reducing poverty and increasing wages for low-income households, the study indicates that securing economic access without jeopardizing food security is a critical first step for policymakers to comprehend. COVID-19, the issue may raise additional issues. Trying to address vulnerabilities like financial insecurity before a crisis helps reduce the Impact on food security. In addition, uneven food distribution and inflation may cause the food supply chain.

COVID-19 outbreak-related events and lockdowns triggered all food security adjustments described here. The pandemic's effects are temporary and will revert to pre-pandemic levels once the number of cases is reduced and limitations are lifted. This effect can emerge as physical access limits, movement restrictions, or fear of contagion. Worry and isolation-induced food alterations may also be reversed once social interactions are reinstated. These issues can be solved in manufacturing if market access obstacles are abolished and the labor movement is unrestricted.

Nonetheless, the data shows that low household income is the main issue. Food costs can spike unexpectedly, leaving low-income households without enough cash reserves to replace many months' worth of lost income or unable to buy in quantity. As a result, customers buy fewer vegetables, fruits, and animal proteins, and producers see decreased demand for these commodities. Consequently, producers confront slow labor flows and a lack of demand due to the closure of the catering sector and a decrease in low-income consumers' spending. Food purchases have been hampered due to labor movement restrictions. Until far, the Indian government's primary role in ensuring farmers' livelihoods has been to increase credit availability, reduce taxes, and give direct payments. The government doubled Public Distribution System allocations and gave monetary aid to unemployed workers to ensure food security. Escalating natural epidemiological dangers of the virus while also affecting consumer and farming livelihoods is the dilemma. It is recommended that existing and future government actions focus on food systems, particularly those that provide the most nutrient-dense foods. The report advises that governments should be prudent in achieving food security through administrative and non-governmental activities. The government can grant interest-free loans to help struggling business owners, farmers, SMEs, and Argo-related sectors grow their operations and feed their people. Partner with existing health programs and non-governmental organizations to expand social protection measures for marginalized groups, especially women and children. COVID-19 has heightened household concerns about the food system's present capacity. To achieve zero hunger, nutrition programs like ICDS, Mid-Day Meal Scheme, and Anganwadi must maintain essential services and provide primary food products to users at home.

In India, food policy has not always been considered the most vulnerable. Instead, corporate agricultural interests have occasionally hijacked food policy, and poor people's food habits have not inspired the state's response. Large-scale agricultural, formal sector suppliers and supermarkets have all been helped. Colonial planning-era prejudices have also bolstered these regulations against informal sector actors. Finally, governments must reassess their trade commitments to ensure food security. However, a more balanced food system less prone to global perturbations like disease pandemics will arise from a greater emphasis on local food production. Even India's national and state governments help migrant workers and informal workers financially and nutritionally. During the shutdown, the government should prioritize food supply chain security.

LIMITATIONS

The current study holds some limitations. The study primarily eliminates those studies published in non-peer-reviewed publications and relevant pieces presented as conference talks and poster presentations. Some bias may have been introduced—in addition to the non-availability of published articles in India's eastern zone. As a result, conducting a meta-analysis is not feasible.

CONCLUSION

As previously stated, the pandemic outbreak grows globally, threatening health and food access. For policy, the findings show that governments and policymakers must help disadvantaged families financially. This help should include direct payments, free food packages, deferred bank obligations, guaranteed income supplements, small business loan guarantees, and expanded credit availability. While these economic choices can help people manage food insecurity during COVID-19, international sanctions can make implementation difficult or impossible. Policymakers can use the findings of this study in other countries to identify areas of household and individual vulnerability for government intervention. With the PMGKY, the Union Finance Minister promised Rs. 1.70 lakh crore package for the poor and needy, in addition to the PDS ration. This scheme has been extended till November 2020 at the cost of Rs. 90,000 crores more (PIB, 2020d). For 80 million migrant laborers and their families, Atmanirbhar Bharat promised free food. On the other side, the Annapurna Dal Bhat Yojana (Jharkhand) and Mukhyamantri Dal Bhat Yojana (Tamil Nadu) provided highly discounted cooked meals to the urban poor (Parajuli, 2020) and others in Kerala, Uttar Pradesh, Maharashtra, Odisha, etc. (D'costa, 2020). The National Food Security Scheme enforced unconditional rationing without eligibility slips. The Indian government should allocate appropriate funds to strengthen the FCI system, which should be more transparent and accountable. Inspections and grievance redressal with the PDS or local government should be improved to maintain smooth system operation and reduce power imbalances. PDS, ICDS, and MDM should be strengthened by adding nutrient-dense grains like ragi, bajra, jowar, etc.

The government should also maintain market stability and control food inflation. To strengthen the food supply system, residents should collaborate with traders, farmers, and others. This disease has hit small and marginal farms hard. So, the GOI can immediately start village-level procurement at the MSP (MPS). Develop a precise model and framework for food aid programs with varied food security problems. The study also employed a systematic review to assess food security and food aid programs, focusing on food-related governance during and after COVID-19.

Compliance with ethical standards:

Funding: External funding was not received for this project.

Statement from Institutional Review Board: Not Applicable

Information Regarding Data Availability: Not Applicable

Conflict of Interest: The authors disclose that they have no conflicting interests.

Ethical Approval: The present study is rcvicw-based research and review. So, it contains Community, National, and individual performance and government measures.

Informed Consent: No consent is required for this study.

REFERENCES

Abi-Habib, M., & Yasir, S. (2020). For India's Laborers, Coronavirus Lockdown Is an Order to Starve. *The New York Times*. https://www.nytimes.com/2020/03/31/world/coronavirus-live-news-updates.html

Agarwal, B. (2021). Livelihoods in COVID times: Gendered perils and new pathways in India. *World Development*, *139*, 105312. doi:10.1016/j.worlddev.2020.105312

Athnere, S., Greeshma, K., Reddy, A. A., & Ashwini, P. (2020). Impact of COVID-19 on agriculture and food security in India: A review. *JPP, 9*(5), 263-270.

Banerjee, O., Darbas, T., Brown, P. R., & Roth, C. H. (2014). Historical Divergence in Public Management of food grain Systems in India and Bangladesh: Opportunities to Enhance Food Security. *Global Food Security*, *3*(3-4), 159–166. doi:10.1016/j.gfs.2014.06.002

Béné, C. (2020). Resilience of local food systems and links to food security–A review of some important concepts in the context of COVID-19 and other shocks. *Food Security*, 1–18. PMID:32837646

Brahmane, M. P., Gaikwad, B. B., Kochewad, S. A., Kumar, M., Kurade, N. P., & Meena, K. K. (2020). *National Lockdown and Agriculture: Impacts and Remedies*. ICAR-National Institute for Abiotic Stress Management Baramati.

Brizi, A., & Biraglia, A. (2020). "Do I have enough food?" How need for cognitive closure and gender impact stockpiling and food waste during the COVID-19 pandemic: A cross-national study in India and the United States of America. *Personality and Individual Differences*, *168*, 110396. doi:10.1016/j.paid.2020.110396 PMID:32982000

Cariappa, A. G., Acharya, K. K., Adhav, C., & Ramasundaram, P. (2020). *Pandemic Led Food Price Anomalies and Supply Chain Disruption: Evidence from COVID-19 Incidence in India*. Academic Press.

Ceballos, F., Kannan, S., & Kramer, B. (2020). Impacts of a national lockdown on smallholder farmers' income and food security: Empirical evidence from two states in India. *World Development*, *136*, 105069. doi:10.1016/j.worlddev.2020.105069

CGIAR. (2020). https://www.cgiar.org/newsevents/news/covid-19-and-food-security-india-and-itsjobs-crisis/

Chatterjee, R. (n.d.). Indian agriculture and role of agricultural extension system to cope up with COVID-19 crisis. *Food and Scientific Reports*, *1*(6).

Chauhan, B. S., Mahajan, G., Sardana, V., Timsina, J., & Jat, M. L. (2012). Productivity and sustainability of the rice–wheat cropping system in the Indo-Gangetic Plains of the Indian subcontinent: Problems, opportunities, and strategies. *Advances in Agronomy*, *117*, 315–369. doi:10.1016/B978-0-12-394278-4.00006-4

De Onis, M., Borghi, E., Arimond, M., Webb, P., Croft, T., Saha, K., ... Hayashi, C. (2019). Prevalence thresholds for wasting, overweight and stunting in children under 5 years. *Public Health Nutrition*, *22*(1), 175–179. doi:10.1017/S1368980018002434 PMID:30296964

Dev, S. M., & Sengupta, R. (2020). *Covid-19: Impact on the Indian economy.* Indira Gandhi Institute of Development Research.

Devereux, S., Béné, C., & Hoddinott, J. (2020). Conceptualising COVID-19's impacts on household food security. *Food Security*, *12*(4), 769–772. doi:10.100712571-020-01085-0 PMID:32837651

DPFP. (2020). https://dfpd.gov.in/food-grain-bulletin.html

Dunn, C. G., Kenney, E., Fleischhacker, S. E., & Bleich, S. N. (2020). Feeding low-income children during the Covid-19 pandemic. *The New England Journal of Medicine*, *382*(18), e40. doi:10.1056/NEJMp2005638 PMID:32227759

Erokhin, V., & Gao, T. (2020). Impacts of COVID-19 on trade and economic aspects of food security: Evidence from 45 developing countries. *International Journal of Environmental Research and Public Health, 17*(16), 5775. doi:10.3390/ijerph17165775 PMID:32785155

FAO. (2021). *The state of food insecurity in the world 2001*. Available: http://www. fao.org/3/y1500e/y1500e00.htm

FAO. (2020a). *Covid-19 Pandemic: Impact on Food and Agriculture*. Food and Agricultural Organisation. https://www.fao.org/2019-ncov/q-and-a/en/

FAO. (2020b). https://www.fao.org/2019-ncov/q-anda/impact-on-food-and-agriculture/en/

FCI. (2020). *Movements - Food Corporation of India*. Food Corporation of India. https://fci.gov.in/movements.php

Food & Agriculture Organization UN. (2020). https://www.fao.org/documents/card/en/c/ca8497en

Gettleman, J., & Raj, S. (2020). Powered by Fear, Indians Embrace Coronavirus Lockdown. *New York Times*.

GHI. (2019). *2019 Global hunger index results by severity. Global hunger index – Peer-reviewed annual publication designed to comprehensively measure and track hunger at the global, regional, and country levels*. https:// www.globalhungerindex.org/results.html

Ghosh, J. (2020). A critique of the Indian government's response to the COVID-19 pandemic. *Economia e Politica Industriale, 47*(3), 519–530. doi:10.100740812-020-00170-x

Gopalan, H. S., & Misra, A. (2020). COVID-19 Pandemic and Challenges for Socioeconomic Issues, Healthcare and National Programs in India. *Diabetes & Metabolic Syndrome: Clinical Research & Reviews*.

Gupta, S., Seth, P., Abraham, M., & Pingali, P. (2021). COVID-19 and women's nutrition security: Panel data evidence from rural India. *Economics and Politics*, 1–28. PMID:35422584

Harris, J., Depenbusch, L., Pal, A. A., Nair, R. M., & Ramasamy, S. (2020). Food system disruption: Initial livelihood and dietary effects of COVID-19 on vegetable producers in India. *Food Security, 12*(4), 841–851. doi:10.100712571-020-01064-5 PMID:32837650

India, N. S. E. (2020). *Macro Reports*. National Stock Exchange. https://www.nseindia.com/resources/publications-macro-reports

Ivanov, D., & Dolgui, A. (2020). Viability of intertwined supply networks: Extending the supply chain resilience angles towards survivability. A position paper motivated by COVID-19 outbreak. *International Journal of Production Research, 58*(10), 2904–2915. doi:10.1080/00207543.2020.1750727

Jhajhria, A., Ankita, K., Balaji, S. J., Jaya, J., Kingsly, I., & Kiran, K. (2020). *Covid-19, Lockdown and Indian Agriculture: Options to reduce the Impact*. ICAR-National Institute of Agricultural Economics and Policy Research New Delhi.

Joshi, P. K. (2016). Pathways to Improve Food Security and Reduce Poverty in Emerging India. *Agricultural Economics Research Review, 29*(2), 171–182. doi:10.5958/0974-0279.2016.00045.8

Kesar, S., Abraham, R., Lahoti, R., Nath, P., & Basole, A. (2021). Pandemic, informality, and vulnerability: Impact of COVID-19 on livelihoods in India. *Canadian Journal of Development Studies. Canadian Journal of Development Studies*, *42*(1-2), 145–164. doi:10.1080/02255189.2021.1890003

Khan, M. I. (n.d.). *COVID-19 lockdown: 50 Public Distribution System shops sealed in Bihar for illegal trade*. Available at: https://www.downtoearth.org.in/news/governance/covid-19-lockdown-50-PublicDistributionSystem-shops-sealed-in-bihar

Kharbikar, H. L., Radhika, C., Naitam, R. K., Daripa, A., Malav, L., & Raghuvanshi, M. S. (2020). Consequences of COVID-19 pandemic and lockdown on food and agribusiness sector in India. *Food and Scientific Reports, 1*(6), 13-18.

Kishore, A., & Chakrabarti, S. (2015). Is more inclusive more effective? The 'New Style'Public Distribution System in India. *Food Policy*, *55*, 117–130. doi:10.1016/j.foodpol.2015.06.006

Kumar, A., Padhee, A. K., & Kumar, S. (2020). How Indian agriculture should change after COVID-19. *Food Security*, *12*(4), 837–840. doi:10.100712571-020-01063-6 PMID:32837635

Laborde, D., Martin, W., Swinnen, J., & Vos, R. (2020). COVID-19 risks to global food security. *Science*, *369*(6503), 500–502. doi:10.1126cience.abc4765 PMID:32732407

Mahajan, K., & Tomar, S. (2020). COVID-19 and Supply Chain Disruption: Evidence from Food Markets in India. *American Journal of Agricultural Economics*. PMID:33230345

Ministry of Human Resource Development. Department of Women and Development. (n.d.). *Annual Report 2019-2020*. Government of India Press.

Mishra, K., & Rampal, J. (2020). The COVID-19 pandemic and food insecurity: A viewpoint on India. *World Development*, *135*, 105068. doi:10.1016/j.worlddev.2020.105068

Moher, D., Liberati, A., Tetzlaff, J., & Altman, D. G.Prisma Group. (2009). Reprint—preferred reporting items for systematic reviews and meta-analyses: The PRISMA statement. *Physical Therapy*, *89*(9), 873–880. doi:10.1093/ptj/89.9.873 PMID:19723669

Mor, N. (2020). *Resources for NGOs During the COVID-19 Epidemic*. Available at: https://www.researchgate.net/publication/340246895_Resources_for_NGOs_During_the_COVID-19_Epidemic

Naja, F., & Hamadeh, R. (2020). Nutrition amid the COVID-19 pandemic: A multi-level framework for action. *European Journal of Clinical Nutrition*, *74*(8), 1–5. doi:10.103841430-020-0634-3 PMID:32313188

Nguyen, P. H., Kachwaha, S., Pant, A., Tran, L. M., Ghosh, S., Sharma, P. K., & Menon, P. (2021). Impact of COVID-19 on household food insecurity and interlinkages with child feeding practices and coping strategies in Uttar Pradesh, India: A longitudinal community-based study. *BMJ Open*, *11*(4), e048738. doi:10.1136/bmjopen-2021-048738 PMID:33883156

Oberoi, S., & Kansra, P. (2019). Factors influencing medical tourism in India: A critical review. *SAMVAD*, *17*, 9–16.

Oberoi, S., & Kansra, P. (2020). Economic menace of diabetes in India: A systematic review. *International Journal of Diabetes in Developing Countries*, *40*(4), 1–12. doi:10.100713410-020-00838-z PMID:32837090

OrgI. F. P. R. I. (2020). https://www.ifpri.org/blog/how-indias-food-based-safety-net-responding-covid-19-lockdown

Pathak, P., Gope, T., & Bader, N. (2020). Effect of COVID-19 on Public Distribution System in India. *International Journal of Community Medicine and Public Health*, *7*(6), 2411. doi:10.18203/2394-6040.ijcmph20202508

Pérez-Escamilla, R., Cunningham, K., & Moran, V. H. (2020). *COVID-19 and maternal and child food and nutrition insecurity: a complex syndemic*. Academic Press.

Rai, R. K., Kumar, S., Sekher, M., Pritchard, B., & Rammohan, A. (2015). A Life-Cycle Approach to Food and Nutrition Security in India. *Public Health Nutrition*, *18*(5), 944–949. doi:10.1017/S1368980014001037 PMID:24866692

Ranganath, V. G. (2015). Food Security: Issues and Concerns. *IUP Law Review*, *5*(4), 7–13.

Ray, A. (2020, May 22). *India's GDP growth in 2020-21 to remain in negative territory: RBI*. https://www.livemint.com/industry/banking/india-s-gdp-growth-in-2020-21-to-remain-in-negative-category-rbi-11590122207688.html

Ray, P., Acharya, K. K., & Thakur, A. (2020). COVID-19 Impact and implication to Agriculture and Food security. *Food and Scientific Reports, 1*(7).

Reardon, T., Mishra, A., Nuthalapati, C. S., Bellemare, M. F., & Zilberman, D. (2020). Covid-19's disruption of India's transformed food supply chains. *Economic and Political Weekly*, *55*(18), 18–22.

SeemaC. (2020). https://indianexpress.com/article/explained/howcoronavirus-lockdown-has-impacted-indian-farmerstheir-yields-6421569/

Shirsath, P. B., Jat, M. L., McDonald, A. J., Srivastava, A. K., Craufurd, P., Rana, D. S., ... Jat, H. S. (2020). Agricultural labor, COVID-19, and potential implications for food security and air quality in the breadbasket of India. *Agricultural Systems*, *185*, 102954. doi:10.1016/j.agsy.2020.102954 PMID:32982021

Singh, D. R., Sunuwar, D. R., Adhikari, B., Szabo, S., & Padmadas, S. S. (2020). The perils of COVID-19 in Nepal: Implications for population health and nutritional status. *Journal of Global Health*, *10*(1), 010378. doi:10.7189/jogh.10.010378 PMID:32582440

Singh, S., Kumar, R., Panchal, R., & Tiwari, M. K. (2020). Impact of COVID-19 on logistics systems and disruptions in food supply chain. *International Journal of Production Research*, 1–16.

Sukhwani, V., Deshkar, S., & Shaw, R. (2020). Covid-19 lockdown, food systems and urban-rural partnership: Case of Nagpur, India. *International Journal of Environmental Research and Public Health*, *17*(16), 5710. doi:10.3390/ijerph17165710 PMID:32784648

Sukhwani, V., Deshkar, S., & Shaw, R. (2020). Covid-19 lockdown, food systems and urban–rural partnership: Case of Nagpur, India. *International Journal of Environmental Research and Public Health, 17*(16), 5710. doi:10.3390/ijerph17165710 PMID:32784648

Udmale, P., Pal, I., Szabo, S., Pramanik, M., & Large, A. (2020). Global food security in the context of COVID-19: A scenario-based exploratory analysis. *Progress in Disaster Science, 7*, 100120. doi:10.1016/j.pdisas.2020.100120 PMID:34173442

UN. (2020). Available at: https://www.un.org/en/un-coronavirus-communications-team/un-working-avert-dual-crises-covid-19-hits-hunger

UNSDG. (2020). https://reliefweb.int/report/world/policybrief-impact-covid-19-food-security-and-nutrition-june2020

Upadhyay, M. K., Patra, S., & Khan, A. M. (2020). Ensuring availability of food for child nutrition amidst the COVID—19 pandemic: Challenges and Way forward. *Indian Journal of Community Health, 32*(2), 251–254. doi:10.47203/IJCH.2020.v32i02SUPP.015

USDA. (2019). *Definitions of Food Security.* United States Department of Agriculture (USDA). Available: https://www.ers.usda.gov/topics/food-nutrition-assistance/foodsecurity-in-the-us/definitions-of-food-security.aspx

WFP. (2019). *2019—The state of food security and nutrition in the world (SOFI): Safeguarding against economic slowdowns and downturns.* https://www.wfp.org/publications/2019-state-food-security-and-nutrition-world-sofi-safeguarding-against-economic

Workie, E., Mackolil, J., Nyika, J., & Ramadas, S. (2020). Deciphering the Impact of COVID-19 pandemic on food security, agriculture, and livelihoods: A review of the evidence from developing countries. *Current Research in Environmental Sustainability, 2*, 100014. doi:10.1016/j.crsust.2020.100014 PMID:34977605

World Bank. (2020a). *GDP per capita (constant 2010 US$).* World Bank Group. https://data.worldbank.org/indicator/NY.GDP.PCAP.KD

World Bank. (2020b). *Unemployment, total (% of the total labor force) (national estimate)—India.* https://data.worldbank.org/indicator/SL.UEM.TOTL.NE.ZS

World Bank. (2020c). https://www.worldbank.org/en/news/feature/2020/04/27/covid19-coronavirus-india-response-health-undernutrition-anganwadi-workers-healthcare

Chapter 7
Curbing Seasonal Migration and Debt Bondage Post COVID-19 Pandemic in Western Odisha, India

Lopamudra Mishra
https://orcid.org/0000-0003-3533-4740
Sambalpur University, India

ABSTRACT

The COVID-19 pandemic has delivered a global economic shock of enormous magnitude. Provision of livelihoods to the retuned migrants is the important challenge faced by various state governments in India. Western Odisha continues to depict a picture of chronic underdevelopment. In this region, the type of migration that dominates is seasonal or circular migration. The aim of the present analysis is to investigate the factors responsible for the seasonal migration of debt bondage (Dadan) from the Western Odisha. The specific objectives of the study are to know the factors responsible for distress migration and to explore how debt-bondage is operating in the economic system. The present study has observed that seasonal migrants of Western Odisha are more likely to be from those households who are poor, socially disadvantaged, less educated, indebted, and landless.

INTRODUCTION

The covid-19 pandemic has resulted in income and employment loss in many states in India. Migrants are returning home by walking, by cycling, by sitting on the top of the trucks which are already loaded with goods in the hot summer of May without food is really painful. More than five lakh migrants have returned home in the state of Odisha. The government as well as the officials are trying their best to manage the unprecedented situation. They have returned from Surat, Andhra Pradesh, Tamil Nadu, Maharashtra, Chhattisgarh, and West Bengal and so on. Now the entire nation is seeing the real picture of distress migration.

DOI: 10.4018/978-1-7998-6896-5.ch007

Migration can be thought as one form of the household investment under uncertainty. In the works of Harris and Todaro (1970), Simon Kuznets (1955), Lewis (1954) and Hicks (1932), the most basic model of migration was originally developed to explain the role of migration in the process of economic development. These studies have explained that wage differentials across markets are responsible for migration. The migration decisions of the individuals are influenced by the known or expected income between the origin from which the migrant is moving and that of the destination. Their path breaking work emphasised on economic growth with the gradual shifts of workers from the lower-paying segments into the higher paying segments. The Human Capital Theory is of the view that when improvements to lifetime earnings are exceeding the costs involved in migration then an individual migrates. (Sjaastad, 1962). Similarly, the families are taking the decision to migrate whenever the total gains out of the migration outweigh the costs involved in migration to the household. (Mincer, 1978, Sandell, 1977). Migration is an investment in human capital (Da Vanzo, J., 1983). Migration can reduce poverty among migrants. (Housen, Hopkins & Earnest. 2013; Lokshin, Bontch-Osmolovski, & Glinskaya, 2010).

Increased wages in the origin, investment of remittances, and an expansion of economic activities in the local economy due to consumption of remittances are the indirect benefits of out-migration (Housen et al., 2013; Mendola, 2012; Zhu et al., 2013). Seema Sangita (2017) investigated the interlinkages between rural to urban migration in India and income and ownership of assets. In the rural India short-term migration plays a very important role in the livelihoods of the migrant households (Breman, 1996; Banerjee & Duflo, 2007). Many authors have also discussed about the child labour problem in the case of children of migrant labourers. The undocumented migrants are most likely to face abuse, discrimination and exclusion in the process of migration (GMG, 2010). When they are children or female, there lies greater risks such as trafficking and being deprived of healthcare facilities and education. In India short term migration among the poor tribal households is common. From Jharkhand poor ST households migrate to work in brick kilns (Shah, 2006). Migrants go to other states to work in the agricultural sector from West Bengal (Rogaly and Rafique, 2003). Migration is expected to have women empowerment in terms of economic independence. But as the study (Krishnaraj, 2005) shows that women migrants have to spend long hours in the work place with very low income. Sometimes the working conditions are also dangerous. The migration rates are very high in the drought prone areas of Bihar, Odisha, West Bengal and Gujarat. An estimated 60,000 people of Bolangir district of Odisha migrated out during the 2001 drought (Wandshcneider and Mishra 2003) alone and informal estimates were about 300,000 in this region (Deshingkar, 2003).

Migration and Western Odisha

Migration does not represent the type of usual investment like investment in fixed assets. The migrants make a sacrifice in the present time in the expectation of future rewards. Migration is not costless. When individuals are migrating it involves costs, which cannot be recovered. The migrants are rational, and these costs are critical as well as consistent with the rational behaviour of the migrants. The migrant's decision to migrate must consider the expected value of the wage differentials of the future and the level of these costs. When the migrant's expected wage differential is more than the level of these costs, he decides to migrate. A person migrates because he expects the benefits to outweigh the costs.

Apart from this cost, the expectation about future and the perception of the migrant regarding the future earnings and the appropriate time for migration plays an important role. In certain circumstances during the lean season of agricultural production, as there is unavailability of job in the agricultural sector and no alternative source of employment is available, so the households have no alternative but to migrate somewhere for their livelihood. Thus, the wage differential what they expect to earn is positive always. Again, whatever they earn at the village of the origin is not sufficient to meet their day to day expenses along with the unexpected expenses. For this reason, they are indebted.

Odisha is located on the eastern coastal part of India. It covers an area of 155.707 Sq. Kms. distributed between the North-western Plateau of Central India and the Bay of Bengal. As far as Odisha is concerned in terms of HDI, its rank is 13th and in terms of the poverty level its rank is 14th among the 14 major states of India. A large number of people of the state of Odisha are unable to secure a meaningful livelihood.

The present study has been undertaken in the three districts of western Odisha. The Western Odisha Development Council (WODC) comprising the districts of Bargarh, Boudh, Deogarh, Bolangir, Jharsuguda, Sambalpur, Subarnapur, Sundargarh, Kalahandi, Nuapada, and Athmallik subdivision of Angul district, continues to depict a picture of chronic underdevelopment. In this region the seasonal or circular migration dominates. The seasonal migrants usually stay at their destination for six months or more at a time.

Figure 1. Map 1: Districts of Western Odisha Development Council

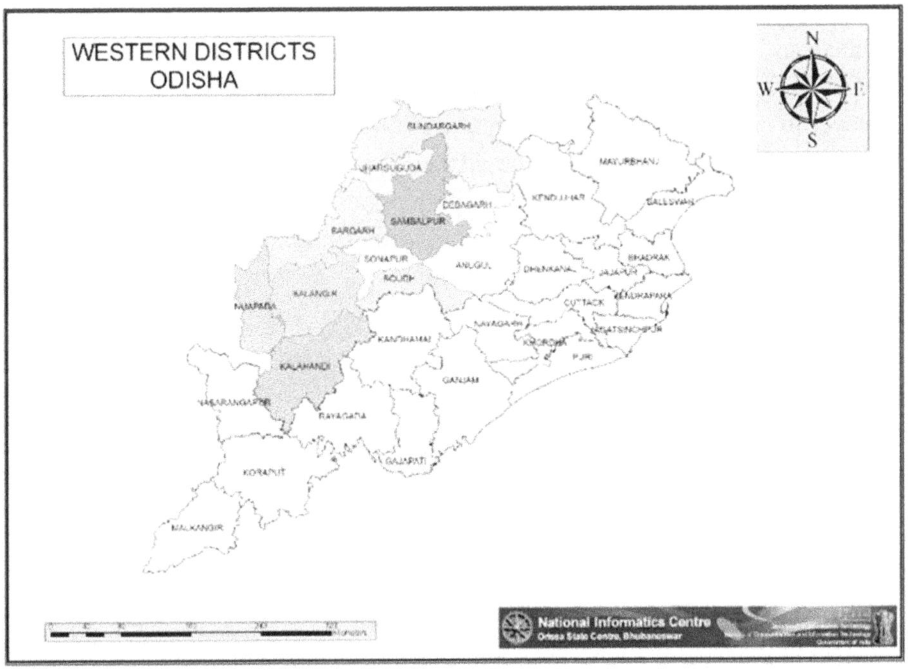

According to the Labour Directorate, Government of Odisha, out of all these western Odisha districts, Bolangir, Kalahandi, Nuapada, Sonepur and Bargarh are the migration prone districts. The migrants of these districts work in different brick kilns in other states. Many households from these districts migrate seasonally to work in brick kilns. In such type of migration, the location of his other economic activity changes but the permanent residence of a person remains the same. The National Commission on Rural Labour (NCRL) of India has mentioned that majority of seasonal migrants are employed in cultivation and plantations, construction sites, brick kilns etc. Improving the well-being is the most important objective of the migrants. In the case of distress migration, migrants, not only have to face the financial constraints but also the structural and cultural constraints. The Government of Odisha is concerned about the prevalence of exploitative labour practices including bondage situation in brick manufacturing activities that engage poor and vulnerable migrant workers. A MOU has been signed between Ministry of Labour and Employment, Government of India and State Labour Department of Governments of Odisha and Andhra Pradesh with the facilitation of ILO (International Labour Organisation) for the welfare of the migrants.

Table 1. Information on interstate migrant workers (March 2013)

District	Number of Migrant Workers	Percent
Bolangir	32437	27.99
Kalahandi	3486	3.01
Nuapada	5306	4.58
Odisha	115874	

Source: Labour Directorate, Government of Odisha

The present analysis investigates the factors responsible for the seasonal migration of debt bondage (*Dadan*) from the Western Odisha. When poor people have no option but to take loan or wage advance from their employer to cover major social expenditures or to get out of the emergency, the concept of debt bondage comes into picture. They face the difficulties of repayment for many reasons. It may be due to high interest rates or low level of income or high prices for agricultural inputs (ILO, 2005). The specific objectives of the study are to know the factors responsible for distress migration and to explore how debt-bondage is operating in the economic system.

Data and Methodology

In the present analysis the study area covers three districts of western Odisha i.e. Bolangir, Kalahandi and Nuapada. These three districts come under the well-known KBK districts of Odisha. According to the information of the District Labour Office, Bolangir, the migration prone blocks of the district are Bangomunda, Turekela, Muribahal, Khaprakhol, Patnagarh, Belpada and Titilagarh. The migrants are going to Andhra Pradesh, Tamil Nadu, Karnataka and Telangana to work mainly in brick kiln operation. The survey conducted by DRDA Nuapada, about 33,000 people migrate to different parts of Odisha and outside the state in search of income and livelihood [1]. Similarly, according to the information of the District Labour Office, Kalahandi the migration prone blocks of this district are Jayapatna, Dharamgarh, Junagarh, Koksara, Kalampur and Narla. Keeping in view the above-mentioned information, six blocks i.e. Muribahal, Patnagarh from Bolangir district, Jayapatna, Koksara from Kalahandi district and Khariar, Komna blocks from Nuapada district were selected for analysis. Accordingly, sample data are collected from these blocks. The migration prone blocks are chosen keeping in view the distance from the district headquarters. As mentioned in the Table 5, the distance ranges within 10km to 80km to make representative samples of the migrants. Migration prone villages were selected purposefully after the pilot survey. Samples from the three districts have been collected by following probability proportional to size of the population. While collecting the samples, care has been taken to make the sample representative of the population. From each village samples are selected using stratified random sampling.

Both primary and secondary data were collected for the purpose. Secondary data were collected from various District Statistical Handbook, Economic Survey, Agricultural Statistics, Statistical Abstract of Odisha. Primary data were collected with the help of a structured questionnaire. A survey method was adopted to collect information on demographic and labour migration related information. Data from 400 households were collected in fifteen villages of six blocks of these three districts. The questionnaire was designed for the survey to measure the most important factors responsible for migration. The household level data of the migrants as well as non-migrants were collected purposefully. The push/pull factors, indicating a pair of moves has been captured by the amount of the debt taken from the labour contractor. The data on non-migrants were also collected to identify the factors responsible for migration. Data were collected for both the migrants as well as non-migrants of the villages. The information on the variables like size of the household, age, education, income of the household, land ownership, loans or advances taken by the household, number of family members who migrate, main reasons for migration, destination, working hours, remuneration per person etc. The present analysis has applied the Logit model.

Study Area

The demographic profile of the three districts is presented in Table 2. These three districts are characterised by the dominance of rural population. In Nuapada district, 94.42 percent of the population live in rural areas. The percentage of socially disadvantaged population is also quite high. The literacy rates of these districts are less than the rate of the state.

Agriculture still dominates to provide employment opportunities to the workers. About 70 to 80 percent of the workers are employed in agricultural sectors in these districts, while for the entire state it is about 62 percent. The percentages of main workers are also markedly below than that of the state.

Net Sown Area (NSA) is an important component of land use of any state. In Odisha, the NSA has declined from 5796 thousand hectares in 2003-04 to 5359 thousand hectares in 2017-18. Similar declining trend has been observed in Bolangir and Kalahandi districts. From the Table 3 it has been observed that the cropping intensity of Bolangir district is the lowest up to 2011-12, but after that it has improved during 2012-14. This improvement is due to both the factors i.e., a decline in net sown area and an increase in gross cropped area.

However, farm yields depend on a technology, quality seeds, fertilisers, pesticides, and irrigation etc. Odisha Climate Change Action Plan (OSDMA) has identified Bolangir, Kalahandi and Nuapada districts as very high-risk zone of drought. Thus, irrigation is the most important critical input in agriculture in these districts. Table 4 presents the net area irrigated, gross area irrigated and their percentage out of net area sown and gross cropped area respectively in the sample districts and Odisha over the years. The net area irrigated out of net sown area in the year 2017-18 are only about 22 percent and 26 percent for Bolangir and Nuapada districts respectively. Similarly, the percentage for gross irrigated area out of gross cropped area are quite low which are about half of the state's percentage of 40.85 percent.

Table 2. Profile of the districts from which samples are collected (2011 census)

Districts		Bolangir	Kalahandi	Nuapada	Odisha
Geographical Area (Sq. Km.)		6575	7920	3852	155707
Distribution of land area (%)		4.22	5.09	2.5	
Population (Figures in the parentheses represent percent)	Male	830097 (50.34)	787101 (49.92)	301962 (49.47)	2,12,12,136 (50.54)
	Female	818900 (49.66)	789768 (50.08)	308420 (50.53)	2,07,62,082 (49.46)
	Total	1648997	1576869	610382	4,19,74,218
	Rural	1451616 (88.03)	1454882 (92.26)	576328 (94.42)	3,49,70,562 (83.31)
	Urban	197381 (11.97)	121987 (7.74)	34054 (5.58)	70,03,656 (16.69)
% of SC population to total population of the district		17.9	18.2	13.5	17.13
% of ST population to total population of the district		21.1	28.5	33.8	22.85
Sex ratio		991	1024	1009	979
Literacy rate(%)		64.7	59.2	57.3	72.87
Workers	Main	402227 (55.82)	376757 (50.11)	151694 (49.66)	1,07,07,543 (61.04)
	Marginal (3 to 6 months)	258074 (35.81)	309753 (41.19)	126786 (41.51)	68,34,046 (38.96)
	Marginal (less than 3 months)	60300 (8.7)	65420 (8.70)	26958 (8.83)	
	Total	720601	751930	305438	1,75,41,589
	Cultivators	166565 (23.11)	144991 (19.28)	94692 (31.00)	4103989 (23.40)
	Agri. Labourers	326416 (45.30)	436733 (58.08)	149834 (49.06)	67,39,993 (38.42)
	Workers in household industry	28650 (3.98)	18453 (2.45)	8641 (2.83)	7,83,080 (4.46)
	Other workers	198970 (27.61)	151753 (20.18)	52271 (17.11)	5914527 (33.72)

Source: District Statistical handbook, Directorate of Economics and Statistics and Statistical Abstract of Odisha

Table 3. Net sown area (NSA), gross cropped area (GCA), and cropping intensity of the three sample districts (in '000 hectare)

Year	Bolangir			Kalahandi			Nuapada			Odisha		
	NSA	GCA	CI(%)	NSA	GCA	CI(%)	NSA	GCA	CI(%)	NSA	GCA	CI(%)
2003-04	335	437	130	364	540	148	158	227	144	5796	7878	135
2004-05	332	449	135	360	536	149	163	246	151	5739	8718	152
2008-09	324	472	146	375	587	162	157	269	171	5604	9071	162
2009-10	328	483	147	377	638	169	157	266	169	5574	9074	163
2010-11	340	488	144	339	608	179	167	272	163	5421	9080	167
2011-12	336	452	134	335	561	168	163	280	172	5292	8801	166
2012-13	290	484	167	332	608	183	157	266	146	5574	9074	167
2013-14	292	489	168	335	617	184	186	291	156	5424	9054	167
2014-15	300	489	163	358	607	170	186	278	147	5496	9011	164
2015-16	306	435	142	366	551	151	189	277	147	5608	8386	150
2016-17	312	475	152	362	603	167	189	276	146	5631	8541	151
2017-18	306	432	141	341	556	163	189	275	145	5359	8361	156

Source: Odisha Agriculture Statistics, Directorate of Agriculture and Food Production, Odisha, Bhubaneswar

Table 4. Net and gross area irrigated in the sample districts and Odisha over the years (in '000 hectare)

Year	Bolangir		Kalahandi		Nuapada		Odisha	
	NAI	GAI	NAI	GAI	NAI	GAI	NAI	GAI
2009-10	52.51 (16.01) *	87.67 (18.14) **	133.55 (35.42)	205.18 (32.17)	44.1 (28.09)	54 (20.31)	2058.85 (36.94)	3038.52 (33.49)
2010-11	62.6 (18.41)	94.39 (19.34)	124.29 (36.66)	209.77 (34.48)	46.59 (27.90)	64.54 (23.69)	2085.21 (38.47)	3105.91 (34.21)
2011-12	52.3 (15.57)	83.76 (18.54)	106.18 (31.70)	146.86 (26.17)	43.8 (26.87)	56.38 (20.16)	2078.9 (39.28)	3087.18 (35.08)
2012-13	37.82 (13.04)	94.7 (19.59)	65.32 (17.33)	175.56 (27.52)	15.25 (9.71)	61.36 (23.08)	1178.73 (21.15)	3365.59 (37.09)
2013-14	60.28 (20.64)	100.66 (20.57)	116.37 (34.74)	200.07 (32.43)	47.54 (25.56)	66.47 (22.84)	2253.67 (41.55)	3521.02 (38.89)
2014-15	42.51 (14.17)	80.1 (16.40)	145.88 (40.75)	223.55 (36.80)	52.72 (28.34)	67.79 (24.40)	2319.96 (42.21)	3461.88 (38.42)
2015-16	61.72 (20.17)	103.75 (23.87)	129.2 (35.30)	182.58 (33.15)	55.97 (29.61)	72.58 (26.16)	2205.72 (39.33)	3422.67 (40.82)
2016-17	90.62 (29.04)	127.56 (26.86)	137.97 (38.11)	206.15 (34.20)	50.83 (26.89)	65.51 (23.73)	2283.09 (40.55)	3409.47 (39.92)
2017-18	66.77 (21.82)	101.14 (23.39)	155.45 (45.59)	233.99 (42.05)	49.86 (26.38)	60.75 (22.12)	2234.91 (41.70)	3415.31 (40.85)

Note: *Figures in the parentheses of NAI indicate the percent of Net Area Irrigated out of Net Area Sown.
**Figures in the parentheses of GAI indicate the percent of Gross Area Irrigated out of Gross Cropped Area.
Source: Odisha Agriculture Statistics, Directorate of Agriculture and Food Production, Odisha, Bhubaneswar

Descriptive Account of Seasonal Migration From the Study Area

The demographic profile of the sample households from the migration prone three districts of western Odisha are presented in Table 5. Four hundred household samples were collected of which 207 were non-migrants and 193 were migrants.

Table 5. Demographic profile of the sample households of the study villages

District	Block	Village	Male	Female	Age Distribution				
					0-5	5-18	18-35	35-55	55 and Above
Nuapada	Khariar(38.4km.) *	Kotipadar	45.45	54.55	11.11	44.83	20.69	20.69	2.68
		Jhitridhola	52.94	47.06	16.67	25.09	31.48	22.22	4.54
	Komna(10.6km.)	Ulva	52.83	47.17	1.89	32.08	26.42	37.74	1.89
Kalahandi	Koksara(60.2 km.)	Lodugaon	46.88	53.12	3.13	14.06	45.31	25.00	12.50
		Ampani	54.41	45.59	2.94	25.00	30.88	27.94	13.24
	Jaipatna(76.9 km.)	Mohanguda	51.85	48.15	8.86	32.91	35.44	18.99	3.80
		Ghantiguda	52.24	47.76	6.06	27.27	46.97	10.61	9.09
Bolangir	Patnagarh(39.8km.)	Dumberpadar	56.98	43.02	3.75	20	40	26.25	10
		Pandamunda	54.74	45.26	6.12	27.55	29.59	23.47	13.27
		Sarmuhana	57.14	42.86	2.86	40.00	28.57	22.86	5.71
	Muribahal (69.4km.)	Budhipadar	49.28	50.72	3.03	30.30	22.73	30.30	13.64
		Goimund	42.5	57.5	2.70	32.50	29.73	29.73	5.34
		Debang	37.84	62.16	2.94	26.47	32.35	26.47	11.76
		Ainlabhata	44.44	55.56	15.38	23.08	46.15	15.38	0.00
		Ghusra Munda	45.33	54.67	10.45	28.36	28.36	22.39	10.45

Note: * Figures in the parentheses indicate distance from the district headquarters
Source: Field survey data

The caste composition of the sample migrants and non-migrants are presented in the Table 6. From the table it is clear that the socially disadvantaged class population are more prone to migrate. On the other hand, the socially better off caste dominates the non-migrants.It has been observed that family migration rather than individual migration dominates in this region i.e., mostly household members in the working age along with their children migrate for their livelihood. The elderly people are left behind at their homes. The flows of migrants are mediated by an elaborate chain of labour contractors *(Seth, Sardar)* and middlemen *(dalal)* who provide information to the labourers regarding their job availability and place of work. They perform the critical functions of advancing loans to the workers and recruiting them to the different brick kilns in the states of Tamil Nadu, Andhra Pradesh and Karnataka.

As far as western Odisha is concerned, the farmers usually do one crop per year except the irrigated area of Sambalpur and Bargarh districts. Here rice production takes place once in a year. Because of this most of the agricultural workers usually get employment opportunity from June to December every year. For rest of the period, they do not have any alternate employment opportunity in the local area. So,they ask for advance to survive during the slack season and come to the crunch of the *Sardar* and *Seth.* As they get a big advance for family matters, the workers become indebted for the next season and are in a cycle of indebtedness and exploitation.

Table 6. Caste-wise distribution of the sample migrants and on-migrants (in percent)

Caste	Migrants	Non-Migrants
SC	55.03	17.2
ST	28.04	20.06
SEBC & others	16.93	62.74

Source: Author's calculation from primary survey data

Figure 2. Flow chart: 1

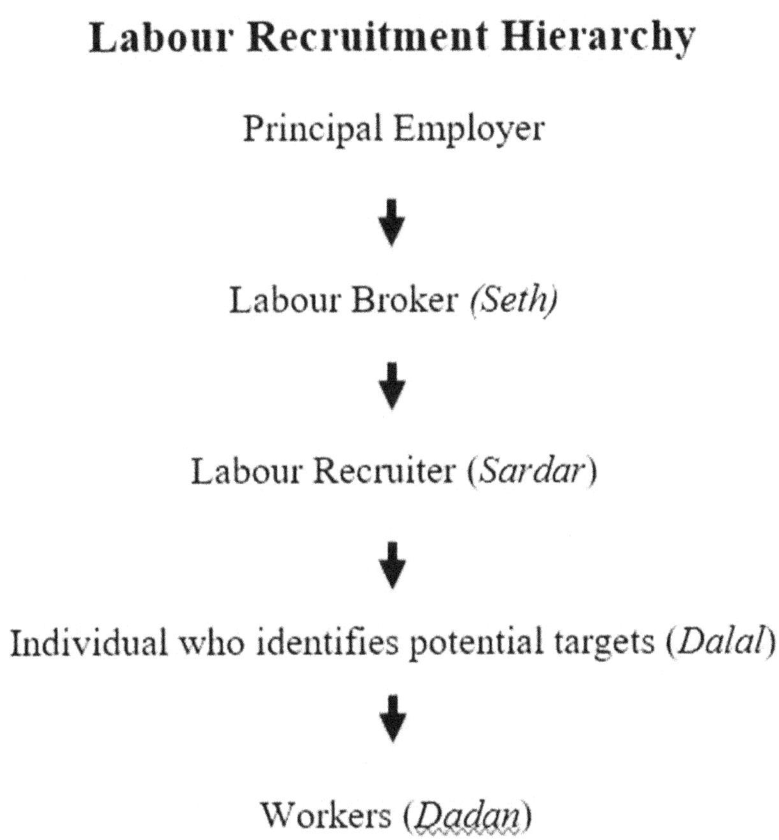

Over the years there has been the creation of five classes: the debt bondage migrant labourer (*Dadan* worker), individual who identifies potential targets (*Dalal*), labour broker *(Seth)*, the labour contractor (*Sardar*) and the principal employer in the destination. The labour broker usually comes to this region just before the local agricultural festival of "*Nuakhai*" with money usually in the month of September.

The labourers are in need of money during this time, and they are paid advance at this vulnerable time of anything between 15,000/- to 18,000/- per person in the working age who are willing to go to work in the brick kilns. Usually, the advances are paid to the 'Pathurias' (consisting of three members of a family). This is because in the making of bricks at least three to four persons are required. One person prepares the malleable paste of mud, one makes the *Gola* (ball of the paste), the third person put that into the frame or brick mould to make the bricks and another person is required to dry it under the sun ray.

Migration will only occur when the net present value (NPV) is sufficiently high to compensate for the irreversibility of the migration decision. A similar argument holds for return migration. However, in this case as they are bonded, the out migration as well as the return migration is determined by the *dadan sardar & Seth* and the workers are trapped in the vicious circle.

About 96.5% of the respondents migrate with other family members and only 3.5% migrate alone to the brick kilns. Of the 96.5%, about 45.7% have reported that some of their family members were there in their respective villages when they migrated. Usually, the old family members and small children were left behind. As the region is well connected with railway communication, the migrants travel to various destination by train in groups. The out migration starts from the month of October and continues till the month of December. The Sardar takes the responsibility of sending them to the destination and usually Titilagarh and Kantabanji are the two most important place from where they leave for their destination. Those who are migrating alone i.e., not with family or friends are usually associated in lifting the bricks. For lifting 1000 bricks, the amount received is 25 rupees to 30 rupees. In a day about 2000-2500 bricks are lifted by any individual.

The work timing differs from person to person. In the morning time they work about four hours on an average i.e., from 6 AM to 10 AM. Then after lunch the work starts from 2 PM to 10PM or 3 PM to12 AM and in some places, it is from morning 6AM till evening 7 PM with a lunch break. Thus, the working hours ranges between 11-13 hours per day. In the first part of the working day, they mix clay, sand and water to make a thick malleable paste with which they can make the bricks and in the second part they make the bricks. Usually, four or five persons of a family engaged in brick making. The male adult of the family prepare the malleable paste in the morning and in the day time one makes the *gola* (ball of the paste), the second person put that in the brick moulds to make bricks, the third person dries them under the sun. When the bricks are completely dried, they are again lifted and burnt. From the study it has been observed that usually women and children are employed in this drying activity.

The migrant families with two three adult male people put their target to make as many as bricks per day say 2000. For 1000 bricks the rate is R.300/-. As a result, they can repay about 600/- rupees per day of the advance that they have taken earlier. Weekly they get some money for their food which is termed as *khairi* It also varies from one brick kiln to another. In some cases, the *khairi* per adult migrant varies between Rs. 200/- to Rs.250/- per week while in some other kilns Rs. 90/- is given as *khairi* for 1000 bricks. *Khairi* i.e., price for food is not given to the children. So, the children who are working in these brick kilns are free labour and they are considered as helping their parents or family members for repaying the debt.

Main Reasons of Migrations

The causes of migration are usually traced to economic, social and environmental factors. However, the economic factors dominate the main reason of migration in western Odisha. The respondents give more importance to the lack of job availability in local areas and availability of works under MGNREGA is not sufficient to meet the requirements of this region as presented in Table 7. Unavailability of job opportunities in the local area for their livelihood is the most important constraint that the people are facing during the months of October to May.

Table 7. Main reasons of migration

District	Block	Village	No Agricultural Land	No Employment Opportunity	No Opportunity under MGNREGA	Better Job Outside	Do Not Get Food Subsidies	Highly Indebted
Nuapada	Khariar	Kotipadar	85.71	100.00	14.29	14.29	14.29	0.00
		Jhitridhola	80.00	60.00	93.33	0.00	0.00	0.00
	Komna	Ulva	91.67	91.67	75.00	16.67	0.00	0.00
Kalahandi	Koksara	Lodugaon	58.33	100.00	75.00	100.00	41.67	50.00
		Ampani	35.71	92.86	50.00	100.00	28.57	50.00
	Jaipatna	Mohanguda	46.15	23.08	100.00	46.15	0.00	46.15
		Ghantiguda	61.54	0.00	100.00	61.54	0.00	61.54
Bolangir	Patnagarh	Dumberpadar	0	100	100	100	0	0
		Pandamunda	52.38	14.29	100.00	52.38	0.00	52.38
		Sarmuhana	20	70	20	30	20	50
	Muribahal	Budhipadar	0	100	100	100	0	0
		Goimund	0	100	100	100	0	0
		Debang	33.33	100	100	100	0	0
		Ainlabhata	60	100	100	100	0	0
		Ghusra Munda	14.29	42.86	28.57	28.57	0.00	42.86
Total			47.44	68.38	69.66	55.98	5.98	22.22

Source: Own calculation of the author from primary survey data

Binary Choice Model (Logit)

To identify the factors responsible for migration, binary choice logit model is proposed and estimated. The Logit model has been applied in the present analysis following McFadden, 1973. Various logit regression models have been fitted to examine the main factors responsible for migration decision in the present analysis. The decision to migrate is influenced by some economic variables and certain social variables. The variables such as age, education, social group, family members in working age, income, land and loan are taken as independent variables in the logit model. In this model the reference category has been the choice of the household not to migrate that is Yi = 0. By taking the dependent dummy variable as = 1 if migrant and = 0 if non-migrant, the significant causes of migration can be analysed for these sample villages.

$$L_i = ln\left[\frac{P_i(Y_i = 1)}{P_i(Y_i = 0)}\right] = B_i X_i$$

To analyse the influence of different variables in the decision to migrate, the following model is proposed.

$$Y_i = \beta_0 + \beta_1(age_i) + \beta_2(edu_i) + \beta_3(income_i) + \beta_4(land_i) + \beta_5(loan_i) + \beta_6(social\ group_i) + \beta_7(fm\ working\ age_i) + \epsilon_i$$

where, Y_i is taken as the dependent variable with $i = 0, 1$.

Y_i (=0) if household is non-migrant and

Y_i (=1) if household is migrant

X_i's are the independent variables.

ε_i - random disturbance term.

For the social group variable SC & ST people are assigned 0 and the rest are assigned as 1. It has been observed that the decision to migrate is not made by the migrant in isolation. The role of *dadan sardar* and other migrants from the same village determine the destination of the migrant. Thus, the migration choices of an individual vary with the characteristics of the groups of which they are part. In the logit model the method of maximum likelihood has been used and z-statistic is used to evaluate the statistical significance. After analyzing the confidence interval of different co-efficient, the conclusions regarding significance of the co-efficient is drawn. The p-values are also used to draw inferences.

The collected primary data is applied to the model as outlined and the result is presented.

Results and Discussion

Average years of schooling of the households are taken to capture the education variable. If the head of the household or any member of the household is educated then, they are aware of the situation faced by the migrants in different working sites. Also, if the average number of years of education is more, there lies an opportunity of getting a decent job. So, they will not prefer for distress migration. The education variable is statistically significant and negative for all three districts considered at a time. This implies that the probability of migration is more in the case of less educated households in this area. The amount of loan taken by the migrants have three components. They are formal (commercial banks, co-operative banks and self-help groups), informal (money lender, friends and relatives) and the third one is again an informal one, but it is in terms of advance payment taken from the *dadan sardar*. From the field survey it has been observed that among the migrants, 11% have taken loan from formal sources, 41% have taken loans from informal sources and all of them have taken advances from the *dadan sardar*. In the formal loan case, the loan taken from the Self-Help Groups dominates the other form of loans. Of the formal sources, 85% of the migrants or their family members are indebted to the Self-Help Groups. As far as informal loan is concerned for the loan taken from moneylender or friends or relatives, the interest rate charge is Rs. 10 for Rs.100 advance per month. Thus, the interest amount become more than the principal amount per year. They borrow from the money lenders for meeting the requirements in emergency as their propensity to save is limited or too small to be mopped up by the banks.

When the migrants take the advance from the *dadan sardar*, they are bound to migrate to the various destinations according to the wish of the *sardar*. In these three districts more than 90% are rural population and for these rural households with a labour surplus, labour migration offers an opportunity for a household to mitigate the advance taken by them. The more the number of family members in the working age, the more is the advance they get as the mode of payment is done on per worker basis.

No interest is charged in this advance amount sanctioned by the *dadan sardar*. The *dadan sardar* gets money from the *seths* who are staying in different parts of India. The calculation of payments is made by the employees in the work site. In almost all cases they have repaid the loan amount and returned. They cannot return without that. If they will try to escape from the work site, they will be punished by the goons of the *seth*. In the year 2013 two migrant labourers of Kalahandi district had tried to escape from the work site as theywere having dispute regarding the payment and place of work. Consequently, the palms of them were chopped off.

The migrants usually repay it by working for long hours. Usually till the onset of monsoon i.e., till the month of June they have to stay there as in the rainy season they cannot make bricks. In most of the cases they cannot return back on their wish, whatever might be the problem in their respective family. For example, during the field survey one of the migrants had taken the advance from the *sardar* and had migrated to Hyderabad to work in a brick kiln along with his wife, his daughter (10 years) and son (3yrs). His wife fell ill there, and she could not work properly. So, they wanted to return back to their village. But the brick kiln owner refused to this and asked for something in guarantee of their return. Their daughter had to stay in the brick kiln and the rest of them returned to the village. In the village the wife died out of illness. After that he again returned to the brick kiln with his son. Like this each migrant has its own story. The migrants are of the view that they cannot get such huge amount of advance at a time from any formal or informal resources without any collateral. However, they do not realise that they are keeping themselves as collateral.

Land holding is the most important asset for rural households and when there is unequal access to this asset, and then it can affect their livelihood. Land holding is also an important source of employment and hence during the lean season the individuals are forced to migrate.

A statistically significant negative relationship between income and migration was observed, which implied that respondents belonging to lower income groups were more likely to migrate temporarily. Further the likelihood of seasonal migration increases with less land being owned by a household. A household with no land or smaller land holdings usually migrate to supplement their income in agricultural lean season. The backward caste people have more tendencies for migration. Similarly, family with more people in working age are more prone to migration. The Mc Fadden R^2 which is one form of pseudo R^2 is also presented for all three districts. The likelihood ratio (LR) statistics represents the impact of all regressors on decision to migrate i.e., for all three districts LR statistic is 316.335 with a p-value of zero indicating together all the regressors have significant impact. The empirical analysis present in this paper shows that seasonal migrants are more likely to be from those households who are poor, socially disadvantaged, less educated, indebted and landless.

In the present scenario of covid-19 pandemic many of these migrants have returned home and the most important challenge the state government is facing is to provide a sustainable livelihood to these people. It has been observed that the people have the skill in working in cotton mills, brick kilns, weaving etc. But they do not get jobs in their home district for their livelihood and so they are forced to migrate. Those who work in brick kilns, as they usually migrate with their family (96.5%), when they return back after six or seven months, their own home is destroyed either by natural calamity or due to lack of maintenance. The need of the hour is to provide employment opportunities for livelihood at their native place. For example, the districts of Sonepur, Bolangir, Bargarh, Sambalpur, are well known for Sambalpuri handloom. But the sad part is that they do not get locally produced quality thread for weaving.

Table 8. Binary choice (logit) model for identifying important factors responsible for migration

Variables	Bolangir			Kalahandi			Nuapada			All three districts		
	Co-Efficient	Z-Statistics	p-Value	Co-Efficient	Z-Statistics	p-Value	Co-Efficient	Z-Statistics	p-Value	Co-Efficient	Z-Statistics	p-Value
Constant	3.046	1.528	0.1265	8.411*	2.878	0.0040	19.335	1.290	0.197	3.768*	3.806	0.0001
Age	-0.020	-0.673	0.5009	-0.074	-1.141	0.2537	-0.109	-0.811	0.4176	-0.021	-1.208	0.2272
Education	0.049	0.592	0.5538	-0.458*	-2.570	0.0102	-0.787	-1.092	0.2749	-0.099*	-2.084	0.0372
Income	-0.001	-0.428	0.6687	-0.001*	-3.516	0.0004	-0.002	-1.627	0.1038	-0.003*	-5.213	0
Land	-4.022*	-6.392	0	-0.384	-1.408	0.1592	-5.572*	-2.179	0.0293	-1.619*	-7.930	0
Loan	0.001*	3.720	0.0002	0.002	0.913	0.3610	0.002*	1.816	0.0504	0.002*	5.587	0
Social group	-3.602*	-3.917	0.0001	-3.217*	-2.785	0.0053	1.789	0.964	0.3348	-2.255*	-5.962	0
Family members under working age	1.388*	3.533	0.0004	1.187*	2.078	0.0377	0.394	0.633	0.5265	0.989*	4.923	0
McFadden R-squared	0.738			0.719			0.553			0.571		
LR statistic 403.090	219.062 (0)			101.618 (0)			96.75 (0)			316.335 (0)		

Note: Yi=1 if migrant and Yi=0 if non-migrant, *indicates significant z-statistics and p-value
Source: Author's calculation from primary survey data

Raw materials like cotton and silk yarn apart dyes are supplied to weavers under cooperative fold by Bhubaneswar based National Handloom Development Corporation (NHDC). They procure yarn from Erode and Coimbatore. If one looks into Odisha economy, cotton is mostly grown in KBK (undivided Kalahandi, Bolangir, Koraput) districts. Over the years area under rice production is being converted to cotton production. In Bolangir and Nuapada districts there is a decline in the growth rate of area under production of rice (-2.56%, -1.05%respectively) and the area under production of cotton has increased markedly (13.32%, 15.10% and 26.82%) in these three districts as shown in the Table 9.

However, many cotton mills of western Odisha are shutdown. Similarly, one sugar factory in Bolangir district was closed due to financial crisis which led not only to unemployment of local people but also to the distress sale of sugarcane as the market for their product did not exist and also, they do not have enough resources to sell their produce in distant market. To overcome such problems the policy makers of the state should look into the facts that in which region what are the agricultural outputs? How many processing units can be established in that region? What are the demands for various raw materials in the region and the maximum extent to which this can be met by the state itself? The state instead of exporting the raw materials, should try to export the finished product so that value addition can be made to that product. This can also add to the employment generation within the state as from the survey it has been observed that MGNREGA is not sufficient to meet the unemployment problem of this region (69.66%). The forward and backward linkages of various economic activities should be identified, and public policy should be determined accordingly. This is because the determinants of public policy depend on the nature and state of the economy.

Table 9. Growth of area under production and amount of production of rice and cotton from 2006-07 to 2014-15 (in percent)

District	Area Under Production		Amount of Production	
	Rice	Cotton	Rice	Cotton
Bolangir	-2.56	13.32	-2.10	19.32
Kalahandi	0.29	15.10	12.87	20.90
Nuapada	-1.05	26.82	2.41	24.57

Source: Author's calculation from secondary data

CONCLUSION

A global economic shock of enormous magnitude has been delivered by the COVID-19 pandemic leading to steep recessions that will affect adversely to many developing countries. India has already started facing the crisis. The pandemic and economic shut down has adversely affected the poor and the vulnerable through job and income losses, illness and food supply disruptions. The migration behaviour of the study area of western Odisha is in line with the New Economics of Labour Migration (NELM) Theory. This theory focuses on migration from the micro level to meso unis i.e., from individual to families or households or other culturally defined units. Thus, the decision to migrate is not merely an individual decision but is a collective decision. The decision to migrate are the result of a joint process involving the migrant and the non-migrant members within the household or families. The government of Odisha has tried its best to provide food, shelter and financial help who were returning home as they have lost their livelihood. The policy makers have to consider additional interventions. The present study has drawn the conclusion that seasonal migrants of western Odisha are more likely to be from those households who are poor, socially disadvantaged, less educated, indebted and landless. Keeping in view all these factors public policy must be formulated and implemented as the determinants of public policy depends on the nature and state of the economy.

ACKNOWLEDGMENT

The present chapter is part of the study' Debt Bondage and Seasonal Migration: A Study of Western Odisha'. The author would like to acknowledge Indian Council of Social Science Research (ICSSR), New Delhi for financial support to undertake the project.

REFERENCES

Banerjee, A., & Duflo, E. (2007). The Economic Lives of the Poor. *The Journal of Economic Perspectives*, *21*(1), 141–167. doi:10.1257/jep.21.1.141 PMID:19212450

Breman, J. (1996). *Footloose Labour: Working in India's Informal Economy*. Cambridge University Press. doi:10.1017/CBO9781139171076

Da Vanzo, J. (1983). Repeat Migration in the United States: Who Moves Back and Who Moves on. *The Review of Economics and Statistics*, *65*(4), 552–559. doi:10.2307/1935923

Deshingkar, P. (2003). Improved Livelihoods in Improved Watersheds: Can Migration be Mitigated. In *Watershed Management Challenges: Improving Productivity, Resources and Livelihoods*. International Water Management Institute.

Global Migration Group (GMG). (2010). *Statement of Global Migration Group on the Human Rights of Migrants in Irregular Situation*. Statement Adopted by the Principles of Global Migration Group in Geneva on 30th September.

Harris, J., & Todaro, M. P. (1970). Migration, Unemployment and Development: A Two-Sector Analysis. *The American Economic Review*, *60*, 126–142.

Hicks, J. R. (1932). *The Theory of Wages*. Macmillan.

Housen, T., Hopkins, S., & Earnest, J. (2013). A Systematic Review on the Impact of Internal Remittances on Poverty and Consumption in Developing Countries: Implications for Policy. *Population Space and Place*, *19*(5), 610–632. doi:10.1002/psp.1743

ILO. (2005). *Global Report on Forced Labour in Asia: Debt Bondage, Trafficking and State-imposed Forced Labour*. ILO.

Lewis, W. A. (1954). Economic Development with Unlimited Supplies of Labor. *Manchester School*, *22*(2), 139–191. doi:10.1111/j.1467-9957.1954.tb00021.x

Lokshin, M., Bontch-Osmolovski, M., & Glinskaya, E. (2010). Work Related Migration and Poverty Reduction in Nepal. *Review of Development Economics*, *14*(2), 323–332. doi:10.1111/j.1467-9361.2010.00555.x

Mendola, M. (2012). Rural Out-migration and Economic Development at Origin: A Review of the Evidence. *Journal of International Development*, *24*(1), 102–122. doi:10.1002/jid.1684

Mincer, J. (1978). Family Migration Decision. *Journal of Political Economy*, *86*(5), 749–743. doi:10.1086/260710

Rogaly, B., & Rafique, A. (2003). Struggling to Save Cash: Seasonal Migration and Vulnerability in West Bengal, India. *Development and Change*, *34*(4), 659–681. doi:10.1111/1467-7660.00323

Sandell Steven, H. (1977). Women and the Economics of Family Migration. *The Review of Economics and Statistics*, *59*(4), 406–414. doi:10.2307/1928705

Sangita, S. (2017). *Poverty and Migration: Evidence of Distress Migration in India*. Paper prepared for IARIW-ICIER Conference, New Delhi, India.

Shah, A. (2006). The Labour of Love: Seasonal Migration from Jharkhand to the Brick Kilns of other States in India. *Contributions to Indian Sociology, New Series*, *40*(1), 91–118. doi:10.1177/006996670504000104

Shanti, K. (2005). *Gender Dimensions in Rural –Urban Migration in India: Policy Imperative*. Paper delivered at 25th population Conference, Tours, France.

Simon, K. (1955). Economic Growth and Income Inequality. *The American Economic Review*, (45), 1–28.

Sjaastad Larry, A. (1962). The Costs and Returns of Human Migration. *Journal of Political Economy*, *70*(5), 80–93. doi:10.1086/258726

Wandschneider & Mishra. (2003). *The role of small rural towns in Bolangir District, India: A village-level perspective*. NRI Report No: 2750, DFID-World Bank.

Zhu, Y., Bell, M., Henry, S., & White, M. (2013). Rural-urban Linkages and the Impact of Internal Migration in Asian Developing Countries. *Asian Population Studies*, *9*(2), 119–123. doi:10.1080/17441730.2013.797296

ENDNOTE

1 Comprehensive District Annual Plan (CDP) 2019-20, Nuapada submitted to Planning and Convergence Department, Odisha, Bhubaneswar.

Chapter 8
Developing Strategies for Restoring the Affected Labor Force in the Post-COVID-19 Period in Rwanda

Eric Ruvuna
Kibogora Polytechnic, Rwanda

Celestin Pierre Rutayisire
Volgograd State University, Russia

Innocent Gahamanyi
Christian University of Rwanda, Rwanda

Fidele Tubanambazi Mweruli
Kibogora Polytechnic, Rwanda

ABSTRACT

This study assessed the impact of the COVID-19 pandemic on labor force and advocated the main strategies to be implemented to restore the affected areas of labor force in Rwanda. The study was guided by three objectives: to explore the status of labor force trends before and during COVID-19 in Rwanda and its implications to the Rwandan economy, to assess the factors that led to reduction in labor force in Rwanda, and thirdly, to determine the strategies to recommend the Government of Rwanda (GoR) to restore the affected labor force sub-sector in the post-COVID-19 period. The trend analyses of the labor force before and during COVID-19 pandemic were drawn and revealed that there were changes in labor force before and during COVID-19 pandemic. Statistics were employed to the data set from National Institute of Statistics of Rwanda (NISR). The multiple regression model was used to express the GDP as a function of employment rate and unemployment rate reveals that the unemployment rate has governed the period of COVID-19 pandemic, and it was statistically significant in contributing negatively to GDP.

DOI: 10.4018/978-1-7998-6896-5.ch008

INTRODUCTION

It was reported that the COVID-19 pandemic was the most global phenomenon disruption since the 1929 great depression and the 2007-2008 financial global crisis which was considered the worst economic disaster (Sogani, 2020). Though the current pandemic is considered as a health-related issue, it has touched the social and economic aspects of people's lives whereby the world labor market was not left behind. For instance, scholars reported that though COVID-19 disrupted many sectors of the global economy, employment was the most shocked sector (Kurmann, Lalé, & Ta, 2020). Thus assessing the effects of COVID-19 pandemic on the employment sector and proposing strategies to mitigate its short and long-term negative impacts is a significant study.

The underlying factor for employment disruption associated with COVID-19 pandemic is the high level of uncertainty. Where there is uncertainty, there is a corresponding level of suspended investment according to economic behavior. This explains the reason for higher labor disruption among the self-employed and informal sector than among wage earners. Noticeable specific impact has been identified among youth due to disrupted education and early/part time employment that favors job learning. The informal sector which constitutes the largest global labor market share of 62 percent (3.3billion) has been hit the most (Sue Enfield Institute of Development Studies, 2021). The highest shock of the impact in the informal sector has been felt in the developing economies. This is attributed to the limited social protection rights including health insurance, contracts at work among others (Sue Enfield Institute of Development Studies, 2021). Research has determined that the existing vulnerable groups including women, children, migrant workers and people with disabilities absorbed the highest shock of the impact (Sue Enfield Institute of Development Studies, 2021). Specific impact was noticed in retail trade, hospitality, service and industry subsectors of the economy.

At the global perspective, the World Economic Forum and IPSOS conducted a survey of 21,000 adults in 28 countries and found that 86 percent of people want to see a more equitable and sustainable world after the pandemic; the results revealed also that 79 percent agreed that they want a new approach to doing things.

A study conducted in the United States of America reports that employment declined by 0.7 million between mid-February and mid-March; Specifically, employment in leisure & hospitality and retail trade was 32.3 million in mid-February and 12.5 million by the end of April which implies a decline of 19.8 million jobs.

An experiment conducted by the congressional research services (CRS) of the U.S authored by Falk, 2020 indicated that respondents were asked whether members of their household experienced a loss in employment income since March 2020(Falk, 2020). Data from the survey showed that in mid-July 2020, half of all adults (18 years and older) lived in a household that had lost some employment income since March 2020.

Ramdoo, 2020 concludes that up to 305 million full-time workers in all economic sectors in the world would be laid off in the second quarter of 2020(Ramdoo, 2020). These losses could be more severe in lower-income countries, given their weaker health bodies, a high number of workers in the informal sector, subsistence salary, etc. She proposed such states should mitigate forthcoming recession for all the economic sectors including the labor market. This augurs well with this study's objective of proposing strategies that can improve the constrained labor industry.

In the U.S., as of the end of April, 2020,70 percent of the workers in hotels became unemployed. Hence, developing strategies that would lead to the betterment of the affected labor force sub sector in the post-COVID-19 era could be the preliminary conditions of expecting a better change of people's lives (WEF, 2020). COVID-19 has surprisingly shocked the world economy by grossly affecting worldwide livelihoods, especially African countries which have shrunk incomes and raised poverty incidences.

Authors are yet to access similar data for Africa. SMEs especially those who have to import their merchandise encountered transportation and social distancing challenges thus affecting both sales and purchases which trickled down to low household purchasing power and the vicious circle of lack continued.

They assessed the remote work and the heterogeneous impact of COVID-19 pandemic on the employment and health in the USA (Angelucci, Kapteyn, Angrissani, & Schaner, 2020). The study used a large; nationally representative and high rate occurrence panel dataset from March to July 2020. Results showed that job losses were up to three times as large for no remote workers. They concluded that 24 percent of non-remote workers and 8 percent of online employees lost their jobs between mid-March and July 2020.

The pandemic antagonized market demand and supply patterns due to restrictions on movements and interactions services, especially in sectors such as hospitality, tourism, transport, and manufacturing for local markets (e.g., nourishment and beverage).

The International Labor Organization (ILO) reported that the COVID-19 crisis led to job loss whereby almost 2.7 billion workers lost their jobs and predicted that 25 million jobs will be affected by the crisis (ILO, 2020). It also indicated that the labor supply declined due to quarantine measures and a fall in economic activity. As a result, it is expected that employment impacts will mean huge revenue decline for workers whereby losses in labor income will globally be in the range between 860 and 3,440 billion USD which will in turn affect the level of consumption of goods and services of the affected workers.

From a continental perspective, during the Great Recession African countries with low- and lower-middle-income economies (LICs and LMICS, respectively) suffered from the economic decline like other developed countries. However, during the pandemic, unlike other LICs and LMICs whose economic growth shrunk to the lowest percentage of 1 in 2019, Africa's economic growth persisted to around 4.5 percent. Earnings and consumption continued to rise, and the share of the population in extreme poverty maintained its slow decline, (WB, 2015).

According to (Battaile, Leonardo, & Vivian, 2015); Africa's fair economic performance can be attributed to mineral prices and her low levels of association which prevented a spillover of the economic crisis from other economic blocks. The explanation for Africa's tenacity during the economic crisis was its sufficient food production which stabilized demand and supply. Debt cancellation was another boost to the survival of the African economies. About 24.3 million workers became unemployed due to COVID-19 effects (National Planning Commission, University of Namibia, April, 2020).

At the regional perspective, The EAC export sector is suffering because of COVID-19 pandemic, like Kenya which was the largest exporter of flowers in Africa in 2019, in only few weeks, their exports fell by a half in only few weeks, leading to one million job loss (Deloitte, May, 2020). Kenyan flower exports to Europe fell by 50 percent, putting about 1 million direct and indirect jobs at risk (Deloitte, May, 2020). The natural resources sector job absorption is low compared to output volumes, but they are well paid, (Andrew & Anthony, 2020).

According to (ZAHID, 2020) African states debts are being forfeited by lenders and receiving financial bailouts from IMF and World Bank and other development partners. While civil servants may not lose jobs due to associated legal consequences, salary delays may be encountered depending on individual state capacity. Already, many top paid officials in Rwanda, Uganda & Kenya have foregone part of their salaries to deal with the effects of the pandemic.

The situation may be different for publicly owned corporations (including utilities). These workers are usually unionized but do not have civil service protections. Reduced product demand and improved payment of outstanding dues from public and private customers will result in delayed pay, dismissals and declined work schedules depending on the length of the economic disruption.

From the National perspective, job creation in Rwanda was considered as the key component of the National Strategy for Transformation one (NST1) where it stipulates that 1,500,000 jobs were anticipated to be created by 2024 through reinforcing growth, creation of jobs for all. The Ministry of Finance and Economic Planning (MINECOFIN) identified high priority sectors to be focused on; to create more jobs. Those sectors include agro-processing, horticulture, and manufacturing, value addition to minerals, construction, tourism, transport, and creative arts (EPRN, 2018). Though the GoR aims at creating more jobs, there is currently a worldwide crisis caused by the COVID-19 pandemic which disrupted both the Rwandan and global economy. The crisis affected the target of creating 1,500,000 jobs as indicated in the NST1, (EPRN, 2018).

The National Institute of Statistics of Rwanda (NISR) reported a decrease in the number of employed people from 3,569,000 in February 2020 to 3,411,000 in March 2020 and continued to decrease to 2,117,416 in April 2020 during the complete lockdown (NSIR, 2020). It was slightly increased in May 2020 to 3,199,000 after the resumption of most business activities.

Therefore, this chapter seeks to inform strategies that would serve as a baseline for Rwanda to restore the affected labor market during the post-COVID-19 period. Moreover, the NISR data were used to confirm the level at which COVID-19 pandemic affected the level of employment in Rwanda from mid-March to August 2020.

Based on the empirical model of employment, strategies were developed to ensure the restoration of the sector in the post-COVID-19 period. Thus, the chapter answered the following questions:

1. How were the labor force trends before and during COVID-19 pandemic in Rwanda and its implications to the Rwandan economy?
2. What were the effects of COVID-19 pandemic on the employment sector in Rwanda?
3. What are the strategies to recommend the GoR to restore the affected workers in the post-COVID-19 period?

This chapter was subdivided into four main sections:

An introduction to the chapter was presented in section one. Materials and methods were explained in section two. Results and discussions were provided in section three. The concluding remarks and recommended strategies were given in the fourth section.

LITERATURES REVIEW

Definition of Key Concepts

A clear understanding on the key terms is necessary for a reader to be able to understand the content of the study. Thus the following key terms were defined and used throughout the process of this study.

Developing refers to the process of doing something. In this study, it involves scientific procedures to come up with an informed opinion on how to restore the affected labor force to the original state before COVID-19.

Strategy development is the process of identifying and finding strategic options most promising and deciding how resources will be utilized for the success of any organization (Google scholar, 2020).

The word "strategy" is derived from the Greek word "stratçgos"; stratus (meaning army) and "ago" (meaning leading/moving). Strategy refers to the action that leaders consider to attain objectives of the organization.

Restoring means putting back anything to its original movement. In this sense, it indicates strategies meant for restoring the labor force to its state before COVID-19.

Labor force is composed of all persons who fulfill the conditions for being among the employed or the unemployed. The unemployed are defined as persons without job but actively seeking employment and currently ready to start work (Economic Policy Institute, 2020).

Employed people are those who have a job, in other words they produce goods or provide services for pay or profit.

Unemployed people are those who are jobless but available and looking for a job.

COVID-19 refers to COVID-19 as a contagious respiratory and vascular disease caused by severe acute respiratory syndrome Coronavirus 2(SARS-COV-2) (Medscape, 2021). It first broke out in China in December 2019. Its common symptoms include fever, cough, fatigue, breathing difficulties, and loss of smell and taste.

Rwanda is a landlocked republic lying south of the Equator in east-central Africa. The capital is Kigali, located in the center of the country on the Ruganwa River Located a few degrees south of the Equator, Rwanda is bordered by Uganda, Tanzania, Burundi, and the Democratic Republic of the Congo. The climate is temperate to subtropical, with two rainy seasons and two dry seasons each year. Rwanda has a population of over 12.6 million living on 26,338 km^2 (Ben, 2019).

Theoretical Review

This study was informed by unemployment theory guided by job creation and job destruction models by Dale and Christopher. Job creation is defined as the employment growth generated by establishing new industries and other investments that expand or start up (Dale & Christopher, 1994) while job destruction refers to the employment decline because of establishment contracting or stinging. The proponents theorize job specific shocks and corresponding unemployment processes and salary dissatisfaction behavior. The proponents advance that an aggregate shock induces a negative coloration between job creation and job destruction, while a dispersed sock induces a positive relationship between job creation and job destruction.

With this in mind, we therefore chose unemployment theory where job creation and destruction models inform the study because it focuses on both job creation and job destruction in the analysis in both short and long runs.

Conceptual Reviews

When the pandemic broke out, social distancing measures such as universal lockdown led to closure of all business save for life saving workers. Even when the measures were relaxed, the shock was too much for especially Small and Medium Enterprises (SMEs), transport, construction and cross border trade and service sectors. These badly affected sectors were not only major labor absorbers but also the major source of labor supply to big companies that require experienced workers. Gender issues shorten because research has determined that new entrants to the job industry and women dominated in the informal sector and SMEs. These worst hit sectors had less or no social security and couldn't afford a recovery fund which comes in the form of a loan. Big companies like Airlines were hardly hit which widened the effect on the labor force. Schools were the first to be closed yet they did not only absorb many workers but were largely among companies that could not afford recovery loans, especially private schools. Schools support growth of cities and so several businesses closed due to school closures.

These explanations enable researchers to formulate the conceptual framework of this research which shows the existing relationship between variables such as dependent and independent variables. For instance, the dependent variable is the employment with two categories viz 1, if COVID-19 affected the status of the employment during the pandemic period and 0, if not. The independent variables were age, working experience, educational level, wage (having two levels Yes if affected and No if not), working hours (having two levels Yes if affected and No if not), aggregate demand (having two Yes if affected and No if not), aggregate supply (with two levels Yes if affected and No if not), Income (with two levels Yes if affected and No if not affected), working remotely (with two levels Yes if changes the working environment and No if not), uncertainty about the end of the pandemic (Yes if affected and No if not), inability to cope with new skills of working remotely (Yes if the personnel was able to cope and no if was not able), employment policies changes (with two levels, Yes if the employment policies were changed and if No if not changed), and type of institutions (having three levels private, public, and self-business owners).

Estimating such an econometric model would provide information on the status of employment and also help to predict about the future possibilities to improve the employment which was hindered by the COVID-19 pandemic by providing the strategies that would be adopted. There are also extraneous variables which are considered to be indirectly related to employment.

Empirical Reviews

On the economic aspect, there were few studies on the effect of COVID-19 pandemic on the socio-economic conditions because this pandemic was mainly considered as a health-related concern though some authors considered it as an economic related issue because it did affect both health and economic systems. Thus, authors tried to review a few existing literatures focusing on the COVID-19 pandemic effects on the labor force.

Ibrahim (2020) conducted a cross section survey to explore the socioeconomic impact of the pandemic on the Nigerian households in Kano state. The study targeted agriculture, private, public service, and trade/craft sectors. The researcher collected data from 404 households using a stratified sampling technique while data analysis was done using a descriptive method (Ibrahim, 2020). Findings revealed that close to 66 percent express displeasure over restriction on national and cross border lockdown. Over half (51 percent) of them suffered domestic violence during lockdown. 99 percent of respondents were not comfortable with stay-at-home order. Close to 95 percent of them were identified to be financially incapable during the lockdown period and about 96 percent said they did not get income support from their employers (especially the private sector workers). Another 92 percent of the respondents did not get palliative support whereas 97 percent said COVID-19 had negatively affected their economic activities.

The author concluded that Nigerian households encountered both social and economic consequences from the pandemic impact on the employment sector. He proposes some measures to mitigate the impact of the pandemic including livelihood opportunities for families that lost revenues and social safety nets program.

America's leading economists through the Berkeley News platform proposed a comprehensive approach that relieves both employers and employees simultaneously; relief and recovery packages (Eduard, April 2020). He proposes a recovery strategic package intended to support the firm's capacity to retain workers and still function and ensure workers' safety and security that adheres to the international labor standards relating to a decent work agenda. The social distancing undermines the social aspect of man thus increasing distress, their job performance and physical health, creating a vicious circle of isolation from business.

Similarly, a study on the impact of COVID-19 on the employment and hours of unincorporated self-employed workers by Charlene and Sabrina used data from the population survey. They determined that much as there was a general impact on all workers, impact varied depending on gender related status of couple, parental, and sex. Working hours for a married woman were severed compared to the working hours of a married man. This was due to the fact that mothers bear a bigger household responsibility than fathers. Fathers of school going children had their hours reduced compared to the fathers without children in school due to school shut down thus increasing the need for child attention at home. A working couple stood an advantage where if one spouse lost a job, the other increased working hours to cover up the income loss of the fired spouse while the unemployed spouse attended to children at home. Thus, school closure has a multiple effect on labor in terms of direct employment to school staff, associated employment for business that come up to serve the school population, and the parenting burden caused by children staying at home competing for the available time to parents for work, and undermining effective equitable, equality and quality access to skills development. Some parents may not afford online associated costs, cannot hire teachers to support children at home and some don't possess the skills to support their children to study online which can create inequality in access to quality education. This trickles down to competitiveness in the labor market creating a vicious circle of inequality.

Based on their research findings, COVID-19 impact is likely to create a long-term negative impact on female labor force on actively reproductive mothers in the self-employment sector in the event of sustained online schooling (Charlene & Sabrina, 2020).

Ellen et al. (2020) carried out a study to assess a socioeconomic impact of COVID- 19 on the Sierra Leone foods system. They found that food insecurity rose sharply from 53.4 percent in August 2019 to 63 percent in June 2020. During the first quarter of 2020, the price for rice and cassava increased by 8 and 17 percent respectively (Ellen, David, & Donald, 2020). Further social constraints arose from basic services such as education, access to electricity and water supply. Employees in these sectors were either fully or partially locked down which exacerbated inequality situations associated with unequal or in some cases, no access at all to service. The lockdown escalated gender issues involving sexual violence and or teenage pregnancy, domestic violence, unequal access to education and in some cases no access at all.

In a similar context, UNDP reported that in Rwanda, the lockdown caused some social protection programs to slow down compared to the period before the pandemic due to containment measures. Specifically, women are more affected where about 68 percent of those benefiting from direct support under the VUP program are affected. Another 52 percent benefiting from financial services under the same program are affected (Fode, 2020).

Research has determined that unemployment is one of the life events associated with psychological disorders. Similarly, COVID-19 impact on the labor force is associated with job loss, loss of friends, school dropout, property auctioning, and general failure to meet social obligation and social safety net system collapse as cited in (Lauterbach, 1987).

Alfred and Simeon (2020) carried out a case study on indicative socio-economic impacts of the Novel Coronavirus (COVID-19) Outbreak in Eastern Africa: The case of Rwanda focusing on external merchandise trade, Small and Medium scale Enterprises(SMEs) and Agriculture(Alfred & Simeon, April, 2020).From the trend analysis, they determined that irrespective of plausible policy responsible, there would still be a negative impact on all sectors in the study, thus proposing more long term innovative policy measures to ensure a fortified economy in the face of the current and similar future crises. They concluded that African economies needed to build resilience and a robust economy.

The world economic forum (WEF) recommended reskilling of workers as a measure against unemployment and uncertainty in the labor industry as well as resilience creation in the economy (World Economic Forum, 2020).

UNECA states that although COVID-19 wave seems to be slowing down in Rwanda and business is active again, the shock on employment is still felt especially in the service industry and business associated with external trade. The main features in the COVID-19 pandemic induced shocks are mainly salary reduction, salary suspension, job loss, and creation of new jobs. The impact and response measures however differ from country to country and business to business (UNECA, 2020). Furthermore, the proponents analyze the impact of dispersed and aggregated shocks on job creation and destruction.

ILO estimated millions of job loss due to COVID-19 pandemic in the informal sector whereas in the first month of the outbreak, 60percent of the income of the informal workers was lost worldwide (ILO, 2020). Africa alone lost 81percent, the Americas declined by 21.5percent and 70 percent in Europe and central Asia.

Paweenawat (2021) conducted a study on the impact of COVID-19 pandemic on the labor market in Thailand. Results showed that the impact of the pandemic is unequal across demographic groups. The author concluded that it may continue to worsen the pre-existing inequality in the Thai labor market if the government does nothing.

OECD answered a question on what have platforms done to protect workers during the COVID-19 crisis? By showing two major problems posed by COVID-19 such as exposure to the virus and income loss. The study focused on platform companies in order the risk of potential income loss and the risk of exposure to the virus while at work. It was noticed from the findings that the platform companies took measures to promote social distancing and/or the safe provision of services and this was reported by more than a half of the companies. In regards to workers working both on location as well as online, 35 percent of respondents reported that their platforms had taken measures to assist them during the pandemic whereby 44 percent of the workers confirmed that they were satisfied with the measures taken (OECD, 2020).

The Asia Foundation conducted a rapid assessment on the impact of the COVID-19 pandemic on employment in Middle-order cities of Nepal (The Asia Foundation, 2021). The findings from the assessment survey reported that job losses looked widespread and, in some sectors, deep whereby only 26 percent of the workers were getting fully paid, with the rest put under partial payment or no-payment jobs. The findings also revealed that 41 percent of women and 28 percent of men had lost their jobs. The sector of construction was the most affected because the lockdowns occurred at the peak of the construction period of March. Karmen revealed the challenges that the labor market faced because of the COVID-19 pandemic in Sub-Saharan Africa (Karmen, 2020). The study reported that most of the informal workers were vulnerable to the shock caused by this pandemic compared to those from formal sector workers as they were not covered by unemployment insurance which indicates that the inability results in immediate loss of income. Regarding formal workers, lockdowns put many of them at risk of unemployment, lost work hours and reduced earnings.

A study on the short-term impacts of the COVID-19 pandemic on the Brazilian labor market using the data from the national household surveys PNAD-Continua and PNAD COVID (Diala, Valentina, Frederik, & Hoon, 2021). They strongly confirmed that the employment sector was heavily affected by the immediate shocks of the pandemic and the affected sectors were construction, domestic services, and hospitality. Majority of workers from these sectors lost their jobs and working hours were declined. To compensate for income loss due to jobs losses for the most vulnerable workers, the government of Brazil had established the temporary emergency aid transfer program. A study on the COVID-19 impact on the labor market in Brazil by Sanyal and CEIC Research Economist confirmed that unemployment rate in Brazil increased to 14.4 percent in Q3 2020 compared to 11.8 percent in Q3 2019 and it was the highest unemployment rate registered by IBGE since it started reporting the indicator in 2012 (Sanyal & Economist, 2020). Yannick studied the adverse impacts of the COVID-19 pandemic on the Cameroonian labor market (Yannick, 2021). Thus, to collect data, a rapid survey was conducted by the National Institute of Statistics on a sample of 1,310 respondents. The findings revealed that many workers suffered job loss (7.47 percent) due to the closure of either partial or total activities. After estimating the logistic regression model, the log of odds shows that workers in private firms are more affected than their peers in public firms and the middle aged are the most affected group. Carmen et al. studied the impact of the COVID-19 pandemic on the labor market of Romania (Carmen, Georgiana, Sorin, Florentina, Corina, & Ionut, 2021). Results showed that the pandemic affected the Romanian workforce because it induced an increase in the number of unemployed people. ILO investigated the impact of the COVID-19 pandemic on the labor market in the occupied Palestinian territory (ILO, 2020). It concluded that the most affected sectors were mining and manufacturing, transportation and storage, hotels, and restaurants while communication, education and health services did not experience changes in employment. Despite the pandemic, the impact in the agriculture sector was positive which was not a surprise because the agricultural activities continued to function. It has been confirmed that more people shifted from other sectors to agriculture which increased the employment rate in this sector because of the pandemic. Daniel and Alexandre assessed the labor market responses to the COVID-19 crisis in the United States and Europe (Danie & Alexandre, 2021). They reported that labor markets have reacted very differently to the crisis across countries. In the US, the impact on unemployment rates increases across all states where they increased in March and April, 2020 and recovered steadily later. Contrary to Europe, unemployment increased far less. Econometric analysis was applied to measure the impact of the lockdowns initiated by the Governments to contain the spread of the virus using data from US states and EU member states. In the case of the US, results reveal that unemployment appears to have been driven mostly by the aggregate shock from the pandemic between March and November, 2020 while in EU unemployment shows little change.

It was noticed that though COVID-19 mainly created negative impacts on the global economy, there are some studies which confirmed that there has been creation of new jobs as a result of COVID-19 pandemic especially those related to online services. Online teachers were hired by different NGOs, compliance online monitoring, home delivery shopping, health workers, and sanitation industries among others (CNBC, 2020).

It is indicated that the global unemployment is estimated to stay above pre-COVID-19 levels until at least 2023 (ILO, 2022).

For instance, it is expected that 207 million people shall remain unemployed in 2022 compared to 186 in 2019. It has also found that in 2022, the global employment participation rate is expected to remain 1.2 percentage points below that of 2019. ILO reported that this change in unemployment was due to the fact that many people left the labor force. Dynan and Powell III (2022) reported that labor demand has continued to be very strong compared to labor supply whereas about 1.9 job openings are available for every unemployed person in the USA. Authors also mentioned that the labor force participation has improved more slowly than expected given the power of labor demand.

Gonzales (2022) emphasized on the men and women Jobs before and after the COVID -19 pandemic.

The author revealed that from February 2020 to January 2022 man workers had regained all the lost jobs due to the covid-19 pandemic while women gained 188,000 jobs in January and remained with more than 1.8 million jobs lost since February 2020 to fully regain all the jobs they lost. He confirmed that it would take women approximately 10 months to regain them.

Research Gap

The empirical works reviewed the effects of COVID-19 pandemic in general with little information on the effects of COVID-19 on employment particularly in Rwanda. Research has determined that the impact of the pandemic differed from country to country (Alfred & Simeon, 2020). This justifies the reason to pay specific attention to the effects of COVID-19 on the labor force status in Rwanda as a baseline for knowledge-based intervention building on informed opinion. After understanding the existing relationship between employment status and the independent variables under consideration researchers therefore proposed strategies that the GoR will adopt to mitigate the caused shocks of COVID-19 pandemic to the labor force sector in the short and long run periods.

MATERIALS AND METHODS

Data Description

The NISR performs the labor force survey four times in a year with aims of providing Quarterly (Q1, Q2, Q3, and Q4) data on the labor force, employment and unemployment. For instance, LF variable for February, May, August and November, 2019 were extracted from the NISR website under link http://statistics.gov.rw/datasource/labour-force-survey-2019 while for February, May, August and November, 2020 were obtained from http://statistics.gov.rw/datasource/labour-force-survey-2020 and http://statistics.gov.rw/statistical-publications/subject/gdp-quarterly-publications. Thus, data are shown in (Table 1) for readers' information.

Sampling Procedures and Sample Size Determination

This study used a target population of 6237 from which a sample has been drawn using of a well-known Slovin's formula for sample size computation as follows:

$$n = \frac{6237}{1 + 6237(0.05)^2} \approx 376$$

With n being the sample size to be selected in the target population of Rusizi district, one of the main cities of Rwanda located at one of the borders of Rwanda and the margin error used here was 5% level of significance. Thus, a simple random sampling method was employed to select the individuals to be included in the sample. After having this sample size, primary data were collected using questionnaire and interview guide and binary logistic regression model was used to model the response variable under study using the independent variables.

Model Specification

This paper develops and tests empirically a type of a regression model of the labor force of binary logistic regression on which strategies to restore the affected labor force was built. Specifically, this model provides detailed information on the intercept and enables also in determining the relationship between employment and its independent variables in order to ascertain the type of relationship between two variables.

For a response variable Y with two measurement levels (dichotomous) and explanatory variable X, let: $\delta(x) = p(X = x) = 1 - p(X = x)$, the logistic regression model has linear form for logit of this probability

$$Logit[\delta(x)] = loglog\left(\frac{\pi(x)}{1-\pi(x)}\right) = \alpha_0 + \alpha_1 x,$$

where the $odds = \dfrac{\delta(x)}{1-\delta(x)}$.

The $odds = e^{(\alpha_0 + \alpha_1 x)}$, and the logarithm of the odds is called logit, so:

$$Logit[\delta(x)] = loglog\left(\frac{\delta(x)}{1-\delta(x)}\right) = loglog[exp(\alpha_0 + \alpha_1 x)] = \alpha_0 + \alpha_1 x.$$

The logit has a linear approximation relationship, and logit = logarithm of the odds.

Constructing econometric model requires information on the dependent and independent variables therefore for the purpose of this chapter employment status of the respondents is considered as dependent variable while age, working experience, educational level, wages working hours, aggregate demand, aggregate supply, income, working remotely, uncertainty about the end of the pandemic, inability to cope with new skills of working remotely, employment policies changes, type of institutions were considered as independent. Thus, based on the above information our econometric model to be estimated is:

$$Logit[p(Y=1)] = \alpha_0 + \alpha_1 x_1 + \alpha_2 x_2 + \alpha_3 x_3 + \ldots + \alpha_k x_k \quad (1)$$

Where:

Y denotes the dependent variable under study having two levels "yes" and "no "expressing whether the COVID-19 pandemic affects the status of the employment and this variable being measured in terms of thirteen independent variables such as age, educational level, working experience, wages, working hours, aggregate, demand, aggregate supply, income working remotely, uncertainty about the end of the pandemic, inability to cope with new skills of working remotely, employment policies changes and type of institutions. In this analogy the independent variables with subscripts described in the model illustrated in equation (1) above, $i = 1, 2, \ldots, 13$. Then α_i for $i = 1, 2, \ldots, 13$ denotes the slope of ith independent variable which is the rate of change in one unit of the dependent variable controlling the other $(k-1)$ remaining independent variables.

ANALYTICAL FRAMEWORK

Trend Analysis of the Macroeconomic Variables

It is the aspect of technical analysis that tries to forecast the future movement of the variables based on past data (Emmanuel, 2018). It is also considered as the technique for extracting a pattern of behavior in a specific time series. When it comes to studying short-term trends (based on monthly or quarterly data) it is crucial to note that the labor market is affected by seasonal factors such as climatic changes to capture variations in the labor market beyond seasonal patterns, it is evident to assess the variations not due to seasonal factors but comparing data for labor force that comprises employed and unemployed. Furthermore, to analyze the trend of the labor force, we used a graphical method of data representation through which reasons behind changes were discussed.

We estimate an econometric model of the labor force that is expected to offer explanations based on its determinants. In the first step, we describe the data and then the statistical methodology to be followed in data analysis.

Trend analysis was used to investigate the tendency of the macroeconomic variables under consideration before and during the COVID-19 pandemic. Variables like GDP growth rates, employment and unemployment were investigated. This comparison served to ensure whether these variables followed a constant, positive, and negative trend before and during the pandemic. The secondary data obtained from the mentioned links of the National Institute of Statistics of Rwanda (NISR) were employed.

Inferential Statistics

It was used to ascertain the relationship between the labor force and its determinants. After confirming the existence of the relationship authors determined the type of the relationship based on which the strategies to restore the affected labor force were developed. Thus, the binary logistic regression model was estimated to investigate the relationship between dependent variable and independent variables.

RESULTS AND DISCUSSION

Trend Analysis of the Macroeconomic Variables

The trend shows quarterly data of GDP growth rates from 2016 to 2020 (Figure 1) as through data, authors confirmed that from the period under consideration, GDP growth rates varied because of various socio-economic changes including changes in macroeconomic and demographic variables. For instance, in 2017, Q1 the rate as 0.3 percent immensely declined due to the fact that activities in the industry sector decreased by 1 percent and some of activities in the service sector include wholesale and retail which decreased by 12 percent. This led to low GDP growth rate in quarter one of 2017. During the period of COVID-19 specifically in the second quarter of 2020 the GDP growth rate heavily declined and became negative i.e. -12 percent. This implies that COVID-19 has negatively affected the economic activities (businesses and investments) because during the outbreak there was disruptions of activities that contributing to the economic growth through paying government taxes such as hotels and restaurants, banks and cooperatives, schools and universities, transport (road and air), closure of touristic sites, closure of churches, closure of sports and entertainment activities, closure of construction activities (houses, roads and others), closure of borders, closure of large and small industries, etc. It worsened during the total lockdown *(Guma Murugo Initiative)* which took 2 months. The GDP growth rate is expected to increase in quarter three because the lockdown measures were softened though some staff are still working from homes and the opening of some universities and others are still waiting to be opened after complying with the ministry of health measures that help to curb the spread of COVID-19.

Briefly, we can confirm that covid-19 has caused the GDP growth rate to decline and become negative since from 2016 to the first quarter of 2020 Rwanda had not experienced such a trend in her history. Thus, Rwandan policy makers are advised to create a conducive environment and or good working environment to enable people to smoothly do their businesses to restore the affected sub sectors that usually contribute to economic growth of Rwanda. For instance, GOR is advised to make sure that those mainly affected businesses return to their normal pace to ensure increment of GDP growth rate in the post COVID-19 period in Rwanda. Evidence shows that the private sector was hardly hit by the pandemic due to the closure of activities whereby customers were no longer interested in purchasing goods and services except consumption goods (foods) as they were uncertain about the situation. Even though the GoR has reduced the measures severity there are still people who think that the pandemic will be aggravated and therefore not ready to invest their money as planned. For instance, they prefer saving rather than investment. As a result, this will affect the country's economy because businesses were not functioning as they used to be.

Trends indicate that both employment to population ratio and unemployment rates (Figure 2) varied frequently in the period before the COVID-19 though the unemployment rate immensely increased from quarter 1 to quarter 2 of 2020 by 13.1 percent to 22.1 percent respectively. This is explained by the fact that most of the people lost their jobs because of the pandemic. Hence, it can be concluded that during the period of the pandemic unemployment rate increased and even in the quarter 3 of 2020 the rate of unemployment is still high though it slightly declined as compared to quarter 2. Regarding the employment to population ratio, it is observed from the data that in quarter 2 of 2020 the rate of employment to population ratio declined as compared to the previous quarter 1 of the same year from 48.3 percent to 43 percent respectively.

It provides quarterly comparisons (Figure 3) of the variables viz employment to population ratio, unemployment rates and GDP growth rates and data show that employment to population ratio was high in the first quarter of 2020 and low in the second quarter of 2020. This low rate of employment to population ratio can be attributed to the fact that people lost their jobs permanently while others got suspended from their contracts in the advent of financial issues to their institutions. This can also be linked to the measures taken by the GoR to curb the spreading of COVID-19 infection rate which has brought the employment rate to decline from 48.3 percent to 43 percent for quarter 1 to quarter 2 of 2020 respectively. Regarding the trend of unemployment rate, it is observed that from the first quarter of 2020 to the second quarter the rate of unemployment highly increased i.e., from 13.1 to 22.1 percent which means an increase of 8 percent. This coincidence might be associated with the GoR interventions specifically in the labor markets towards the curbing of the spread of the Corona virus such reducing the number of employees at work in order to respect social distancing among employees, many private companies (transport, tourism, construction and real estate, hotels and restaurants), universities, schools suspended their staff contracts. Consequently, the labor force sector was heavily affected by the pandemic due to the loss of jobs by many employees. In the second quarter of 2020, the estimated GDP growth rate in 2020 was negative at -12.4 percent which was very lower compared to the previous quarter of the same year. This is explained by the ongoing economic disturbances caused by the COVID-19 outbreak.

Determinants of the Labor Force Sub-Sector in Rwanda

Using the binary logistic regression model, researchers estimated the effects of COVID-19 pandemic by measuring the employment status using the independent variables illustrated in section of model specification and the extracted output from SPSS version 21 software revealed sufficient evidence of the independent variables on the dependent variable.

From the Table 2 representing the variables in the model, the researchers found that on the total of thirteen independent variables namely Age coded as "Age", working experience coded as "Work.Exp", inability to cope with new skills of working remotely coded as "inability", Uncertainty about the end of the pandemic coded as "uncertai", wages coded as "Wages", working hours coded as "Whours", aggregate demand coded as "AggDe", employment policies changes coded as "EMPolicy", aggregate supply coded as "AggSup", income coded as "Icome", type of the working institution coded as "Type. Ins", education coded as "Education", and household size coded as "HHSize" respectively in the model, only three among these explanatory variables are statistically significant to the dependent variable which are "Working experience", "Working hours", and "type of the institution through which the people under study were working for." Such decision was made in accordance of comparing the p-values (sig. values) and the cutoff (marginal error) which is 5%. This indication is revealed by noticing that the corresponding p-values of these three independent variables Working experience", "Working hours", and "type of the institution through which the people under study were working for, are all less than 5%.

Strategies for Restoring the Affected Labor Force Sub-Sector in the Post-COVID-19 Period

After examining changes in trends for GDP growth, employment and unemployment rates, effects of COVID-19 pandemic on employment were investigated. Through modelling the labor force, strategies to restore the affected labor force sector in Rwanda were developed and listed below.

1. Creating a conducive environment for business activities to retake place once again such as infrastructure readiness in order to limit the spreading of COVID-19, increase buses to ease transport in the city of Kigali because when people easily move businesses activities are restored and employment opportunities are created.
2. The National Bank of Rwanda (NBR) should advocate for facilitating people to get bank loans at lower interest rates to strengthen their affected business. The time of reimbursement should be long.
3. The GoR should continue to focus on the creation of new job opportunities as indicated in the Rwandan Employment Policy that aims to decline the unemployment rate among youth and fresh graduates.
4. Establishing anti unemployment clubs in Rwanda.
5. Reinforcing jobs creation related projects to strengthen the most affected labor force areas.
6. GoR should encourage reskilling programs to reinforce adaptability and diversity among citizens because COVID-19 has dictated creation of new jobs (mainly those done through online like e-commerce, virtual meetings, online education, etc.) and approaches to working methods.
7. Private and public institutions should make sure that their employees are enough equipped with needed computer skills to perform remotely office work whenever needed.
8. GoR needs to promote a piece rate system to ensure those online workers' daily contribution amounts to value for money. It will also create working opportunities and facilitate firms to work longer hours through shifts which may trickle down to faster industrial growth through attracting investors.
9. GoR and all employers should up-skill their employees to prevent job loss and low productivity while maintaining organizational competitiveness and employee relevancy in the labor market.
10. For the government to create more jobs, there is a need to accelerate direct and indirect investment. To get funds for this, GoR should introduce a reimbursable taxation system where tax on income is charged and reimbursed after three months. This will promote savings for investment on both sides of the employee and GoR, while enhancing the population's purchasing power to attract investment, which in turn will create more jobs.
11. GoR should levy a non-refundable income tax on the working population to take care of the unemployed population. The levied tax should be invested in job creation acceleration activities to absorb more jobseekers.
12. GoR should enhance safety net strategy by introducing a savings strategy contributed by both employees and employers to cater for unemployment benefits. This will not only avail money to the Government for investment but also increase retirement packages.

CONCLUSION

This study focuses on developing strategies to restore the affected labor force in the post COVID-19 period in Rwanda. Results of the study confirm that in the second quarter of 2020, GDP growth rate was negative and unemployment rate increased. The fact was that many people lost their jobs (contract suspension) while others were sent home and received a small portion of their salaries. Furthermore, results of the binary logistic regression model revealed that the main variables that affected the employment status during the COVID-19 pandemic were "working experience", "working hours", and "type of the institution through which the people under study were working for while other remaining ten explanatory variables such Age, Educational level, Wages, Aggregate demand, Aggregate supply, Income, Working remotely, Uncertainty about the end of the pandemic, Inability to cope with new skills of working remotely and Employment policies changes were found to be statistically insignificant to the change of the employment status.

Based on the findings of the study, authors developed strategies to restore the affected labor force sector in the post COVID-19 period in Rwanda which are shown in the previous section. Therefore, authors recommend establishing the proposed strategies to restore the affected labor force sector in the post COVID-19 pandemic period in Rwanda.

ACKNOWLEDGMENT

Authors acknowledge the National Institute of Statistics of Rwanda for availing data at their disposal.

REFERENCES

Alfred, R. B., & Simeon, S. (2020, April 13). *Google scholar*. Retrieved November 10, 2020, from Google scholar: https://ssrn.com/abstract=3586622

Andrew, M., & Anthony, M. (2020). *The impact of the COVID-19 crisison trade: Recent evidence from EastAfrica;* https://www.brookings.edu/wp-content/uploads/2020/07/EAC_COVID_Mold_Mveyange.pdf

Angelucci, M., Kapteyn, A., Angrissani, M., & Schaner, G. (2020). *Remote Work and the Heterogeneous Impact of COVID-19 on Employment and Health.* NBER Working Paper Series-27749. Available from https://ideas.repec.org/p/nbr/nberwo/27749.html

Battaile, W. F., Leonardo, H., & Vivian, N. (2015). *Debt Sustainability in Sub-Saharan Africa: Unraveling Country-Specific Risk. World Bank.* doi:10.1596/1813-9450-7523

Ben, D. (2019, December 23). *Who invaded Rwanda from the North starting the Rwandan civil war?* Retrieved November 23, 2020, from Mvorganizing.org: https://www.mvorganizing.org/who-invaded-rwanda-from-the-north-starting-the-rwandan-civil-war/

Carmen, V. R., Georgiana, R. L., Sorin, B., Florentina, C., Corina, I., & Ionut, L. P. (2021). Impact of the COVID-19 Pandemic on the Romanian LaborMArket. *Sustainability*, 1–23.

Charlene, M., & Sabrina, W. (2020, July). *Repec*. Retrieved November 29, 2020, from Repec Website: https://ideas.repec.org/p/iza/izadps/dp13443.html

CNBC. (2020, May 31). *CNBC*. Retrieved November 07, 2020, from CNBC: https://www.cnbc.com/2020/05/31/new-jobs-created-as-a-result-of-the-coronavirus-pandemic.html

Dale, T., & Christopher, A. (1994). Review of Economic Studies: Job Creation and Job Destruction in the Theory of Unemployment. Academic Press.

Danie, G., & Alexandre, O. (2021, April 1). *Labour market responses to the Covid-19 crisis in the United States and Europe*. Retrieved May 21, 2021, from https://www.ceps.eu/: https://www.ceps.eu/wp-content/uploads/2021/04/WD2021-01_Labour-market-responses-to-Covid.pdf

Deloitte. (2020). *Economic impact of the COVID-19 pandemic on East African Economies*. Nairobi: Deloitte Insights.

Diala, A. M., Valentina, F., Frederik, G. T., & Hoon, L. (2021, March 5). *The Short-Term Impact of COVID-19 on Labor Markets, Poverty and Inequality in Brazil*. Retrieved April 22, 2021, from IMF elibrary: https://www.elibrary.imf.org/view/journals/001/2021/066/article-A001-en.xml

Dynan, K., & Powell, W., III. (2022, April 1). *US employment and wages are rising briskly amid strong labor demand*. Peterson Institute for International Economics. Retrieved May 21, 2022, from https://www.piie.com/blogs/realtime-economic-issues-watch/us-employment-and-wages-are-rising-briskly-amid-strong-labor

Economic Policy Institute. (2020, March). *Google scholar*. Retrieved January 23, 2021, from www.google.com: https://www.epi.org/newsroom/useful_definitions/

Ellen, J. S., David, C., & Donald, K. (2020, June 16). *UNDP*. Retrieved November 10, 2020, from UNDP Website: http://www.UNDP-rba-COVID-assessment-Sierraleone.pdf

Emmanuel. (2018, April 10). *Academia.edu*. Retrieved October 09, 2020, from Academia.edu: https://www.academia.edu/35421416

EPRN. (2018). *Policy Dialogue: NST 1- Creating 1,500,000 Decent and Productive Jobs: challenges and policy actions*. EPRN.

Falk, G. (2020, November 9). *Congressional Research Service*. Retrieved March 20, 2021, from crsreports.congress.gov: https://crsreports.congress.gov/product/pdf/IN/IN11457

Fode, N. (2020, June). The Socio-Economic Impact of COVID-19 in Rwanda. *COVID-19 in Rwanda*.

Gonzales, M. (2022, February 17). *Nearly 2 Million Fewer Women in the Labor Force*. SHRM. Retrieved May 21, 2022, from https://www.shrm.org/resourcesandtools/hr-topics/behavioral-competencies/global-and-cultural-effectiveness/pages/over-1-million-fewer-women-in-labor-force.aspx

Google Scholar. (2020, April 1). Retrieved June 2020, 2020, from CMI Website: https://www.managers.org.uk/

Google Scholar. (n.d.). Retrieved October 20, 2020, from Google scholar: https://en.wikipedia.org

Ibrahim, I. B. (2020). *Research gate*. Retrieved November 10, 2020, from Research gate: https://www.researchgate.net/publication/344581589

ILO. (2020a, April). *ILO Monitor: COVID-19 and the World of Work*. ILO.

ILO. (2020b). *Impact of the COVID-19 Pandemic onthe Labour Market in the Occupied Palestinian Territory*. International Labour Organization.

ILO. (2022, January 17). *ILO downgrades labor market recovery forecast for 2022*. ILO. Retrieved May 15, 2022, from https://www.ilo.org/global/about-the-ilo/newsroom/news/WCMS_834117/lang--en/index.htm

ILO. (2020c). *COVID-19 and the world of work. Second edition: Updated estimates and analysis*. https://www.ilo.org/wcmsp5/groups/public/---dgreports/---dcomm/documents/briefingnote/wcms_740877.pdf

Karmen, N. (2020, June 10). *Africa Portal*. Retrieved July 09, 2020, from https://www.africaportal.org/features/labour-market-challenges-covid-19-pandemic-sub-saharan-africa/

Kurmann, A., Lalé, E., & Ta, L. (2020). *The impact of COVID-19 on U.S. Employment and Hours: Real-Time Estimates with Homebase Data*. Available from https://www.lebow.drexel.edu/sites/default/files/1588687497-hbdraft0504.pdf

Lauterbach, W. (1987). Psychological Impacts of Unemployment: Theory, Research Methodology, Assessment and Help. *Health Systems Research*, 23.

Medscape. (2021, June 25). *What is COVID-19?* Retrieved June 12, 2021, from Medscape Website: https://www.medscape.com/answers/2500114-197401/what-is-covid-19

Mwai, C. (2020). *COVID-19: How recovery funding will be disbursed*. Available from https://www.newtimes.co.rw/news/covid-19-recovery-funding-disbursed

National Planning Commission, University of Namibia. (2020). *Estimating the Economic Impact of COVID-19: A case study of Namibia*. Windhoek: University of Namibia.

NSIR. (2020). *Labor Force Survey Trends-February 2020(Q1)*. https://www.statistics.gov.rw/publication/labour-force-survey-trends-february-2020q1

OECD. (2020, September). *OECD Policy Responses to Coronavirus (COVID-19)*. Retrieved October 15, 2020, from https://www.oecd.org/coronavirus/policy-responses/what-have-platforms-done-to-protect-workers-during-the-coronavirus-covid-19-crisis-9d1c7aa2/#section-d1e187

Paweenawat, S. W. (2021). *The Impact of COVID-19 on the labour markets in Thailand*. ERIA Discussion Paper Series, No.378. Bangkok: University of the Thai Chamber of Commerce, Thailand.

Ramdoo, I. (2020, June). *IGF*. Retrieved September 15, 2020, from https://www.igfmining.org/: https://www.iisd.org/system/files/publications/covid-19-employment-mining-key-points-en.pdf

Report, S. A. (2020). *Tourism sector recovery plan COVID-19 Response*. https://www.tralac.org/documents/resources/covid-19/countries/3992-south-africa-tourism-sector-recovery-plan-covid-19-response-august-2020-request-for-comments/file.html

Sanyal, R., & Economist, C. R. (2020, July). *COVID-19 Impact: Brazil's Labor Market Puzzle.* Retrieved September 20, 2020, from https://info.ceicdata.com/covid-19-brazils-labour-market-puzzle: https://info.ceicdata.com/covid-19-brazils-labour-market-puzzle

Sogani, A. (2020, July). *The Great Lockdown vs The Great Depression and the 2008 Global Financial Crisis.* Retrieved September 11, 2021, from E-internationals Relations: https://www.e-ir.info/2020/07/02/the-great-lockdown-vs-the-great-depression-and-the-2008-global-financial-crisis/

Sue Enfield Institute of Development Studies. (2021, February). *Covid-19 impact on employment and skills for the labor market.* Retrieved March 11, 2021, from google.com: https://opendocs.ids.ac.uk/

The Asia Foundation. (2021). *A rapid assessment on the impact of the COVID-19 pandemic on employment in Middle-order cities of Nepal.* The Asian Foundation.

UNECA. (2020, April 9). *Tralac.* Retrieved October 15, 2020, from Tralac: https://www.tralac.org/docments/resources/COVID-19/3293-COVID-19-protecting-african-lives-andeconomies-uneca-april-2020/file.html

WB. (2015). *An analysis of issues shaping Africa's economic future.* https://www.worldbank.org/content/dam/Worldbank/document/Africa/Report/Africas-Pulse-brochure_Vol12.pdf

WEF. (2020). *An overwhelming majority of people want real change after COVID-19.* Available from https://www.weforum.org/agenda/2020/09/sustainable-equitable-change-post-coronavirus-survey?utm_source=facebook&utm_medium=social_scheduler&utm_term=COVID-19&u

World Economic Forum. (2020, October). https://www.weforum.org/agenda/2020/10/

Yannick, F. D. (2021). The adverse impact of the Covid-19 pandemic on the labor market in Cameroon. *African Development Review*, 31–44. PMID:33821111

Zahid, H. (2020). *What about public sector wage bill cuts to finance coronavirus response?* https://blogs.worldbank.org/governance/should-public-sector-wages-be-cut-finance-coronavirus-response

APPENDIX

Table 1. Quarterly data on GDP growth rates, employment to population ratio, and unemployment rate

Period	Years	Quarter	GDP Growth Rates (%)	Employment to Population Ratio (%)	Unemployment Rate (%)
Before COVID-19	2016	Q1	10.7	42.8	13.2
		Q3	3.2	41.1	18.8
	2017	Q1	0.3	45	16.7
		Q3	6.7	43.4	17.8
	2018	Q1	9.8	44.8	16
		Q3	7.1	47.3	14.3
	2019	Q1	6.1	44.9	14.5
		Q2	12.3	45.9	14.5
		Q3	10.9	43.9	16
		Q4	8.4	46.5	15.4
	2020	Q1	3.6	48.3	13.1
During COVID-19	2020	Q2	-12.4	43	22.1

Source: NISR (2020)

Table 2. Determinants of employment during COVID-19 pandemic

Variables	B	S.E.	Wald	df	Sig.	Exp(B)
Agc	-11.132	184.905	0.004	1	0.952	0
Work.Exp	20.989	2497.748	0.193	1	0.004	1304314253
Inability(1)	-53.3	27478.82	11.567	1	0.998	1.4051E+23
uncertai(1)	-8.657	40327.49	6.168	1	1	0
Wages(1)	-41.162	30182.73	.	1	0.999	7.52672E+17
Whours(1)	13.038	28551.11	3.781	1	0.003	459399.569
AggDe(1)	-83.26	8661.887	2.27	1	0.992	0
EMPolicy	-89.6		0.264	2	1	
EMPolicy(1)	-301.957	26891.04	0.271	1	0.991	0
EMPolicy(2)	375.843	29154.2	0.687	1	0.99	1.68E+163
AggSup(1)	-226.543	6255.592	2.429	1	0.971	0
Icome(1)	21.674	9534.854	0.193	1	0.998	2586395286
Type.Ins				3	1	
Type.Ins(1)	409.871	74010.59	0.338	1	0.001	1.01E+178
Type.Ins(2)	79.767	102713.7	0.002	1	0.005	.1.08 E+178
Type.Ins(3)	435.43	73381.92	0	1	0.008	1.27E+189
Education			0.006	2	1	
Education(1)	-58.693	32890.8	.	1	0.999	0
Education(2)	99.557	54382.72	4.136	1	0.999	1.73E+43
HHSize			0.001	2	1	
HHSize(2)	444.769	92324.75	.	1	0.996	1.45E+193
HHSize(4)	-45.992	79369.26	1.393	1	1	0
Constant	161.094	108003	0	1	0.999	9.16E+69

Source: SPSS Output

Figure 1. Trend of GDP growth rates before and during COVID-19 pandemic
Source: Own constructed

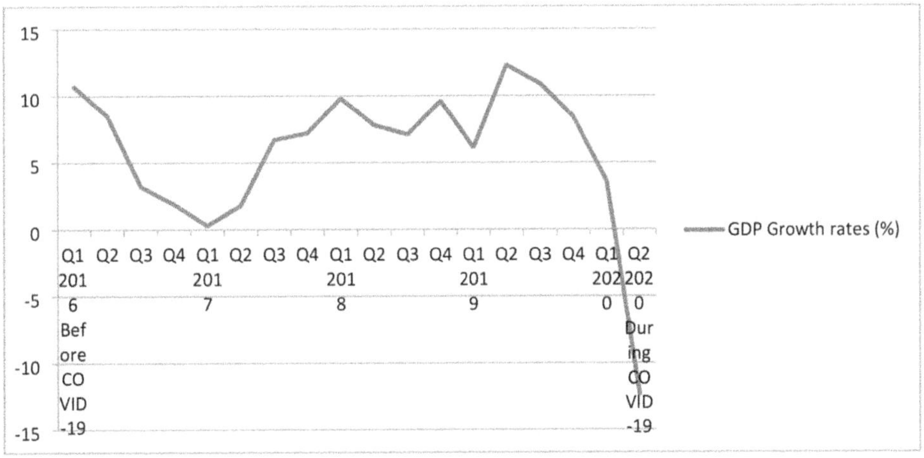

Figure 2. Trends of employment to population ratio and unemployment rates before and during COVID-19 pandemic
Source: Own constructed

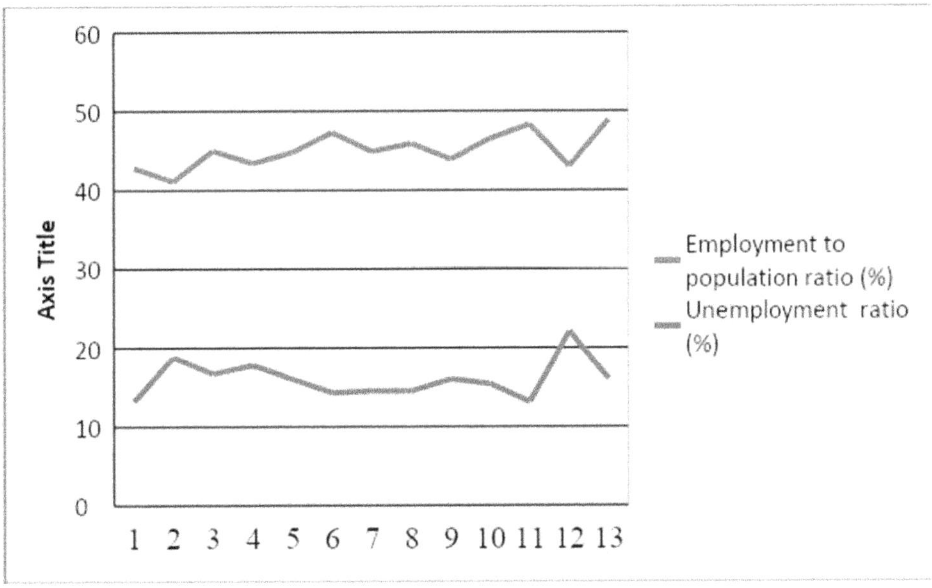

Figure 3. Trends of GDP growth rates, employment to population ratio, and unemployment rates before and during COVID-19 pandemic
Source: Own constructed

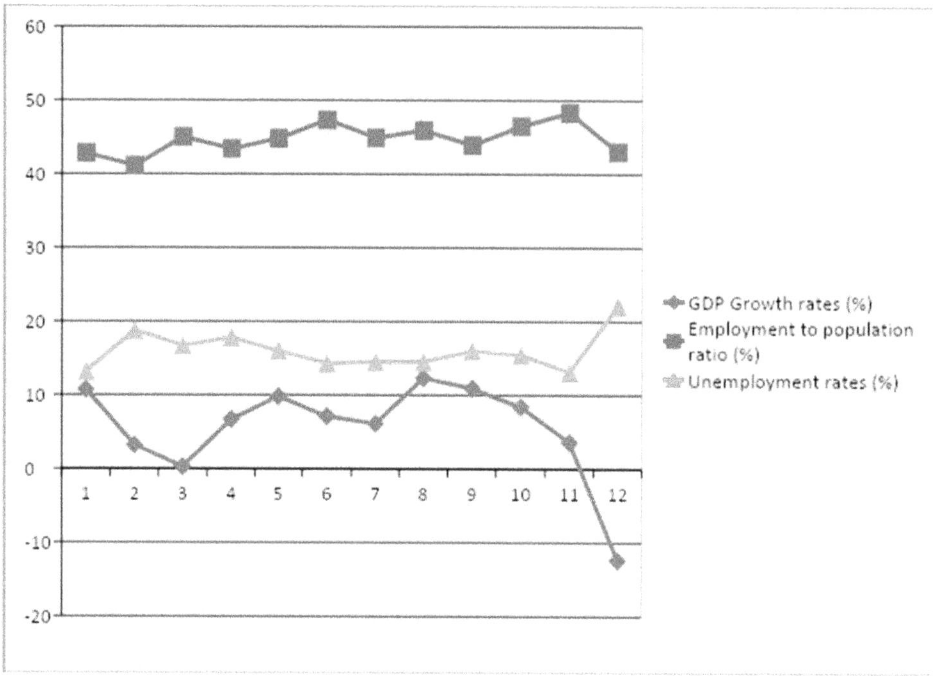

Chapter 9
Digital Education During COVID-19 in Odisha: Challenges and Prospects

Minati Sahoo
https://orcid.org/0000-0002-6061-8035
Central University of Odisha, India

Karishma Rana
https://orcid.org/0000-0001-8699-6301
Central University of Odisha, India

ABSTRACT

One of the worsts hit by the COVID-19 pandemic has been the education sector, which has led to the closure of all educational institutions. Hence, an effort has been made in this study to examine various issues and challenges of digital education in Odisha. The study found that most of the educational institutions in Odisha have gone for online teaching. Additionally, to promote e-learning, various digital platforms have been provided by the state and central governments. But digital education in Odisha is facing many challenges like uneven access of internet and digital gadgets, low tele density, lack of support structures, low computer literacy, and less competency. Additionally, power cut, financial constraints, lack of parent's involvement in the process are some of the issues that are adding woes to the effectiveness of digital education in teaching and learning process. Hence, there is need to evolve a judicious mix of normal and digital education with revised curricular post-COVID-19 to provide more learning opportunities for the all-around development of the students.

INTRODUCTION

The newly detected corona virus pandemic has become a global health crisis and is moving like a wave to every continent except Antarctica. It was declared as a pandemic by the World Health Organization on 11th March 2020 to take immediate actions to detect, treat and reduce transmission to save people's lives.

DOI: 10.4018/978-1-7998-6896-5.ch009

More than 10,474,029 cases of Covid-19 have been found over 215 countries and territories, resulting in around 5,09,000 deaths and over 57,16,000 recoveries as on June 2020. In 2021 we are living with the second wave of the corona pandemic with the fear of third wave in the coming future. More than 203,944,144cases of Covid-19 have been found over 215 countries and territories, resulting in around 4,312,902 deaths and a total of 4,394,596,684 vaccine doses have been administered as August 2021. But Covid-19 is not merely a health crisis with the potential to create devastating social, economic and political crises in both developed and developing countries (Nicola et al., 2020). The United Nation's framework for immediate socio-economic crisis said that "The Covid-19 pandemic is far more than a health crisis affecting societies and economies at their core. It will most likely to increase unemployment, poverty and inequalities at a global scale making achievement of Sustainable Development Goals even more urgent" (UN Sustainable Development Group, 2020, pg. 03). The widespread transmission of the covid-19 pandemic put challenges for the economic development of the almost all economies of the world but the worst hit in terms of achieving the sustainable development goals specifically for developing countries. One of the major challenges for achieving SDGs are poverty and hunger because this pandemic situation first time rise the extreme poverty level in 2020 where additional around 124 million people were pushed back to poverty (United Nations Sustainable Development Goal Report, 2021). Along with poverty covid-19 pandemic also adversely affected the progress in health and reduced the life expectancy. Around 90% of the nations are still facing the disruption in one or more essential health services. This emergency situations and urgent needs of medical services creates shortage in the supply of doctors, nurses and other health workers. Universal access to quality education is one of the major key for ensuring human development, eradication of poverty and increasing standard of living. According to United Nations Sustainable Development Goal Report, 2021 around 260 million are still out of school globally in 2018 and covid -19 pandemic adds fuel to the fire again. In 2020, due to severe outbreak of the virus there was temporary school closure in almost all countries which impacted around 91% of the students worldwide. Based on UN report, nearly 369 million children who rely on school meals faced problem for searching other sources of daily nutrition requirements.

Every country are trying to slow down the transmission of the virus by testing and treating infected people, limiting travel and social distancing by cancelling mass gathering sports and social events and educational institutions. On March 18, 2020, the UNESCO estimated that 107 countries had implemented national school closures affecting 862 million children and young people, roughly half the global student population related to Covid-19 pandemic (Viner et al., 2020). Government of India announced 21 days lockdown from 25 March followed by Janata curfew to fight against Covid-19. The country is now fighting with this pandemic with 3.2 crore cases, 4.29 lakh deaths compared to 5,74,926 cases, 17,038 deaths in the first wave of Covid-19 pandemic. But all the educational institutions across the nation are prohibited to open putting students, teachers and parents in the stress and it not only disrupting the ongoing teaching-learning process but also cancellation or re-scheduling examination starting from primary schools to different universities. There is a wide adoption of technology for the teaching learning process during the pandemic willingly or unwillingly. UNESCO (2020) has reported that around 320 million students have been affected due to corona virus in India. Department of Higher Education in this regard said "Institutions shall promote the digital learning among students so that they can continue their learning by making full use of available digital/e-learning platforms and access to these resources were made available free of cost". This will help the students for the ample utilisation of the e-resources ensuring social distancing norms. Online platforms like Microsoft team, Google classroom, Video conferencing (Google meet, Zoom, Slack, Cisco, Webex, Hangout) Canvas, Blackboard are new era tool in the hand of the teachers for their teaching learning process. Some studies have found some positive impact of this lockdown on the learning process. Burgess and Sievertsen (2020) described that families are the central to education and widely agreed to provide major inputs into a child's learning. So this lockdown will widen up the opportunity to involve and learn values from family. Students can plan themselves and practice self-paced learning (Tripathi, 2020). Besides, digitalisation will lead to promptly introduction of innovations in academia and higher education that would have normally taken several years due to the various contradictory administrative regulations (Strielkowski, 2020). However there are many problems beset with the digital learning (Dhoot, 2020). The digital mode of the teaching-learning process is often discriminatory to poor and marginalized students (Manzoor, 2020). Lack of parental guidance, when both the parents are working is another challenge for most of the children and young learners (Pokhrel, 2021). Being a developing country with lack of conducive environment and poor infrastructure like access to technology, internet connectivity, it is very important for the teacher to deliver content to meet the expectation of the student (Gopal, 2021).

Objective of the Study

The objective of this study is:

- To highlight the various challenges and prospects of digital education in Odisha.
- To put some effective suggestions for the teaching-learning process during the pandemic situation.

BACKGROUND

The covid-19 pandemic has affected almost every country, every sector around this world. Government of India tried their best to deal with the new normal seamless support to the students during this pandemic situation by transforming and modifying the conventional classroom learning to new era online and blended learning. Jena, 2020 found that covid 19 pandemic positively affected the educational system by making them more technology oriented, by reaching to a huge mass at the same time. They also found this pandemic situation enhance digital literacy. Radu, 2020 found that more than 60% of the students indicated that the internet connectivity and availability of digital equipment like computer, phone, tablet etc are satisfactory. They did not face any problem while the accessing the digital education. But the communication among the teacher- student was not found satisfactory because of lack of proper content and pedagogy for digital education. But most of the developing countries are facing problem for transforming the traditional education system towards new normal due to lack of proper infrastructure, connectivity issue, technological illiteracy, poverty etc. Dawadi et.al 2020 found in their study in Nepal that the major adverse impact of covid19 on educational sector is that the inequality and discrimination created among the students and widen the gap between the advantaged and disadvantaged children in terms of access and avail the learning opportunity in the lockdown period. Absence from school for a quite long period may reduce the skill and educational competency among the school going students. Carlsson, Dahl, Ockert and Roothet (2015) in their study found that just 10 days of extra schooling increased the test score of students significantly. The Covid-19 pandemic is likely to increase the dropout rate among students. The marginalised, poor and tribal students are more vulnerable for drop outs because of two reasons: firstly, the loss of jobs of their parents due to lockdown who are mainly casual labourers. So due to the income stress of the family some of the parents may not be able to afford the educational expenses of their children. Secondly, children are not interested to go to the school because of the gap in the physical mode of schooling habit. Thus longer the closure of the schools greater will be the drop-out rate among students (Buckler et.al, 2020). It will take lots of effort on the part of the govt. to again re-enrol and re-engage. Onyema et al. (2020) in their study found that around 70% of the student agreed that the lack of computer, internet connectivity, electricity issues are some of the important factors for the poor accessibility and engagement of the student in the learning process during the period of school closure. Odrizola et al. (2020) found that continued spread of disease, travel restrictions and the closure of educational institutions significantly affected the social life, educational progress and mental health of the students (Chaturvedi et al., 2020). Around 51.4% of the students reported that they did not effectively utilise the lockdown period for their study. But the closure of the educational institutions is not a obstacle for most of the developed country where the use of technology and the infrastructure to obtain and access the facility of online education. Gupta (2020) found that the rescheduling of the exam may reduce the students' performance due to the long gap between the lessons taught them in the class and their final examination. It also affects the next session progress of the students. Mahapatra (2021) found that after the lockdown the ultimate responsibility of learning activities of their children puts on their parents. This home schooling puts additional burden to the parents who are already occupied with lots of other works like work from home burden, financial burden due to temporary unemployment, management of household works etc. The situation is more critical for those parents who does not have necessary educational qualification to assist their children for home task. This lockdown period also cause gender disparities by putting additional burden to the female member of the house. Machado (2019) found that women are expected to dedicate more time for the home learning of their children. This digital education is also discriminatory for the students who are differently-abled. The children with neuro developmental disorder such as autism and intellectual disability required more focus of the teacher for behaviour and vocational therapy. But most of the special education institutions in India are not equipped to serve such students through the online mode of education through digital platform (Mahapatra, 2021).

DATA SOURCES AND METHODOLOGY

Odisha has been selected as the study area for present research as the state is considered to be one of the least developed states in terms of quality of life (Parashar, 2018). It is also the most backward state in India (Ministry of Finance, 2013). This is based on the underdevelopment index that includes ten sub-components i.e. monthly per capita consumption expenditure, education, health, household amenities, poverty rate, female literacy, percent of SC-ST population, urbanisation rate, financial inclusion and connectivity. The state suffers from high incidence of poverty, low average per-capita monthly consumption expenditure, high infant mortality rate, low life expectancy & lowest HDI among major states of India. The state even witnesses acute regional & social disparities in development with large rural-urban divide (Economic Survey of Odisha, 2017-18). The state has the third highest tribal population in the entire country accounting for 9.66% of total tribal population of India. Odisha is considered as the native of the tribal as 40% of the states total population is tribal population according to Census 2011 (Economic Survey of Odisha, 2017-18). The study has been based on secondary sources of data retrieved from official websites like WHO, UNESCO, University Grant Commission, Odisha Primary Education Programme Authority, Department of Higher Education under MHRD, Ministry of Rural

Development, All India Survey of Higher Education Report (AISHE), TRAI, and Odisha Economic Survey. Some e-journals and e-contents are also referred to analyse the issues and challenges faced by students as well as teachers while adopting virtual learning. This study is both descriptive and analytical in nature. Descriptive statistics like averages, percentages has been used to analyse the data.

MAIN FOCUS OF THE CHAPTER

This study aims to analyse the challenges and prospect of digital education in Odisha amid Covid-19. Before discussing the challenges, it is important to have a bird-eye view of the education institutions in terms of its number and number of enrolment in Odisha. This is shown in Table 1.

Table 1. Number of educational institutions and enrolments in Odisha

Number of elementary schools	58,344
Number of secondary schools	9872
Number of universities	28
Number of colleges	1062
Number of colleges per lakh population	23
Number of enrolment in elementary level	56,23,940
Number of enrolment in secondary level	12,48,344
Number of Enrolment in Higher Secondary level	5,79,339
Under graduate enrolment	780144
Post graduate enrolment	83077
Enrolment in M.Phil.	1161
Enrolment in Ph.D.	3722

Source: OPEPA (2017) and Ministry of Human Resource Development (2019)

Table shows that there are around 58,344 elementary schools and 9,872 secondary schools with around 56 lakhs elementary enrolment, 12 lakhs secondary and 5 lakhs higher secondary enrolment. With regard to higher education in Odisha, there are 28 universities, 1062 colleges with 780144enrolment under graduate, 83077 under post graduates and 4883 under M.Phil. & Ph.D. scholars. There is 23 colleges per one lakh population which is lower than national average of28 colleges ranges from 7 colleges in Bihar and 53 in Karnataka with average enrolment of 682.

Now with regard to mode of education, Table 2 reveals that the number of students opted for regular mode and distance mode of taking education. It also shows that greater numbers of students are preferred regular, face-to-face mode of education than distance mode. There is no provision of research in distance mode in Odisha. This is not only the scenario of Odisha but almost all the states in India. This also provides hints that most of the students prefer to have traditional face to face mode of education.

Table 2. Number of enrollment according to mode of education in Odisha

Number of Enrolment	Regular Mode	Distance Mode
Under graduate	752030	28114
PG Diploma	93290	2674
Diploma	125515	4003
Post graduate	61886	21191
M.Phil.	1161	-
Ph.D.	3722	-

Source: Ministry of Human Resource Development (2020)

Table 3 explains the enrolment picture of the under graduate and post graduate students of Odisha. It shows that COVID-19 pandemic has reduced the enrolment in remarkably which reduced the enrolment from 7.5 lakh to 7.1 lakh in regular mode but it increased the enrolment in distance mode for both UG and PG students (Figure 1) as during corona pandemic mass closer of different educational institute and risk of attending physical class made the students to opt for distance mode of education.

Table 3. Enrolment of student before and during COVID-19 in Odisha

Year	UG Regular	UG Distance	PG Regular	PG Distance
Before COVID-19				
2017-18	765592	27956	55196	18037
2018-19	752030	28114	61886	21191
Average	758811	28035	58541	19614
Amid COVID-19				
2019-20	717633	29475	70447	28108

Source: AISHE Annual Report, Govt. of India

Many state governments across the country, including Odisha has shut down schools, colleges and universities. Education experts declared this year as a "zero academic year" due to the corona pandemic. As per the current scenario, since there is uncertainty when the schools and colleges will re-open, many of the educational institutions have gone for digital education. This has made both teachers and students to adopt online mode of teaching. But the question arises, how far this online system of education is effective in Odisha. What are the challenges and prospects that this mode of teaching? Hence an analysis of those challenges and prospects of digital education are discussed below:

Figure 1. Distance mode enrollment in UG and PG courses
Source: AISHE annual report, Govt. of India

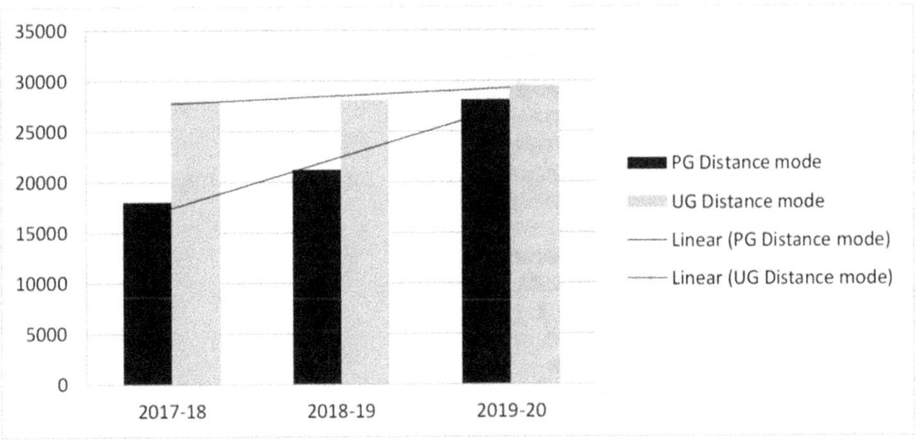

Challenges of Digital Education

1. Uneven access to digital connectivity

Uneven access to digital connectivity has put a threat to fundamental right of education in states like Odisha. This is one of the greatest challenge that digital mode of education would be facing when teaching learning process shifts from traditional class to online mode. Access to digital connectivity can be based on tele-density and internet subscribers. Tele-density is the number of telephone connection per hundred populations living in a particular area. Figure 2 shows the state wise tele- density in India.

Figure 2 shows that the overall tele density of India is 87.84% for the year 2021. Tele density of 8 states namely West Bengal, Odisha, Bihar, Uttar Pradesh, Madhya Pradesh, Assam, north east states and Rajasthan has lowest score compared to the national tele density. Bihar has the lowest tele-density with 53.315 of telephone subscribers and Delhi has the highest tele density with 279.72% of subscribers. The Data for Andhra Pradesh includes Telangana, Madhya Pradesh includes Chhattisgarh, Bihar includes Jharkhand, Uttar Pradesh includes Uttarakhand, North-East includes Arunachal Pradesh, Sikkim, Manipur, Meghalaya, Mizoram, Nagaland & Tripura States as taken by TRAI, 2021.

Figure 3 shows the tele-density in Odisha and India. It shows the overall tele- density in Odisha is 80.28% which is comparatively lower with respect to India with the tele-density of 93.27%.

Within the state also, there is a huge rural urban disparity in the telecom development. The tele-density in the rural area is 61.8 and it is higher than the national tele-density but far below compared to the urban tele-density which is 163.7 and 166.6 in India (Figure 4).

This implies that the status of telecom infrastructure is adequate and as per the national average. So the students in the urban area can have better access to tele-communication and can use the benefits of digital learning but it surely creates obstacle for the students belong to the remote and village area with very low tele-density as it is the basic requirement for having access for the online classes.

Figure 2. State wise tele-density
Source: Telecom Regulatory Authority of India (2021)

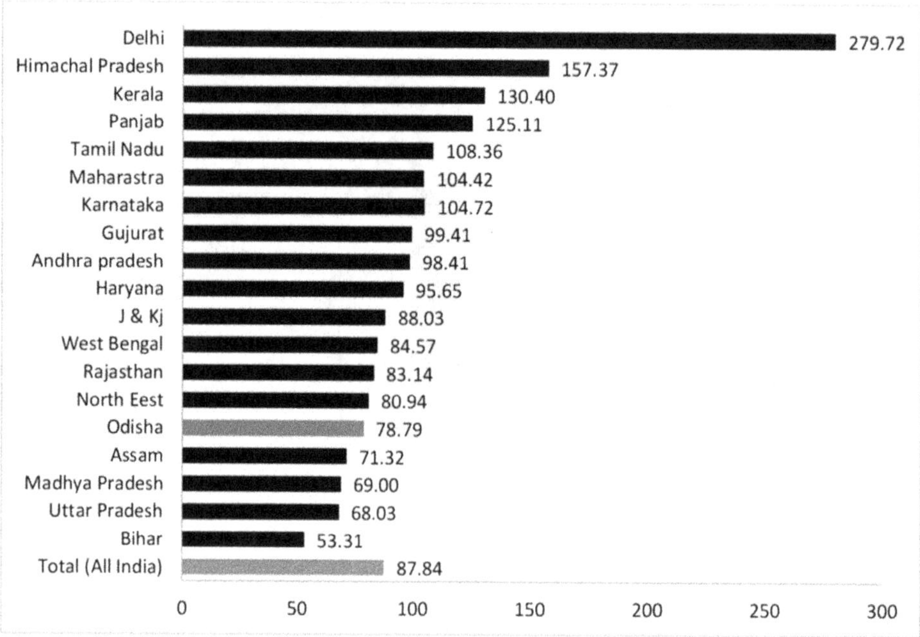

Figure 3. Tele-density: Odisha and India
Source: Government of Odisha (2020)

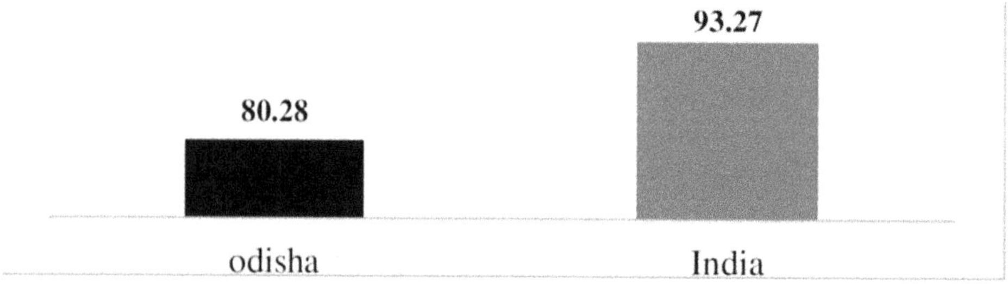

Figure 4. Rural-urban tele-density in Odisha
Source: Government of Odisha (2020)

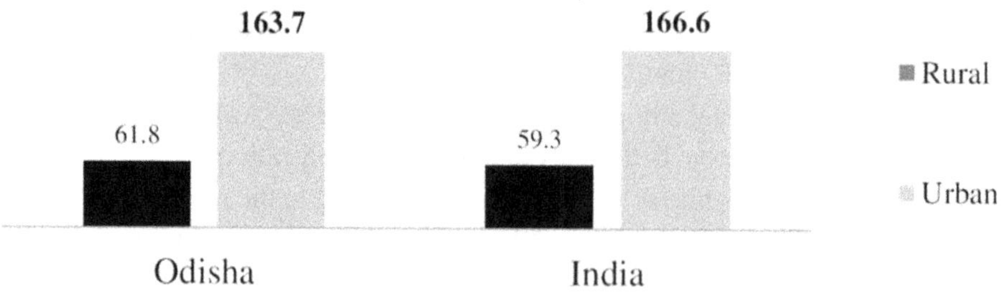

Distribution of internet access can be known from the number of internet subscribers. Figure 5 shows the number of internet subscribers per 100 populations in a particular area. It is one of the major factors for having access to online classes. But the table shows that only 38.02 percent of people in India have access to internet which is quite low and it is again low 28.22 in Odisha. The picture is even worst when we look into the rural Odisha (figure 6). The internet user is only 16 per 100 populations. But in urban area 83.3% people having access to internet, i.e., they are able to access digital classes but most of the people live in remote and rural area which creates anxiety among the students about their classes and career. Interestingly, between 2017 and 2018, the total volume of wireless data used in Odisha jumped 138 pc from 474 million GB to 1,134 million GB. Still rural pockets remain way behind in its reach to data. Thus, there is significant urban-rural difference in the state both for Tele-density and Internet subscription.

Figure 5. Internet subscribers per 100 population
Source: Government of Odisha (2020)

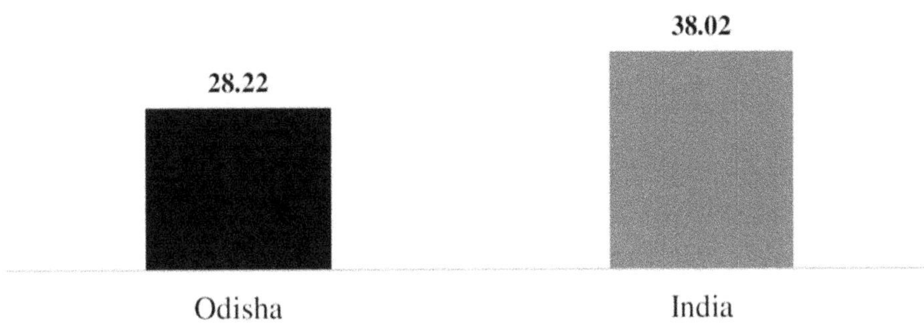

Figure 6. Internet subscribers per 100 population in urban-rural area
Source: Government of Odisha (2020)

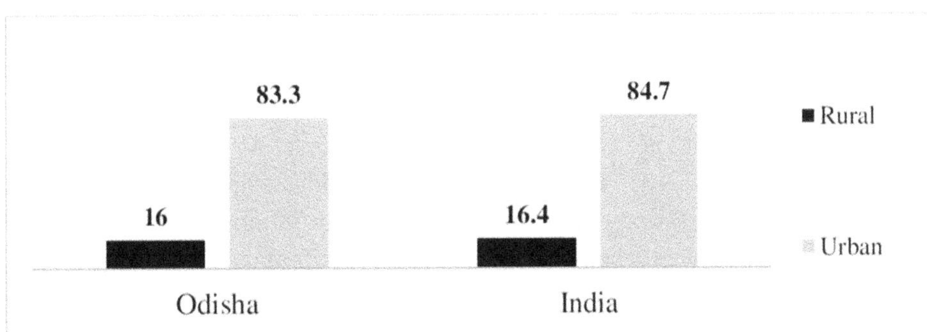

2. Lack of devices for digital education

Since access to phone, tabs, computer and internet are an integral part of digital education, statistics are certainly not in favour of Odisha students. Considering school education in Odisha where 56.23 lakhs of students are studying in 58,344 Government schools including both primary and upper primary schools. Out of which only 3621 schools are private schools including both aided and unaided schools (Government of Odisha, 2020). Figure 7 reveals that education in government institutions is still one of the major source of education in Odisha.

Figure 7. Distribution of enrolment in elementary and secondary school according to educational institutions
Source: OPEPA (2017)

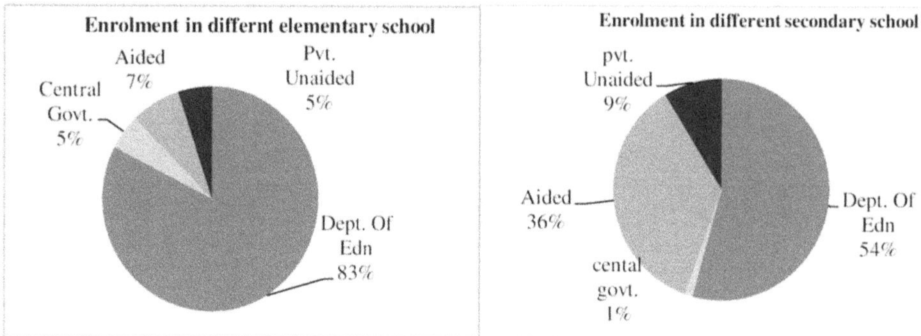

But it is found that government school in rural areas lacks basic infrastructure(The new Indian Express, 2020). In this pandemic situation, online teaching-learning during lockdown has deprived many students from learning opportunity through virtual classes. Whereas in urban areas, mostly the private schools with adequate infrastructure exist. This makes it possible for the students in urban areas with mobile connectivity, internet and availability of gadgets to be able to learn and innovate amidst of pandemic crisis. But lakhs students in rural areas studying in government school with poor or no access to smart phone, computer and internet along with many teachers lacking computer efficiency makes it impossible to achieve the desired goal of education through digital learning. Convenor of RTE forum from Odisha, Mr. Anil Pradhan said "the impact of digital learning has been minimal in the state limited to three coastal districts of Odisha. Again it has been limited to WhatsApp forwarded materials from respective educational institutions".

Not only the educational institutions mostly Government institutions are deprived of devices for digital education, even challenges are also from the side of students. As per report of National Sample Survey (NSS) on education 2017-18, only 4.3% households in Odisha have computers and Only 17.2% households in urban areas possess computers. In rural Odisha, the numbers are woefully short. Just 1.8 per cent households have computers at home. Now this raises an important question that how can students manage online education in such circumstances? According to a study, around 42% learners were mostly suffering from stress, depression, and anxiety due to poor internet connectivity (32.4%), absence of a favourable environment and separate room to study at home i.e.12.6% (Kapasia et al., 2020).

3. Discriminatory in nature

Digital learning process is also found to be often discriminatory. Many students from remote areas and marginalized sections denied online learning due to the lack of electricity and poor internet connectivity

It is also found that women students, from families with financially stressed or where education is not prioritised will be doubly disadvantaged. Mishra and Mishra (2013) found that impact of e-education vary according to gender and boys have more positive impact than girls. Manzoor (2020) found digital education further creates obstacle for the physically challenged students mainly hearing impaired and blind students. The immediate shift to the online learning amidst of the pandemic without proper planning in states like Odisha where the foundation for online education is not properly built and the curriculum was not designed for such initiatives created risk and discrimination and make them passive learner.

4. Low Ability and lack of interest among students for digital education

Most of the students from rural and remote areas in the state have remain untouched due to the digital divide and discouraging computer literacy rate. Only 25.5 per cent people have ability to operate computer in urban Odisha, whereas 13.4 per cent in rural Odisha have ability to operate computers. Moreover, only 7.4 per cent individuals, above five years age, in rural areas and 29.3 per cent individuals in urban areas have the ability to use internet.

Studies have shown that many students those who have access losing interest due to low attention span, power cut during summer, financial constraints of households for recharging data pack and lack of involvement of parents in the process (Mishra, 2020; The New Indian Express (2020). Another study shows that students used the WhatsApp group for getting study the materials from teachers and as well as friends. However, fewer learners followed institutions/teachers' website and YouTube lives for study materials (Sain and Saha, 2020). This pandemic also created uncertainty in learning progress or assessment due to cancellation or re-scheduling the examination (Goyal, 2020).Even, the research activities of different institutions have been affected. In many cases where data from the field are needed, the students cannot visits the field because of the fear of being infected. Even for the secondary data also where the investigator need to visit various offices, libraries which are not available online has also slowdown. There is a negative impact on the project work as well (Gupta, 2020).

Prospects of Digital Education in Odisha

Though covid-19 global health crisis has put a lot of stress in the educational sector to provide learning opportunity to the students with uneven access to technology, internet, lack of competency but it also provide some new dimension to our traditional teaching-learning process. It is found that various educational institutions are using different platforms for e-lectures such as Team link, YouTube live, Skype, Google meets/hangout, Google classroom, WhatsApp etc. The learners also followed many platforms for e-learning and study materials during this lockdown period like Swayam, Dedicated TV channels, Odisha Shiksha Sanjog, Diksha, e-pathsala, National Repository of open Educational Resources, National Institute of Open Schooling with some other IT initiatives are provided by State and Central government. This crisis has opened up the new ways of learning and assessment for future education system that will be based on blended learning model where both online and face-to-face delivery becomes a norm (Mishra, 2020; Tripathi, 2020). Another opportunity is virtual internship, which allows the students to go beyond the curriculum and learn about the practical uses of their professions. It also helps the students to understand the need of automation; this will further allow them to digitalise their fields in near future (Kumar, 2020). This crisis made every house a school and every parent a teacher as there is no boundary between the bedroom and classroom which allow the students to learn by themselves make them self-paced learner (Nanda and Khanna, 2020). There is massive rise in the tele-conferencing opportunities like meetings, seminars and conferences which minimise the geographical barriers among different students and resource persons (Mishra, 2020). State Project Director of Odisha School Education Programme Authority (OSEPA) Mr. Bhupendra Singh Poonia agrees there are hurdles in reaching out to students online but feels it is the right time to encourage such learning to get a picture of how many students at grassroots don't have access to online education and plan for future (The New Indian Express, 2020).

Initiatives Taken by Government of India on Education Amid COVID-19 Pandemic

To break the chain of the spread of covid-19 pandemic Govt of India declared a nationwide lock-down on 16 March 2020. As educational sectors are more vulnerable due to mass gathering so this lockdown adversely affected the lockdown. But almost all state govt. have taken measures to provide educational opportunities to the students through online mode. Traditional education system transformed to technology oriented online education. During lockdown period teaching- learning opportunities are provided through tools like WhatsApp, Zoom. Google meet, google classroom, Microsoft team, telegram, YouTube live, hangouts, Facebook etc. The digital initiatives of MHRD is a comprehensive platforms to ensure safe learning among the secondary and higher secondary students during the COVID-19 pandemic. Some of the digital initiatives of MHRD and UGC for secondary and higher education are:

Secondary Education

- **Diksha:** It is a web portal for e-learning contents for the elementary and secondary school students. It is a curriculum based portal with the content created by more than 250 teachers in multiple languages designed under the guidance of NCERT and CBSE . This portal has more than 80,000 books starting from class 1 to 12. It is very user friendly and accessed through mobile apps downloaded from google play store. This can also be used in offline mode.
- **E-Pathshala:** It is an e-learning app created for the elementary and secondary school students including classes from 1 to 12. It is designed by NCERT for providing learning facilities in a wide varieties of subjects in multiple languages covering Hindi, English and Urdu. This app contains books, videos, audio and various other learning materials for the students and teachers. This portal is a store house of 1886 audios, 2000 videos, 696 e-books and 504 flipbooks. Mobile app is available and downloadable from google play store.
- **National Repository for Open Educational Resources:** It is a single window search for multiple repository including e-books, videos, interactive modules. It is a curriculum based repository including 401 collections, 2779 documents, 1345 interactive modules, 1664 audios, 2586 images and 6153 videos for both elementary and secondary school students from class 1 to 12.

Higher Secondary Education

- **E-Gyan Kosh:** It is a national digital repository to provide digital education through storing and sharing of various learning materials. It is developed by the Open and Distance Learning Institutes of India with copy right contents of Indira Gandhi National Open University (IGNOU).

- **Gyan Darshan:** It is a wed based TV channel specially designed to meet the learning needs of the distance learners with various e- contents of different subject oriented contents and knowledge.
- **Swayam:** It is a national platform for online and distance education for secondary and higher education levels. It covers 1900 courses to provide Massive Open Online Courses with 140 universities approved credit transfer system. It covers both school education from class9 to 12 and higher education including under graduate, post graduate programmes. A wide varieties of subjects including humanities and social sciences, engineering, law and management, agriculture, medicine, performing arts etc.
- **E-PG Pathshala:** It is specially designed web based portal for the post graduate students. They can access this portal freely for books, online courses, study materials through online mode. The main importance of this platform is students living with low internet facility can also access this portal.
- **Swayam Prava:** It is also another web based 24*7 dedicated TV channel to provide educational access through 32 DTH channels for transmitting educational contents. It provides learning opportunities to a varieties of users including school students, under graduate, post graduate students, out o0f school children, vocational courses and teacher training facilities.
- **E-Adhyayan:** It is a platform that provide access to 700+ e-books for various post graduate courses including a varieties of subject disciplines. It only provide access to those books included in e- pathshala courses.
- **E-Pathya:** It is one of the blended platform which provide both online and offline access to various learning materials for post-graduation students. It is a component of e-PG pathashala.
- **National Digital Library of India (NDLI):** It is a e-content repository on multiple disciplines for a wide varieties of user access including teachers, students, researchers, library professionals, differently abled users and for other lifelong learners. It is designed and developed by Indian Institute of Technology Kharagpur. The main focus of this platform is to help the students to prepare for different competitive and entrance exams. It helps to learn knowledge from best practises all over the world. It also helps the researcher for inter linked exploration from a wide varieties of sources. It is very user friendly by single window search facilities and provision of access through mobile apps.
- **E-Yantra:** It mainly designed for science and engineering learning through hands on training and experiences on embedded systems. It has about 380 labs for providing better learning experiences.
- **FOSSEE:** It stands for Free and Open Source Software for Education. It designed to open source learning for education as well as professional use.
- **Virtual Labs:** It is a curriculum based web source experiments for remote operation. It has more than 100 virtual labs consisting 700+ web based experiment facilities. It provides remote access to virtual labs foe multiple disciplines of science and engineering. It serves to a wide varieties of learners including under graduate students, post graduate students as well as research scholars.
- **National Educational Alliance for Technology:** It is a public private partnership wed based platform for providing skill to the learners about the latest technology for pedagogical development in a single platform.
- **SAKSHAT:** It is a web based portal for all up to date knowledge in education to meet the learning need of the students, scholars, academicians and other lifelong learner by providing all latest news, press releases, events and achievements etc. It is a single platform to gain multiple knowledge through online learning.

Research Purpose:

- **E-Sodh Sindhu:** It is a e-platforms of e-journals, e-journal archives and e-books on long term access basis. It has a wide repository of more than 10000 e-journals, more than 3135000 e-books. It provide access to full-text electronic journals, bibliographics and factual data base for the academician and research community at minimal subscription charges.
- **Sodh Ganga:** It is the largest Indian research repository designed for the M.Phil. and Ph.D. research scholars to deposit their theses and dissertation and make them available and accessible freely for whole research community. The repository has the feature to capture, index, disseminate and store the research work electronically submitted by the researcher of different Indian universities.
- **VIDWAN:** It is a national portal for database and national research network which includes researchers, scientists, faculty members and experts working at various prestigious academic institutions and research and development institutions in India.

SOLUTIONS AND RECOMMENDATIONS

The corona pandemic not only has make the economy standstill but also has affected the education sector adversely and the uncertainty situation in education sector puts parent, teachers and students under lots of pressure about their learning, examination and career. This calls for some stronger measures and the education sector has been taking some transformation to tackle the urgent need like adoption of the digital teaching through WhatsApp, video conferencing, zoom, teams, google classroom and e-learning through Swayam, dedicated TV channels, Odisha Shiksha Sanjog because education industry is more vulnerable since mass gathering cannot be avoided in classrooms but the achievement of the desired goal is far away. But online education are no substitutes for classroom lectures in Odisha because of various reasons like low tele-density, low access to computers and smart phone, poor internet connectivity, frequent power-cut, low computer literacy, financial stress and gender gap which creates digital divide and discrimination. Over and above the body language and eye contact of the teacher is also an important aspect for the effective classroom which is missing in the online classes. The practical classes and laboratory work cannot be held online. As one of the least developed state Odisha is not fully equipped to make education for all through digital platform. But this pandemic is no doubt an opportunity for the education sector to grow and opt new platforms and techniques. So both state government and central government need to develop strong backbone for the digital education which may reduce the digital divide and help to access the benefits and opportunities of the e-learning for all. Some of the suggestions are:

- Government of India including state government should develop strategies to deal with this pandemic situation with equitable learning opportunity by taking into consideration various drawbacks like remote region students, poor network issue, technological backwardness, marginalised, minorities and tribal students.
- For effective deliberation of teaching learning opportunities among students of the higher education level various open learning sources should be considered. Many platforms in online sources offer multiple subject specific programmes on different levels of assessment, certification and

methodology which can be used and approved by different higher education institution for better learning opportunities to the students.

- Various educational institutions, research organisation should organise webinars, e-conferences, e-workshops, capacity building programmes and training to both teachers, students and researchers to enhance their learning ability, research capability and pedagogical innovations in the wave of this covid-19 pandemic situation.
- At the current scenario of 2021 amid covid-19 pandemic government should think of reopening of the different schools, colleges, universities and other educational institutions with proper protocols to further spread of this virus. Measures like social distancing by phase wise and shift wise educational activities with 40-50% of students and teachers, provision of mask, sanitizer should be taken.
- This pandemic open up ways by transferring traditional educational system into more technology oriented. Thus Government should think of some infrastructural development in the remote areas, rural and poor communities to enhance the digital accessibility of the students. Government and other stakeholders should contribute to reduce the interstate and intra state internet and digital gap.
- Awareness should be developed among the school going adolescent students and parents for the use of technology in the right ways to acquire the maximum benefit of the digital learning. As this is a completely new mode of learning for most of the school students so teachers should develop required competencies and abilities to engage the students in the class effectively.

FUTURE RESEARCH DIRECTIONS

This study only confined to detailed explanation only for Odisha with reference to India. This study is based only on the secondary data but the direct responses from the students and other stakeholders may be more helpful for deriving a true picture of this situation.

CONCLUSION

Covid-19 pandemic has affected every sector in the whole world from the core. Due to world-wide and nation-wide lockdown, the education sector has also been affected adversely. But the world is now moving towards new normal. The education sector is also transforming from face to face mode to the online and blended mode of teaching learning process. But most of the states bare not completely ready for the adoption of the new mode of education in the form of proper technological infrastructure for education, curriculum modification, competency among the teachers for digital mode of teaching learning process etc. So the detailed discussion about the problems and challenges face by the students and teachers is very much important to cope with the new normal with suggestive strategies. The idea about the positive impacts is also noteworthy for determining the sustainability of the digital mode of education. The analysis of the various provision of the govt. for helping the students and the faculties to continue their education is also helpful for analysing the comprehensive scenario of the education amid this pandemic situation.

REFERENCES

Buckler, A., Chamberlain, L., Stutchbury, K., & Hedge, C. (2020). *Minimising 'distance' in distance learning programmes during a global health crisis: Framing an international education response to COVID-19*. UKFIET. https://www.ukfiet.org/2020/minimising-distance-in-distance-learning-programmes-during-a-global-health-crisis-framing-an-international-education-response-to-COVID-19/

Burgess, S., & Sievertsen, H. H. (2020). *Schools, Skills and Learning: The Impact of COVID-19 on Education*. https://voxeu.org/article/impact-covid-19-education

Carlsson, M., Dahl, G. B., Öckert, B., & Rooth, D. (2015). The effect of schooling on cognitive skills. *The Review of Economics and Statistics*, *97*(3), 533–547. doi:10.1162/REST_a_00501

Chaturvedi, K. (2020). COVID-19 and its impact on education, social life and mental health of students: A survey. *Children and Youth Services Review*. Advance online publication. doi:10.1016/j.childyouth.2020.105866 PMID:33390636

Dhoot, P. (2020). Impact of COVID-19 on Higher Education in India. *International Journal of Creative Research Thoughts, 8*(6), 1263-1273. https://www.ijcrt.org/papers/IJCRT2006171.pdf

Economic Survey of Odisha-2017-18. (n.d.). Planning and Co-ordination Department. Directorate of Economics and Statistics, Government of Odisha.

Gope, P. C., Gope, D., & Gope, A. (2021). Higher Education in India: Challenges and Opportunities of the COVID-19 Pandemic. *Asian Journal of Distance Education*, *16*(1), 54–73. doi:10.5281/zenodo.4643552

Government of Odisha. (2020). *Odisha Economic Survey 2019-20*. Planning and Convergence Department. Directorate of Economics and Statistics. https://pc.odisha.gov.in/Download/Economic_Survey_2019-20.pdf

Goyal, S. (2020). *Impact of Coronavirus on Education in India*. https://www.jagranjosh.com/general-knowledge/impact-of-coronavirus-on-education-in-india-1587642880-1

Gupta, A., & Goplani, M. (2020). Impact Of COVID-19 On Educational Institution In India. *Purakala (UGC Care Journal), 31*(21), 661-671. https://papers.ssrn.com/sol3/papers.cfm?abstract_id=3679284

Gupta, S. (2020). *The Impact of the Coronavirus SARS-CoV-2 on the Education Sector in India*. http://confluence.ias.ac.in/the-impact-of-the-coronavirus-sars-cov-2-on-the-education-sector-in-india/

India Today Web Desk. (2020). *Covid-19: 4 negative impacts and 4 opportunities created for education*. https://www.indiatoday.in/education-today/featurephilia/story/covid-19-4-negative-impacts-and-4-opportunities-created-for-education-1677206-2020-05-12

Jena, P. K. (2020). Impact of Pandemic COVID-19 on Education in India. [IJCR]. *International Journal of Current Research, 12*(7), 12582–12586. http://journalcra.com/article/impact-pandemic-covid-19-education-india

Jena, P. K. (2020). Impact of Covid-19 on higher education in India. *International Journal of Advanced Education and Research.*, *5*(3), 77–81. https://papers.ssrn.com/sol3/papers.cfm?abstract_id=3691541

Kapasia, N., Paul, P., Roy, A., Saha, J., Zaveri, A., Mallick, R., Barman, B., Das, P., & Chouhan, P. (2020). Impact of Lockdown on Learning Status of Undergraduate and Post graduate Students During COVID-19 Pandemic in West Bengal, India. *Children and Youth Services Review*, *116*, 105194. Advance online publication. doi:10.1016/j.childyouth.2020.105194 PMID:32834270

Kumar, D. N. S. (2020). *Impact of Covid-19 on Higher Education*. Higher Education Digest. https://www.highereducationdigest.com/impact-of-covid-19-on-higher-education/

Machado, L. S. (2019). Parent in science: The impact of parenthood on the scientific career in Brazil. In *2019 IEEE/ACM 2nd international workshop on gender equality in software engineering (GE)* (pp. 37–40). IEEE

Mahapatra, A. Sharma, P (2020). Education in times of COVID-19 pandemic: Academic stress and its psychosocial impact on children and adolescents in India. *International Journal of Social Psychiatry, 67*(4), 397–399. doi:10.1177/0020764020961801

Manzoor, A. (2020). *Online Teaching and Challenges of COVID-19 for Inclusion of PWD in Higher Education*. https://dailytimes.com.pk/595888/online-teaching-and-challenges-of-covid-19-for-inclusion-of-pwds-in-highereducation/

MHRD Notice. (2020). *COVID-19 Stay Safe: Digital Initiatives*. https://www.mohfw.gov.in/pdf/Covid19.pdf

Ministry of Finance. (2013). *Report of the Committee for Evolving a Composite Development Index of States*. Working Papers id:6728, e Social Sciences. https://finmin.nic.in/sites/default/files/Report_CompDevState.pdf

Ministry of Human Resource Development. (2019). *All India Survey of Higher Education 2018-19*. Department of Higher Education, Government of India. http://aishe.nic.in/aishe/viewDocument.action?documentId=262

Mishra, K. (2020). *Covid-19: 4 negative impacts and 4 opportunities created for education*. https://www.indiatoday.in/education-today/featurephilia/story/covid-19-4-negative-impacts-and-4-opportunities-created-for-education-1677206-2020-05-12

Mishra, S., & Mishra, S. (2013). Impact of E-Education on School Going Children. *International Journal of Humanities and Social Science Invention.*, *2*(7), 58–61.

Nanda, P. K., & Khanna, P. (2020). *Every House a School, Every Parent a Teacher as Covid-19 Impacts Education of 300mn Students*. https://www.livemint.com/news/india/every-house-a-school-every-parent-a-teacher-as-covid-19-impacts-education-11585140662556.html

Nicola, M., Alsafi, Z., Sohrabi, C., Kerwan, A., Al-Jabir, A., Iosifidis, C., Agha, M., & Agha, R. (2020). The Socio-economic Impact of Coronavirus Pandemic (COVID-19):A Review. *International Journal of Surgery*, *78*, 185–193. doi:10.1016/j.ijsu.2020.04.018 PMID:32305533

Oneyma. (2020). Impact of Coronavirus Pandemic on Education. *Journal of Education and Practice*, *11*(13), 108–121. https://genbase.iiep.unesco.org/workspace/applis/epidoc/fichiers/EPIDOC/38698_52821_56584_1_PB.pdf

OPEPA. (2017). *Status of Elementary Education & Secondary Education in Odisha 2017-18*. Dept. of School and Mass Education, Government of Odisha. http://osepa.odisha.gov.in/webadmin/pdf_link/udise%20booklet%202017_11_29_24am8046c2c2aa57e4cc68d42dc129f0b444.pdf

ParasharB. K. (2018). https://www.hindustantimes.com/lucknow/uttar-pradesh-among-states-with-lowest-quality-of-life-says-study/story-goJLFpONnWKCr2YwZuz3CJ.html

Rado. (2021). The Impact of the COVID-19 Pandemic on the Quality of Educational Process: A Student Survey. *International Journal of Environmental Research and Public Health*, *18*(11), 6177. https://www.mdpi.com/867768 PMID:34200515

Sain & Saha. (2020). E-class, an alternative of classroom teaching. *International Journal of Creative Research Thoughts, 8*(5), 2902-2910. https://www.ijcrt.org/papers/IJCRT2005381.pdf

Saraswati, D. (2020). *Impact of COVID-19 on the Education Sector in Nepal: Challenges and Coping Strategies*. https://eric.ed.gov/?id=ED609894

Strielkowski, W. (2020). *COVID-19 Pandemic and the Digital Revolution in Academia and Higher Education*. https://www.researchgate.net/publication/340684703_COVID-19_Pandemic_and_the_Digital_Revolution_in_Academia_and_Higher_Education

The New Indian Express. (2020). *Rural Odisha: No state for online education*. https://www.newindianexpress.com/cities/bhubaneswar/2020/may/17/rural-odisha-no-state-for-online-education-2144400.html

Tripathi, A. (2020). *Positive Sides of Lockdown-Digital Inclusion*. https://timesofindia.indiatimes.com/blogs/agyeya/positive-sides-of-lockdown-digital-inclusion/

UNDP. (2020a). *A UN framework for the immediate socio-economic response to COVID-19*. https://unsdg.un.org/sites/default/files/2020-04/UN-Framework-for-the-immediate-socio-economic-response-to-COVID-19.pdf

UNDP. (2020b). *A Strategic Framework for a immediate socio-economic response to Covid-19 in Yemen 2020-21*. https://www.arabstates.undp.org/content/rbas/en/home/library/crisis-response0/a-strategic-framework-for-and-immediate-socio-economic-response-.html

UNESCO. (2020). *Education: From disruption to recovery*. Retrieved from https://en.unesco.org/covid19/educationresponse

Viner. (2020). *School closure and management practices during coronavirus outbreaks including COVID-19: A rapid systematic review*. doi:10.1016/S2352-4642(20)30095-X

World Health Organisation. (2020). *A UN framework for the immediate socio-economic response to COVID-19*. https://unsdg.un.org/resources/un-framework-immediate-socio-economic-response-covid-19

ADDITIONAL READING

Aleksander Aristovnik, D. K. (2020). Impacts of the COVID-19 Pandemic on Life of Higher Education Students: A Global Perspective. *Sustainability*, *12*(8438), 1–34. https://scholar.google.com/scholar?start=10&q=role+of+digital+education+in+covid19&hl=en&as_sdt=0,5#d=gs_qabs&u=%23p%3DwhQLs2Puyj4J

Amina Charania, U. B. (2021). Constructivist teaching and learning with technologies in the COVID-19 lockdown in Eastern India. *British Journal of Educational Technology*, *52*(4), 1–16. doi:10.1111/bjet.13111 PMID:34219752

Chandra, Y. (2021). Online education during COVID-19: perception of academic stress and emotional intelligence coping strategies among college students. *Asian Education and Development, 10*(2), 229-238. https://www.ncbi.nlm.nih.gov/pmc/articles/PMC8236909/

Charania, A., Bakshani, U., Paltiwale, S., Kaur, I., & Khan, N. N. (2021). Constructivist teaching and learning with technologies in the COVID-19 lockdown in Eastern India. *British Journal of Educational Technology*, *00*(4), 1–16. doi:10.1111/bjet.13111 PMID:34219752

Dutta, D. A. (2020). Impact of Digital Social Media on Indian Higher Education: Alternative Approaches of Online Learning during COVID-19 Pandemic Crisis. *International Journal of Scientific and Research Publications*, *10*(5), 604–611. doi:10.29322/IJSRP.10.05.2020.p10169

Madhu Arora, L. M. (2020). Factors affecting digital education during COVID-19: A statistical modeling approach. *IEEE*. https://scholar.google.com/scholar?start=10&q=role+of+digital+education+in+covid19+in+india&hl=en&as_sdt=0,5#d=gs_qabs&u=%23p%3DZRFcafKZ_k4J

KEY TERMS AND DEFINITIONS

Digital Education: A new mode of education using various digital tools in the teaching learning process.

Educational Expenses: Expenditure required for obtaining a degree including, books, fees, materials, and other stationeries.

Educationally Disadvantaged: A person/group who is deprived of basic requirements for their learning progress.

Online Platform: A range of facilities available on the internet for education.

Pedagogy: Science of teaching that includes teaching method, materials, and practices.

Self-Paced Learning: A method of learning where the learner is accountable for his/her learning progress.

Technological Illiteracy: A situation of inability of a person/group to understand access and use the required technology effectively.

Chapter 10
Impact of COVID-19 on the Fiscal Health of India:
A Sub-National Analysis From Odisha State

Sushanta Kumar Mahapatra
https://orcid.org/0000-0002-0831-3621
The ICFAI Foundation for Higher Education (IFHE) (Deemed), Hyderabad, India

Pareswar Sahu
Barpali College, Barpali of Sambalpur University, India

ABSTRACT

With the emergence of COVID-19 within Odisha, preventive measures like partial or total lockdown of the state have been undertaken by the government to control its spread despite the provision of health-related infrastructure. Among the 14 major states of India, Odisha is a poor state. However, the spread of the pandemic has become massive. In this context, this chapter attempts to examine the fiscal health of India at the sub-national level from the state of Odisha. The revenue generation capacity declines to a larger extent while expenditure responsibilities in terms of health expenditures expand tremendously. Consequently, the state has to face serious difficulties in sustaining its fiscal balance. This chapter observes that the fiscal health of the state deteriorated to a larger extent during the lockdown period than the pre-lockdown period. In such a critical situation, the state needs to plan effective strategies to raise the level of income through fiscal policy allowing economic activities compromising the sanitization measures of the pandemic.

INTRODUCTION

The emergence of COVID 19 across the globe has retarded the fiscal health of the economy due to excessive health expenditures and lack of revenue generation on account of partial and total lockdown of the economy (Baldwin, Richard and Beatrice Weder di Mauro 2020). The governments of almost all countries have used nationwide lockdown, fully or partially, as a preventive measure against the spread

DOI: 10.4018/978-1-7998-6896-5.ch010

of corona virus (Arun Kumar 2020) resulting loss of economic activities throughout the countries. The economic deterioration of countries has become a debatable issue among the academicians, social scientists, researchers and policy makers (Kumar, Arun 2020; Baldwin, Richard and Beatrice Weder di Mauro 2020; McKibbin, Warwick and Roshen Fernando 2020). In this juncture, the sub-national level of government being a unit of the country having low revenue potentiality and prime responsibility to provide better health faces greater challenges to fight with the pandemic. The sub-national level of government in India is no exception to it. In Indian federalism health is a subject of the Sub-national level (state) government[1]. It is the prime responsibility of the state to protect its people from the pandemic. However, the revenue potential of the state is low relative to its expenditures (Mahamallik and Sahu 2015). Among the divided fourteen major states of India[2], Odisha is the fourth lowest state in terms of per capita income and own revenue capacity to meet its revenue expenditure during 2018-19 (Table l and 2). Further, the socio-demographic output indicators show its weak performance (Table 3). However, the spread of the pandemic has become massive in Odisha which is not only a shock to human lives but also to the fiscal health of the state. In this context attempts are made in this chapter to examine the fiscal health of India at sub-national level from the perspective of the state of Odisha. Literature examined the economic impact of influenza (Meltzer *et al* 1999), the impact of 1918 Spanish flu epidemic on the economic performance of Sweden (Karlsson and Nilsson 2014), global economic effects of COVID-19 (Jackson *et al* 2021), socio-economic consequence of COVID-19 (Brodeur *et al* 2020), the effect of COVID 19 on Indian economy (Chaudhary *et al* 2020; Dev and Sengupta 2020), the impact of preventive measures used to reduce the spread of COVID 19 on marginal sections of the society (Ray *et al* 2020), income, output and employment (Arun Kumar 2020; McKibbin, Warwick and Roshen Fernando 2020; Baldwin, Richard and Eiichi Tomiura 2020; Mann, Catherine L. 2020), economic activity, fiscal and monetary policy (Cochrane, John H. Cochrane 2020) and bank's regulatory actions (Beck, Thorsten 2020; Cecchetti, Stephen G. and Kermit L. Schoenholtz 2020). This chapter observes that the fiscal health of the state is deteriorated to a larger extent during lockdown period than pre-lockdown period.

CONTEXT

The outbreak of COVID 19 has retarded the globe medically and economically. It is found that globally the total number of confirmed cases suffering from corona virus and number of deaths due corona virus as of 28th November 2020 were 61299371 and 1439784 respectively (WHO 2020). The top seven largest economies of the world (The US, China, Japan, Germany, Britain, France, and Italy), which account for 60% of world GDP, 65% of world manufacturing and 41% of world manufacturing export, have found the exponential growth cases of the disease. It is argued that since these economies are part of global value chains, their deterioration will produce supply chain contagion in all nations of the world (Baldwin, Richard and Beatrice Weder di Mauro 2020). The world output was projected to grow at -4.9 per cent in 2020. India is no exception to the suffering of the pandemic[3] and its economy withstanding the nationwide full or partial lockdown throughout the country for more than eight months since March 24, 2020 as a preventive measure for the disease (Ray *et al* 2020). Among 32 States and Union Territories of India, the highest percentage of confirmed cases of the disease (20.8%) is found in Maharashtra followed by Tamilnadu (12%) and Rajasthan (8.4%) respectively during 18th March to 11th April 2020 (Table 4). The total number of confirmed cases of corona disease and deaths resulting from it were 9351109 and 41322 respectively as on the 28th November, 2020, (WHO 2020). The Gross Domestic Product of India was projected to decline by 10.3 per cent in 2020 (Government of Odisha 2021). Strategic monetary and fiscal policies are recommended as panacea to be rescued from the adverse effect of the economy (Fornaro and Wolf 2020). The government of India used monetary policy, direct cash transfers and food security measures to boost the economy (Congressional Research Service 2020). Partial impact of monetary policy on the growth performance in India is observed (Chakraborty and Harikrishnan 2022). The monetary policy may fail to raise the level of income at a very low rate of interest since the expansion of money supply can not reduce the interest rate to investment which in turn will raise the level of income. Further, even at a low rate of interest, investment may not expand due to lack of confidence of investing enterprises on the demand with the rising fear for corona virus on the part of the people. The fiscal compression during 2021-22 hinders the economic recovery of the country (Mundle and Sahu 2021). Accommodative fiscal policy is recommended for the development of the country (Chakraborty and Harikrishnan 2022). The fiscal policy is the appropriate tool to fight the situation with opening up the economic activities. Elsewhere, it is argued that there is a dire need of effective fiscal policy that targets the sources of shocks, public health being the prime matter of consideration (Faria e Castro 2020; Dupor, B. 2020). The direct cash transfer increases the level of income but it depends on the level required to meet the demands. The cash transfer is a meager one. Further the food security has no direct impact on the economy. The analysis of pandemic of states in India indicates that the disease may hit the rich state most. Since there is supply chain connections between rich and poor states there is possibility for the poor states to be suffered worst. Odisha being a poor state as stated earlier suffered from both medical and economic deterioration ground. As per the report of National Health Mission, Odisha 2020, COVID 19 was found for first time in Odisha on the 15th March 2020 and it increased tremendously from 3rd April 2020 (Figure 1). The number of confirmed cases and deaths on corona disease in Odisha are 317789 and 1730 respectively as of the 28th November, 2020 (Government of Odisha 2020). The spread of the disease increased the burden of the state through raising the health expenditure. Initially the government fully lock downed the state since 24 March 2020 for 21 days and subsequently partial lockdown was done at a time throughout the state or at different places to prevent the disease[4]. Strict disciplinarian action is taken against the persons and officials violating the rules related to COVID 19 (The Hindu, March 31, 2020). The increased strict disciplinarian action taken by officials of the State in protecting its people from the pandemic resulted in rising administrative expenditures. Further, as an adverse economic repercussion of the preventive measure of the pandemic on the economy, the Gross State Domestic Product (GSDP) of Odisha declined by -4.92 per cent during 2020-21(Government of Odisha 2021). In this context, this chapter attempts to re-examine the possibilities of deterioration of fiscal health of Odisha using secondary data collected from the website of Reserve Bank of India from 1980-81 to 2020-21.

THEORETICAL FRAMEWORK

There is a debate regarding the effect of fiscal deterioration represented by increased borrowing on the growth of the economy. While the classical and neoclassical economists are against financing expenditures through borrowing, the Kenysian School appraises the effect of borrowing on the economic growth. The Ricardian School argues for a neutral effect of fiscal deficit on economic growth (Rangarajan and Srivastava 2005).

The classical economists argued that there is always full employment in the economy and even if there is unemployment for a temporary period of time that can be automatically corrected through flexibility in the wage and interest rate. Supply always creates its own demand. The interference in the economy through imposition of too much taxation, borrowing and expenditure responsibilities adversely affect the income, output and employment of the economy. It indicates to reduce the revenue and fiscal deficits for the development of the economy. The financing of expenditures through borrowing reduces the rate of saving and investment and hence adversely affects growth in both closed and open economy as viewed by the neoclassical economists. Since there is full employment of resources in a closed economy increased consumption reduces the saving. Even if the rate of interest and investment is not affected in an open economy, the reduction of national saving is recovered through external borrowing and decline in export. Hence in both closed and open economy saving declines and consumption increases resulting fall in investment and exports.

Market failure in the economy during the Great Depression of the 1930s encouraged Keynes to argue for the government interference through taxation and expenditure responsibilities to raise the level of income, output and employment. The wage rate flexibility mechanism did not work properly due to excessive pressure of trade unions. The reduction in the level of wage rate could not enable to absorb all the job seekers required for full employment at the given wage rate. Keynes argued when revenue generation falls short of expenditure responsibilities deficit financing through borrowing becomes necessary to raise the level of demand to attain full employment level of income and output. The investment financed by borrowing leads to expansion in output through investment multiplier effect. Even if the multiplier effect is reduced to some extent due to increase in the rate of interest with the presence of fixed money supply and increased demand for money, the rise in demand for goods and services increases the profit of private investment and calls for further investment at any given rate of interest before full utilization of resources.

As per the Ricardian School, fiscal deficits have neutral impact on the economic growth. Deficits at any time are equivalent to the present value of future taxation. The equality between the present value of spending and the present value of taxation has no effect on the economy since the household's spending decision is based on the present values of their income which accounts the present value of future taxation.

These Schools of thought vary in behavioral responses from the individuals. Individuals, who behave under money illusion, have high propensity to consume out of current disposable income in Keynesian world. In the universe of Ricardo, individuals are farsightedness, altruists and fully informed. Rationale individuals inhabit in the neoclassical world. The above three types of individuals as characterized by different schools reside in an economy with different size. The relevance of the theory depends on the relative size of individuals residing in an economy. However, in Indian economy as observed by social scientist's fiscal deficits have detrimental effect on its economic growth (Lahiri 2000; Mohan 2000; Rao 2002; Rangarajan and Srivastava 2005).

FISCAL HEALTH IN ODISHA

Almost all countries of the world are federal in structure with different degree (Oates 1972). The federal structure of governance is characterized by multiple levels of governments[5] each with constitutional resource and responsibility share. The structure and the principles of resource and responsibility sharing between levels lead to fiscal imbalance between different levels (vertical imbalance) and across the same levels (horizontal imbalance) of government (Mahamallik and Sahu 2015). For economic development of the country these imbalances have to be rectified since fiscal imbalances do not enable each level of government to provide common minimum level of basic public goods in accordance with the preference of the people. Even if constitutional body exists[6] to rectify the imbalances in countries still there are fiscal imbalances with different degrees in different countries across the globe (Rao and Sen 1996; Rangarajan and Srivastava 2004a; Rangarajan and Srivastava 2004b; Mahamallik and Sahu 2015). Since vertical and horizontal imbalances are complementary and supplementary in nature, the interdependence and co-operation between levels of government is of utmost importance to reduce these imbalances (Sahu and Mahamallik 2019). If the Federal government would spend in proportion to its collection of revenue in each state, the vertical imbalance might not affect the horizontal imbalance. When the spending of the Federal government is less than its proportionate revenue collection in a state, the fiscal health of the state is deteriorated. If the deteriorating state is a poor state, it becomes poorer. As a consequence, the fiscal imbalance across states increases. The increased horizontal imbalance puts pressure on the Federal government in transferring more revenues towards the state. The pressure again encourages the Federal government to raise more revenue from the state to care of their fiscal health leading to raising of vertical imbalance (Rao and Sen 1996). Further, insufficient revenue generation with less effort and mismanagement of public expenditures drags a state to debt insolvency in providing common minimum level of public goods to its people. Sound fiscal health of a state is crucial for improvement in the fiscal performance of the National and Sub-national level of governments to have economic development in the country. India has a federal structure of governance with Central government at the national, 30 state governments and a number of urban and rural local governments at sub-national level with constitutional division of resources and responsibilities. Even if there exists a constitutional body[7] and perennial efforts are undertaken by it to reduce the fiscal imbalances (Rao and Sen 1996; Rajaraman and Majumdar 2005), still there is persistent rising fiscal imbalances in the country (Mahamallik and Sahu 2015). Mahamallik and Sahu (2015) examined the vertical fiscal imbalance through own revenue, total revenue, revenue expenditures and total expenditures of the Centre and state and horizontal imbalance across fourteen major undivided states using co-efficient of variation of own revenue as percent of revenue expenditures of the state, total receipts and revenue expenditures as percent of total expenditures of the state and per capita of own revenue, total receipts, total expenditures and revenue expenditures of state during 1980-81 to 2014-15.

The deterioration of state finances due to discretionary government policies (Rao 2002) and public finance management during COVID 19 in India (Mukherjee and Badola 2021) have been examined in literature. Rao (2002) observed the sharp deterioration in state finances during 1980-81 to 2000-01 due to low growth of federal transfers to states, implementation of the recommendations of Fifth Pay Commission and deterioration in state's own fiscal performance. The deterioration is reflected through sharp rise in revenue, fiscal and primary deficits, indebtness, contingent liabilities and revenue expenditures and decline in own revenue, share in central transfers and capital and maintenance expenditures of 25 Indian states. Mukherjee and Badola (2021) examined the public finance management of the central and 16 major states of India during the time of COVID- 19 (2020-21 to -2021-22) using secondary data on state's own revenue, central transfers, revenue expenditures, capital expenditures and total expenditures from 2017-18 to 2021-22. They have found that the public finance management in India has been a challenging task due to lower revenue mobilization and higher expenditure responsibilities. The fiscal health of Odisha has been examined in literatures using deficit, revenue and expenditure indicators (Jena 2011; Jena 2019). Jena 2011 found that during 2001 to 2010-11 even if fiscal discipline is maintained to some extent, the state lacks strategic prioritization and operational efficiency in public expenditure management. Jena 2019 argues that the maintenance fiscal discipline through controlling expenditures has led to shrinking fiscal with lower growth of own revenue and high dependency on federal transfers. These analyses of the fiscal performance relate to an economy with demand constraint. This chapter by using three sets of indicators available in literatures with a longer time period (1980-81 to 2020-21) analyses the fiscal health of the state between the existence of demand (1980-81 to 2019-20) and both demand and supply constraint economy (2020-21). The three sets of indicators used are: (1) Deficits (Revenue deficit, fiscal deficit, primary deficit) as percentage of GSDP; (2) Revenue receipts (state's own tax, state's own non-tax, state's own revenue, total revenue receipts of state, federal transfers to state) as percentage of GSDP and (3) Expenditures (revenue expenditures, total expenditures, revenue account social and economic expenditures and capital account social and economic expenditures) as percentage of GSDP. Despite the policy measures undertaken by both the central and state government there is larger fiscal deterioration during the existence of demand and supply constraint situation in the state.

PRE-LOCKDOWN PERIOD

Fiscal health of Odisha was to some extent on the verge of improvement before lockdown period as per theories discussed earlier. Further, it was quite good on the ground of remedial measures prescribed by the recommendations of the Finance Commissions to maintain macro-economic stability and debt sustainability for states[8]. Empirical analysis shows that before lockdown with the occurrence of the pandemic, Odisha has been able to maintain revenue surplus and fiscal deficit below the target (3.5% of GSDP) of Fiscal Responsibility and Budget Management (FRBM) Act since 2005-06 (Figure 1). It corroborates to government of Odisha 2020 (Government of Odisha, 2020). There is rise in revenue receipts and decline in revenue expenditures from the previous year (2004-05). The estimation shows that (1) the total revenue as per cent of GSDP has increased tremendously from 16.55% during 2005-06 to 19% during 2019-20 (Figure 2) and (2) the total revenue expenditure as per cent of GSDP has declined 16% during 2005-06 to 15% during 2012-13 and then increased to 18% during 2019-20 (Figure 3). One percent rise in state's own revenue due to rationalization of taxation and introduction of value added tax during 2005 and 3% increase in federal transfers on account of rise in volume of central shared taxes from 32% of divisible pool to 42% from 13th to 14th Union Finance Commission have enabled the total revenue to expand[9]. Federal transfer being a significant portion (on an average 53% from 2003-04 to 2019-20) of total revenue of the state and an increase of three times of state's own tax, it is solely responsible for increase in total revenue receipts. The decline in revenue expenditure is attributed to curtailment of revenue account social and economic expenditures. The revenue surplus and decline in the repayment of central government loans keep the fiscal deficit of the state below the target of FRBM act. The fiscal stability helps to enlarge the size of developmental activities. The developmental revenue expenditure of Odisha grew more than 2 times in a span of 6 years (2014-15 to 2019-20 (GoO 2020).

However, to meet the sizeable chunk of revenue expenditure the state mainly depends on the transfers of funds from the Centre as stated earlier. The declines in revenue account social and economic expenditures in turn reduces the own tax of the state which further expands the fiscal dependency of the state on Centre to meet revenue expenditures. As a consequence, it arises a vicious circle in the fiscal dependency syndrome of the state indicating weak fiscal performance of the state. Elsewhere, the weak fiscal performance of the state was observed during 1976-77 to 2018-19 due to low dormant own tax capacity and inappropriate public expenditure management (Sahu and Mahamallik 2020).

Figure 1. Deficits of Odisha (% of GSDP)
Note: RD =Revenue Deficit, FD = Fiscal Deficit and PD = Primary Deficit
Source: https://finance.odisha.gov.in/Budgets

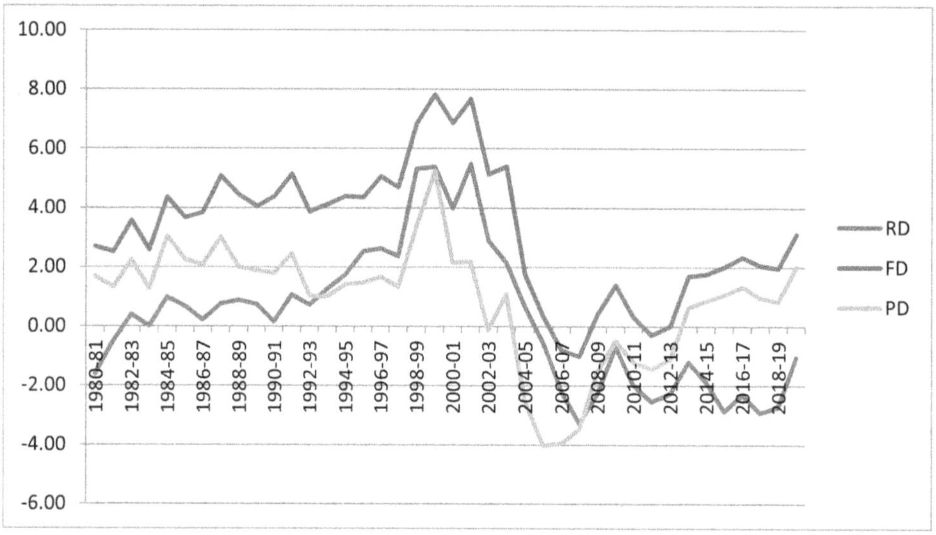

Figure 2. Revenue receipt of Odisha (% of GSDP)
Note: OWT =Own Tax, OWNT = Own Non-Tax, TOWR = Total Own Revenue and TR = Total Revenue
Source: Same as Figure 1.

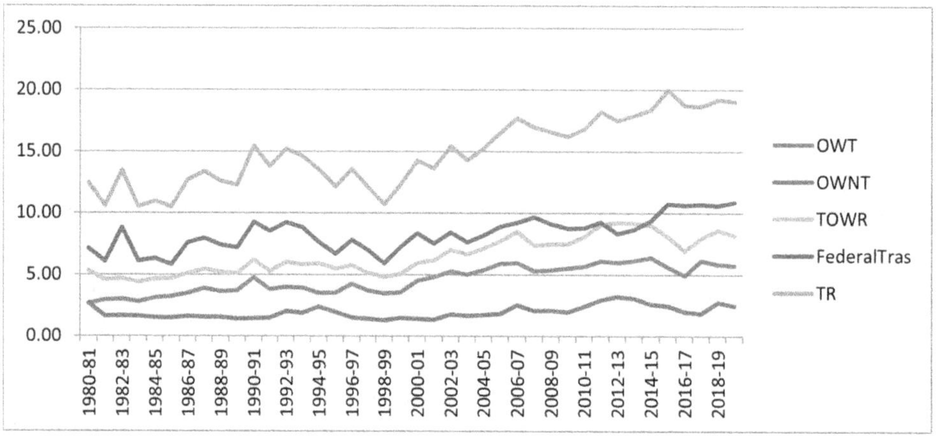

Figure 3. Expenditure of Odisha (% of GSDP)
Note: TEXP = Total Expenditure, REXP = Revenue Expenditure, CEXP = Capital Expenditure, R_SS = Revenue account Social Services, R_ES = Revenue account Economic Services, C_SS = Capital account Social Services and C_ES = Capital account Economic Services
Source: Same as Figure 1.

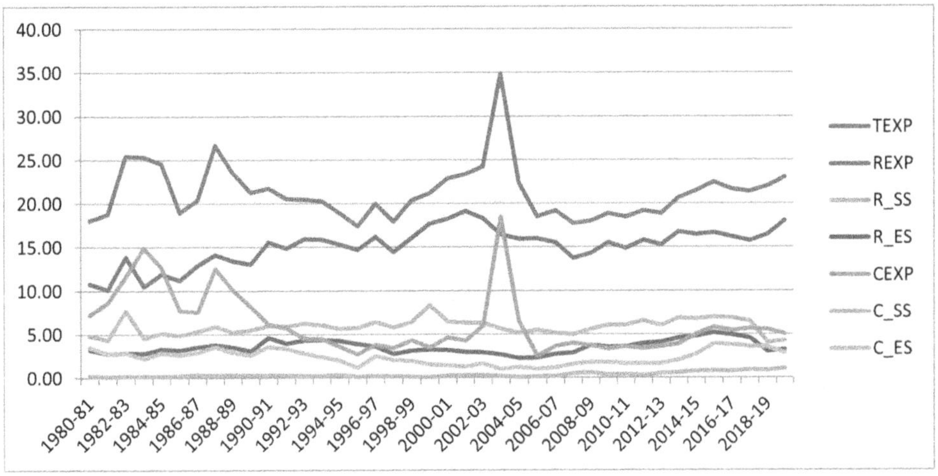

LOCKDOWN PERIOD

With the introduction of full or partial lockdown of the economy, there has been increase in the rates of deficit indicators (Revenue and Fiscal Deficit) of the budget 2020-21 showing sign of further deterioration in the existing weak fiscal performance of the state before lockdown (Table 1). The average estimation from the year 2005-06 to 2019-20 shows that the total revenue, revenue expenditures and total expenditures of the state are 18, 16 and 20 per cent of GSDP respectively. The excess of total revenue over revenue expenditures has led to revenue surplus as reflected by negative revenue deficit (RD) of -2% during 2005-06 to 2019-20. In the same manner, fiscal deficit (FD) of around 2% is found due to excess of total expenditures over total revenue in the same period. The generation of revenue surplus has enabled the state to reduce FD to below the target of Fiscal Responsibility Budget Management Act (3% of GSDP). However, during the lockdown period (2020-21) the total revenue of the state has declined by 2% than pre-lockdown period due to reduction in own tax revenue by the same percentage as that of total revenue as a consequence of total or partial lockdown of the economy. The federal transfer which contributes to the total revenue of the state has contracted by 1% due to reduction in the collection of central shared taxes. On the other hand, revenue expenditures and total expenditures have increased by 3% and 5% during lockdown than the pre-lockdown period. It is observed that there has been risen in revenue account expenditure on education (0.46%), health (1.02%), rural development (1.38%) and administration (0.3%) and pension (0.83%). The reduction in own tax revenue and federal transfers on the one hand and the increase in revenue expenditures and total expenditures led to rise in RD and FD by 5% and 7% respectively[10].

As a result of total closed down of all economic activities throughout the state the revenue generation totally banned. In the same manner the revenue generation of the Central government also stopped leading to decline in the state's share in central taxes. The increase in total expenditures is attributed to rise in health expenditures,of the state. The state increased the health infrastructure. Quarantine centers were opened in the area of each local government (Gram Panchayat) at village level for COVID suspected persons. To meet the expenditure needs five lakhs rupees have been sanctioned to each Gram Panchayat. Two hospitals with 500-bed in each have been set-up for treatment of COVID-19 patients in collaboration with Kalinga Institute of Medical Sciences and SUM Hospital (The Economic Times March 27, 2020). For sanitization facilities the primary health center and additional primary health center were given 10 and 5 lakhs rupees respectively. In economic sphere the government came forward to protect the poor from starvation. In order to meet the expenditure needs of COVID 19, 70 per cent salaries of the Chief Minister, Cabinet Ministers, MLAs, chairpersons of corporations and the elected representatives of all local bodies have been postponed (India Today April 1, 2020). Further, 200 crores rupees has been allocated to increase the public health fund.

The contribution of manufacturing sectors towards its economy has totally stopped. Agricultural activities have been adversely affected. Staying at home farmers could not attain the agricultural field. Pest damaged the unharvest crop. The ripen products get damaged without harvest. Further whatever ripens products is there in home get ruined due to lack of marketability. When stored, they are damaged by pests. Irrigation is hampered in the absence farmer's supervision. Lack of transportation facility made the situation tougher for the farmers to sale their products in different parts of the state. The contribution of trade sector reduced to a large extent. Overall, the epidemic has brought out a sharp degradation in economic activities within the state. The extent of expectation of the state to mobilize own revenue declines to a large extent. Elsewhere it is argued that lockdown costs significantly to the economy (Motkuri 2020; Chakraborty and Thomas 2020). On the other hand, there is rise in unexpected expenditure due to the pandemic. The resources of Indian states have decreased with their large immediate expenditure needs (Rao 2020). It encourages state to go for larger borrowing which will add to increasing fiscal deficit. It is argued that the fiscal deficit target of FRBM should not be considered while making expenditures on containment of COVID 19 since the rise in fiscal deficit would not be inflationary due to low demand (Kumar, Arun 2020; Chakraborty and Thomas 2020). However, if the pandemic continues for a longer period of time, huge amount of resources will be required to handle the circumstances which in turn raise the fiscal deficit to a larger extent. It may lead to debt unsustainability for the state. No such step has been taken by the state to increase the revenue instead of resorting to debt. Printing of money is recommended to finance the deficit (Chakraborty and Thomas 2020). It is an exogenous factor for sub-national level in a fiscal federalism. In such a critical situation, the state needs to plan effective strategies to raise the level of income through fiscal policy allowing economic activities compromising the sanitization measures of the pandemic. Although the state has allowed some economic activities after April 20, 2020, still stringent conditions have been imposed by the authorities. It will have little positive impact on the economy.

Table 1. State finances of Odisha

	% of GSDP								
Year	OWT	OWNT	TOWR	FT	TR	TEXP	REXP	RD	FD
2005-06	5.88	1.80	7.68	8.87	16.55	18.50	15.99	-0.57	1.95
2006-07	5.96	2.54	8.50	9.21	17.71	19.13	15.49	-2.22	1.42
2007-08	5.30	2.05	7.36	9.64	16.99	17.71	13.71	-3.28	0.72
2008-09	5.37	2.10	7.48	9.12	16.59	17.97	14.27	-2.32	1.37
2009-10	5.51	1.95	7.46	8.74	16.20	18.86	15.51	-0.69	2.66
2010-11	5.67	2.42	8.09	8.76	16.85	18.44	14.87	-1.98	1.59
2011-12	6.09	2.92	9.01	9.24	18.23	19.13	15.76	-2.47	0.91
2012-13	5.98	3.22	9.20	8.29	17.49	18.83	15.24	-2.25	1.34
2013-14	6.11	3.07	9.18	8.67	17.93	20.65	16.75	-1.18	2.72
2014-15	6.38	2.60	8.98	9.36	18.34	21.45	16.45	-1.89	3.11
2015-16	5.61	2.46	8.08	10.73	20.00	22.42	16.64	-3.36	2.42
2016-17	4.94	2.00	6.94	10.64	18.72	21.63	16.19	-2.53	2.91
2017-18	6.11	1.84	7.95	10.70	18.66	21.35	15.73	-2.93	2.69
2018-19	5.84	2.75	8.59	10.58	19.17	21.95	16.44	-2.73	2.77
2019-20(RE)	5.72	2.47	8.19	10.86	19.05	23.01	18.00	-1.05	3.96
Average	**5.77**	**2.41**	**8.18**	**9.56**	**17.90**	**20.07**	**15.80**	**-2.10**	**2.17**
2020-21	5.03	2.53	7.55	8.65	16.21	25.34	19.39	3.18	9.13

Note: The sign '(-)' and '(+)' indicates surplus and deficit respectively. OWT = Own Tax, OWNT = Own Non- Tax, TOWR = Total Own Revenue, FT = Federal Transfers, TR = Total Revenue, TEXPT = Total Expenditure, REXP = Revenue Expenditure, RD = Revenue Deficit and FD =Fiscal Deficit.

Source: Same as Figure 1.

CONCLUDING OBSERVATIONS

With the spread of COVID 19 within the state of Odisha, the government has taken perennial efforts to control its spread and protect the masses from the pandemic. It has undertaken full or partial lockdown of the economy as a panacea in the absence of availability of medicine for the disease besides providing health related infrastructure. While the partial or full lockdown of the economy reduces the revenue generation capacity, provision of extra health expenditure due to COVID 19 raises the expenditure burden on the state. Further, with the decline in the mobilization of resources by the central government, the federal transfers to state contracts. As a consequence, the state has to resort to borrowing to meet the unexpected revenue expenditure needs on the health sector of the state. The decline in revenue generation capacity and the use of borrowing for activities that do not generate income for its repayment deteriorates the fiscal health of the state. In this juncture, the state has to allow economic activities compromising sanitization measures to expand its income generation capacity through fiscal measures.

Table 2. Per capita net state domestic product (NSDP) at current 2011-12 base price in rupees during 2018-19

State	Per Capita NSDP
Haryana	236147
Karnataka	212477
Kerala	204105
Gujarat	195845
Tamil Nadu	193964
Maharashtra	191736
Punjab	154313
Andhra Pradesh	151173
Rajasthan	110606
West Bengal	101138
Odisha	99196
Madhya Pradesh	90165
Uttar Pradesh	66512
Bihar	40982
All-India per capita NNI	126521

Source: https://www.rbi.org.in/Scripts/AnnualPublications.aspx?head=Handbook of Statistics on Indian Economy

Table 3. Revenue capacity of states during 2018-19

State	TOWR%REXP
Haryana	70.7
Gujarat	68.6
Maharashtra	68.3
Karnataka	62.6
Tamil Nadu	62.5
Kerala	59.5
Punjab	52.2
Uttar Pradesh	50.2
Andhra Pradesh	49.9
Rajasthan	47.3
Odisha	45.2
Madhya Pradesh	41.3
West Bengal	41.1
Bihar	25.2
All States and UTs	51.9

Note: TOWN and REXP are same as Table 1.

Source: https://www.rbi.org.in/Scripts/ccasionalPublications/A Study of State Finances

Table 4. Socio-demographic characteristics of states (as per 2011 census)

State	Area	Pop	Density	Sex Ratio	Urban	SC and ST	IMR	LER (2011-15)	Hospital	Bed
Andhra Pradesh	11.2	8.0	308	992	8.6	7.7	43	69	1	98
Bihar	3.8	9.9	1102	918	3.6	7.0	44	68.4	3	30
Gujarat	8.0	5.7	308	1084	7.8	5.1	41	69.1	2	107
Haryana	1.8	2.4	573	930	2.7	2.0	44	69.1	8	143
Karnataka	7.8	5.8	319	926	7.2	5.7	35	69	17	429
Kerala	1.6	3.2	859	995	4.9	1.4	12	75.2	10	297
Madhya Pradesh	12.5	6.9	236	908	6.1	10.4	59	64.8	1	89
Maharashtra	12.5	10.6	365	947	15.5	9.3	25	72	3	206
Odisha	**6.3**	**4.0**	**269**	**979**	**2.1**	**6.6**	**57**	**66.9**	**6**	**61**
Punjab	2.0	2.6	550	883	3.2	3.5	30	72.1	8	220
Rajasthan	13.9	6.5	201	987	5.2	8.4	26	67.9	8	136
Tamil Nadu	5.3	6.8	555	975	10.6	5.9	22	71	3	215
Uttar Pradesh	9.8	18.9	828	961	13.6	16.6	57	64.5	9	141
West Bengal	3.6	8.6	1029	963	8.9	10.4	32	70.5	2	124

Note: POP = Population, SC and ST = Schedule Caste and Schedule Tribe Population, IMR = Infant Mortality Rate, LER= Life Expectancy Rate. IMR is per one thousand life births, Hospital (Private and Public) and bed in hospital are per one lakh population. Area, population, urbanization, SC and ST population are in percentage terms.

Source: https://www.rbi.org.in

Table 5. State wise corona disease cases during 18 March to 11 April, 2020

STATE/UT	Confirmed	Active	Recovered	Deceased
Arunachal Pradesh	1	1	0	0
Dadra and Nagar Haveli	1	1	0	0
Mizoram	1	1	0	0
Manipur	2	1	1	0
Tripura	2	2	0	0
Goa	7	6	1	0
Puducherry	7	6	1	0
Andaman and Nicobar Islands	11	1	10	0
Ladakh	15	4	11	0
Jharkhand	17	16	0	1
Chhattisgarh	18	9	9	0
Chandigarh	19	12	7	0
Assam	29	28	0	1
Himachal Pradesh	32	24	46	2
Uttarakhand	35	30	5	0
Odisha	51	38	12	1
Bihar	61	45	15	1
West Bengal	126	105	16	5
Punjab	158	126	20	12
Haryana	179	141	36	2
Karnataka	215	170	39	6
Jammu and Kashmir	224	214	6	4
Kerala	374	228	143	13
Andhra Pradesh	405	389	10	6
Gujarat	432	379	34	9
Madhya Pradesh	451	373	39	39
Uttar Pradesh	452	402	45	5
Telangana	487	430	45	12
Rajasthan	678	559	16	3
Delhi	903	862	27	14
Tamil Nadu	969	915	44	10
Maharashtra	1666	1368	88	110
Total	8027	6885	886	256

Source: https://www.covid19india.org/

Figure 4. Day wise trend of COVID-19 positive cases in Odisha (15 March to 9 April 2020)
Source: Website of National Health Mission, Odisha.

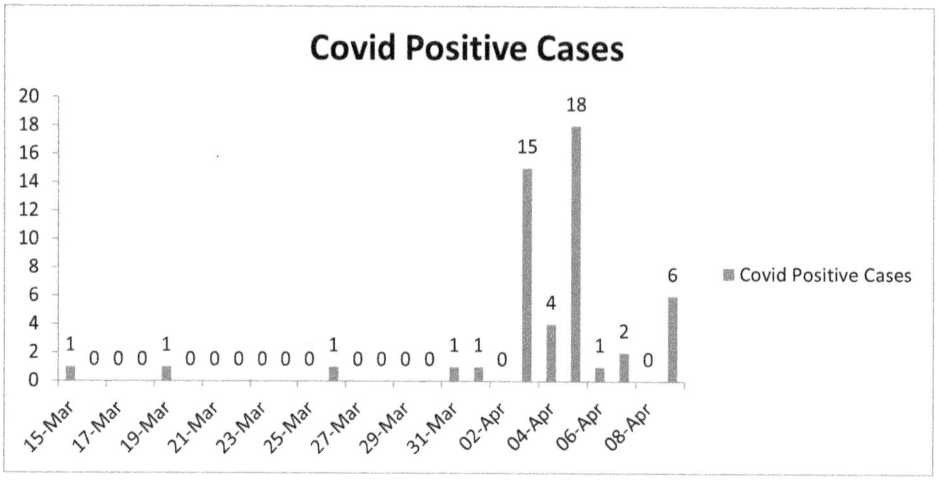

REFERENCES

Baldwin, R., & Tomiura, E. (2020). Thinking ahead about the trade impact of COVID-19. In R. Baldwin & B. Weder di Mauro (Eds.), *Economics in the Time of COVID-19*. Centre for Economic Policy Research Press.

Baldwin, R., & Weder di Mauro, B. (2020). *Economics in the Time of COVID-19*. Centre for Economic Policy Research Press.

Beck, T. (2020). Finance in the times of coronavirus. In R. Baldwin & B. Weder di Mauro (Eds.), *Economics in the Time of COVID-19*. Centre for Economic Policy Research Press.

Brodeur, A., Gray, D., Islam, A., & Bhuiyan, S. J. (2020). *A Literature Review of the Economics of COVID-19*. Discussion Paper Series, No. 13411. IZA Institute of Labour Economics.

Cecchetti, S. G., & Schoenholtz, K. L. (2020). Contagion: Bank runs and COVID-19. In R. Baldwin & B. Weder di Mauro (Eds.), *Economics in the Time of COVID-19*. Centre for Economic Policy Research Press.

Chakraborty & Thomas. (2020). COVID-19 and Macroeconomic Uncertainty: Fiscal and Monetary Policy Response. *Economic and Political Weekly, 40*(15), 10-12.

Chakraborty, L., & Harikrishnan, S. (2022). COVID-19 and Fiscal- Monetary Policy Co-ordination: Empirical Evidence from India. *Economic and Political Weekly, 57*(4), 18-21.

Chaudhary, M., Sodani, P. R., & Das, S. (2020). Effect of COVID-19 on Economy in India: Some Reflections for Policy and Programme. *Journal of Health Management, 22*(2), 169–180. doi:10.1177/0972063420935541

Cochrane, J. H. (2020). Coronavirus monetary policy. In Economics in the Time of COVID-19. Centre for Economic Policy Research Press.

Congressional Research Service. (2020). *Global Economic Effects of COVID-19*. CRS Report prepared for members and committees of congress, R46270. https://crsreports.congress.gov

Dev, Mahendra, & Sengupta. (2020). *Covid-19: Impact on the Indian Economy*. Working Paper, No. 13. Indira Gandhi Institute of Development Research.

Dupor, B. (2020). *Possible Fiscal Policies for Rare, Unanticipated, and Severe Viral Outbreaks. Economic Synopses, 1-2(6)*. doi:10.20955/es.2020.6

Economic Times. (2020). *Odisha announces Covid-19-dedicated hospitals with 1,000 beds*. https://economictimes.indiatimes.com/industry/healthcare/biotech/healthcare/odisha-announces-countrys-first-covid-19-dedicated-hospitals-with-1000-beds/articleshow/74832053.cms?from=mdr

Engage, E. P. W. (2020). Controlling the Corona Virus: Examining Nation States and their Approach towards Fighting Viral Diseases? *Economic and Political Weekly*. Available at https://www.epw.in/engage/article/controlling-coronavirus--nation-states-viral-diseases

Faria e Castro. (2020). *Fiscal Policy during a Pandemic*. Working Paper 2020-006D. Research Division Working Paper Series, Federal Reserve Bank of St. Louis. doi:10.20955/wp.2020.006

Fornaro, L., & Wolf, M. (2020). *Covid-19 Coronavirus and Macroeconomic Policy: Some Analytical Notes*. CREI/UPF and University of Vienna. http://www.crei.cat/wp-content/uploads/2016/07/CMP.pdf

Government of Odisha. (2020a). *Odisha Economic Survey 2019-20*. Planning and Convergence Department, Directorate of Economics and Statistics.

Government of Odisha. (2020b). *Odisha Economic Survey 2020-21*. Planning and Convergence Department, Directorate of Economics and Statistics.

Government of Odisha. (2020c). *The number of Confirmed Cases and deaths of corona disease*. Available at https://statedashboard.odisha.gov.in/

Jackson, J. K., Weiss, M. A., Schwarzenberg, A. B., Nelson, R. M., Sutter, K. M., & Sutherland, M. D. (2021). *Global Economic Effects of COVID-19*. Congressional Research Service, No. R46270. Available at https://crsreports.congress.gov

Jena, P. R. (2011). Public Expenditures Management at Sub National Level: A Perspective from the State of Orissa. *Orissa. Economic Journal (London)*, *43*(1&2), 237–262.

Jena, P. R. (2019). *Living under Fiscal Rules: Fiscal Management Response and Resource Allocation Choices for State of Odisha*. Working Paper, No. 264. National Institute of Public Finance and Policy.

John, T. (2020). How Prepared Is India to Control the COVID-19 Pandemic? *Economic and Political Weekly, 55*(11), 13-15.

Karlsson, M., & Nilsson, T. (2014, July). The impact of the 1918 Spanish flu epidemic on economic performance in Sweden: An investigation into the consequences of an extraordinary mortality shock. *Journal of Health Economics, 36*, 1-19. Available at https://www.sciencedirect.com/science/article/abs/pii/S0167629614000344

Khemani, S. (2007). Does delegation of fiscal policy to an independent agency make a difference? Evidence from intergovernmental transfers in India. *Journal of Development Economics*, *82*(2), 464–484. doi:10.1016/j.jdeveco.2006.04.001

Kumar, A. (2020). Impact of COVID-19 and What Needs to Be Done. *Economic and Political Weekly*, *LV*(14), 10–12.

Lahiri, A. K. (2000). Budget Deficits and Reforms. *Economic and Political Weekly, 35*(46), 4048-4054.

Mahamallik, M., & Sahu, P. (2015). Paradox of Fiscal Imbalances: Recommendations of Fourteenth Finance Commission. *Artha Vijnana*, *57*(4), 301–320. doi:10.21648/arthavij/2015/v57/i4/111493

Mandle & Sahu. (2021). Fiscal Compression, Jeopardised Recovery, the Humanitarian Crisis and Reforms. *Economic and Political Weekly, 56*(21), 39-46.

Mann, C. L. (2020). Real and financial lenses to assess the economic consequences of COVID-19. In R. Baldwin & B. Weder di Mauro (Eds.), *Economics in the Time of COVID-19*. Centre for Economic Policy Research Press.

McKibbin, W., & Fernando, R. (2020). The economic impact of COVID-19. In R. Baldwin & B. Weder di Mauro (Eds.), *Economics in the Time of COVID-19*. Centre for Economic Policy Research Press.

Meltzer, M. I., Cox, N. J., & Fukuda, K. (1999, September-October). The Economic Impact of Pandemic Influenza in the United States: Priorities for Intervention. *Emerging Infectious Diseases*, *V*(5), 659–671. doi:10.3201/eid0505.990507 PMID:10511522

Motkuri, V. (2020). COVID19 Cases and Testing: A Cross Country Analysis. Nabakrishna Chaudhary Center for Development Studies, Bhubaneswar.

Mukherjee, S., & Badola, S. (2021). *Public Finance Management in India in the Time of COVID-19 Pandemic*. Working Paper, No. 337. National Institute of Public Finance and Policy.

Oates, W. E. (1972). The Fiscal Federalism, Harcourt Brace Jovanovich Inc.

Rajaraman & Majumdar. (2005). Equity and Consistency Properties of Twelfth Finance Commission Recommendations. *Economic and Political Weekly, 40*(31), 3413-3420.

Rangarajan & Srivastava. (2004a). Fiscal Transfers in Australia: Review and Relevance to India. *Economic and Political Weekly, 40*(27), 3709-3722.

Rangarajan & Srivastava. (2004b). Fiscal Transfers in Canada: Drawing Comparisons and Lessons. *Economic and Political Weekly, 39*(19), 1897-1909.

Rangarajan & Srivastava. (2005). Fiscal Deficit and Government Debt: Implications for Growth and Stabilization. *Economic and Political Weekly, 40*(27), 2919-2934.

Rao, M. G. (2002). State Finances in India: Issues and Challenges. *Economic and Political Weekly, 37*(31), 3261-3271.

Rao, M. G. (2004). Linking Central Transfers to Fiscal Performance of States. *Economic and Political Weekly, 39*(18), 1820-1825.

Rao, M. G. (2020). The Key Strategy is Fiscal Empowerment of States. *The Hindu.*

Rao, M. G., & Sen Tapas, K. (1996). *Fiscal Federalism in Theory and Practice in India.* Indian Council of Social Science Research.

Ray, Subramanian, & Vandewalle. (2020). India's Lockdown. Policy Insight, No. 102. Centre for Economic Policy Research.

Sahu, P., & Mahamallik, M. (2019, December). Centre-State Relation in India: Issue of Cooperative Federalism. *Madhya Pradesh Journal of Social Sciences, 24*(2), 94–106.

Sahu, P., & Mahamallik, M. (2020, December). The Rhetoric of Fiscal Performance: A Study of Odisha, India. *Artha Vijnana, 62*(4), 336–355.

The Hindu. (2020). *Coronavirus | Odisha says cost of treatment will be borne by the State.* https://www.thehindu.com/news/national/other-states/coronavirus-odisha-says-cost-of-treatment-will-be-borne-by-the-state/article31211494.ece

Today, I. (2020). *Odisha Govt to defer salaries of CM, ministers to counter economic impact of Covid-19.* https://www.indiatoday.in/india/story/odisha-govt-to-defer-salaries-of-cm-ministers-to-counter-economic-impact-of-covid-19-1661946-2020-04-01

World Health Organization. (2020). *The Number of Cases of Corona Disease.* Available from https://covid19.who.int/?gclid=Cj0KCQiAh4j-BRCsARIsAGeV12B-WrtLBICk1963VqpTEMlXEurjro8s-jB39Y24yGpEgdmyFjytf58aAqwnEALw_wc

ENDNOTES

1. Public health, sanitation, hospitals and dispensaries are listed in item 6 of List II (State List) of Seventh Schedule of the Indian Constitution.
2. The fourteen major states of India are Andhra Pradesh, Bihar, Gujarat, Haryana, Karnataka, Kerala, Maharashtra, Madhya Pradesh, Odisha, Punjab, Rajasthan, Tamil Nadu, Uttar Pradesh and West Bengal.
3. Earlier it was found that over 1000 people died due to H1N1 virus in 2019. Elsewhere, it is mentioned that epidemic results from lack of development, unregulated market and poor hygienic conditions (EPW 2020,). Unlike earlier epidemics it is moderate killer but mighty spreader (John 2020).
4. The full lockdown fully banned cross boarders, travels, all educational and other institutions. It made all the industries shut down for an uncertain period. Further, the government closed down all shops except daily needs shop, working place, temples, public gathering, visiting place, market except few hours of operation and construction works. People were ordered to stay at home. But keeping in mind the spread of the disease which has no clear cut source and certainty regarding its containment, the government increased the extent of lockdown to 19 more days from 14th April to 3rd May 2020. Any kind of social gatherings (like marriage receptions), religious functions and parties are regulated by local authorities. Places like swimming pool, gym and cinema halls across the state are closed. Non-essential official gatherings such as seminars, workshops and conferences have been cancelled.

[5] For instance in India and Australia, there are three levels: (1) Central government at the national level, (2) State government at sub-national level and (3) Local self-government at sub-national level. The term National, Central and Federal have been interchangeably used.

[6] The commonwealth Grant Commission in Australia, the National Finance Council in Malaysia, the Revenue Mobilization Allocation and Fiscal Commission in Nigeria and the Finance Commission in India are the constitutional bodies to mediate revenue transfers from Federal government to Sub-national government (Khemani 2007).

[7] As per the article 280 of the constitution of India, a Finance Commission is to be constituted in every five years or earlier, if necessary, by the order of the President of India to recommend measures: (1) to distribute the net proceeds of the central government between the Centre and state and inter se distribution of state's share across states, (2) grants in aid to states and (3) relating to any other matters for sound finance of the country.

[8] The 11th and 12th Union Finance Commission recommended Medium Term Fiscal Restructuring Programme (MTFRP) and Fiscal Responsibility Budget Management Act (FRBMA) respectively for fiscal improvement of States through incentive linked grants in the former and debt write of in case of later. As per the MTFRP, a state is entitled to receive incentive linked grants provided it maintains: (1) the gross fiscal deficit as 2.5 per cent of gross state domestic product, (2) zero revenue deficit, (3) interest payment as less than 18-20 per cent of the revenue receipts, (4) wages and salaries less than 5 per cent of increase in consumer price index, (5) less than 10 per cent increase in interest payment per year and reduction of explicit subsidies to less than 50 per cent over the five year period (Rao 2004). FRBMA enables a state in receiving relief from debt and interest rate reduction provided it fulfills the conditions such as: (1) zero revenue deficit by 2008-09; (2) fiscal deficit as 3 per cent of gross state domestic product or interest payment as 3 per cent of revenue receipt; (3) commitment of targets of annual reduction in revenue and fiscal deficit; (4) annual statement on prospect for state economy and related fiscal strategy and (5) special statements with budget giving in detail the number of employee in government, public sector, aided institutions and related salaries (Rajaraman and Majumdar 2005)

[9] The total own revenue and federal transfers as per cent of GSDP have increased from 7% and 8% to 8% and 11% respectively during 2003-04 to 2019-20.

[10] The data for major heads of revenue and expenditures of Odisha for the year 2020-2021 have been estimated as per the average difference between the actual and budget estimate as given by Jena 2019.

Chapter 11
Indian Agriculture During COVID-19:
Prospectus and Challenges

Rajender S. Godara
https://orcid.org/0000-0002-7568-0819
Lovely Professional University, India

Durafshan Jaihon Fetrat
Department of Business and Administration, Economics Faculty, Takhar University, Takhar, Afghanistan

Azatullah Nazari
Department of Business Administration and Economics Faculty, Takhar University, Takhar, Afghanistan

ABSTRACT

The purpose of this chapter is to summarize the initial evidence based on various research articles and sources. The results show that the effects of the agricultural epidemic can be categorized into supply, demand, labor, food security, food safety, and trade. COVID-19 by affecting the supply chain, demand and liquidity, firms, and by affecting the supply of labor, consumption of goods, and services and especially by reducing the income of consumers and producers of agricultural products in the short- and long-term affects the household economy as well as influences the economy of the agricultural sector. The market for some products in other countries has also been weakened, and part of the export of agricultural products has been affected both directly and indirectly. This chapter examines the impact of the Corona crisis on India's agricultural sector. The effect of the shock caused by the corona crisis on the supply chain of agricultural products, including consumption, production, distribution, and trade, as well as other economic effects are examined.

DOI: 10.4018/978-1-7998-6896-5.ch011

INTRODUCTION

The agricultural and allied sector carries immense importance for the Indian economy. It contributes nearly one-sixth to the Indian national income and provides employment to nearly 50% of the workforce. It is fundamental for ensuring food security of the nation and also influences the growth of secondary and tertiary sector of the economy through its forward and backward linkages. The performance of agricultural sector greatly influences achievements on many other fronts. For instance, World Development Report 2008 released by World Bank emphasises that growth in agriculture is, on average, at least twice as effective in reducing poverty as growth outside agriculture. Agricultural growth reduces poverty directly, by raising farm incomes, and indirectly, through generating employment and reducing food prices. In other words, a thriving agricultural sector is a boon for most sectors of the Indian economy.

The economic implications of the novel Coronavirus (COVID-19) pandemic have brought the agricultural sector into sharp focus and heightened its responsibility to feed and employ thousands who might have lost livelihoods. At this time when most sectors of the economy are reported to be under significant stress, the agricultural sector continues to be promising and cushioning the economy. The area sown under all major kharif crops is expected to be higher than corresponding period during the last year. Since the agricultural sector continues to be one of the bright spots amidst this pandemic, there is a need of prioritising agricultural sector during this time to ensure speedy economic recovery of the country.

Undoubtedly, the outbreak of the Corona virus is one of the most universal phenomena in human history, the dimensions of which have affected everyone on the planet. It can be argued that today, the concern of all governments around the world is to plan to control this disease and manage its economic consequences. According to the World Health Organization, as of Nov 09, 2020, more than 50,266,033 people worldwide have been infected with the diseaseincluding 1,254,567 deaths, with India accounting for 8,553,657 and the number of deaths from this disease in the country has been 126,611 until that date (WTO, 2020). This has led to one of the most unprecedented government controls on day-to-day operations around the world. Fear of the spread of the virus has left many economic activities in a coma. Estimates show that the shock caused by the disease was far greater than the Great Depression of 2007-2008 and could largely lead to a change in economic thinking, as did the Great Depression of 1928 (Arumugam, Kanagavalli, & Manida, 2020).

The agricultural sector is of special importance in the country's economy due to providing food security and providing a livelihood for a part of the country's population directly and indirectly. Examining the consequences and actively preparing for them is one of the most important ways to reduce anxiety and stress about crises (Odisha, 2020). COVID 19 is a negative event for the economies of most countries in the world, and most of the problems created or predicted in India are similar to those in other parts of the world. However, due to the period of several months since the outbreak of this disease in the world and about two months in India, it is not enough time to make a definite statement about the effects and possible damages of this disease (Jain, Baghla, & A, 2020). Although some assumed that the prevalence of COVID 19 had no effect on the agricultural sector and its producers due to the constant human need for food, which accounts for the bulk of agricultural production, but this crisis has affected the activities of the agricultural sector as well as has affected other economic sectors. The COVID 19 crisis on the agricultural sector of the country, in a situation where this sector is facing major problems and challenges such as lack of investment, low productivity, market inefficiency, and production, increases the severity of the vulnerability of this sector (Rawal, Kumar, Verma, & Pais, 2020).

Production characteristics of most agricultural products have forced the producers of this sector to continue their activities and expenses. Because gardens, farms, and livestock does not have the ability to be abandoned, while the livelihood of farmers is endangered if abandoned (Wani, 2020). To study the real effect of coronavirus on the country agricultural economy, it is necessary to evaluate the data related to supply chains, supply and demand of agricultural products, which itself is affected by such things as energy demand and prices, and the past and present goods of this sector (Ali & Khan, 2020).

Agriculture, the only sector to clock a positive growth of 3.4 per cent at constant prices in 2020-21, during the first wave of the novel coronavirus disease (COVID-19), could be severely impacted due to the ongoing second wave.

The primary reason is that COVID-19 is running riot in the country's rural hinterland, where most agricultural activity takes place, during the second wave.

During the first wave, there were some supply chain issues related to the produce's transport from the primary mandis to the secondary and bigger markets. But this time around, there are several concerns about taking the produce even to the primary mandis due to rising COVID-19 cases in rural areas and imposition of lockdowns.

The COVID-19 crisis has bought to the fore some of the persistent problems that Indian agriculture faces. Despite the impressive strides made toward improved access to institutional credit, dependency on informal credit sources remains high, especially among smallholder farmers. The government has to step in to ensure farmers can access fresh credit for the *Kharif* season. The other important dynamic that policymakers and the wider development community need to look at is preserving the role of women in agriculture. The surplus labor in rural areas can potentially undermine the status of women in agriculture, and push them further into economic exclusion.

The SHG movement that includes SHG federations and women-owned FPOs should be utilized to improve market price realization for women farmers and improve the engagement of women in value-addition activities such as low value processing. The push for market reforms has put the focus on the transformative role of FPOs in agriculture marketing. The dilution of the ECA and APMCs provides a huge opportunity for FPOs to link directly with buyers across the country and also to develop more direct-to-consumer supply chains, and in the process, improve their incomes.

COVID-19 has made visible, long ignored realities of the Indian economy – its fragility, regional and spatial concentration and deep structural inequality. It has also highlighted areas of deep resilience and strength. In 2020, it was India's long ignored rural economy and more specifically agriculture that withstood the COVID-induced economic shock. India's halting efforts at putting in place the foundations of a welfare state for rural India through the Mahatma Gandhi National Rural Employment Guarantee Act (MGNREGA) provided a source of much needed income, and in doing so demonstrated the one truth that we often forget in our debates on growth in the Indian economy – a strong welfare architecture is the foundation of a strong economy. COVID-19 also made visible the precarious nature of the informal economy and its deep interlinkages with rural India. It was to rural India and to agriculture that workers returned when India's cities failed to provide them livelihood.

For too long India's economy has been understood in false binaries of formal vs informal, rural vs urban, farm vs non-farm, growth vs welfare and policy has failed to understand the interlinkages that the experience of COVID-19 has now made visible. Any debate on repair and recovery of the economy now and post COVID-19 will need to recognize this critical failing in our policy debates.

This research examines the impact of the Corona crisis on India's agricultural sector. After this introduction, a picture of the agricultural situation in the country is presented. The effect of the shock caused by the corona crisis on the supply chain of agricultural products, including consumption, production, distribution, and trade, as well as other economic effects are then examined. In the end, policy conclusions and suggestions will be presented.

METHODOLOGY

In fact, this is a descriptive study in which we have used secondary sources. The data used in this study were collected from various sources such as websites of governmental and non-governmental organizations, books, magazines, newspapers. It is noteworthy that in this research, we have used products including APEDA, i.e. Agricultural and Processed Food Products Export Development Authority, to show quantitative data of the agricultural sector. That is, in each part where the data is discussed and a descriptive or inferential analysis is performed, it is based on APEDA Agri Exchange (https://agriexchange.apeda.gov.in/) information and items including APEDA.

The number of agricultural products including APEDA that we used in this study reaches 36 agricultural products which are divided into the following 6 sections: Floriculture, Fresh Fruits & Vegetables, Processed Fruits & Vegetables, Animal Products, and Other Processed Foods & Cereals. In fact, in our inferential analysis, we have studied the effects of the corona virus on these six major groups of agricultural and food products. From an analytical point of view, this research has covered four areas of production, distribution, consumption, and trade of the agricultural sector during the outbreak of Coronavirus.

A PICTURE OF THE AGRICULTURAL SITUATION IN INDIA

Agriculture in India is one of the most private economic sectors and high percentage of it is fully competitive and accounts for 15.96% of production and 41.49% of employment (Bank, 2020). This sector is a key element in ensuring food security and its instability will create many challenges in the growth and development of the country's economy. Agriculture, no matter how vulnerable to natural disasters, is the most resilient economic sector to artificial disasters. Due to the pivotal role of the agricultural sector as drivers of many economic sub-sectors of the country such as industry (food industry, wood industry, textile, and clothing industry, etc.) and services (trade, hotel, and restaurant, transportation, warehousing, etc.) (Kumar, Arabinda, & Ku, 2020). The goal for this sector should be such that in the current situation and the possibility of its continuation, the agricultural sector is the main factor of the positive growth of the national economy with the optimal use of all software and hardware capacities and sustainable production requirements (Sahoo & Samal, 2020). Figure 1 shows the growth rate of Indian's agricultural sector between 2010and2020. Despite the fact that in this decade, severe fluctuations have been imposed on the country's economy, but the agricultural sector has grown by 44.88% and in recent years its growth has reached 3.4 percent (PRS Legislative Research, 2020).

Therefore, the agricultural sector has been the stronghold of macroeconomics in critical conditions and has helped the resilience of the country's economy. In the face of the outbreak of the Coronavirus, the agricultural sector is also expected to suffer less damage than the industrial and service sectors.

Figure 1.

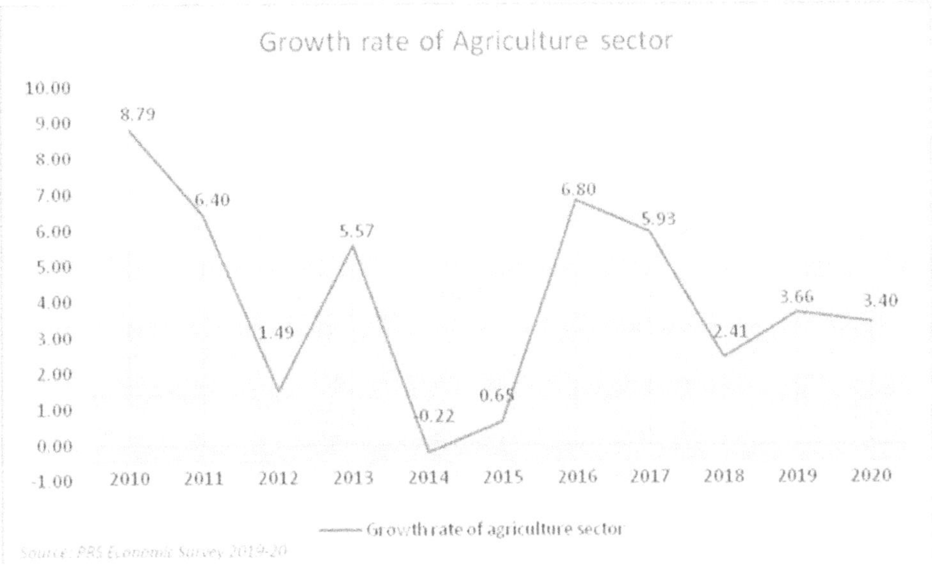

SUBJECT ANALYSIS

Given the importance and impact of the outbreak of COVID 19 on foreign trade in agricultural products we start the analysis from this section. For this purpose the situation of exports and imports of agricultural products before the outbreak of COVID 19 (before Jan 03, 2020) can also be significant.

Table 1. Comparison of the trade balance of the agricultural sector in 2020 and 2019

Type of Trade	Agriculture Sector				Percentage of Changes	
	2019-20		2020-21			
	Weight (In MT)	Value (In US$ Bill)	Weight (In MT)	Value (In US$ Bill)	Quantity	Value
Export	6224790.70	5.52	8212926.27	5.55	+31.938999	+0.543478
Import	1633243.25	1.36	1227588.83	1.14	-24.837354	-16.17647
Trade balance	4591547.45	4.16	6985337.44	4.41	+52.134711	+6.009615
Source: Directorate General of Commercial Intelligence and Statistics (DGCIS)						

Table 1, using data from April to July 2019 and 2020, shows the fluctuations in the import and export of agricultural products and the trade balance of agricultural products.

As you can see, the export of agricultural products in 2020 shows increase compared to 2019. In contrast, imports in 2020 have decreased compared to 2019. Increase in exports and decrease in imports in 2020 and 2019 can be seen in quantity and value. There can be a huge difference between quantity and value fluctuations for various reasons, including price changes and changes in consumer preferences.

The increase in exports and the decrease in imports in 2020 have led to a positive change of 6% in value and a 52% change in quantity of the balance of trade.

Table 2.

April-July 2019-20			April-July 2020-21		
Product	**Quantity**	**US$ Bill**	**Product**	**Quantity**	**US$ Bill**
BASMATI RICE	1435021.9	1.56	BASMATI RICE	1680813.6	1.5
BUFFALO MEAT	368362.96	1.06	NON BASMATI RICE	2999254.8	1.18
NON BASMATI RICE	1711429.9	0.7	BUFFALO MEAT	241176.24	0.72
GROUNDNUTS	134789.73	0.15	FRESH ONIONS	952866.25	0.2
MISCELLANEOUS PREPARATIONS	122208.99	0.21	MISCELLANEOUS PREPARATIONS	121487.19	0.19
CEREAL PREPARATIONS	113564.28	0.18	GROUNDNUTS	140075.08	0.17
GUARGUM	148978.81	0.18	CEREAL PREPARATIONS	102494.22	0.16
PROCESSED FRUITS, JUICES & NUTS	119568.5	0.14	PROCESSED VEGETABLES	118407.56	0.15
PROCESSED VEGETABLES	83869.13	0.13	PULSES	138710.71	0.13
FRESH ONIONS	704046.24	0.15	PROCESSED FRUITS, JUICES & NUTS	95083.82	0.12
FRESH GRAPES	42154.53	0.05	JAGGERY & CONFECTIONERY	233823.95	0.11
OTHER FRESH FRUITS	128680.85	0.07	ALCOHOLIC BEVERAGES	66572.86	0.09
OTHER FRESH VEGETABLES	229461.88	0.09	GUARGUM	73516.23	0.08
ALCOHOLIC BEVERAGES	47779.65	0.08	OTHER FRESH VEGETABLES	173996.38	0.08
JAGGERY & CONFECTIONERY	81120.53	0.06	OTHER FRESH FRUITS	131151.02	0.07
PULSES	85706.08	0.09	MAIZE	349651.63	0.07
DAIRY PRODUCTS	21933.87	0.08	MILLED PRODUCTS	125737.39	0.07
COCOA PRODUCTS	9312.71	0.06	CUCUMBER AND GHERKINS	68185.33	0.07
CUCUMBER AND GHERKINS	48546.56	0.05	DAIRY PRODUCTS	14448.77	0.06
MILLED PRODUCTS	93144.19	0.05	FRUITS & VEGETABLES SEEDS	4101.57	0.04
MAIZE	135139.26	0.05	FRESH GRAPES	32783.13	0.04
FRUITS & VEGETABLES SEEDS	3704.61	0.05	WHEAT	139309.79	0.04
SHEEP/GOAT MEAT	6201.58	0.04	COCOA PRODUCTS	6384.42	0.04
NATURAL HONEY	20658.07	0.03	NATURAL HONEY	19393.27	0.03
MANGO PULP	23232.68	0.02	FRESH MANGOES	17323.27	0.03
POULTRY PRODUCTS	124195.82	0.03	MANGO PULP	25515.26	0.03
FLORICULTURE	6382.3	0.03	POULTRY PRODUCTS	89664.13	0.02
WHEAT	69413.68	0.02	FLORICULTURE	3303.33	0.02
OTHER CEREALS	53449.28	0.03	OTHER CEREALS	39860.98	0.02
FRESH MANGOES	42966.98	0.05	ANIMAL CASINGS	3506.35	0.01
ANIMAL CASINGS	3742.86	0.02	SHEEP/GOAT MEAT	1749.11	0.01

continues on following page

Table 2. Continued

April-July 2019-20			April-July 2020-21		
Product	**Quantity**	**US$ Bill**	**Product**	**Quantity**	**US$ Bill**
OTHERS (BETEL LEAVES & NUTS)	3969.93	0.01	ALBUMIN(Eggs & Milk)	871.59	0
ALBUMIN(Eggs & Milk)	688.08	0	OTHERS (BETEL LEAVES & NUTS)	1064.11	0
WALNUTS	543.13	0	CASEIN	360.35	0
OTHER MEAT	494.85	0	WALNUTS	187.69	0
PROCESSED MEAT	214.25	0	PROCESSED MEAT	90.91	0
CASEIN	112.09	0	OTHER MEAT	4.01	0
Total	**6224790**	**5.52**	**Total**	**8212926**	**5.55**
Source: DGCIS					

Table 2 shows the amount and value of imports and exports of all APEDA Products agricultural items. In the above tables, we can clearly see the changes in the amount and value of different products in the two years (2020 and 2019), which show the change in prices and consumer preferences. For example, the export of Basmati Rice and Buffalo Meat in 2019 is 1435021.9 with a value of 1.56 and 368362.96 with a value of 1.06, respectively, but in 2020 the export of these two products has decreased to 1680813.6 with a value of 1.5 and 241176.24 with a value of 0.72. In contrast, exports of Non-Basmati Rice and Fresh Onions in 2020 compared to 2019 show an increase.

Figure 2.

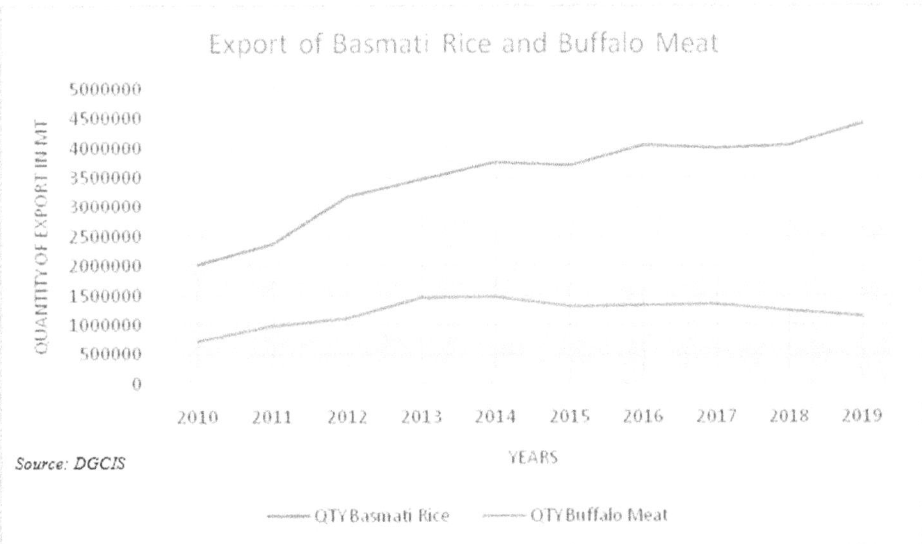

Source: DGCIS

As you can see in the graph above, the amount of Basmati Rice and Buffalo Meat exports has always had a positive and upward growth in the last 10 years, and since 2010 we have not seen a decrease in the exports of these two products.

Figure 3.

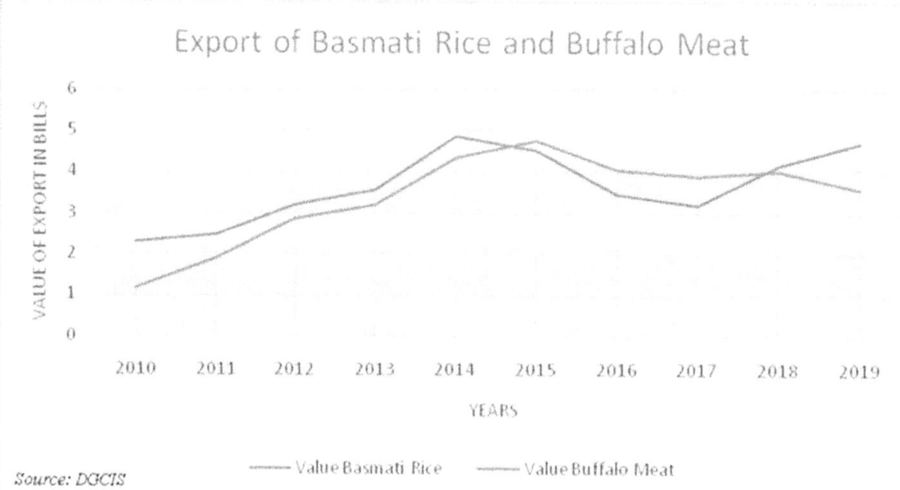

Source: DGCIS

The graph above shows the total export value of Basmati Rice and Buffalo Meat over the past 10 years. According to the data, the export value of Basmati Rice has decreased from 2014 to 2017 and has been on the rise since 2017. From 2015 to 2017, it decreased and then went up, and fluctuations in the total value of exports indicate price changes in the global market for these products.

Figure 4.

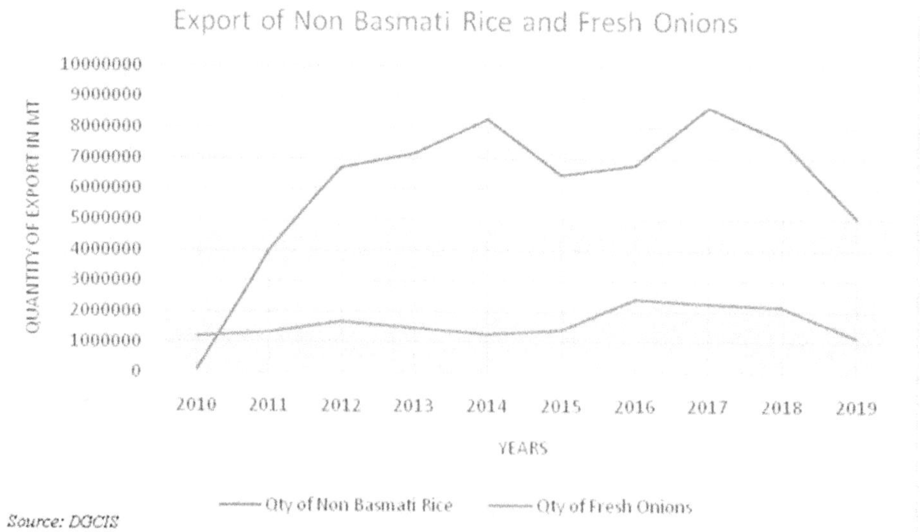

Source: DGCIS

As you can see in the graph above, Non-Basmati Rice and Fresh Onions, despite the fluctuations between 2014 and 2016, has started a downward trend of uniformity from 2017.

Based on the above evidence, we can say that major changes in exports, imports and agricultural trade balance will be observed in 2020, which is defined by the effects of the Corona virus. Excessive changes in the value and amount of exports can also reflect the effects of the Corona virus on consumer behavior and price changes. The effects of the Corona virus as a whole have led to an increase in exports of APEDA products, causing the trade balance to jump in a positive direction.

Table 3 shows the imported items of APEDA agricultural products between April-July. What we faced in the export sector has also happened in imports. This means that the COVID-19 shock has caused the import of some APEDA agricultural items to increase and others to decrease.

Table 3. India import Statistics: APEDA Products (Quantity in MT and Value in US$ Bill)

April-July 2019-20			April-July 2020-21		
Product	**Quantity**	**US$ Bill**	**Product**	**Quantity**	**US$ Bill**
Pulses	801937.4	0.36	Pulses	494769.3	0.33
Other Fresh Fruits	282048.02	0.25	Alcoholic Beverages	273452.7	0.2
Alcoholic Beverages	226164.16	0.24	Other Fresh Fruits	174770.24	0.16
Miscellaneous Preparations	102409.72	0.14	Miscellaneous Preparations	57846.61	0.09
Cocoa Products	29978.78	0.09	Cocoa Products	24392.92	0.08
Processed Fruits, Juices, and Nuts	25556.4	0.06	Cereal Preparations	28942.12	0.04
Cereal Preparations	25157.66	0.04	Fruits & Vegetables Seeds	4010.52	0.04
Fruits and Vegetables Seeds	3889.71	0.05	Jaggery& Confectionery	29133.78	0.04
Maize	71608.92	0.02	Processed Fruits, Juices & Nuts	14112.72	0.03
Jaggery and Confectionery	23056.96	0.03	Others (Betel Leaves & Nuts)	8734.91	0.03
Fresh Onions	22	0	Other Cereals	77352.78	0.02
Walnuts	2902.47	0.01	Albumin(Eggs & Milk)	3435.81	0.02
Albumin (Eggs and Milk)	3879.9	0.02	Walnuts	5552.15	0.02
Other Cereals	5556.74	0	Dairy Products	6790.25	0.01
Others (Betel Leaves and Nuts)	3756.33	0.01	Casein	1156.36	0.01
Processed Vegetables	11026.96	0.01	Processed Vegetables	5661.64	0.01
Dairy Products	3761.56	0.01	Floriculture	879.12	0.01
Floriculture	2818.75	0.02	Maize	12916.99	0
Casein	182.12	0	Fresh Grapes	496.96	0
Fresh Grapes	1021.29	0	Non-Basmati Rice	831.66	0
Non-Basmati Rice	1905.22	0	Poultry Products	72.2	0
Poultry Products	234.01	0	Groundnuts	713.97	0
Other Meat	422.59	0	Guar gum	198.38	0

continues on following page

Table 3. Continued

April-July 2019-20			April-July 2020-21		
Product	**Quantity**	**US$ Bill**	**Product**	**Quantity**	**US$ Bill**
Other Fresh Vegetables	626.38	0	Other Meat	99.43	0
Guar gum	498.6	0	Natural Honey	82.11	0
Milled Products	1463.23	0	Milled Products	608.59	0
Natural Honey	181.73	0	Processed Meat	57.89	0
Sheep/Goat Meat	51.57	0	Other Fresh Vegetables	397.56	0
Groundnuts	420	0	Sheep/Goat Meat	10.44	0
Wheat	523.77	0	Cucumber and Gherkins	79.72	0
Processed Meat	42.05	0	Fresh Onions	29	0
Mango Pulp	28.63	0	**Total**	**1227588.83**	**1.14**
Cucumber and Gherkins	109.62	0			
Fresh Mangoes	0	0			
Total	**1633243.25**	**1.36**			
Source: DGCIS					

India has always been a net importer of agricultural products and foodstuffs. On average, in the last decade, 6397065 MT of agricultural products have been imported into the country every year, although the amount of food imports in 2019 was about 5868143 MT. The import deficit in recent years has been affected by the outbreak of the Corona virus, which has raised food security concerns.

Some of the changes we have seen in the import and export of APEDA agricultural products are due to the quarantine policies adopted by India's trading partners. Since the export of agricultural products has experienced an increase, it shows that the import of these products is not hindered by India's trading partners and the decline in imports, along with the decline in domestic demand for imported agricultural products, reflects the strict import policies of the Indian trading partners to prevent the spread of the corona virus. This means that the fear of trading partners from transmitting the virus to their country through interaction with the exporting or importing country has led to the closure of land and air borders, which has also disrupted trade activities with countries.

Closing the borders will push the goods back to the domestic market, and because COVID 19 takes several months, this problem will continue. On the other hand, by reducing the country's revenues, reducing foreign exchange earnings can have a negative impact on the import of basic goods. If export restrictions continue, some agricultural products will lose their sales market, and consumer confidence in target markets of India's food health will decline, and it will be very costly and time-consuming to restore market and consumer confidence. This poses a serious threat to India's global agricultural market in the future. The largest import and export destinations of APEDA agricultural products are Netherland, USA, Bangladesh, Germany, United Arab EMTS, U.K, Afghanistan, Iran, etc.

THE EFFECT OF THE COVID-19 CRISIS ON THE SUPPLY CHAIN

The agricultural supply chain includes a complex network of interrelationships between factors such as inputs, producers, transportation, conversion industries, trade, and so on. Shock from the corona virus has a greater impact on the end of the chain, which includes consumption and trade, and may not have a significant effect on the beginning of the chain, including the production and even distribution of these products. However, a reduction in consumption or trade with a time lag can have significant effects on manufacturer or distributor decisions. Figure 5 shows the initial estimate of the impact of the outbreak of coronavirus on the agricultural supply chain in India. Due to the time of the outbreak, the agricultural, livestock and horticultural sectors have not been harmed much, because the decision to produce agricultural products was made before the outbreak of the virus.

In the distribution sector, due to the fact that the distribution of agricultural products is not banned, this sector has not been harmed much. But on the consumption side, estimates suggest that declining consumption has reduced the incomes of suppliers of agricultural products and food. Also, due to the control and restrictions imposed on the country's customs bases, the trade sector has also been affected. Of course, since the country is under quarantine, efforts are being made to import agricultural and food products as in the past, so as not to face food shortages and food security is not endangered. An outbreak of coronavirus in the Indian agricultural supply chain is shown in the figure.

Figure 5. Area of possible effects of COVID-19 on agricultural supply chain of India

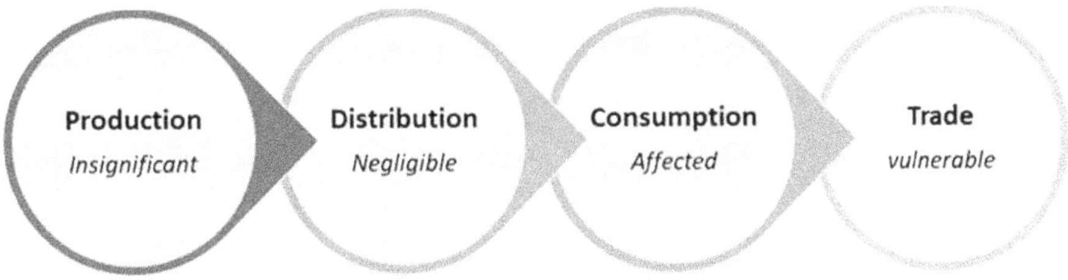

Although the agricultural sector is inherently highly immune to this crisis, but the consumer sector has been affected by this phenomenon. For example, the price of a kilogram of corn has fallen by 50 cents since the outbreak of the virus and the price of soy by 60 cents in the United States. As a result, global corn prices have fallen to their lowest level since January 2018, falling to less than $ 340 per ton in March 2020. A similar trend has occurred for soybeans. Agricultural prices in India have also fallen by 20 percent. Perishable products have also seen their prices fall by about 15 to 20 percent due to declining demand.

On the other hand, the spread of this virus has caused significant changes in the diet and consumption of people. Due to the excess demand for food that exists in the last month of each year, consequently, the prices this month are higher than the average of eleven months. But from February to May 2020, a strange thing happened in many food items, and that is the sharp fluctuations and the opposite direction to previous years. In the charts for 2018 and 2019, if you notice, the price changes are relatively smooth and do not fluctuate much. During the same period, the fluctuations of 2020 have been more intense and the opposite of previous years. For example, in the chicken meat group, suppliers of this product have seen a 9.18% price reduction per kilogram of goods sold. But in the cereals group, the selling price of rice was 14.17% higher than the trend of previous years. Therefore, the continued prevalence of this virus can significantly alter the food basket.

Figure 6.

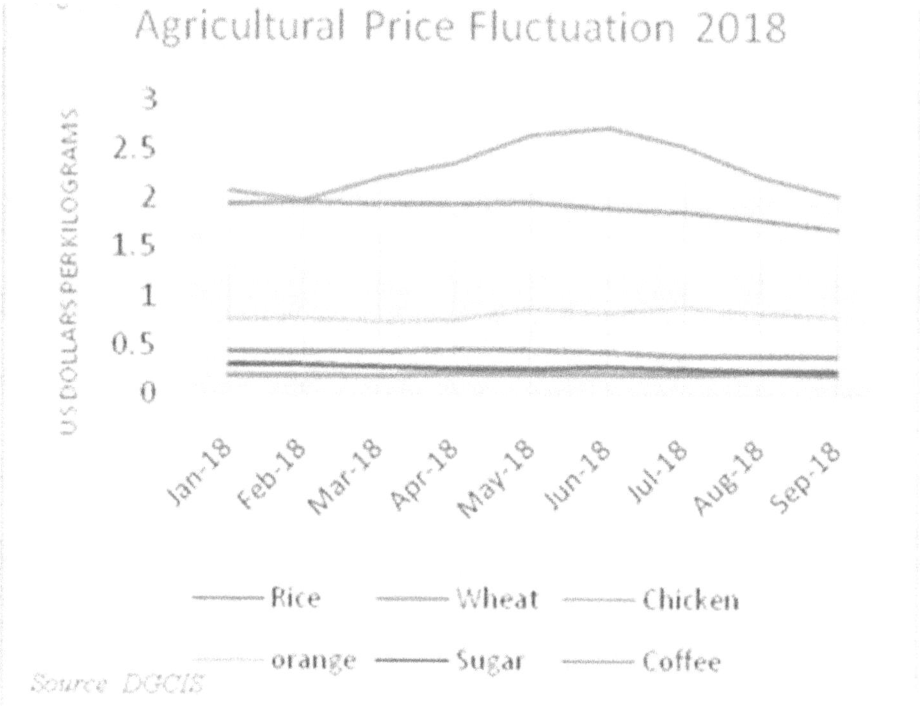

Closure of many food-related businesses such as restaurants, catering activities, hotels, etc., whose food supplies are from the agricultural sector, as well as the presence of people in-home quarantine, has changed the pattern of food consumption in Becomes a country. This shift in the pattern of food can affect consumers, producers, investors, and value chain actors.For example, the consumption of industrial bread used in delicatessens is expected to decrease compared to the consumption of home-made bread. The same situation applies to the demand for many goods such as canned food and other semi-finished foods produced by the food industry, which in the short and medium-term will have a negative effect on the sustainability of agricultural production and in the event of damage to this part of the food production chain are costly. The escalation of uncertainty will lead to a change in the pattern of expectations of consumers, producers, investors, and value chain players. Finally, due to unpredictability in the short term, the error of the planning system, and the economic management of activities will cause problems. It may neutralize the policies and executive strategies of the government.

Figure 7.

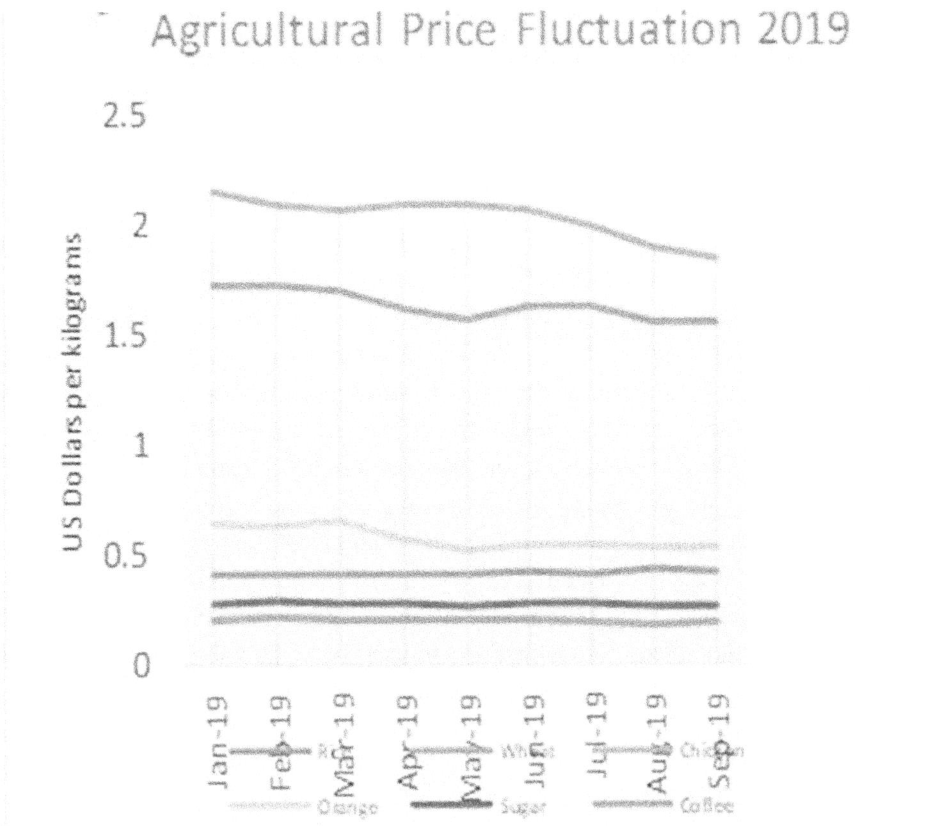

Figure 8.

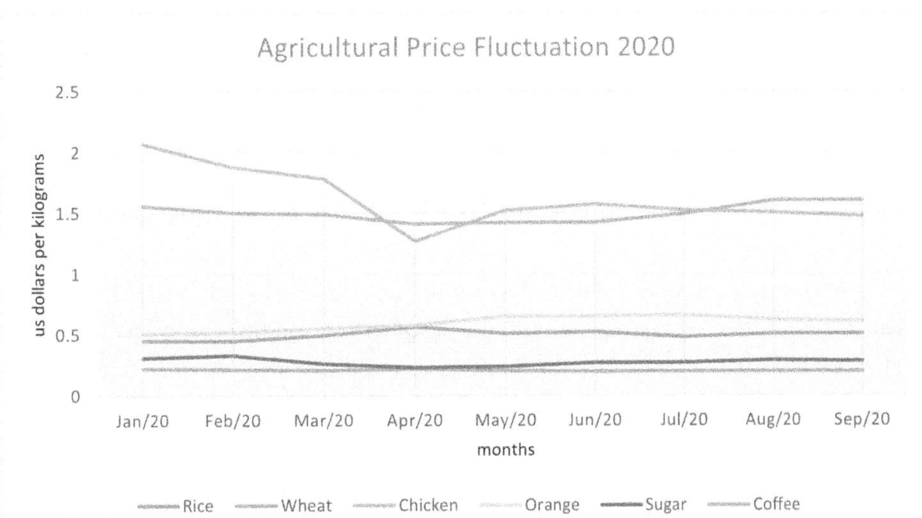

Source: DGCIS

OTHER ECONOMIC EFFECTS

The decline in government foreign exchange earnings, along with the reduction in tax revenues due to business closures and some other government revenues, leads to a significant reduction in public resources. The negative effect of the intensification of recession and inflation in the country and its effect on the stability and competitiveness of the players in the value chain of agricultural activities is more than other expected economic sectors. Therefore, it is expected that the allocation of development credits to the agricultural and rural sectors will decrease, as has happened at other times with a decrease in government revenues (Deshpande, 2017).

Acknowledging the impact of the Corona crisis on the economic downturn and increasing poverty, and in the context of an inflationary economy and the spread of poverty in rural areas (the main center of agricultural production), it is expected that in order to sustain production, part of the agricultural and rural sector (small and medium-scale) to be supported effectively and intelligently in critical situations. A high percentage of agricultural operators in the country are small-scale agriculture. These farmers face difficulties in financing, investing in technology, using new production methods, using machinery, and selling markets. Therefore, providing their livelihood and financing in the context of the Corona crisis and the effects of this crisis on the country's economy is facing problems (Bochtis et al., 2020).

The corona crisis can also disrupt the production and processing cycle of the various livestock, agricultural, horticultural, and aquatic products that are used by weakening and eliminating the active agricultural workforce in various activities.

CONCLUSION AND POLICY PROPOSALS

There is no doubt that the spread of the coronavirus will have a profound effect on the human lifestyle. This phenomenon can also change many economic paradigms. Likewise, the economy's pendulum movement also accelerates from west to east. Therefore, the economic effects of this phenomenon are more significant than other cases, and for this reason, many countries around the world have considered significant support packages to overcome this crisis. Among the economic sectors, the agricultural sector will also be affected, although it is less affected than the industrial and service sectors.

The COVID-19 crisis has had a major impact on the global economy and trade. Countries are still fighting the pandemic, and its repercussions for food supply chains are still unfolding. While agricultural trade has proven more resilient than trade in other goods owing to the essential nature of food products, additional disruptions to supply chains could start to undermine this resilience, with damaging consequences. There is currently no supply-related reason why the ongoing health crisis should turn into a food crisis. However, disruptions to food supply chains constitute a risk for global food security. Governments' trade policy choices will play a major role in shaping how the situation evolves. Transparency remains crucial for food security. Incomplete or insufficient information creates uncertainty that, in turn, leads to sub-optimal policy decisions. Sharing timely information on trade-related measures, as well as making information available on production, consumption, stocks and food prices, would help markets function efficiently and contribute to ensuring global food security.

At the national level the impact of COVID-19 and the resultant lockdown had been quite harsh on agriculture and allied sector in majority of districts. Among various subsectors, rabi crops were least affected as its harvesting was on the verge of completion but allied sectors such as poultry, fisheries and pig/goat/sheep sector witnessed a drastic fall in demand due to misplaced rumours leading to declining production as well as declining farm gate prices. However, prices of agriculture inputs were estimated to be rising mainly due to disruption in supply chain and closure of shops and markets. Although banking activities were exempted from lockdown, yet basic banking services viz, loans, deposit and recovery were severely hampered in majority of the sample districts in the country. However, the silver lining was the increase in digital banking transactions in majority of the sample districts. The microfinance sector and MSME sector were the biggest casualty with disruption in more than four-fifths of the sample districts thereby seriously hampering the livelihood in the unorganised sector which provides maximum employment in the rural areas. The activities of FPOs and FCs also came to complete halt. However, these rural institutions including SHGs grabbed the opportunities provided by the situation of stitching face masks, PPEs and preparation of sanitizers thereby helping the society as also earning some income for their members. Further, FPOs in close coordination with local administration in some of the districts were quite instrumental in door to door delivery of fruits, vegetable and dry rations to the needy there by extending a helping hand to the 34 society. These rural institutions like SHGs and FCs were also active in creation of awareness in rural areas about COVID 19 and its preventive measures. Trade of agricultural products: The outbreak of the corona virus, in addition to a few percent decrease in imports of agricultural products, has also led to an increase in exports of these products. This situation has led to an increase in the positive balance of agriculture. This means that the current state of trade in agricultural products is satisfactory and every effort must be made to maintain this state. We must realize that the fear of trading partners from transmitting the virus to their country through interaction with India can lead to the closure of land and air borders, which will also disrupt business activities and have an adverse effect on the country's agricultural exports. For example, the rejection of some export agricultural products and their supply to the domestic market will cause a drop in the price of these products in India. Undoubtedly, agricultural exports as a powerful driving force can lead to a boom in production. On the other hand, the import of agricultural products can deprive domestic products of a comparative advantage. Global estimates show that each dollar of agricultural exports can lead to $ 1.27 added value in supply chain businesses. Therefore, it is recommended that export restrictions and barriers be reviewed. The creation of such barriers leads to disruption of the supply chain of agricultural products and leads to the collapse of value chains. On the other hand, the economic downturn caused by this virus in the world has led to a decrease in the economic power of countries and, consequently, the value of the national currency in these countries will decrease; this will eventually make importing these products more expensive.

Falling Prices for Agricultural Commodities: Falling commodity prices are weakening investment and reducing GDP growth in exporting countries, but as demand falls, agricultural commodity prices are expected to fall as well, which is potentially a good opportunity for importers, traders, and consumers.

The Rotting Possibility of Most Agricultural Products: The possibility of spoilage of most agricultural products, especially summer crops and greenhouse products (such as ornamental flowers), and the reduction of buyers due to the Corona conditions, especially for the special events (birthdays, Eid, Valentine's Day, etc.) have caused them not to be sold and destroyed.

Decreased Production: With staying home after the corona outbreak, leaving the job due to fear of contracting the disease or quarantining the labor supply has decreased. If the corona crisis persists, the production of some agricultural products, such as ornamental flowers, will be considered unnecessary and production will be severely reduced. Also, with the people staying at home and of course with the change in consumption pattern, the production of a significant part of the products of food industries such as canned food, compote, etc. will be reduced. Therefore, production is reduced in the agricultural sector, especially related services (in the wholesale and retail chains) and conversion industries.

Consideration of the Consumer Sector: The economic downturn caused by the outbreak of the Coronavirus has significantly affected companies supplying agricultural and food products. Declining demand has reduced the prices of some food products and caused significant losses to agricultural and food businesses. Therefore, special measures to continue the production and business sustainability of retailers and food suppliers should be on the agenda of policymakers. For this purpose, it is recommended that the insurance ceiling be extended to cover the risk of the virus.

Household Support: Foodstuffs cover almost a large percentage of household expenditures, but due to the recession, households have difficulty meeting part of their food expenses. Credit packages and cash payments must be operationalized to ensure that households receive adequate food.

Export Management of Agricultural Products: Due to possible restrictions imposed by other countries and concerns about declining export earnings Export Management includes continuous monitoring of India's export target markets in terms of products and extraction of export barriers and benefiting from the advice of the Ministry of Foreign Affairs for export Commodities to alternative markets are essential. In case of repatriation of agricultural goods exported to the domestic market, it is necessary for the government to be ready to buy goods such as milk, eggs, etc. so as not to damage production because repairing such damage to production can take up to two years.

Development and Modification of Health Protocols: In order to reduce the threat of food exports and raw materials in the agricultural sector and to create confidence of export destination countries in the context of the Corona crisis and rapid development of health and quarantine protocols in the country's export bases in line with the Corona crisis. There is also more emphasis on monitoring and controlling the production process of agricultural products based on health and healthy food standards and providing reports in order to reassure foreign business partners.

Changes in Consumption Patterns: The post-corona global community will experience a different lifestyle and food basket. Meanwhile, the role of foods that supply and strengthen the human immune system is expected to play a significant role. Therefore, the necessary mechanisms should be created to prepare for these changes in the production and supply of agricultural products and food.

Possibility of Inflation After the Disease Subsides: Since this disease leads to a recession in economic activity. As a result, as the income of the people in the society decreases, the demand will decrease and consequently the price of food products will decrease. But after this crisis, due to the recovery of economic conditions and the restoration of revenues, will lead to an increase in market demand. Because the decision to produce happens with a time lag, prices are likely to rise. However, due to the reduction of producers' incomes due to the reduction of consumption, the producers may plan to reduce production in the future, which will exacerbate the problem of excess demand. Therefore, production intervention to reduce supply fluctuations and the use of storage mechanisms can play an important role in regulating the market of agricultural and food products in the future.

Ensuring the Stability of the Supply Chain: In trade policies, ensuring the stability of the supply chain, and in particular the supply chain of products whose production inputs are dependent on imports, must be more considered. Action should be taken regarding food and basic imported goods, especially the provision of the required currency and, if necessary, the reduction of import barriers, including the reduction of import duties.

Supporting Agricultural Businesses: Stimulating food demand is essential to maintain food security and strengthen the supply side. Lending to provide agricultural inputs, reduce marketing and sales costs can also help sustain agricultural production and resilience. It is worth noting that even the agricultural sector and the production of basic commodities such as cereals, which are considered less vulnerable, face a lack of liquidity for cultivation. Also, the use of idle economic capacities with maximum facilitation in licensing the applicant business units in the agricultural sector can play a role to improve the situation and reduce the damage to businesses in this sector.

Supporting Complementary Industries in the Food Production Chain in the Agricultural Sector: Maximum care should be taken to maintain and activate the basic infrastructure and key sectors, especially the food production industries. These industries have an effective role in reducing waste and increasing production efficiency in the agricultural sector, so helping these firms to survive in crisis by helping to finance and credit these firms and put their products in the livelihood basket for the poor can be to be considered.

Support for Agricultural Activities Based on Geography Relocation: Problems of parts of agricultural activities that are based on relocation in the geography of the country, such as combine owners and beekeepers, may be in the form of transportation subsidies, tax exemptions, partial loan forgiveness etc. can be solved. Facilitating their relocation (by considering issues related to the Corona crisis) can also help reduce the problems of such activities. It is worth mentioning that the set of measures that lead to cost reduction and the continuation of production and consumer price reduction can be considered as opening the way for new conditions.

The Position of the Agricultural Sector in Post-Corona: The outbreak of the corona virus will further strengthen the position of this sector and lead to a change in mental patterns towards this sector. Since the outbreak of this virus has affected the trade of agricultural and food products, it is not possible to hope for the import of these products forever because in critical situations, importing products can lose its originality. Therefore, it is expected that the agricultural sector played a special role in the post-corona economy.

REFERENCES

Agri Exchange, A. P. E. D. A. (2020). *India export Statistics*. Retrieved from APEDA Agri Exchange: https://agriexchange.apeda.gov.in/IndExp/PortNew.aspx

Ali, J., & Khan, W. (2020, August 15). Impact of COVID-19 pandemic on agricultural wholesale prices in India: A comparative analysis across the phases of thelockdown. *Waley*, 1-6. doi:10.1002/pa.2402

Arumugam, U., Kanagavalli, G., & Manida, M. (2020). COVID-19: Impact of agriculture in India. *Aegaeum Journal*, *8*(5), 480–488.

Bank, W. (2020, June 21). *Employment in services*. Retrieved from The World Bank: https://data.worldbank.org/indicator/SL.SRV.EMPL.ZS?locations=IN

Bochtis, D., Benos, L., Lampridi, M., Marinoudi, V., Pearson, S., & Sørensen, C. G. (2020, October 05). AgriculturalWorkforce Crisis in Light of the COVID-19 Pandemic. *Sustainability (Basel)*, *12*(12), 1–13. doi:10.3390u12198212

Deshpande, T. (2017). *State of Agriculture in India*. PRS Legislative Research.

Industry, M. o. (2020). *Directorate General of Commercial Intelligence and Statistics*. Retrieved from Ministry of Commerce and Industry: http://www.dgciskol.gov.in/

Jain, P., Baghla, K., & A, R. (2020). Effect of corona / COVID19 on the agricultural sector in India. *The Pharma Innovation Journal, 9*(5), 41-45. Retrieved 04 03, 2020, from www.thepharmajournal.com

Kumar, A., Arabinda, K., & Ku, S. (2020, July 07). How Indian agriculture should change after COVID-19. *Springer, 20*(12), 837-840. doi:10.1007/s12571-020-01063-6

Odisha, G. o. (2020). *Covid-19: Impact on Agriculture & Allied Sectors in Odisha (Odisha Economic Survey 2019-20)*. Government of Odisha.

Organization, W. T. (2020). *COVID-19 and agriculture: A story of resilience*. Geneva: World Trade Organization. Retrieved from https://www.wto.org/

PRS Legislative Research. (2020). *Economic Survey 2019-20*. New Delhi: PRS Legislative Research. Retrieved from https://www.prsindia.org/sites/default/files/parliament_or_policy_pdfs/Economic%20 Survey%202019-20%20Summary.pdf

Rawal, V., Kumar, M., Verma, A., & Pais, J. (2020). COVID-19 Lockdown: Impact on Agriculture and Rural Economy. New Delhi: Society for Social and Economic Research. doi:978-81-937148-7-4

Sahoo, J., & Samal, K. (2020, July 26). Impact of COVID-19 on Indian Agriculture. *Agriculture Letters, 1*(3), 45-46. Retrieved from https://agletters.in/

Singh, K. S., & Rosmann, M. (2020). Government of India Issues Three Ordinances Ushering in Major Agricultural Market Reforms. USDA.

Srinivasan, N., Tagat, V., & Sriniva, G. (2020). *Indian agriculture during and after the pandemic*. MSC.

Wani, A. (2020). Impact of COVID-19 Lockdown on Agriculture in India: A Review. *International Journal of Scientific Research, 09*(06), 1727–1728. doi:10.21275/SR20627172107

WHO. (2020). *Weekly Operational Update on COVID*. Geneva: Health Emergencies Programme. Retrieved from https://www.who.int/emergencies/diseases/novel-coronavirus-2019

WTO. (2020). *WHO Coronavirus Disease (COVID-19) Dashboard*. Retrieved from World Health Organization: https://covid19.who.int/?gclid=Cj0KCQiA7qP9BRCLARIsABDaZzhiVe7ydEgHNhDWQ TYF9k5tNnVmOYnx7J70fI-gy7CyCWdZzMy9JLIaAq8LEALw_wcB

Chapter 12
Inter-Relationship of Health, Communication, and Commerce:
A Study of the Healthcare Sector in Odisha, India

Sourav Gupta
Central University of Odisha, India

Minati Sahoo
https://orcid.org/0000-0002-6061-8035
Central University of Odisha, India

ABSTRACT

The Covid-19 has given a new dimension to the healthcare industry of India. The pandemic has exposed the limited health capacity of the states including Odisha. Hence an attempt has been made to evaluate the performance of healthcare services in Odisha. Further, it will also analyze the content of the advertising campaign used to popularize the health packages. It will critically study the communication approach, design and angles of the campaign and find out how they have been prepared to influence the people with pre-conceived desired aims. The study will be based on the secondary sources. The study infers that the performance of the government health sector is not up to the mark and the private hospitals have manipulated with the guidelines to attract the people through their campaign. Hence, measures to be taken to improve healthcare sector and to regulate manipulations by the private sector.

DOI: 10.4018/978-1-7998-6896-5.ch012

1. INTRODUCTION

The pandemic Covid-19 has infected over 32 million people globally (World Health Organization, 2022). The case of corona has been on rise despite of the various lockdown measures. Further after the relaxation of the lockdown measures, there has been a rapid rise in cases across countries (International Monetary Fund, 2022). The number of cases in India has risen to over 4.3 millions, within a period of six month (Worldometer, 2022). The outbreak of this pandemic has put to test the resilience and effectiveness of the health systems. It has also taught for an urgent need of a strong health workforce which is considered to be an important part of a strong health care system (ILO, 2022).

In India, Odisha was one of the first states to Covid-19 as a State disaster even before the declaration of it as National disaster (Das, 2020). The state was first to come up with an online portal for Covid-19 pandemic. Similarly, it has been the first in announcing a number of innovative policy interventions like imposing lockdown in the entire state, opening Covid-19 special hospitals with public-private-partnership and providing ₹50 lakh insurance cover to all health workers engaged in the fight against Covid-19 (Orissa Economic Association, 2020). It has also announced that in case of death in harness the state would honour the health workers as martyrs. In order to boost the morale of health professionals engaged in the fight against Covid-19, advance payment of salary for health professionals was announced by the State Government. The state had also got a thumbs up from World Health Organisation and UNESCO, as the teams found that the hospitals in the state have been operating with 96 per cent compliance in all parameters (Bhatia, 2020).

But, the months of June and July has changed the course of the state and its battle against coronavirus. Returning of about one million migrants from various states has completely made the situation worst for the Government. The state started to see a sudden surge in coronavirus cases from 35,000 active cases as on 24 Sep 2020 to more than 12 lakhs as on June 2022 (Government of Odisha, 2022). Earlier, in 2020, despite of spending around INR 1,900 crore on Covid control and healthcare infrastructure, the state government has to face under criticism for its mishandling of the crisis.

2. CONCERN OF THE STUDY

The Covid-19 has given a new dimension to the healthcare industry of India. On one hand the government both at the Centre and state have struggled to provide proper care to the people in accordance to the WHO guidelines. For the common people, especially in the rural areas, there has been few or no option of getting any substantive treatment. So far there are 48 dedicated Covid-19 hospitals with 7,328 beds and 710 ICU beds (Barik, 2020). The Covid-19 pandemic has exposed the limited health capacity of the state. While people were provided special care for Covid-19, there were instances of death due to non-Covid-19 diseases owing to lack of adequate healthcare facilities. Despite of hard efforts by the state government for hiring health professional during the pandemic, still there is only one doctor for every 5,500 people (Kar, 2020).

The private hospitals, however, has converted the pandemic into an opportunity to multiply profit by coming up with special Covid-19 packages. The packages have also been promoted and marketed aggressively through mass media, particularly social and online media, in an effort to popularize them. Recent studies have also shown that the business of the private health sector has increased during the Covid-19 period. That makes it imperative to look back at the marketing and promotional strategies in which media plays a big role as effective communication leads to mobilization of people. According to Mheidly and Fares(2020), 'Media channels become windows through which the public looks for accurate information, scientific sound facts, government decisions, and reactions of the general public'.

People have been facing a lot of health concerns during the Covid-19 pandemic situation. There are two kinds of people presently, symptomatic and asymptomatic. The SOP and government guidelines for treatment of these two categories have been changing also with the pandemic getting worse with each passing day. The issue of mental health is also getting worse with people losing jobs, young teenagers missing campus life and women getting confined to four walls of the home. The situation has also led to knowledge gaps due to misinformation and disinformation (Igoe, 2020). Hence an attempt has been made to evaluate the performance of healthcare sector in Odisha. Further, it has also analyze the content of the advertising campaign used to popularize the health packages. It had critically study the communication approach, design and angles of the campaign and find out how they have been prepared to influence the people with pre-conceived desired aims. The objectives of the study are:

- To examine the performance of healthcare sector in tackling Covid-19 in Odisha.
- To analyze the advertising campaigns of the Covid special packages of the private hospitals-text and design and assess the effectiveness of communication campaigns in mobilizing business

3. REVIEW OF LITERATURE

3.1. Advertising and Health Communication

Advertising has been conceptualized as a form of impersonal communication where the message is communicated by the mass media. As there is no immediate feedback so the nature of advertising is held to be impersonal. (Belch and Belch, 2002). Persuasion is integral to Advertising. The objective of advertising is to persuade the target audience i.e. clients to buy and accept a product, service, idea, etc. Advertising is paid publicity by manufacturing or producing units offering products and services. This feature of advertising distinguishes advertising from other forms of marketing communication. Publicity is also different from advertising. (O' Guinn et al, 2003). Advertising as a form of marketing communication deals with products, services and ideas which are both tangible and intangible in nature.

The idea of health communication is popularized by WHO especially in the context of rural health awareness. It involves use of media to share messages of good health practices among the poor people in particular and is done with a missionary zeal. However, conventionally advertising has played the role of an important catalyst and its main role has been to present the Unique Selling Proposition, the strength of the products and services and lure people into buying them. There is a clear distinction in following of ethical norms in case of advertising and health communication. While health communication has evolved from a noble and ethical foundation, advertising has been accused of violating its professional code of ethics as we see in case of making absurd claims in health drinks and children's foods. In fact, that number of codes of ethics is in place for advertising speaks a lot about the profession. The question of ethics gain significance in case of advertising of health services. According to Solomon et al (2016):

'One of the most frequent discussions that arose with the development of healthcare marketing was due to the concern that advertising will lead to a situation in which the medical activity will turn into an overly commercial one. Of course, this is quite difficult to avoid, considering that the medical units providing services and healthcare have the right to make their own activities known and inform consumers on the health services they provide. In the past, it was considered that advertising and promotion were below the dignity of the medical profession and that the only way to gain new patients was by recommendation from satisfied patients and other clinicians' positive assessments. Such thinking is no longer compatible with the current patients' requirements, which want to be more and more informed. It is interesting to study how the ethical considerations are maintained while studying advertisements.

3.2. Covid Health Package

The media gave its whole hearted support in providing exhaustive coverage to the Covid packages introduced by the private hospitals. It is quite expected as these hospitals are good sources of advertising revenue for the media. The media reports comprehensively outlined the salient features of the packages. According to a report by Orissa diary.com on AMRI Bhubaneswar package, it will, 'support to such patient with remote monitoring, as patients stay in the comfort of their homes' (Orissa Diary, 2020). This underlines the spirit of the package.

The report further quotes senior officials as:

'The package will include online and telephonic consultations, monitoring of health parameters through instruments provided by AMRI, along with Emergency support service, in case the patient's condition worsens, informed Ms. Nilanjana Mukherjee, AVP, Operations & Administration and Unit In-charge, AMRI Hospitals-Bhubaneswar. Under the package, a "well-being kit" will also be provided, which will help patients to keep regular track of their vitals even at home, she said. This way, patients will be able to seek consultation and round-the-clock screening at a fraction of the cost of hospitalisation, Ms Mukherjee added. "Besides masks, gloves and sanitizer, the well-being kit will include a pulse oximeter, a BP monitor, and a digital thermometer, devices that a COVID-19 positive patient will need to keep an eye on their health parameters, she said.'

It further cites:

'Mr Rupak Barua, Group CEO, AMRI Hospitals, said, "A number of patients even with mild symptoms are now opting for home care treatment. Since they will also need to be monitored regularly under the supervision of doctors, we have designed the 'Virtual Home Care', where doctors will offer treatment guidelines and regularly monitor as patients stay homes. This way, their recovery will be quick and screening will ensure the patient can be shifted to the hospital; immediately, if condition worsens." He further said that AMRI Hospitals has set up a special portal for the package, where patients can regularly upload their health update, which will be screened by doctors every day. "Our doctors will interact with patients online and over telephone twice a week while nurses will keep in touch with patients on daily basis," he added. AMRI has already tied up with a number of top corporate houses to provide services under the package to the employees of their organisations.'

Thus, it can be observed that the private hospitals are taking aggressive marketing steps to find clients for their packages. Not only are they tying up with corporate but also encouraging mild symptom patients to take up. Almost all the reports on such packages have reported similar trend. A business standard reports on Apollo package goes like: 'Once it starts screening and identifying positive cases, consideringthat many Indian homes have 6-7 people who share commonaccommodation and toilet, Apollo will launch Project Stay I. This is a strategy to create medical rooms in hotels or hostels with light medical supervision for quarantine and creating a barrier before they come into the hospitals. It is expecting almost 80 per cent of the cases might get cured here, while the rest will be moved to the main hospitals for further treatment.' (Business Standard, 2020). The government guidelines have been subtly transformed into a package as is evident from the above lines.

4. THEORETICAL FRAMEWORK

4.1. Hypodermic Needle Theory

The hypodermic needle theory is a part of the total effects theory of mass media developed by social scientists after they were convinced of the media's all pervasive influencing power during the second world war. The rise of Nazism in Germany leading way to propaganda communication and subsequent second world war reinvented the scope of media and integrated with daily public life. The social scientists propounded that media has tremendous capacity to bombard people with information and influence their opinion. In fact, the process of communication by mass media to the society was compared to that of a firing of bullet by a gun or injection by a syringe both of which leads to a spread of content inside the target. That is why the theory has been coined as Hypodermic Needle Theory and also known popularly as Magic Bullet Theory. With increase in media literacy levels, the theory has given way to multi step flow theory which argues that media may not always be effective in influencing people but in developing countries like India, the pandemic led to infodemic which is an ideal setting for media influence.

4.2. Functional Theory of Attitude Change

The four personality functions identified by communication scientist Elihu Katz are Utilitarian, Knowledge, Ego defence and value expression. According to Katz (1960) these functions constitute an attitude system. The function of advertising is to create a discrepancy between the need met by the attitude and the attitude. If the former is strong, change will be likely while if the latter is strong, change will be resisted. The basic premise of functional theories is that advertising implements change in attitude through persuasionin parity with the functional aspect of attitude. Advertising strategy recognizes the functional attitude of the individual and creates a disparity between the attitude and one or more of the attitude functions. Basically the theory centres round the fact that a change in attitude is integral to the basis of its motivation, which is again the functional aspect of the attitude of the individual.

5. METHODOLOGY

The study is basically based on the secondary sources for the analysis. To examine the performance of healthcare sector in Odisha, analysis has been based on data and information provided by the Department of health and family welfare, Government of Odisha and Survey Organisations. To analyse the health guidelines by WHO and Ministry of Health and Family Welfare and the health packages offered by private hospitals in Odisha between April to September 2020, relevant literature has been surveyed. Besides,

Qualitative Content Analysis was carried out of the special Covid-19 packages of private hospitals of Kolkata, Bhubaneswar, Hyderabad and Mumbai. In all, 15 advertisements published in print, electronic and social media were collected randomly as per purposive sampling as selected private hospitals were only offering Covid care packages. Two techniques of qualitative content analysis-thematic analysis and appeal analysis has been done. The appeal analysis is analysis of the catchlines, slogans and images to find out the area or points where the advertisements are attempting to influence. Thematic analysis identifies major themes which the advertisement addresses. Both the analysis results are used to tally whether they are in accordance to the government guidelines and ethical in nature in that context.

The sample advertisements were qualitatively analysed to bring out the appeal of the ads i.e. to which psychological aspect of the target audience are they appealing to and how the appeals may motivate the consumers to adopt the idea. The advertisements were studied in the light of the guidelines and packages to find out the emerging themes. The thematic analysis was tested to ensure 'soundness of fit' (as per Schilling 2006) and treated as a subjective process (Kracauer 1952). The soundness of fit lies in the analysis of themes and subjects used in the advertisements for effective communication. The third technique used is Semiotic analysis, a conventional technique of content analysis where symbols and texts act are decoded as signifier and signified. The inherent meaning of the signs, symbols, texts, figures, colours and graphics have been decoded and their social semiotic analysis has been applied to construct the significance.

6. RESULT AND DISCUSSION

6.1. Performance of healthcare sectorin Odisha in tackling Covid-19

The Covid-19 pandemic has affected the entire economy and lead to an economic crisis (ICRISAT, 2020). There has been a rapid rise in the number of corona cases in all the states including Odisha. Figure 1 shows that there has been a significant rise in the number of Covid-19 positive cases and now it has crossed the mark of 3,16,001. Same situation is also seen in case of death and active cases. But within this recovery cases are also on rise where as of now 3,07,374 cases have been recovered.

Government of Odisha during last decade has taken several reform measures to strengthen the delivery of health care services. For this, additional resources were allocated through National Health Mission and also under state budget to address local health issues and marginalised communities. With the effective policy formulation, various National Health Surveys have shown significant improvement in many key health indicators. Now, the Covid-19 crisis has put to test the effectiveness of the public health care delivery facilities in Odisha. The present study will assess the performance of healthcare sector in tackling Covid-19 in Odisha on the basis of following points:

6.1.1. Strategy of Governance

The state government sought permission to screen international passengers and put up a portal on 3rd March for mandatory registration. This was followed by fourteen days of home quarantine/ isolation with an incentive of INR 15,000 on successful completion. Different committees constituting senior bureaucrats were formed by the state for transportation of essential goods and services, procurement of medicine and equipment during Covid situation. Lockdown in a phased manner was firstly announced by Odisha from March 21. The state then extend the lockdown period. Even there was suspension of train and air traffic into the state. Further to address the shortage of N95 masks and Personal Protective Equipment, all the possibilities were explored by officials and they coordinated with the Union government to ensure timely delivery. The state also invoked National Security Act against attacks on/dishonouring of doctors, healthcare personnel. The state police have also shown great tenacity in maintaining cyber safety and sternly handling mischief mongers and those violating rules. Social media, humour and creativity were used to spread awareness.

Figure 1. Cumulative summary of Covid-19 cases in Odisha
Source: Ministry of Health and Family Welfare, Government of Odisha, 2020

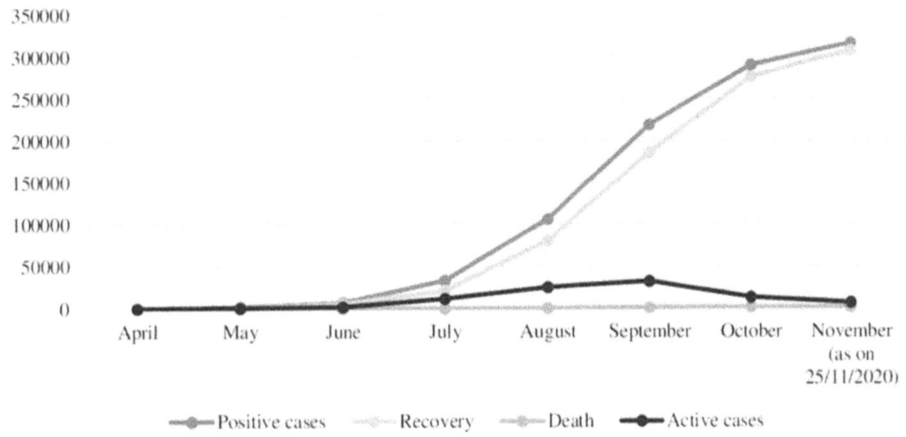

6.1.2. Health Facilities

There was only one testing centre on 16 March 2020 when Odisha reported its first case. But today, it is conducting more than 4,500 tests per day in 15 testing centres. It is also planning to increase testing to 15,000 per day. Initially, Covid-specific wards were opened in four existing hospitals but to prevent transmission, decision was taken to have exclusive Covid hospitals. Further, this was done when Odisha had only five cases. Testing capacity during the initial phase was limited but gradually it got expanded. On average, more than 4,000 tests per day were conducted. Further, in partnership with public sector and private organisations, exclusive Covid hospitals were set up. As on 1 June 2020, there were 34 Covid hospitals with around 5,493 beds. Most of the cyclone centres were being used as quarantine centres. Odisha has declared Covid-19 as a ‘disaster’. This will help to adequately empower officials to control the spread of the corona. Today, the state has 48 Covid hospitals spread across the state with 7328 beds, and 710 ICUs. It has also set up 17,647 temporary medical camps with 8,26,079 beds for quarantine and isolation of people returning from other states.

6.1.3. Capacity Building/Training Programmes for Health Personnel

The existing health staffs for Covid-19 consists of about 8000 doctors, nurses, pharmacists, and other health workers. But since it was difficult to manage with the existing health professionals, about 1,039 medical graduates and other professionals were engaged. Besides, 500 medical students were also trained. Even 1,72,499 health personnel were also trained by the state government to deal with the corona crisis. According to Labour and ESI Secretary Anu Garg, 'A total of 8,023 doctors, 8,296 staff nurses, 4,105 paramedical staff and laboratory technicians, 4,114 AYUSH doctors, 4,905 ambulance drivers, 1,35,820 health workers and 7,236 sanitation workers have been drafted into Covid workforce. Also, 108 doctors, 64 staff nurses and 61 pharmacists from ESI and private sector hospitals have been trained in Covid management. Around 8,325 MBBS, AYUSH and nursing students, who had volunteered for Covid crisis, have been trained in providing care to the patients', as per Health and Family Welfare Secretary N B Dhal. About 33,900 temporary medical camps were set up in different panchayat areas for returned migrants. Those in charge of those camps were provided training to deal with children and women and also traumatised migrants. Even 753 counsellors have been preparedfor psychological support and 2,471 volunteers were trained to provide necessary support in Covid-19 management (The Economics Times, 2020).

6.1.4. Participation of other Stakeholders

In anticipation of reverse migration to rural areas, the State has delegated powers of district collectors to sarpanches of Gram Panchayats. This was done to ensure smooth return and proper monitoring under quarantine. The government has undertaken all expenses during quarantine, and even announced a relief of INR 2,000 per person on completion of quarantine. Women self-help groups were asked to preparer usable face masks, and also food required to be served to those who are quarantined. These groups have also helped in spreading of awareness about social distancing and safety in rural areas (WHO, 2020).

6.1.5. Provision of Financial Incentives

The Government of Odisha has announced a INR 2,200 crore package for the economically weaker sections of the society to deal with the impact of the Covid crisis. An advanced disbursement of resources to beneficiaries; pensioners in cash and ration stocks for card holders for three months were ensured by the State. The cash-in-hand mode was used to reduce the chances of corruption and also to minimise crowding at banks. For the welfare of health workers, a financial package of INR50 Lakhs was announced by State Government (WHO, 2020).

Current efforts to combat Covid-19 can be explicated in view of Odisha's blueprint for achieving Universal Health Coverage (UHC), which was laid down by announcing Biju Swasthya Kalayan Yojana (BSKY) in 2018. The scheme aims at providing free healthcare to all citizens of Odisha, irrespective of income, caste and social status at the public health institutions. Additionally, 71 lakh economically vulnerable households can avail healthcare services from the empanelled private hospitals with financial coverage up to INR 5 lakh per family and INR 10 lakh to women members. Moreover, the state has been taking prompt action to enhance healthcare workforce which stands at 9.6 per 10,000 population against the World Health Organisation's prescribed norm of 23. These efforts are significant and will complement other efforts introduced, to improve the performance of the health care system in the state (Rout, 2020).

Though Odisha's strategies to fight Covid-19 are well designed drawing inferences from the philosophy of UHC (Garikipati, 2020), there are a number of implementation challenges that the health system is facing and need to be set right. Several people have over the last few days complained that patients were being denied admission in hospitals, despite the fact that they were suffering from serious health problems. This has been despite of the order issued by the state, asking all healthcare facilities to ensure necessary medical services are provided to those in need. Large scale vacancies and reluctance of doctors to work in underdeveloped districts and rural areas have thrown the healthcare system out of gear. More concern is required towards the pandemic's spread in many tribal-dominated districts where the health infrastructure and the communication network are very poor. Even after the state government had pressed more medicos into the service during the pandemic, the ratio stands at one doctor for every 5,500 people. Another challenge that the state is facing is the non-availability of competent human resources to deal with a dynamic virus. Creation of beds and other facilities are not enough. An adequate personnel to provide proper treatment to those admitted in such centres are very pertinent (Kar, 2020).There were also instances of mismanagement of hospitals (The New Indian Express, 2020). Though the State Government has pumped in funds and ramped up efforts to contain the pandemic in the Covid hotspot, lack of adequate protective gear continues to hamper patient care in many hospitals. Thus these are some of the challenges that state are dealing with despite of all the hard efforts in tackling the corona crisis.

6.2. Qualitative Analysis of the Advertisements of the Health Packages

In view of the present scenario of COVID-19 positive cases, the state government of Odisha in August 2020 came up with a set of guidelines to be followed strictly by the private hospitals having 30 beds or more for treatment of the coronavirus affected patients. In an official notification, the Health and Family Welfare department stated that the state government has created many Dedicated Covid Care Centre (DCCC), Dedicated Covid Health Centre (DCHC) and Dedicated Covid Hospitals (DCH) to take care of mild symptomatic, moderate and severe cases. But, considering the present scenario of positive cases, the state will need more number of Dedicated Covid Health Centre and Dedicated Covid Hospitals. In order to manage the situation, the private hospitals with 30 beds or more have to abide by the following guidelines:

'All asymptomatic or mild cases shall be sent to institutional quarantine/home isolation or any paid CCC run by the private hospital. All the private hospitals having 30 beds or more shall designate minimum of 10% of all beds to be reserved for the COVID patients with an option to convert the entire hospital as a COVID hospital. However, they have to intimate the Collectors and DM of the district concerned and the State level authorised officer for data updating. They have to appoint one Authorised Medical Officer who will coordinate with state authorities. Such reserved beds must include appropriate numbers of ICU beds with ventilators dedicated for COVID patients (at the rate of 10% of all available beds). There must be a separate fever clinic and facility for isolation of suspected cases.

When the suspected cases come out to be positive they shall be shifted to the COVID beds provided the patient wants to take the services of hospital on payment of fees. Only those patients who want to pay on their own or covered under their own insurance shall be treated in the hospital. No reimbursement or payment of any kind towards treatment of such patient will be made by the government. The hospital must provide all possible treatment as per the guidelines for management of Covid-19 patients issued by Ministry of health. As the COVID patients usually have high anxiety, they must be handled very gently and proper and regular counselling shall be done regarding the status of disease and the outcome of treatment. Adequate number of the consumables like Oxygen, PPEs, Sanitisers must be made available. The Infection prevention & control measures must be taken as per Govt. of India guidelines so that the infection never spreads to the other non-COVID patients. The staff managing the patients shall take utmost care and preventive measures so that they themselves do not contract the disease. They will work for 14 days and go for quarantine for another 14 days after which they can again come back to patient duty.All the tests must be done at the approved rate notified by the government. The hospital will charge reasonable fees from patients and refrain from collecting exorbitant fees, failing which strict action will be taken against the hospital. The institution will develop mechanism for collection of bill amount on a day to day basis so that a lump sum amount never remains pending. Dead body disposal shall be done as per the state and Central government guidelines. All patients' data shall be uploaded in the designated portal or social media group in the appropriate format. The hospital shall regularly share all information to the government regarding availability of facility, patient information, line of treatment, availability of beds, price charges. The hospital shall provide the COVID-19 test result to the patient. The hospital shall allow one willing attendant of the patient to remain in the earmarked place on the hospital premises while ensuring prevention of cross infection. The hospital shall create a help desk accessible physically and telephonically for counselling the relatives of patients and share information on status of health to attendant of the patient regularly. The hospital shall put CCTV in the patient treatment area for management, facilitation and screening of footage by appropriate authority as and when required.' (Odisha bytes, 2020).

As it is evident from the above guidelines that it is quite challenging to set up a Covid set up in a hospital. All the government hospitals are not equipped to do it. And given the rate at which Covid-19 was spreading in India, it was always going to be short of logistics and care quantitatively-there will always be shortage of beds and wards. The private hospitals in metro cities like Kolkata, Mumbai, Bhubaneswar and other urban centres of India came up with special Covid-19 isolation packages based on the government guidelines. However, although it was based on the guidelines, the aggressive promotions and media coverage of these packages hint towards a money making mechanism. The following is an example of a way the packages were analysed (Figure 2).

From the above figure, it is pretty evident that the private hospitals were trying to convert the pandemic into a profit making venture by setting up and marketing the special Covid-19 special care packages. The present study analyses the advertisement content of these packages. The advertisements were specially designed by the private hospitals and they have their own specialized way of attracting the target consumers. The study decodes the advertisements qualitatively and attempts to find out its underlying relationship with the guidelines.

6.2.1. Appeal analysis of advertisements

The concept of Appeal is derived from the Rhetorical Triangle proposed by Aristotle according to whom the three main aspects or appeal of communication are Ethos, Logos and Pathos. Ethos being the communication which creates credibility for an idea, logos being the tools & techniques of communication which appeals to the logical mind of audience and pathos signifies the emotional appeal which is likely to lead the audience towards acceptance and adoption of the idea. Thus, basically advertising appeals are created by ad professionals to attract attention and persuade people to act in a desired way. The communication strategy is likely to be successful if it has a n appeal comprising credibility, emotion and logic.

Figure 2. Way of package analysis
Source: www.thequint.com

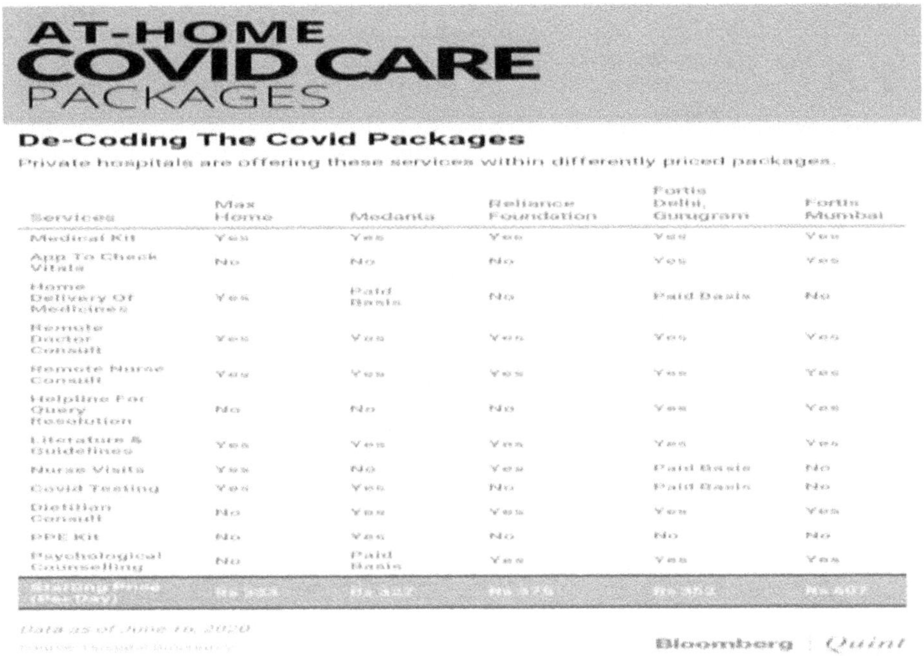

AT-HOME
COVID CARE
PACKAGES

De-Coding The Covid Packages

Private hospitals are offering these services within differently priced packages.

Services	Max Home	Medanta	Reliance Foundation	Fortis Delhi, Gurugram	Fortis Mumbai
Medical Kit	Yes	Yes	Yes	Yes	Yes
App To Check Vitals	No	No	No	Yes	Yes
Home Delivery Of Medicines	Yes	Paid Basis	No	Paid Basis	No
Remote Doctor Consult	Yes	Yes	Yes	Yes	Yes
Remote Nurse Consult	Yes	Yes	Yes	Yes	Yes
Helpline For Query Resolution	No	No	No	Yes	Yes
Literature & Guidelines	Yes	Yes	Yes	Yes	Yes
Nurse Visits	Yes	No	Yes	Paid Basis	No
Covid Testing	Yes	Yes	No	Paid Basis	No
Dietitian Consult	No	Yes	Yes	Yes	Yes
PPE Kit	No	Yes	No	No	No
Psychological Counselling	No	Paid Basis	Yes	Yes	Yes
Starting Price (Per Day)	[illegible]	[illegible]	[illegible]	[illegible]	[illegible]

With time, advertising and marketing have undergone a sea change with introduction of modern ideas, change in social value systems and technological advancements. New appeals have surfaced which imparts a greater degree of creativity, persuasion and effectiveness in advertising.Table1 qualitatively portrays the various kinds of appeal reflected in the advertisements:

Out of the standard advertising appeals, some of them were not discussed because in a grave and serious matter like Covid-19 pandemic they are not applicable. Except when Amitabh Bachhan was himself admitted in Nanavati Hospital, no celebrity actually endorsed any particular hospital or package in lieu of money. The use of celebrity endorsement is very common in advertising campaigns. However, it seems that in pandemic situation neither the hospital nor the celebrity was interested to break legal and ethical parameters to indulge in creating in endorsement appeal. It is worthwhile to mention that when the government had pointed out objectionable elements in a instant noodle the brand ambassadors, both eminent actors of the Bollywood film industry, were also indicted in a related legal case. Similarly Covid package is not a product which has gender or youth implications to it. It is a matter of life and death and therefore the advertisements cannot go overboard. Use of music, humour, body shaming etc is also pointless and therefore was not considered.

The appeals basically denote the mood of the advertisement that Is the psychological, legal and human aspects which the advertisements aspire to touch upon to create a degree of influence on its target audience, the clients. Usually in health communication, *Fear Appeal* plays a major role. The hospitals come up with preventive and corrective measures using the fear psychosis in the mind of the people as in ailments of heart, liver and kidney. In this case as Covid-19 has taken the shape of a pandemic and the mysterious fear which is already inside everyone. Also in a pandemic situation it is not possible legally

Table 1. Mapping of different standard appeals in advertising

Sl. no.	Campaign	Content	Type of Appeal	Analysis
1	Isolation Package	Isolation facility for Covid patients in the hospital	Adventure Appeal	Venturing out of home and comfort zone
2	Covid Test	Testing for Covid	Bandwagon Appeal	Testing is hailed to be the convention
3	All Packages by Corporate Hospitals	Private Hospitals having corporate structure	Brand Appeal	The hospitals are aggressively promoting their brand names and exclusivity
4	N.A.	N.A.	Endorsement Appeal	No brand ambassadors have been used for endorsing
5	All Packages by Corporate Hospitals	The Virus Covid-19	Fear Appeal	An underlying fear of death is looming large in the society
6	N.A.	N.A.	Humour Appeal	No humorous tone is used in grave issue
7	N.A.	N.A.	Shaming/Perfection Appeal	There is no scope
8	N.A.	N.A.	Gender Appeal	There is no scope
9	N.A.	N.A.	Music Appeal	There is no scope
10	All Packages by Corporate Hospitals	Life and health	Emotional Appeal	Emotion is associated with insecurity, vulnerability and hope
11	Isolation Package, Stay at Home	Utility, necessity	Linguistic Appeal	The smart language reflects positive vibe and attracts patients by instilling confidence
12	All Packages by Corporate Hospitals	Utility, necessity	Rational Appeal	In accordance with the government guidelines
13	Isolation package	Lack of availability of the facility	Scarcity Appeal	Availability of Covid ward is not adequate, far less than positive cases
14	N.A.	N.A.	Sex Appeal	There is no scope
15	Isolation Package	Comfort and care	Snob Appeal	The elites want to afford the luxury of buying the comfort
16	Covid Test	Testing is trend	Inclusion Appeal	Everyone wants to be in the group of tested
17	Covid Test	The numbers of test is on rise	Statistical Appeal	The number of testing, positive and recovery is on the rise
18	N.A.	N.A.	Youth Appeal	Covid can occur at any age

Source: Compiled by authors

or ethically to use the fear appeal directly in the advertisements. However, as the fear factor is already there it has been a hidden appeal in all the advertisements. However, as it is implicit and not explicit therefore officially it cannot be attributed as the major appeal. The appeal which therefore officially takes the attribution for the major appeal is the *Rational Appeal*. In rational appeal the advertisement appeals to the reasoning ability of the client where he/she arrives at the logical conclusion after thinking that the product or service should be purchased. In this case the Covid-19 guidelines issued by the World Health Organization and the Ministry of Health & Family Welfare, Government of India have been the rationale behind the code of conduct to handle the Covid-19. The different state governments have made slight adjustments to the guidelines but the spirit remained the same. The advertisements of the Covid packages were designed based on the guidelines and made sense which no one could deny. Educated people and scholars critique the persuasive role of the advertising in a negative light, as if, they try to lure people into buying things by inflating their qualities. As the advertisements were in accordance with the government guidelines, the credibility of their content was not questioned. However, it cannot be denied that emotional appeal which mostly comprises emotion aroused from the fear of death is also a strong appeal. An excerpt from an opinion piece goes like: 'Health is the buzzword in this pandemic time than ever before, and brands are displaying their "healthy" efforts to entice consumers with a series of new campaigns displaying renewed interest in a trend that talks about boosting immunity and nutrients, killing germs to increase safety against disease and improving health. The threat of infection, disease, immunity, and death is a frightening syndrome for human being and any brand that is able to tap that apprehension can entice them with a booster to improve their health, immunity, or stop the spread of diseases. It is a sure way to secure a place in the heart of the consumers. In this time of uncertainty, when people do not know how much they will be impacted, it makes it easy to catastrophise and create panic.' (Brand Equity, 2020).

The *linguistic appeal* in this case lies in presentation of the facilities in medical terms which emerged during this period like the Home Isolation. There is no major experimentation in the language of advertisement. However, a few hospitals have categorized the packages into further sub categories indicating the level of attention like ILS Hospital's Risk Care, Standard Care etc. While most of the hospitals have coined the term 'Home Care' AMRI has termed it Special Covid Care. Infact, AMRI's catchline goes like, 'Special Covid care and beyond….'.

Statistical Appeal which goes a long way to influence people's behaviour and attitudes has played a significant role in the background as the mass media has continuously updated the figures for Covid positive cases, recovery rate and death rate. The figures have created a conducive mentality in the psyche of the people where acceptance of the advertisements has become more likely. *Brand Appeal* is another appeal widely used in the advertisements with the private hospitals using their brand names, corporate identities, logos and slogans to instil confidence in the clients by suave and state of the art presentation. The brand name has played a pivotal role here as most of the content were of same nature but it was the name which mattered. The people have an image construction of different hospitals awakened by the name. The sense of venturing out of home and going for a costly home isolation package at a private hospital, this entire proposition is mostly out of compulsion however it is hard to believe that people able to afford such a package do not have isolation facility at home. So a little bit of Adventure Appeal and Bandwagon Appeal, the latter being the urge of falling in line, cannot be ruled out. Snob Appeal is also included to a very small extent which is often seen among elites visiting hospitals and getting admitted on frivolous grounds, much like spending vacation. The following figure 3 the qualitative trends of the appeals in the 15 advertisements studied:

6.2.2. Thematic Analysis of Advertisements

It was observed that isolation and quarantine emerged as the main backbone of the Covid treatment. There were basically two types of quarantines, home quarantine and hospital quarantine. It is understandable that in the beginning hospital quarantine was mandated but due to the increasing number of positive patients and scarcity of Covid hospitals the concept of home quarantine or home isolation came especially for those who had enough space in their homes for the arrangement. However, although government hospitals had scarcity of Covid wards, the private hospitals immediately lapped up the opportunity and introduced special home isolation packages. The concepts of isolation and quarantine are the main theme of the advertisements. The word 'Care' has featured prominently alongside the word home isolation. Care is something the private hospitals boast of and charge for. In fact, the entire fundamental of these advertisements is care which the people are actually looking for to escape the deadly blow of the Covid-19. Care appears in different forms and idioms like home care, standard care, risk care, special care etc. Care is a constant factor. Care here includes a supply of range of medical equipment, termed as Covid kit, like the N-95 mask, oximeter, thermometer, antibiotics and vitamins. It also includes regular monitoring by doctors.

A technological theme which emerges from the advertisements is medical care through remote mode. Distancing has been one of the major aspect of tackling the onslaught of the Covid-19 pandemic. While some have critiques the term social distancing and recommended using physical distancing instead implying that socializing is possible over technological platforms like the social media and telephone. The hospitals also followed the same methodology in designing their packages and followed modern technology like telemedicine, doctor on call via phone, helpline numbers and online video conference. The idea of the theme is to conduct the care on a remote mode where the patients don't have to actually go out amidst in the pandemic to the hospitals and avail hospital care in their homes itself. That reduces the risk factor and also serves the purpose of isolation. Therefore remote health care is an important theme.

Figure 3. Qualitative dominance of appeal
Source: Compiled by authors

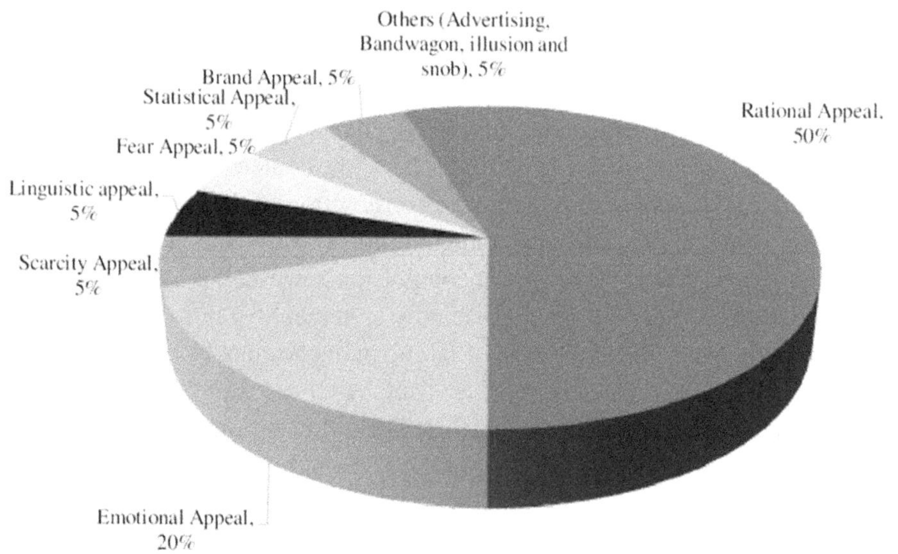

6.2.3. Semiotic Analysis of advertisements

Semiotics of the use of signs and symbols are very conventional and proficient in advertising. They denote the signifier i.e. the symbol and the signified i.e. the meaning. The signs and symbols are in the form of figures, graphics, colours and logos which have constructed social meanings and communicates the people (figure 4).

Figure 4. An example of the advertisement sample
Source: Orissa Diary (2020)

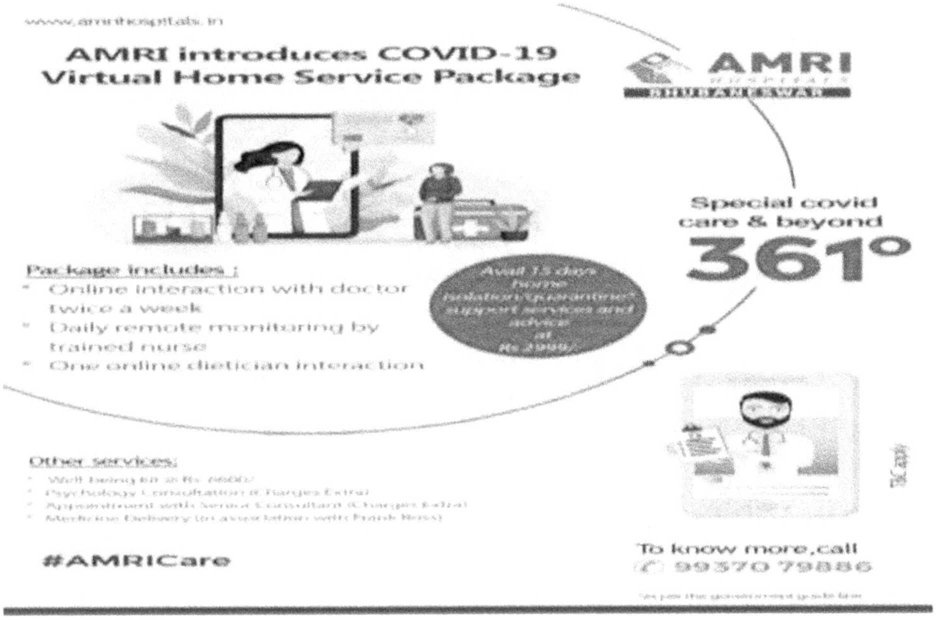

The samples studied have reflected wide use of semiotic instruments which have been enumerated in the following table 2:

Thus from above it has been found that Covid-19 government guidelines has been used as the private hospitals as the Unique Selling Proposition in the advertisements of the special Covid packages. The advertisements instil a confidence among the people that adequate care will be taken. There are minor deviations from government guidelines viz. some hospitals are offering packages of 14 days while some of 15 days. The pricing of the packages are a clear indication that the private hospitals have converted it into a profit making venture. The efforts to make money are quite evident. The packages are indirectly cashing on the fear factor associated with Covid-19.The advertisements are attractive due to their innovative content and design and due to the increase in the impact of the pandemic they are likely to be successful in luring the target audience i.e. the patients to avail the health care packages. A few items, medicines, number of consultations, period of care, addition of general medicines have been included in the packages which have elevated the cost and are not included in the guidelines and SOP. The issue of mental health which is an important issue in Covid have not been included in packages. The packages are implemented based on remote mode following the principles of distancing based on modern

Information & Communication Technology. The cultural aspects of the advertisements viz. the use of English language, signs and symbols clearly indicate that it is western in nature and targeted towards elites and educated intelligentsia.

Table 2. Semiotic analysis of advertisements

Sl no.	Semiotic used	Signifier (Meaning)	Signified (Analysis)
1.	Graphics of House	Homely care	Isolation facility at your own home
2.	Graphic of family	Homely care	The comfort of family proximity
3.	Graphic of Hospital premises	Hospital care	Specialized and professional care
4.	Graphic symbol of telephone	Helpline Number	Consultation available over phone
5.	Graphic of doctor & patient	Medical Treatment	Trust and professional care
6.	Graphic of doctor with patient file	Medical treatment	Professional time
7.	Rising Sun, window corner	Home and familiarity	Homeliness and ray of hope
8.	Red Colour	Strength	Trust
9.	Blue Colour	Positivity	Hope
10.	Green	Nature	Medical treatment
11.	Text-361 degree	Catchline	Extra care
12.	Text –Special Covid care and beyond…	Slogan	Extra care

Source: Compiled by authors

7. CONCLUSION AND SUGGESTIONS

Odisha has undoubtedly done well so far in tackling the Covid-19 crisis. Patient preparedness, step by step practical, sensitive and humane approach; delegation of powers to sarpanches, alertness, and human resource management have been the highlights of the state's crisis management strategy. Timely coordination with Centre and other states helped in procurement of necessary equipment. The Covid-19 government guidelines have been used as the private hospitals as the Unique Selling Proposition in the advertisements of the special Covid packages. The advertisements instil a confidence among the people that adequate care will be taken. There are minor deviations from government guidelines viz. some hospitals are offering packages of 14 days while some of 15 days. The pricing of the packages are a clear indication that the private hospitals have converted it into a profit making venture. The efforts to make money are quite evident. The packages are indirectly cashing on the fear factor associated with Covid-19.The advertisements are attractive due to their innovative content and design and due to the increase in the impact of the pandemic they are likely to be successful in luring the target audience i.e. the patients to avail the health care packages. A few items, medicines, number of consultations, period of care, addition of general medicines have been included in the packages which have elevated the cost and are not included in the guidelines and SOP. The issue of mental health which is an important issue in Covid have not been included in packages. The packages are implemented based on remote mode following the principles of distancing based on modern Information & Communication Technology.

During the lockdown period, there were several cases of mistreatment of non-corona patients. Hence appropriate steps should be undertaken to prevent these ill-treatment. Moreover, this crisis has spurred the need to invest more on public health. There is highly need of upgradation and more expansion of health infrastructure and facilities at the district and block-level. The crisis has further highlighted the need for comprehensive primary care in rural areas particularly tribal region. Given the slower revenue projections due to the economic downturn, resources from the district mineral fund and other potential sources may be explored for health development in the state. The government hospitals should boost up their infrastructure and facilities so that they can also provide Covid care packages to the common people at a much cheaper rate. The advertisements may be controlled and verified by the government so as to prevent marketing of unnecessary matters which are really not that important. For e.g., some general medicines are being marketed as 'well-being kit'. The Post-covid care period is also being stretched and charged for in some cases. A standardization of the packages may be done and an uniformity in their prices should be brought about.

REFERENCES

Barik, S. (2020), Bed shortage in COVID-19 hospitals forces Odisha to change strategy. *The Hindu.* https://www.thehindu.com/news/national/other-states/bed-shortage-in-covid-19-hospitals-forces-odisha-to-change-strategy/article32599863.ece on 26/09/2020

Belch, G. E., & Belch, M. A. (2002). *Advertising and Promotion: An Integrated Marketing Communications Perspective*. McGraw Hill/Irwin.

Bhatia, A. (2020), Here's What Odisha Is Doing To Fight COVID-19 Battle Successfully. *SwCH India.* swachhindia.ndtv.com/heres-what-odisha-is-doing-to-fight-covid-19-battle-successfully-44523/

Bytes, O. (2020). Odisha Govt Caps treatment costs for Covid-19 patients in Private hospitals. Retrieve from https://odishabytes.com/odisha-govt-sets-norms-for-private-hospitals-to-treat-covid-19-patients/ on 28/11/2020

WHO. (2022). *Covid 19.* WHO. https://covid19.who.int/table on 04-06-2022 on 04/06/2022

Das, A. (2020), How Odisha and Kerala are leading from the front in war against Covid. https://www.livemint.com/opinion/columns/opinion-how-odisha-and-kerala-are-leading-from-the-front-in-war-against-covid-11587810374135.html on 26/09/2020.

Diary, O. (2020). AMRI introduces Covid-19 Virtual home service facility. Retrieve from https://orissadiary.com/amri-introduces-covid-19-virtual-home-service-facilities/?utm_source=nyoooz&utm_medium=post

Equity, B. (2020). Quality or Variety: Brands thriving with a health kick Retrieve from https://brandequity.economictimes.indiatimes.com/news/marketing/opinion-quality-or-variety-brands-thriving-with-a-health-kick/77903060 on

Garikipati, N. (2020). Odisha's quiet success in war on Covid-19 pandemic. Policy Circle, Retrieve from https://www.policycircle.org/life/odishas-quiet-success-in-war-on-covid-19-pandemic/ on 28/11/2020

Government of Odisha. (2022), *Covid Dashboard*. State Dashboard. https://statedashboard.odisha.gov.in

Igoe, K. J. (2020). *Developing Public Health Communication Strategies—And Combating Misinformation—During COVID-19.* Harvard Press. https://www.hsph.harvard.edu/ecpe/public-health-communication-strategies-covid-19/

International Monetary Fund. (2020). *Policy Responses to Covid-19.* IMF. https://www.imf.org/en/Topics/imf-and-covid19/Policy-Responses-to-COVID-19

Kar, S. (2020). Low testing, poor health services – how scrambling to fight Covid after good start.

Kassarjian, H. (1977). Content analysis in consumer research. *The Journal of Consumer Research, 4*(3), 19–27.

Kolbe, R. H., & Burnett, M. S. (1991). Content analysis research: An examination of applications for improving research reliability. *The Journal of Consumer Research, 18*(3), 243–264. doi:10.1086/209256

Kracauer, S. (1952). The challenge of qualitative content analysis. *Public Opinion Quarterly, 16*(Winter), 631–642. doi:10.1086/266427

Mheidly, N. and Fares, J. (2020). Leveraging media and health communication strategies to overcome the COVID-19 infodemic. *Journal of Public Health Policy.* DoIhttps://doi.org/ doi:10.1057/s41271-020-00247-w

O'Guinn, Thomas, Allen, Chris Semenik, Richard J. (2003). *Advertising and Integrated Brand Promotion*, 3e. South-Western College Publishing.

Orissa Economic Association. (2020). *Covid-19 and the economy of Odisha-Challenges and the way forward.* OEA.http://www.orissaea.in/COVID-19/COVID_19%20and_The%20Economy_of_Odisha_OEA.pdfon 26/09/2020

Roberts, M., & Pettigrew, S. (2007). A thematic content analysis of children's food advertising. *International Journal of Advertising, 26*(3), 357–367. doi:10.1080/02650487.2007.11073018

Rout, S. K. (2020). How Odisha is managing COVID-19 in framework of Universal Health Coverage. News Click. https://www.newsclick.in/Odisha-Managing-COVID-19-Framework-Universal-Health-Coverage on 28/11/2020

Schilling, J. (2006). On the pragmatics of qualitative assessment: Designing the process for content analysis. *European Journal of Psychological Assessment, 22*(1), 28–37. doi:10.1027/1015-5759.22.1.28

Standard, B. (2020). Apollo Hospital plans 5000 isolation rooms, Covid-19 treatment on anvil. *Business Standard.* https://www.business-standard.com/article/current-affairs/apollo-hospitals-plans-5-000-isolation-rooms-covid-19-treatment-on-anvil-120032601351_1.html on 28/11/2020

The Economics Times. (2020). Odisha trains 1.72 lakh health personnel to combat Covid-19 in state. *The Economic Times.* https://economictimes.indiatimes.com/news/politics-and-nation/odisha-trains-1-72-lakh-health-personnel-to-combat-covid-19-in-state/articleshow/75643447.cms on 28/11/2020

The New Indian Express. (2020). In addition to COVID-19, hospital mismanagement stress for patients in Odisha. *The New Indian Times.* https://www.newindianexpress.com/states/odisha/2020/aug/04/in-addition-to-covid-19-hospital-mismanagement-stress-for-patients-in-odisha-2178869.html on 28/11/2020

WHO. (2020). *From governance to community resilience: Odisha's response to Covid-19.* WHO. https://www.who.int/india/news/feature-stories/detail/from-governance-to-community-resilience-odisha-s-response-to-covid-19 on 28/11/2020

Worldometer (2022), *Covid-19 Coronavirus Pandemic.* Meters. https://www.worldometers.info/coronavirus/?utm_campaign=homeAdUOA?Si

Chapter 13
New Normal Manufacturing Industry Post-Pandemic 2020

Muskaan Arora
Thapar School of Liberal Arts and Sciences, Thapar University, Patiala, India

Archana Goel
Chitkara University, India

ABSTRACT

Manufacturing industry plays a paramount role in the world economy, accounting for almost 16% of the global GDP in 2018. Manufacturing has been identified as the key driver of dynamic growth and development of the country. The COVID-19 pandemic has caused immense devastation around the world. Due to the downturn in the manufacturing industry along with the factory blackout, the Coronavirus epidemic reduced the global FDI by 5 per cent -15 per cent. The aim of this chapter is to highlight the need to understate the vital role of manufacturing industry in the Indian context. It will further discuss and elaborate on the impact of the 2020 pandemic on the manufacturing industry and would suggest a framework to manufacturing industry how it can come back in a new normal position post-COVID-19 scenario. Manufacturers who acknowledge this new standard discussed in the present chapter and will operate on it will have enough growth opportunities and can have long-term sustainable success.

1.0 INTRODUCTION

Manufacturing Industry plays a paramount role in the world economy, accounting for almost 16% of the global GDP in 2018. Manufacturing has been identified as the key driver of dynamic growth and development of the country (Rele, 2020). The most important production sectors where India has established its expertise are steel industry, electronics, automotive, health sector, engineering industry, textiles, food processing industry and many more (Deshmukh, 2016). The manufacturing sector generates several job opportunities both directly a well as indirectly. It also has a billowing and productive impact on many other industries, such as agriculture. Therefore, the government has taken a lot of initiatives across the world to develop this industry. The contribution by the retail sector towards India's GDP is

DOI: 10.4018/978-1-7998-6896-5.ch013

about 10% due to which the Global Retail Development Index (GRDI), 2019 has ranked India at the number 2 position. One of the major initiatives taken in 2015 to promote the manufacturing industry includes 'Make in India' to expedite the production of goods in India. Its purpose was to lessen India's dependence on exporting countries by manufacturing products in its own country. FDI in the nation has pursued an ideal pattern since the launch of Make in India which led to the development of investment-favourable policies which finally the opened the path of FDI allowances in various industries. The FDI inflows to India have amounted to $286 billion in the last five years, which is almost 46.9% of the total FDI earned in our country.

The COVID-19 pandemic has caused immense devastation around the world. It has contributed to an extensive human loss around the globe. In December 2019, COVID-19 originated in Wuhan. Due to the downturn in the manufacturing industry along with the factory blackout, the Coronavirus epidemic reduced the global FDI by 5 per cent -15 per cent (UNCTAD). Airlines Automobiles and Oil industries majorly faced the adverse impact of pandemic 2020 on its Foreign Direct Investments.

The imposed lockdown for maintaining social distancing drained the manufacturing sector. Many manufacturing companies across the globe, including India, have shown concerns for their raw material supply (Pratheeesh and Arumugasamy, 2020). It was quite common to see the order getting cancelled almost around in every sector except the essential industries. Companies have declined their production operations and have also postponed the launch of new products following the pandemic outbreak. In addition to finished goods, India also imports almost 70% of its television components and other consumer durable items such as air conditioners, refrigerators, and washing machines. Sales of these products was disrupted due to supply disruption. Supply chains were disrupted, stopping the flow of raw materials, intermediate and finished goods. One reason for this could be the lack of money to buy the goods as everyone was sitting at home for three months and another reason could be the shutdown of their businesses. The left-over cash was spent on purchasing essential goods only.

Moreover, the Chinese suppliers have raised the prices of some components by almost 2%, and more than 15% for TV panels. The significant disturbances caused by COVID-19 are incomprehensible. Furthermore, the well-being of a worker has been a considerable problem too, and physical contact was hazardous. Large number of workers, particularly semi-skilled and unskilled workers, migrated to their homelands, after the announcement of lockdown by the Government authorities. They didn't want to re-join their work because of the fear that the government might impose lockdown again, without informing. The shortage of workers led to the suspension of assembly lines or curtailment of their operations. Moreover, the employees carried out their administrative activities from the homes, but that too on a small scale. It led to the deterioration in the stock of raw materials, work in progress and finished products.

Additionally, the slower pace of banking activities, reduced work schedules, crowded and busy lines of communication contributed to delayed cash transactions which raised lot of financial risks for the manufacturing industry. Therefore, Governments and manufacturers should be sensitised with this situation and respond rapidly. For both academicians and practitioners, these disturbances have tremendous consequences.

Although the immediate impact is daunting, if not harsh, manufacturers should take actions to ensure their survival and then relative stability will come as the conditions improve. Though, the leaders in manufacturing industry are already progressing and implementing the reforms. India's role post-COVID-19, especially in the industrial sector, is of great interest. It is a hope and speculation from the rest of the world that India would emerge as one of the preferred centres for the manufactured goods vis-a-vis China. It is a sensible and rational ambition for the country. But this is a result, not a planned strategy. Though the global epidemic has devastated people and threatened to take lives, our priority should be to ensure that the causalities are reduced and also, the management should devise future strategies in compliance with the rapidly evolving global dynamics. It is well said that "there is light at the end of every tunnel", every disaster brings its own set of prospects and opportunities. New statistics indicate that manufacturing output in India has declined to almost zero levels. This pandemic, on the other hand, has the potential to build the path for India to enter into new production ways in the entire industry. When India plays its cards correctly, it can intensely reverse its prosperity in the decades ahead. The Coronavirus epidemic is like a tsunami expanding across the globe with a moving epicentre and never-ending aftershocks.

Today, everybody is hoping to resume a semblance of production activities, and leaders are planning to face the new standard, such as how digital transformation will provide the industry with a swift recovery. This chapter is an attempt to throw light on measures taken by manufacturers to combat the impact of COVID 19 havoc. This chapter aims to highlight the need to understate the vital role of the manufacturing industry in the Indian context. It will further discuss and elaborate on the impact of Pandemic 2020 on the manufacturing industry. It would suggest a framework to manufacturing industry on how it can come back in a new normal position post-COVID-19 scenario. Manufacturers, who acknowledge the new standard policies discussed in the present chapter and operate on it, will get enough growth opportunities and can have long-term sustainable success in the future.

2.0 2020 PANDEMIC REPERCUSSIONS ON THE MANUFACTURING SECTOR

The recent lockdown in the country has put a lot of strain on all sectors, including the manufacturing industry, which has shown a decline of about 27.4% (See Fig 1). Even before the lockdown, the industry was not in a great shape and in the smaller organisations with lesser retaining control, and lower profitability, the situation was even worse, due to larger amount of uncertainty. This can be compared to 'root beer game' effect in the Supply Chain Management, whereby a market incident can lead to a highly intensified reaction from the suppliers which further will lead to short term overproduction and average discount sales. This effect causes blocking of distribution channels which reduces the prices of offloaded goods though provided volume support, but hit the profitability.

The recent pandemic has affected the manufacturing sector in many ways. Few of them are as follows (See Fig. 2)

1. Low or no production

The government directives all around the globe, including India, announced the lockdown to control coronavirus. Thus, with very little labour and slow movement of Cargoes, production got halted in the manufacturing industry, thereby, decreasing the scale of operations, and affecting the production volumes (See fig 3). Moreover, the cost and quality of the products got impacted, which drastically reduced the profits of the business. It adversely affected the turnover over a period, which slowed down to a crawl leading to the shutdown of various small organisations.

Figure 1. Contraction in manufacturing sector during pandemic
Source: HIS/Market Monthly Data

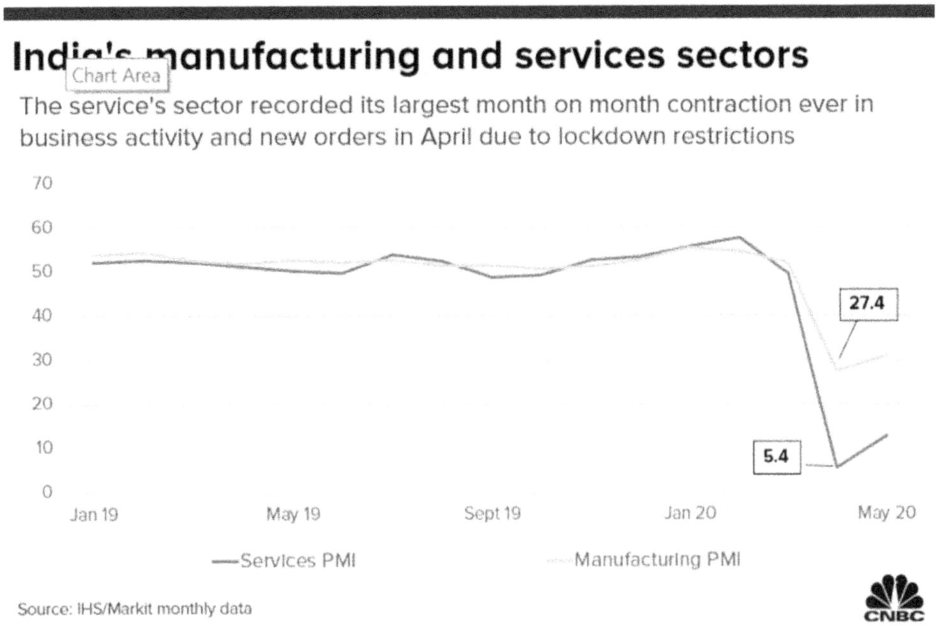

Figure 2. 2020 Pandemic effects on manufacturing sector
Source: Authors Own Compilation

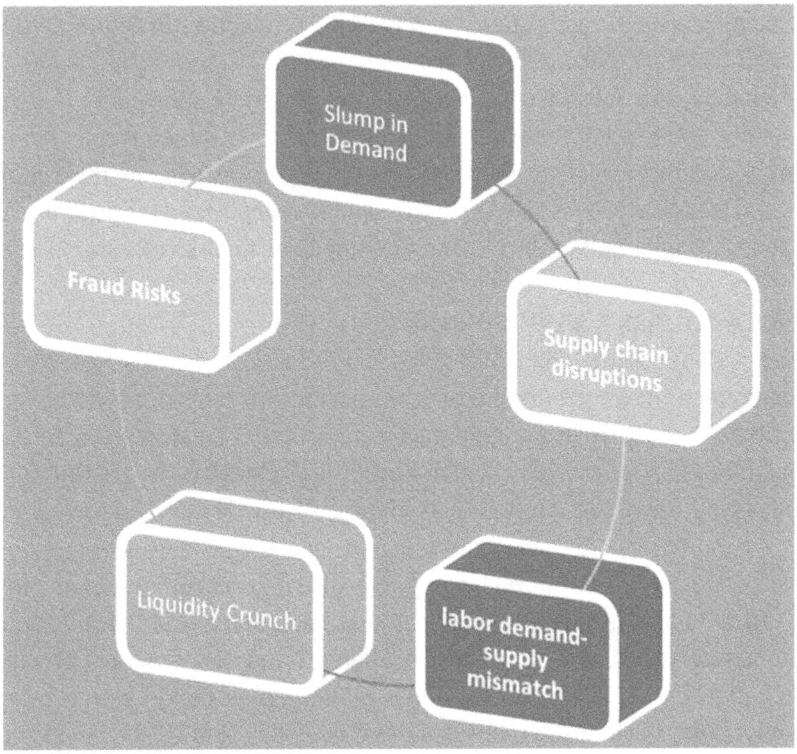

Figure 3. Epidemic effects on production
Source: National Statistics Office, Government of India

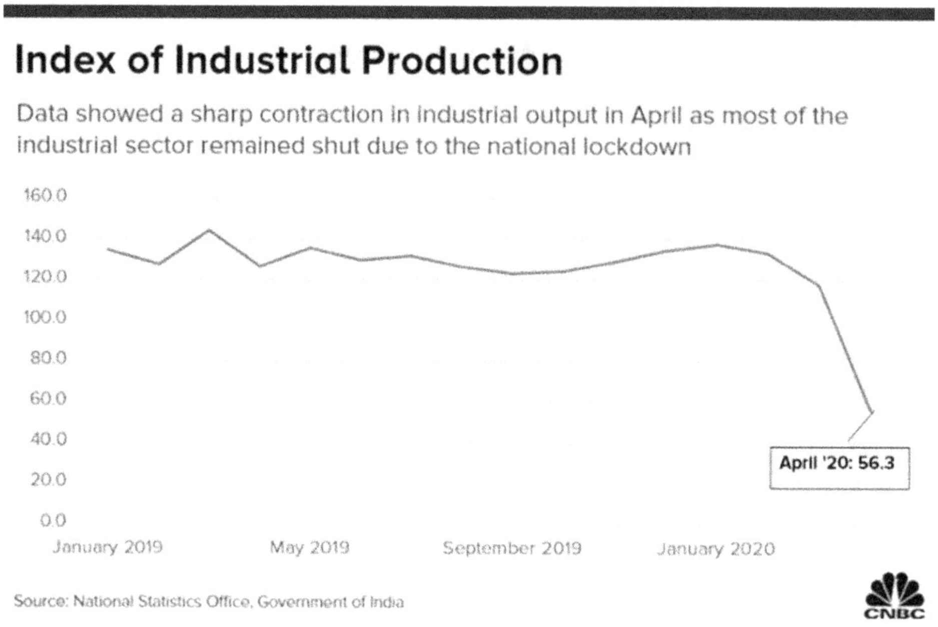

2. Slump in demand

Even though manufacturing organisations step up their production in future, a drop in the demand would be a matter of concern. With reduced or no income due to retrenchments and salary cuts, end consumers can often delay the purchasing of non-essential products, thus going to slow the demand for finished goods. Finally, due to all of these disturbances, the end consumer usually begins deferring non-essential transactions and disconnects from consuming processes by delaying their demands (See Fig 4). Demand shock would lead to a decrease in potential business revenue and profitability. It, combined with increased uncertainty, would result in the closing of companies and the disruption of the supply chain.

3. Transportation woes/ Supply chain disruptions

Due to the quarantine in the surrounding nations, during this period, limited export-import movements have exacerbated the crisis in the manufacturing sector. The slowdown in manufacturing had lowered the demand for logistics services, which further brought down prices through warehouses and freight. Constraints on air travel and international flights worldwide have led to a slowdown in the flow of goods, putting an end to first and last-mile transport and intermodal movement of goods. The declines in the capacity of carriers and shortages of goods distribution equipment due to disruptions have had a significant effect on intra-Asia trade routes. A sharp and unexpected drop in freight volumes had caused significant carriers to announce service cancellations and delays, and consequently, empty sails to and from India had taken place. The uncertainties in the logistics had led to a cascading effect. The transporters not only struggled to place their vehicles for loading, but they were also under pressure to adjust their quotes for carrying goods, as they also faced lower attendance, with their operational risks increasing steeply. Upon re-opening of manufacturing operations around the globe, the supply of cargo vessels/carriers would reduce, and this will not only lead to delayed shipping but also raised logistic costs which all together aggravated the problems in the manufacturing industry.

Figure 4. Covid 19 effect on consumer demand
Source: Reserve Bank of India

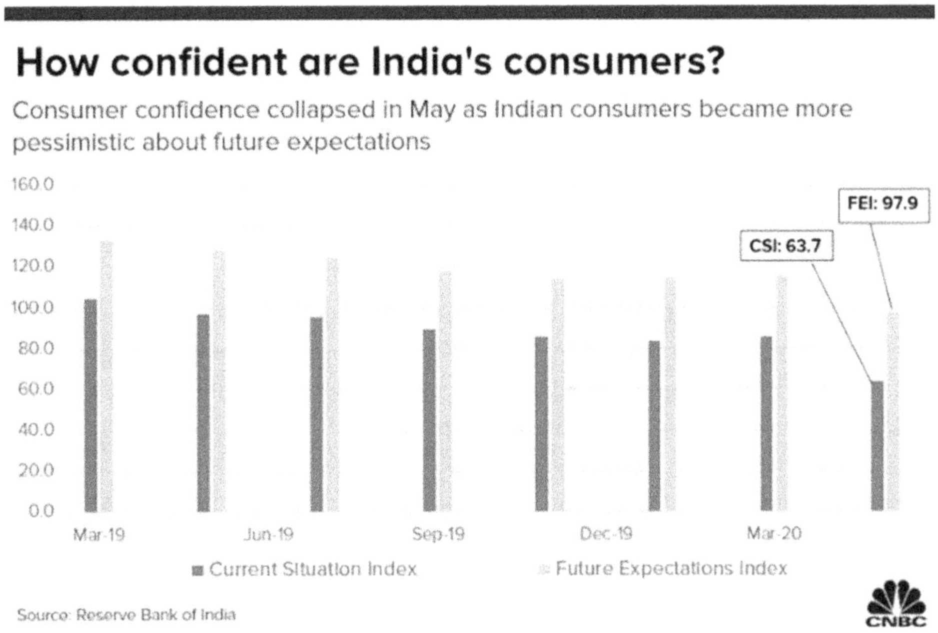

4. Increased labour demand-supply mismatch

As per the International Labour Organisation, 2.7 billion workers worldwide are affected by the COVID-19 pandemic due to lockdowns. With a significant dip in the market, Indian companies looked at layoffs, although temporarily. The temporary relocation of workers to their homes led to a shortage of workers. For labour-intensive industries such as textiles manufacturing, agriculture, hospitality and mining, labour costs are a crucial figure in the supply chain. The manufacturing companies had to bear higher transportation costs because of a shortage of labour to load and unload goods, which further raised operating risks.

5. Liquidity Crunch

The Indian economy was stressed by labour capital/liquidity crisis due to production slowdowns amid global lock-downs and ongoing payments for fixed costs. Further, low demand, distribution network disruption and significantly decreased productivity and sales have made liquidity a significant concern for the government as well as manufacturers. Moreover, factories with reduced capacity build inventories that couldn't be distributed. Also, many producers' have increased repayment period from thirty days to ninety days. Smaller businesses, to avoid risks, considered those conditions which put pressure on the cash conversion cycle. Cash flow pressures persisted even after the lockdown due to the decreased demand, resulting in reduced inventories, with MYMEs having the worst hit cash flow problems could see a rise in NPA levels due to non-repayment.

6. Increasing Fraud Risks in the Manufacturing Sector

During these turbulent times, both the supply chain and the distribution side of the manufacturing sectors were under pressure. They faced enormous, unprecedented challenges due to the disturbances in the supply chain, labour shortage problems, stressful liquidity situations, too unpredictable demand and logistical difficulties, and many other uncertainties associated with the pandemic. All these challenges enhanced fraud risks; some of them are as follows:

a) Sales and distribution

Diversion of goods, expected to be sold in one channel to another channel, to claim unfair benefits from price arbitrage between the two channels • Fictitious sales recorded under the programme to claim higher benefits under the said programme • Fictitious sales recorded to claim benefits from volume/slab discounts that are not currently carried out in the supply chain.

b) Sale of damaged and expired products

To meet the growing demands for critical goods, defective and expired products were placed into circulation in the distribution chain by altering the date of manufacturing or altering the packaging of the products.

c) Artificial inflation of prices

The hoarding of vital goods, which causes superficial scarcity, were sold at rates higher than those stipulated.

d) Counterfeiting

Owing to the perceived disparity between demand and the availability of critical goods, there is a strong likelihood of counterfeit products being injected into the supply chain. The general public may not be able to distinguish discrepancies between genuine and potentially fake products and therefore ends up purchasing potentially counterfeit products.

3.0 RECENT STRATEGIES FOR NEW NORMAL MANUFACTURING INDUSTRIES

It is true that the covid epidemic has created havoc on humans and continues to claim the lives of people. So our priority should be to reduce the casualties and build the plans that are in line with the rapidly evolving global dynamics. As the saying goes, “there is light at the end of every tunnel,” every crisis has its collection of opportunities. Fresh figures show that India's manufacturing output has fallen to almost zero. But then, on the contrary, this disease outbreak has the potential to pave India's much-awaited journey into the manufacturing industry. All appreciation lies to the developments in technologies, like the Internet of Things (IoT), Machine Learning, robotics, digital technologies, 3D Printing, Artificial Intelligence and Robotics which could facilitate the world of manufacturing.

a) **3D printing service**- It is a process of manufacturing three dimensional solid things from a digital image. This latest manufacturing technology uses the virtual model to manufacture items by printing layers of materials. It offers cost-effectiveness with its emphasis on lean production. Digital Manufacturing Network has only augmented over the past few months in all types of industries such as aerospace automobile, healthcare, defence, and others in the wake of COVID-19. It has tremendous potential in India with mega-projects coming up. HP has partnerships with leading industrial companies such as Siemens and BASF to accelerate the design and production of 3D printed at scale. The entire 3D printing community has come unitedly to help fight this pandemic.
b) **Internet of Things (IoT)**: The Internet of Things also plays a vital role in the digital transformation process. The introduction of essential IOT technologies in the manufacturing sector is called the Industrial Internet of Things (IIoT) which is a big disruptor. With the growth of IoT in consumer technology, the industrial sector has also begun to introduce this new sensor network and Actuators for data processing, tracking, selection and process optimisation over the digital infrastructure. Indian companies have a lot of opportunity in this field, like many large companies. Indian Rail Network will roll out locomotives with tools such as remote diagnostics and constructive predictive maintenance, and these trains will be part of a broader ecosystem linked to the new technology.
c) **Digital Technologies**: With the rise of the digital era, Indian manufacturing firms have begun to incorporate digital technology in their manufacturing processes, which will help to improve productivity. It is projected that 65 per cent of manufacturing firms will have a high degree of digitalisation by the end of 2020. For its commercial vehicles, Ashok Leyland uses machine learning techniques and its newly developed telematics unit to boost the efficiency of vehicles, drivers and so on.
d) **Artificial Intelligence (AI)** – Manufacturing plants and factories must accept automation to remain significant in the long run. AI-driven machines add tremendous value to the manufacturing process by allowing tasks to be automated, improving production quality and bringing machine interaction closer to human interaction.
e) **Robotics manufacturing** – Robots operate with human employees. They can therefore play a vital role to optimise the assembly operations and improve the production cycles via precision, speed, reach and any material handling capability. Robots empower human workers as their deployment enables them to be educated in new skills and thereby achieve a competitive advantage among the workers. Though stand-alone robotic workstations are already commonplace even in Indian companies, autonomous robots use improved senses, dexterity and intellect to optimise tasks or work human workers.

India needs to improve its current infrastructure to support manufacturers and potential firms planning to set up their plants in the country. We need to be on par with the kind of facilities and amenities that China has had in place for many years. It includes improving roads, highways and also provide stable power and electric supply for manufacturers to sustain a steady flow of production. The world of advanced technology will transform the four building blocks of manufacturing industry to New Normal Post Pandemic 2020.

Material: The global supply chain for raw materials relies heavily on one source. It will be subject to significant disruption, with most countries/industry announcing either move to alternative, near-shore or domestic locations. It will create new opportunities for countries such as India to become a manufacturing hub. However, this necessitates a well-organised plan to produce the right quality products, achieve economies of scale, and finally reduce costs. Advanced Technology can help to achieve this plan by which the entire supply chain can be automated and managed remotely, at any time, anywhere.

Machines: There is also an excellent sign for traditional factories or brownfields, as emerging technology platforms offer the opportunity to digitise non-digital assets and protect existing investments.

The whole new world of Industry 4.0 gives life to devices that are highly intelligent and wired, establishing a truly digital supply chain. It combines communications, IT, data and physical elements around the value chain and helps turn conventional plants into smart factories.

Manpower: Skilled labour has always been a problem, but it will become even more challenging in today's world where people needs have shifted to remain safe and secure. Remotely linked robots to computer systems, equipped with Machine Learning algorithms, can operate manufacturing facilities with minimal human assistance. Also, the safety and protection of on-duty staff are equally important, particularly in remote and hazardous areas. Today, connected and wearable devices help employees manage and track their workers on a single dashboard in real-time. It helps to provide urgent support and relief to staff in emergencies.

Methods: People, procedures and business processes are going to undergo a full transformation. The combined power of computers & automation enables remote monitoring, fault detection and control of machines for their maintenance and predictive on-demand maintenance activities. It also allows the standardisation of quality of products at a reduced cost of output.

4.0 GOVERNMENT MEASURES TO BOOST MANUFACTURING INDUSTRY

The COVID-19 disease outbreak has taken the industry and everyday human activities around the world to a standstill. It has affected the manufacturing sector very severely due to lockdowns in many nations around the globe. China is well famous with the name of the world's factory' as 'Made in China' tag can be observed all around the world. While China is re-opening its economy after the COVID19 quarantine process, the manufacturing epicentre of China is entering into an unprecedented scenario in which businesses and customers from all over the world are suspending or discontinuing business orders and corporate deals.

Companies of Korea are withdrawing their investments from China due to a Corona Pandemic. There are also similar buzzes from Japan to pull out their investment from China. Their government official has pledged $2.2 billion as an economic stimulus package to help its producers switch output out of China, as the economic effect of COVID-19 disrupts vital supply chains. China's regulated economy and increasing global trade disputes with the U. S. further make it extremely difficult, particularly in today's times. Therefore, the entire world is rethinking its overreliance on China's entire logistics chains. If the China manufacturing zones gets 'de-concentrated, developing nation India has more chances to be benefitted from this. India presents a viable replacement destination for companies seeking relocations from China. Indian central government, state industry departments are already examining proposals at different levels. This could be seen alongside with formation of new policies by Indian authorities to promote its manufacturing industry.

1. It is a highly favourable time for India to upsurge as a manufacturing hub. NITI Aayog and the Promotion of Industry department are preparing to offer incentives to attract international manufacturing organisation. Therefore, to promote mobile phone manufacturing in India, the government had declared three policies in March with incentives totalling Rs. 48,000 crore and the production-linked incentive (PLI) scheme has a significant share close to Rs. 41,000 crore with sops to be spread over three years.
2. Rs 1,70,000 crores funding by the government to the transportation industry, includes expenditure in bridges, highways, railway, ships, docks and aviation safety. With national highway projects ongoing post-lock relaxation by the government, the completion of these activities at a faster speed is a significant concern, as it will help manufacturers expect improved transport and logistics availability for their stock.
3. The government has announced to create 100 million manufacturing jobs by 2022 in the "Make in India" programme. Also, Rs 6,940 crores have been allocated for the coming eight years. Additionally, 100 per cent Foreign Direct Investment is permitted in this sector through the automatic route.
4. The drive to reduce corporation taxes has resulted in India to be one of the lowest corporate tax rates globally, which is at 15 per cent for a new upcoming manufacturing organisation in India. It clearly shows the goal of the Indian government to grow the manufacturing industry as a significant share of national GDP.
5. India has projected USD 1.5 trillion in spending to develop capability and increase its infrastructure over the next five years.
6. The goal of doubling the current port capacity of 1500 MT, which has itself doubled over the last five years, is a positive one as rising port freight, shipbuilding capacity and the usage of portland for renewable energy production would further drive the manufacturing agenda.
7. The qualifying suppliers of listed 53 essential bulk drugs will get financial benefits for their increased revenue over the base year (2019-20) over a term of 6 years.
8. Out of 53 listed bulk drugs, 26 are bulk-based ferment drugs, and 27 are bulk-based chemical synthesis drugs.
9. The bonus rate would be 20% (of incremental market value) for bulk-based fermentation drugs and 10% for bulk-based chemical synthesis drugs.
10. Jump in India's place from 77th to 63rd in the World Bank's Ease of Doing Business Index testifies to India's government capacity and effort.

5.0 SUGGESTIONS TO GOVERNMENT TO NEW NORMAL MANUFACTURING SECTOR

When China met with severe criticism not only for covering up the initial outbreak of the virus but also for spreading lies and disinformation in the aftermath, India was admired at the international level. Many world leaders from Brazil, Nepal, Afghanistan, including the President of the United States, have openly expressed gratitude to India for its support and compassion during this epidemic hardship. India has the potential to see itself as a manufacturing centre, not only because of the COVID-19 pandemic but also because of China's rising wage levels. Over the years, salaries have increased to $6.5 per hour in China, an improvement of $1.5 from 2016 prices. "India is well ready to take advantage of China's worsening competitiveness, as workers' wages in most Indian countries are considerably lower than in China" (Economic Survey of India). However, India faces intense competition from countries such as Vietnam, Bangladesh, Myanmar, Indonesia and even Ethiopia. These nations tend to be other potential options for businesses searching for younger investment destinations. India is required to get ready rapidly if it is to regain prosperity and maximise their market share in the manufacturing sector since the window of opportunity is going to close as all other nations will leap in to grab the opportunity of the crisis. India has the requisite labour pool, but it needs to drive the business acumen towards consumer demand for long-term subsistence.

The recent policy initiatives of the Indian government, such as the lowering of corporate tax and the introduction of the Goods and Services Tax, have further aided in attracting the manufacturers. However, the manufacturing industry of India itself is brimming with a plethora of challenges. Tax and customs laws, labour legislation, transportation and sexism in the export industry are some of them.

To address the problems, we need to discuss potential options where the government wants to go forward with some crucial reforms to encourage investment and improve India's manufacturing sector.

1. The Indian market size is vast, and it offers to give manufacturing sector a lift due to its large population. For example, if a commodity is manufactured in Vietnam, the product will be exported due to a low-consumption environment. In the other hand, if the manufacturing industry is based in India, the demand is readily open. Mobile production is a perfect example of this.
2. India should look at offering subsidies to improve jobs. There ought to be a relief for exporters to compensate for the cost of state taxation. Simplified permits and single port clearances, in addition to solving bottlenecks related to the transport sector and growing logistics capability, will benefit the nation. It also needs to step up the process of negotiating further Free Trade Agreements with countries as well as with different regional groupings.
3. More specific laws for the purchase of land for business and labour changes require immediate consideration. The government has moved to integrate 44 labour laws into four labour codes, but officially only the Wages Code has been approved by Parliament. The other three codes – Workplace Relations, National Welfare, Health & Working Practices – are also outstanding. Karnataka has changed its land acquisition legislation and made it possible for corporations to buy land directly from farmers. Gujarat has declared that it will assign land to corporations within seven days and the government will give all the requisite permissions within 15 days. Tamil Nadu, Maharashtra and Telangana are designing dedicated reward programmes for electronics manufacturers. Given these state-specific steps, the central government would have to take the lead in crucial institutional reforms and policies for a long term boosting for the manufacturing industry
4. The introduction of the National Investment Clearance Cell and National Logistics Strategy announced in the Union Budget 2020-21 would create a more desirable investment scenario. The Central Government has opened its doors to multinational companies who are looking to restore and/or diversify their industrial supply chains in the post-COVID-19 environment. Some policy-makers have taken measures to reduce investment bottlenecks and improve investment.
5. The potential of the SEZ Act, 2005 was a crucial opportunity overlooked by India. As a catalyst for foreign investment in India's manufacturing environment through tax and fiscal incentives, the Act has been the flag-bearer for the growth of India's services industry. However, the crooked rise

and surplus capacity in the SEZ areas currently in place shows that the programme has not borne the expected effects to the degree envisaged.

6. Rather than focusing on these problems, the time is ripe either for the revival of the SEZ strategy or to allow for alternative, productive use of such aggregated land for manufacturing units, post-de-notification. The re-imagination of these areas as jobs and economic enclaves (as per the Baba Kalyani report) and the re-imagination of the tax benefits, as well as the explicit distribution of incentives for the manufacturing sector, would make it possible for the policy to achieve its initial, specified objectives. However, tax cuts and associated benefits might not be enough. Becoming tax-friendly and industry-friendly, by definition, is more important. Critical considerations include the simplification of the GST code and the enhancement of tax transparency and certainty of tax policy and practise. While tariff barriers on imports can promote local manufacturing, mutually beneficial trade agreements with other countries and regions would go a long way towards boosting India's manufacturing ambitions.

6.0 CONCLUSION

The continuing pandemic of COVID-19 caused temporary closures at numerous production facilities around sectors, leaving the supply chain cycle across the globe badly affected. Now that factories have resumed activities, the main emphasis is on returning to the average rate of production. It is not a simple job, but the Smart Automation technologies of Industry 4.0 are emerging to the assistance of businesses, not just to help them regain full productivity quicker, but also to improve operating productivity. The technology exists, and companies that are rapidly transiting to digital infrastructure will emerge more robust and resilient. Some automated additions in the organisation will set workers free for other demanding activities. At the same time, others will stand them collaboratively to execute tasks that are too complex or too risky for humans to perform repeatedly. Smart Automation improves the quality of the product and its efficiency as producers do not have to think about downfall and the loss of sales that goes with it.

REFERENCES

Deloitte. (2016). Global manufacturing competitiveness index: report. London: *Deloitte Touche Tohmatsu Limited*. https://www2.deloitte.com/global/en/pages/manufacturing/articles/global-manufacturing-competitiveness-index.html

Deshmukh, S. G. (2016). Manufacturing Competitiveness: Research Opportunities. *International Journal of Global Business and Competitiveness*, *11*(1), 1–6.

Deshmukh, S. G., & Haleem, A. (2020). Framework for Manufacturing in Post-Covid-19 World Order: An Indian Perspective. *International Journal of Global Business and Competitiveness*.

Financial Express. (2020). Coronavirus brings business competitors on one table. *Financial Express*. https://www.financialexpress.com/industry/coronavirus-brings-business-competitors-on-one-table-cci-allows-firms-to-work-together/1933729/

Pratheeesh, J. T., & Arumugasamy, G. (2020). Impact of Coronavirus in Indian economy and banking sector-an overview. *Studies in Indian Place Names*, *40*(18), 2090–2101.

Rele, S. (2020). Emerging outbreaks and epidemic threats: The practicality and limitations in the development and manufacturing of treatments for Coronavirus (COVID-19). *Polymorphism*, *4*, 45–52.

Chapter 14
The Socio-Economic Impact of the Pandemic on the Micro-, Small-, and Medium-Scale Enterprises

Ca Shilpa Vasant Bhide
Department of Management Sciences, Savitribai Phule Pune University, India

ABSTRACT

The micro small and medium scale industry in India is an important sector, as it has contributed tremendously to the economic as well as social development. It has not only encouraged entrepreneurship but has also been instrumental in generating employment. The sector supports large-scale industries as it offers a wide range of products and services. The Covid 19 pandemic is having an impact on the sector such as loss of profit and revenue, loss of employment, and working capital problems. The chapter covers the impact in three stages: pre-pandemic, during the lock down, post-lock down and post-pandemic. It studies the remedial measures undertaken to revive and sustain the sector. It traces the risks, challenges, and opportunities for the sector. The chapter focuses on the journey of the MSMEs Sector from before the pandemic to the current situation and tries to analyse what lies ahead.

INTRODUCTION

The micro small and medium scale industry in India is a key sector as it has contributed tremendously to the economic as well as social development. It has not only encouraged entrepreneurship but has also been instrumental in generating employment. The sector supports the large scale industries as it offers a wide range of products and services. (Annual Report 2019-2020).Micro, Small and Medium Scale Enterprises is one of the key sectors contributing to the Gross Domestic product and exports.

DOI: 10.4018/978-1-7998-6896-5.ch014

Micro, Small and Medium Enterprises (MSMEs) manufacture steel products, chemicals, spare parts, auto components, and products supplied to the Original Equipment Manufacturers for OEMs, ceramic tiles, brass metal industry. The Micro Small and Medium Scale Enterprises sector not only manufactures engineering products it is also involved in the manufacture of Agro based products such as honey and beekeeping, bamboo and cane, processing of fruit, vegetable, pulses, cereals. Not only manufacturing the Micro Small and Medium Scale Enterprises sector is in the service sector as well such as maintenance of electrical goods. It has an urban as well as rural presence. Products such as coir, khadi, auto components are manufactured by the Micro, Small and Medium Enterprises

The Micro Medium and Small scale industries act was passed in the year 2006 to address various legal issues of the sector and also promote their development. The act defined the Micro, Medium and small Scale industry. The Micro Small and Medium Scale Enterprises Act, classified the Micro Small and Medium Scale Enterprises as the Manufacturing Sector and Service sector. The act was passed in 2006 and covers definition of the micro small and medium scale units, payment to the Micro Small and Medium Scale Enterprises. The objective of the Micro Small and Medium Scale Enterprises act is to protect the interests of the entrepreneurs and encourage the Micro Small and Medium Scale Enterprises

The Definition of Micro Small and Medium Scale enterprises before 2020 were as follows, the parameters were changed in the Pandemic. However the grievous definition was based on the Investment in Plant and Machinery.

Table 1. Manufacturing sector

Enterprise Category	Investment in Plant and Machinery
Micro Enterprise	Not Exceeding Rs 25 Lakhs
Small Enterprise	More than Rs 25 Lakhs but less thanRs 5 Crore
Medium Enterprise	More than Rs 5 Crore but less than Rs 10 crore

Source: Micro Small and Medium Scale Enterprises ACT 2006

Table 2. Service sector

Enterprise Category	Investment in Plant and Machinery
Micro Enterprise	Not Exceeding Rs 10 Lakhs
Small Enterprise	More than Rs 10 Lakhs but less thanRs 2 Crore
Medium Enterprise	More than Rs 2 Crore but less than Rs 5 crore

Source: Micro Small and Medium Scale Enterprises ACT 2006

There are various schemes and portals created for encouraging and supporting the micro small and medium scale enterprises sector such as the MSME Samadhaan which is a Portal created by Office of DC (MSME), Ministry of Micro, Small and Medium Enterprises (MSME) Micro and Small Enterprises (MSEs) can file their applications online regarding delayed payment on this portal. There are a number of schemes, packages and training programs offered through government agencies. Loan, funds and resources are made available to support the sector.

During the Covid Pandemic the Parameters of the Classifications changed,which are highlighted later in the chapter. The change in the classification was done to help the Micro Small and Medium Scale Enterprises face the challenges posed by the pandemic and help their sustenance and survival.

Covid 19 Pandemic

Covid 19 is caused by Corona Virus or SARCoV-2. It is a respiratory pathogen. Corona Virus is an infectious disease, which can lead to death . The World Health Organisation detected the first case in Wuhan, China on 31st December 2019. Scientists globally are working on it to find a cure in the form of a vaccine.

In India in march 2020, 44 confirmed cases of corona virus were detected. The states previously affected were Delhi, Haryana, Jammu, Kerala, Ladakh, Punjab, Rajasthan, Tamil Nadu, Telangana, Uttar Pradesh. There were both foreign and indian nationals. The infections spread to other states such as Maharashtra, honorable Prime Minister of India Me. Narendra Modi announced a Janata Curfew on 22nd MArch 2020, between 7 am to 9 pm. The citizens were urged to stay in homes and maintain social distancing only personnel in essential services were excluded. The honorable Prime Minister as per the powers of Section 6 (2) (i) issued an order for lockdown from 25th March 2020 for a period of 21 days. The order was issued for all states and union territories. The nationwide lockdown was in 4 Phases namely:- Phase 1 was between 25 March 2020 and 14 April 2020, it was for a period of 21 days. Phase 2 was between 15 April 2020 and 3 May 2020for a period of 19 days. The Phase 3 was from 4 May 2020 to 17 May 2020 for 14 days in duration. The last Phase 4was from 18 May 2020 to 31 May 2020 for 14 days. This was followed by 6 phases of unlock which were Unlock 1.0 from 1 June 2020 to 30 June 2020 for 30 days, followed by Unlock 2.0 from 1 July 2020 to 31 July 2020 for a period of 31 days then Unlock 3.0 for 1 August 2020 to 31 August 2020 for 31 days, which was followed by Unlock 4.0 between September 2020 and 30 September 2020 for a duration of 30 days. Next was Unlock 5.0 from 1 October 2020 to 31 October 2020 for 31 days. And then Unlock 6.0 from: 1 November 2020 - 30 November 2020.

The covid 19 pandemic is having an impact on the sector such as loss of profit and revenue, loss of employment, working capital problems. The chapter covers the impact in three stages: - Pre Pandemic, During the Lockdown , Post Lockdown and Post Pandemic. It studies the remedial measures undertaken to revive, sustain the sector. It traces the risks, challenges and opportunities for the sector. The chapter focuses on the journey of the MSMEs Sector from before the pandemic to the current situation and tries to analyze what lies ahead.

The impact can be understood by looking at the Pre Pandemic times, during the lockdown and post lockdown. One can even speculate, the situation of the Micro Small and Medium Scale enterprises would be post the pandemic. The pandemic has certainly had an impact on the Micro Small and medium scale enterprises sector. The impact has social as well as economic repercussions.

PRE-PANDEMIC: MICRO, SMALL AND MEDIUM SCALE ENTERPRISES

In the Pre Pandemic time, the Micro Small and Medium Scale Enterprises was a major contributor to the Indian Economy in terms of contribution to the Gross Domestic Product, employment generation, exports. The pre pandemic time is before march 2020, which was the time when the pandemic lockdown had not started.

Micro Small and Medium Scale enterprises have been described as the key sector in India. As per the Micro Small and Medium Scale Enterprises Annual Report of 2019-2020, the Estimated number of Micro Small and Medium Scale Enterprises in the Rural area involved in the manufacturing are 114.17 lakhs whereas in the urban area are 82.51 lakhs, the estimated number of enterprises in Trade and other services are 210.71 lakhs and around 226.49 lakhs in the urban area.,As per the annual report on Micro Small and Medium Scale Enterprises of 2019-2020. The estimated number of Enterprises are as follows:

Table 3. Estimated number of enterprises (in Lakhs)

Activity	Rural	Urban
Manufacturing	114.17	82.51
Trade and other services	210.71	226.49
Total	324.88	309

Source: Annual Report Micro Small and Medium Scale Enterprises 2019-2020

The number of enterprises in Rural and Urban Areas are shown in the table below. The figures are in Lakhs

Sector	Micro	Small	Medium	Total
Rural	324.09	0.78	0.01	324.88
Urban	306.43	2.53	0.04	309
Total	630.52	3.31	0.05	633.88

Source: Annual Report Micro Small and Medium Scale Enterprises 2019-2020

As per the annual report on Micro Small and Medium Scale Enterprises of 2019-2020..there are 324.09 micro units in the rural areas, 0.78 lakhs Small scale units and 0.01 lakhs medium scale units in the rural area. On the other hand there are 306.43 lakhs Micro units in the Urban areas, 2.53 small scale and 0.05 medium scale units in the urban area. It can be observed that more than 90% of the Micro Small and Medium Scale Enterprises comprise the Micro Units.

Table 5. Estimated employment in the micro small and medium scale enterprises sector (in Lakhs)

Activity	Rural	Urban	Total
Manufacturing	186.62	173.88	360.5
Trade and Services	311.17	438.23	749.40
Total	497.79	612.11	1109.9

Source: Annual Report Micro Small and Medium Scale Enterprises 2019-2020

The Micro Small and Medium Scale Enterprises sector generates employment opportunities for a large number of people with varied educational backgrounds. The employment opportunities are generated for undergraduates to graduates, diploma holders with technical and non-technical backgrounds. It can be noted from the above table that 186.62 lakhs are employed in the manufacturing sector of the Micro Small and Medium Scale Enterprises sector in the rural areas and 173.88 lakhs in the urban areas. For trade and other services, it is 311.17 lakhs and 438.23 lakhs in the Rural and urban areas respectively, as of the year 2019-2020.

Table 6. Micro small and medium scale enterprises employment generation in urban and rural areas numbers in Lakhs

Sector	Micro	Small	Medium	Total	Share%
Rural	489.3	7.88	0.6	497.78	45
Urban	586.88	24.06	1.16	612.1	55
Total	1076.18	31.94	1.76	1109.88	100

Source: Annual Report Micro Small and Medium Scale Enterprises 2019-2020

It can be further observed that the Micro Units generate employment to the extent of 489. Lakhs in the rural and 586.88 lakhs in the urban areas, which is again more than 90% of the total employment generated.

Table 7. State wise distribution of the enterprises

State/ UT	Number in Lakhs	Share (in%)
Uttar Pradesh	89.99	14
West Bengal	88.67	14
Tamil Nadu	49.48	8
Maharashtra	47.78	8
Karnataka	38.34	6

Source: Annual Report Micro Small and Medium Scale Enterprises 2019-2020

It can be inferred that Uttar Pradesh has 89.99 lakhs Micro Small and Medium Scale Enterprises, followed by West Bengal, Tamil Nadu and Maharashtra. The presence of the sector is Pan India, there are Micro Small and Medium Scale Enterprises in Uttar Pradesh, west Bengal, Maharashtra, Andhra Pradesh, Karnataka. The top five are listed below along with the percentages. There are 14% Micro Small and Medium Scale Enterprises in Uttar Pradesh, and West Bengal each followed by Maharashtra and Karnataka.

As per the Annual report of Micro Small and Medium Scale Enterprises and with reference to the information published in CSO the share of Micro Small and Medium Scale Enterprises in the Gross Value added as 32.35% in the year 2011-2012, it was 32.82% in the year 2012-2013, it was 32.71% in

2013-2014, it went down to 32.21% in 2014-2015. The percentage share of Micro Small and Medium Scale Enterprises in GVA was 32.06% in the year 32.03 and was 31.83% in the year 2016-2017.

Similarly share of Micro Small and Medium Scale Enterprises in the Gross domestic product was 30% in 2011-2012, 30.40% in the year 2012-2013, 30.20% in 2013-2014, 29.70% in 2014-2015, 29.20% in 2015-2016, and 28.90/% in 2016-2017.As per the website of the CII, Micro Small and Medium Scale Enterprises contribute around 6.11% of the manufacturing GDP and 24.63% of the GDP from service activities as well as 33.4% of India's manufacturing output. As per the Ministry of Micro, Small and Medium Enterprises, Government of India. The number of Micro Small and Medium Scale Enterprises in 2000-2001were 10.11 it rose to 42.87 million in the year 2010-2011, the number of Micro Small and Medium Scale Enterprises rose 633.88 lakhs in 2019-2020. Similarly, the employment in million was 23.87 in 2000-2001 it increased to 96.52 in 2010-2011, in the year 2019-2020, the employment was 1109.88 lakhs. It can be observed that the employment generation has happened tremendously over the last two decades. This employment also includes self-employment of the entrepreneurs as well. The gross output from the Micro Small and Medium Scale Enterprises' sector was Rs 261297 crores in the year 2000-2001, in 2010-2011 the gross output was Rs 1653622 crores.

A twelve-digit unique identification number was provided by the ministry of Micro Small and Medium Scale Enterprises was started for the benefit of the Micro Small and Medium Scale Enterprises sector.

As per the Udyam registration portal, by the end of December 2019, 74,17,612 micro units were registered, 9,17,096 small and 35,739 medium scale units were registered on the portal.

The database of the Udyam registration reveals that by the end of December 2019 2,86,82,655 persons were employed by the micro enterprises, 1,50,28,301 and 29,50,906 persons were employed by the small and medium scale enterprises. The data of course covers those enterprises which had the registration.

From October 2015 to December 2019 the Udyog Aadhaar portal reveals that 41% of the Micro Small and Medium Scale Enterprises comprise of manufacturing units and those involved in the service sector were 59%. In the Micro sub sector of the Micro Small and Medium Scale Enterprises 40.61% were manufacturing units and 59.38% were service. Similarly, during the same time period 45.3% of the small scale and 56.77% of medium scale were manufacturing units, whereas 54.56% of the small scale and 42.22% of the medium scale were involved in service sector

Till December 2019 the investment in the Micro Units was Rs 3,27,40,957, in the small scale it was Rs 60756586 and in Medium Scale it was 2,27,33,213. It can be observed that the total investment in the Micro Small and Medium Scale Enterprises sector was RS11,62,30,756 as per the Udyog aadhar portal statistics.

As per the information of the PIB up to December 2019 the exports of the Micro Small and Medium Scale Enterprises were 49.81% of the total exports.

DURING THE LOCKDOWN: MICRO, SMALL AND MEDIUM SCALE ENTERPRISES

There are immense challenges faced by the Micro Small and Medium scale enterprises. These challenges are faced during the lockdown by the owners / entrepreneurs and the employees. The government is also taking remedial measures to mitigate the losses; several measures were announced by the government. The lockdown in India began on 24th March 2020, after which all the business units were shut down. The confirmed cases of Covid 19 as on 22nd March 2020 were 353 and 7 deaths as per the World Health

Organization website .The lock down period lasted till the end of May 2020. The lockdown period was extended several times. After May 2020, the lockdown was relaxed with certain businesses and activities commenced but with restrictions. The lockdown was done to ensure that the spread of the Covid 19 will not take place. Entire cities and towns were subdivided into zones according to the severity of the cases and infections. Businesses in high risk zones with infections and cases were totally shut down, whereas in low and medium risk zones businesses and shops were allowed to function for a limited period. The Micro Small and Medium Scale Enterprises sector has large varieties of Products and services. Right from food processing to manufacture of spare parts are produced by the manufacturing Micro Small and Medium Scale Enterprises. As far as the service sector is concerned there are small shops such as and other services.

Except for the food processing units, medical shops and all the other enterprises were shut down. Food processing units such as dairy business and grocery shops were operating for a limited time, for 2 to 3 hours daily in some areas.

The enterprises involved in manufacturing of products other than food processing and essential items were closed down.

Previously as well there has been the pandemic or epidemics such as the SARS, Bird or Avian Flu, the epidemic of H1N1 in the last two decades, major studies on the impact of the pandemic situations on businesses particularly the Micro Small and Medium Scale Enterprises sector had been previously conducted.

During the outbreak of SARS, many businesses such as retail, banking and finance suffered heavy financial losses in Hong Kong due to the shutdown. Airline companies like Cathay pacific suffered an 87% drop in air traffic as compared to the earlier year. The small and medium scale companies in Australia expected a loss of 1Million dollars and its growth was expected to drop by 0.3percent. The epidemic created obstacles for the managers. There were not only financial losses by epidemics and disease but the loss of human resources is lost, Barclay's bank in Zambia lost more than a quarter of its staff to HIV/AIDS (Day et al., 2004). Epidemics like HIV/AIDS in African countries have not only affected the GDP rate as there was a decrease in the agricultural contribution. It also had a severe impact on human resources, loss of life in a family greatly impacts the income-earning capacity of the family, if the family is involved in agriculture the agricultural production will be impacted. (Agbola et al., 2004). Major natural disasters and Man-made environmental damage and disasters are some of the major global risks faced by the SME Sector (Asgary et al., 2020). The impact of HIV/AIDS resulted in the absenteeism of the labor force. An increase in illness and deaths lead to lesser revenue, increased costs, and low productivity (du Bruyn, 2008). Epidemics, pandemics, and diseases impact economically such as in the reduction of savings, and rising household expenses, the social impacts are labor shortage, job losses, more demand for food, and children being withdrawn from school. (Fauk et al., 2017). The Covid 19 pandemic may lead to economic recession. Due to the social distancing, travel restrictions, and lockdown resulting in a fall in the workforce, jobs may be lost. In a study, 80% of respondents anticipated a decrease in turnover. For the manufacturing sector, working from home is not considered a viable option (Nicola et al., 2020).

Some businesses will thrive, but for the manufacturing sector there will be labor shortage, disruption in the supply chain, and output will be reduced.(Kanupriya, 2020; Nicola et al., 2020). There is a huge informal sector in India, which has 90% of the working population, this sector has migrant laborers as well. They have no job security, no paid and sick leave. The pandemic will increase poverty as these people are out of job. (Buheji, Mohamed & Cunha, Katiane. (2020). (Buheji et al., 2020). In Srilanka sectors like agriculture, manufacturing and service are badly affected leading to an estimated decrease in the GDP and employment (Deyshappriya, 2020). The pandemic has impacted the Micro units in Brunei as people are afraid of being infected in public. There are restrictions on the movement leading to the temporary shutdown of the business. There are some business operations carried out from home (Salleh, 2020).

It is expected that there will be fall in the sales leading to losses and defaults. Liquidity will go down creating working capital issues. The solvency of firms will be affected. (Socioeconomic Impacts of COVID-19: Reflections from the Basque Country, n.d.)

Capital turnover and the supply chain will be impacted adversely for the small-scale regional enterprises, however, certain businesses might have a positive impact such as the food industry, and businesses which are done online. (Tashanova et al., 2020)

In a study on the Namibian economy, it is expected that loss of income and jobs, business trading hours and loss of demand would affect the GDP as well and a robust fiscal stimulus will have to be given to the informal sector. (Julius et al., 2020) The business in Turkey does not depend on China but also on Italy and other affected countries, it is estimated that the GDP will drop and workers will lose income. It is estimated that there will be bankruptcy and high unemployment. The government announced a 15.4 billion dollar economic stimulus. (Açikgöz & Günay, 2020). The pandemic will have negative impacts on the economy and society. Economic loss can lead to instability of the economy as there will be higher costs, shutdown, and a long-term burden. (Qiu et al., 2017). Small businesses are estimated to be the hardest hit, there are going to be cash flow problems and an impending recession, and the governments will have to work along with the banks and other financial institutions to help the small business (Baker & Judge, 2020)

The performance of Micro Small and Medium Scale Enterprises is going to get affected adversely, there will be reduced sales and low production. Cash management will be a key to survival. (Sultan & Sultan, 2020). Measures taken for the prevention of Covid 19, have negatively impacted the supply chain (Min et al., 2020). It can be observed that many sectors such as airline manufacturing were affected by the previous epidemic including the micro small and medium-scale enterprises sector These enterprises faced many challenges during the period. Discussions with the owners of the enterprises as well as studies conducted during the earlier pandemics revealed the following problems or challenges: - No Production, Labor shortage, No Revenue and Sales, payments of Salary and other bills, Problems of Working Capital, nonpayment of loan Installments.

The white paper published by the North Orissa Chamber of Commerce & Industry, reveals that the Micro Small and Medium Scale Enterprises will face problems such as low demand, lower liquidity, low inputs and inventory, shortage of manpower, export issues, temporary shut down and shortage of funds, absenteeism of employees and negative impact on orders. Micro Small and Medium Scale Enterprises have been facing problems due to the pandemic situation. There was a large exodus of skilled employees which had an impact on the businesses especially the Micro Small and Medium Scale Enterprises as per the news article published in business standard in may 20,2020

Months of isolation have a psychological impact on the people who are under stress and that leads to domestic violence, and physical and psychological abuse, which becomes a social issue. (M.S. et al, 2020). (Kumar et al., 2020; Min et al., 2020). As per statista.com during the month of April 2020, 14.4% job loss happened in the age group of 40 to 44 years, the impact of job losses was 13.9% for persons between the age group of 35 to 39 years, whereas it was 12% for persons between the age group of 45 to 49 years. Months of lockdown, isolation, loss of jobs in many cases, and domestic violence have become social issues.

It can be observed that social and economic impact goes hand in hand, one influences the other and vice versa. E.g. job loss leads to economic problems and psychological problems for the individual and a social problem for the society. It can be inferred from the various studies undertaken in the previous epidemic and pandemics that there is a profound impact on the socio-economic situations of the different economies and there is an effect on the business and sectors such as the Micro Small and Medium Scale sectors.

During the months of lockdown, several Measures were announced by the Government of India. Governments both at the national and state level introduced fiscal measures and liquidity-enhancing measures. Some of the measures can be counterproductive in the long run (Jose et al., 2021)

First of all the definition of Micro Small and Medium Scale Enterprises or the classification of Micro, small, and medium scale enterprises was changed with effect from 1st July 2020.

A Composite Criteria of Investment in Plant & Machinery/equipment and Annual Turnover was made applicable. The classification of micro, small and medium scale enterprises for both service and manufacturing sectors is now the same.

Table 8. Manufacturing sector

Enterprise Category	Investment in Plant & Machinery/equipment and Annual Turnover
Micro Enterprise	Not more than Rs.1 crore and Annual Turnover ; not more than Rs. 5 crore
Small Enterprise	Not more than Rs.10 crore and Annual Turnover ; not more than Rs. 50 crore.
Medium Enterprise	Not more than Rs.50 crore and Annual Turnover ; not more than Rs. 250 crore

Source: https://Micro Small and Medium Scale Enterprises.gov.in/know-about-Micro Small and Medium Scale Enterprises

Table 9. Service sector

Enterprise Category	Investment in Plant and Machinery
Micro Enterprise	Not more than Rs.1 crore and Annual Turnover ; not more than Rs. 5 crore
Small Enterprise	Not more than Rs.10 crore and Annual Turnover ; not more than Rs. 50 crore.
Medium Enterprise	Not more than Rs.50 crore and Annual Turnover ; not more than Rs. 250 crore

Source: https://Micro Small and Medium Scale Enterprises.gov.in/know-about-Micro Small and Medium Scale Enterprises

The primary objective of changing the classification is to benefit the Micro Small and Medium Scale Enterprises sector. Various loans and schemes can be availed by the sector. Not only the classification was changed but various schemes, funding and packages were announced for the sector.

The finance minister Ms Nirmala Sitaraman announced a package to make the Micro Small and Medium Scale Enterprises sector " Antmanirbhar" or so as to say self reliant

The following important measures were announced apart from the revision of the definition.

1. Rs 20,000 crores were approved as a subordinate debt, for providing equity to support the Micro Small and Medium Scale Enterprises, it is expected that it will help around 2 lakhs Micro Small and Medium Scale Enterprises who are under stress due to the covid 19 pandemic situation.

2. An equity infusion was approved to the extent of Rs 50,000 crores through the Fund of Funds or the FOF, for establishing a framework for capacity augmentation, which can help the Micro Small and Medium Scale Enterprises to list their institutions on stock exchanges. This will help them to raise funds through the secondary market.
3. For meeting operational liabilities, procurement of raw materials and for restarting the businesses a collateral free automatic loans of Rupees three lakhs crores were announced.
4. As mentioned above the definition of the micro small and medium scale enterprises was changed. This was primarily done to avail them maximum benefits.
5. For creating more opportunities for the domestic businesses global tenders in procurements were disallowed upto Rs 200 crores.
6. The dues by the government and public sector towards the Micro Small and Medium Scale Enterprises are to be cleared within 45 days

The emergency credit line guarantee scheme was made applicable from june 2020. This is a comprehensive package of Rs20 lakhs crore, which will address working capital needs, operational needs and for restarting businesses, which were shut down due to the pandemic.

The scheme provides a guarantee up to Rs 3 lakhs crores, the working capital term loan has tenure of 48 months and has for 12 months the principal moratorium. The scheme also specifies eligibility criteria. It is interesting to note that once the scheme was announced the number of credit enquiries increases. The credit inquiries in all regions metropolitan, semi urban, urban and rural increases in June 2020 as compared to May 2020

As per the Micro Small and Medium Scale Enterprises pulse outlook report published in October 2020 report the credit inquiries jumped up 1.9 X as compared to the February volumes for the Public Sector banks, there was an increase of 1.2 x for NBFCs as compared to February, and 0.9x as compared to February for Private banks in March 2020. The same report reveals that the loan disbursements increased in June 2020, showing that the Micro Small and Medium Scale Enterprises are taking advantage of the Scheme.

The impact of the Covid 19 Pandemic on the Micro Small and Medium Scale Enterprises sector is revealed by studying the Micro Small and Medium Scale Enterprises Pulse reports. The rate of nonperforming assets increased from 11.4% in June 2019 to 12.8% in June 2020 for all lenders put together i.e PSU banks, Private Banks and MBFCs.

For PSU banks NPA rates showed a rise from 17.5% in June 2019 to 18.6% in June 2020, for the private sector banks the NPA rate was 4.6% in June 2019 to 5.8% in June 2020. For Non Banking Financial Companies or NBFC the rise in NPA was significant, it was 5.8% in June 2020 and the NPA Rate became 9.7%. NPA rates have increased slightly for most of the sub-segments. Another important parameter that can be observed is the CIBIL Micro Small and Medium Scale Enterprises Rank or the CMR, it indicates that the one term loan had missed payments between 9% to 11% during the pre covid time, post Covid it had gone up to 30%, indicating a rise of 20% in the missed payments by the borrowers to the lenders.

POST LOCKDOWN: MICRO, SMALL, AND MEDIUM SCALE ENTERPRISES

Risks, Challenges and opportunities for the Micro Small and Medium Scale Enterprises sector and the possible remedy to revive the sector and the risk management must be understood and studied. There will be challenges and risks, the economy may go down leading to recession at the Macro level, loss of profit, jobs at the Micro level. Thus the impact can be observed at both macro and micro level.

As per the Reserve Bank of India, Governors Statement in August 6, 2020, the real Gross Domestic product is estimated to be negative in the year 2021, it can be observed that during June 2020, the merchandise exports are falling consecutively for the fourth time in a row. Imports also fell indicating weak demand and low crude oil prices internationally. However there was a surplus trade balance in June 2020 which was 0.8 million US dollars, which was noticed after a gap of 18 years. Containment of Covid 19 infections was seen in some parts and spread of infections in other parts were posing as risks, volatility in the global market was an important risk factor to the economy. The economic activity in India was recovering from June 2020 onwards as compared to April to May 2020, when the major part of lockdown was in effect. The agriculture sector also showed good prospects due to the good monsoon prospects as well as the expansion of the Kharif crop area by 13.9 percent as compared to July 2019. However the industrial production seemed to be overall in fall. The other important risk was the fresh spread of infections forcing lockdowns again for some time in some parts of the country, As per the Governor's Statement published by the Reserve bank of India in October 2020, the real gross domestic product of the country is expected to decline by 9.5%. However, the manufacturing purchasing managers index rose to s56.8 in September 2020, which is indicating that there is a possibility of a bounce back by the manufacturing sector as whole

The lockdown opened up in Phased Manner post June 2020, initially the businesses were asked to open but with strict sanitization restrictions, there were restrictions on the number of people in the company, they had to maintain distance, use masks and hand sanitizers. The sanitization measures were followed also for the employees returning from work places and were asked to self quarantine. For the Micro Small and Medium Scale Enterprises there are still problems related to low productions, less orders from large scale companies, and loan repayments. On 14 September 2020, India had confirmed 4,754,356 COVID-19 cases and 78,586 deaths, and recovered cases were 3,700,000. In case one person contracts the entire business unit is shut down. Micro Small and Medium Scale Enterprises still is facing a challenge for payment of salary to their employees. The pandemic persists but the Micro Small and Medium Scale Enterprises have to work with caution and with sanitization measures. The government has issues ``Guidelines on preventive measures to contain the spread of COVID-19 in workplace settings ". These measures focus on use of masks, social distancing, and quarantine in case of an infection.

In this post lockdown period what is actually happening as far as the Micro Small and Medium Scale Enterprises are concerned. As per the Micro Small and Medium Scale Enterprises Pulse Reports States like Bihar, Jharkhand, Punjab and Kerala are taking a lead in the bounce back, followed by Maharashtra and Delhi. Micro Small and Medium Scale Enterprises with a strong financial structure will be resilient from the risk perspectives Economy may head towards recession, and hence there has to be an aggressive, well targeted fiscal as well as monetary measures which can give stimulus to the economy. The impact of the Micro Small and Medium Scale Enterprises sector can be tremendous, there can be an estimated shrinkage up to 20% in the manufacturing sector, a drop of 20% in exports. (Sahoo & Ashwani, 2020).

There are risks in the new normal as they say, the Micro Small and Medium Scale Enterprises will face challenges nut there will be opportunities as well. There can be solutions to at least some of the problems and challenges

Cash management and digital marketing will help the Micro Small and Medium Scale Enterprises in their revival. (Sultan & Sultan, 2020) Government measures and increases in government spending can control the economic crisis posed by the pandemic, however, there has to be proper implementation of the policies and measures with regard to expenditure and revenue in order to have a long-term resilient impact on the economy. (Dzigbede & Pathak, 2020; Jose et al., 2021).

The Micro Small and Medium Scale Enterprises sector creates national wealth and boosts the economy. Self-improvement, innovative business models, digitization, and using intellectual property can boost the sector. A crisis can be used as a powerful challenge to bring about change (Csath, 2020).

For survival many Micro Small and Medium Scale Enterprises are resorting to a temporary reduction in manpower, loaning of employees to other businesses, deferred payments, diversifying in new products, putting on hold expansion plans, and sourcing from new suppliers, however there many Micro Small and Medium Scale Enterprises who have not thought of any strategies to overcome the problem as per the White paper Published by: North Orissa Chamber of Commerce & Industry.

Not everything was negative in the Covid 19 pandemic, people resorted to pursuing hobbies, and online learning (Kumar et al., 2020). This would lead to new opportunities which Micro Small and Medium Scale Enterprises can explore.

CONCLUSION

Post Pandemic: Micro, Small and Medium Scale Enterprises

The larger question is what lies ahead? Where do we go from here? How many of these Micro Small and Medium Scale Enterprises who are the backbone of the economy by generating employment and contributing to the Gross domestic product will sustain and survive. Some of them may not be able to bear the brunt and will permanently shut down. As mentioned earlier there is a global impact and an impending global recession. As per the world bank forecasts the global economy will shrink by 5.2%, which is the deepest recession since World War 2. Many economies across the world will see a decline in their per capita output. What will be the future for the Micro Small and Medium Scale Enterprises especially in India, the North Orissa Chamber of Commerce and Industry conducted a survey of Micro Small and Medium Scale Enterprises in the state of Orissa to understand the influence of the Covid 19 pandemic on the Micro Small and Medium Scale Enterprises in Orissa and published a white paper, as per the white paper submitted by the North Orissa Chamber of Commerce and Industry 96% of the respondents have faced the challenges and do not believe in permanent closure of their businesses. 56% respondents have put their growth and expansion plan on hold. They are waiting for the markets to recover, stabilize. They are looking at the market with positivity. 27% of the respondents are diversifying into new business ventures by using innovative methods.

So the Micro Small and Medium Scale enterprises are showing a positivity, there trying to find new avenues and strategies to overcome their challenges.

It can be noticed that the relief and remedy measures through long term and short term loans, working capital aid, tax reliefs and benefits can go a long way in bringing the turnaround in the Micro small and medium scale enterprises.

The micro small and medium scale industry in India is an important sector as it has contributed tremendously to the economic as well as social development. It has not only encouraged entrepreneurship but has also been instrumental in generating employment. The sector supports the large scale industries as it offers a wide range of products and services. The Covid 19 pandemic is having an impact on the sector such as loss of profit and revenue, loss of employment, working capital problems the impact be traced from comparing: - Pre Pandemic situation, During the Lockdown situation, Post Lockdown situation and Post Pandemic situation, which is about the future. The remedial measures are undertaken to revive, sustain the sector. There will be immense risks, challenges and at the same time opportunities for the sector. The journey of the MSMEs Sector from before the pandemic to the current situation can help us understand what will be the future and how the micro small and medium scale enterprises must prepare themselves. Of course the government policies and interventions to mitigate the loss and other remedies for the revival of the sector are important, but it seems to see how the Micro Small and Medium Scale Enterprises face the challenges and mitigate the risks and become Atma Nirbhar.

REFERENCES

Açikgöz, Ö., & Günay, A. (2020). The early impact of the Covid-19 pandemic on the global and Turkish economy. *Turkish Journal of Medical Sciences*, *50*(SI-1), 520–526. doi:10.3906ag-2004-6 PMID:32283904

Agbola, F. W., Damoense, M. Y., & Saini, Y. K. (2004). South Africa. *International Journal of Social Economics*, *31*(7), 721–731. doi:10.1108/03068290410540909

Asgary, A., Ozdemir, A. I., & Özyürek, H. (2020). Small and medium enterprises and global risks: Evidence from manufacturing SMEs in Turkey. *International Journal of Disaster Risk Science*, *11*(1), 59–73. doi:10.100713753-020-00247-0

Baker, T., & Judge, K. (2020). How to help small businesses survive COVID-19. SSRN *Electronic Journal*. doi:10.2139/ssrn.3571460

Buheji, M., da Costa Cunha, K., Beka, G., Mavrić, B., Leandro do Carmo de Souza, Y., Souza da Costa Silva, S., Hanafi, M., & Chetia Yein, T. (2020). The extent of COVID-19 pandemic Socio-economic impact on global poverty. A global integrative multidisciplinary review. *American Journal of Economics*, *10*(4), 213–224. doi:10.5923/j.economics.20201004.02

Csath, M. (2020). Crisis situations: How should micro, small and medium enterprises handle them with a long term view? *Development and Learning in Organizations*, *35*(3), 10–12. doi:10.1108/DLO-04-2020-0086

Day, B., Burnice Mckay, R., Ishman, M., & Chung, E. (2004). The new normal: Lessons learned from SARS for corporations operating in emerging markets. *Management Decision*, *42*(6), 794–806. doi:10.1108/00251740410542357

Deyshappriya, N. P. R. (2020). Economic impacts of COVID-19 macro and microeconomics evidences from Sri Lanka. SSRN *Electronic Journal*. doi:10.2139/ssrn.3597494

du Bruyn, R. (2008). A proposed reporting framework for HIV/Aids disclosure by listed South African companies. *Meditari Accountancy Research*, *16*(1), 59–78. doi:10.1108/10222529200800004

Dzigbede, K. D., & Pathak, R. (2020). COVID-19 economic shocks and fiscal policy options for Ghana. *Journal of Public Budgeting, Accounting & Financial Management*, *32*(5), 903–917. doi:10.1108/JPBAFM-07-2020-0127

Fauk, N. K., Mwakinyali, S. E., Putra, S., & Mwanri, L. (2017). The socio-economic impacts of AIDS on families caring for AIDS-orphaned children in Mbeya rural district, Tanzania. *International Journal of Human Rights in Healthcare*, *10*(2), 132–145. doi:10.1108/IJHRH-01-2017-0002

Jose, J., Mishra, P., & Pathak, R. (2021). Fiscal and monetary response to the COVID-19 pandemic in India. *Journal of Public Budgeting, Accounting & Financial Management*, *33*(1), 56–68. doi:10.1108/JPBAFM-07-2020-0119

Julius, E., Nuugulu, S., & Julius, L. H. (2020). Estimating the economic impact of COVID-19: A case study of Namibia. Unpublished. https://doi.org/doi:10.13140/RG.2.2.30419.32806

. Kanupriya. (2020). COVID-19: A Socio-economic perspective. *FIIB Business Review*, *9*(3), 161–166.

Kumar, S., Maheshwari, P, Prasanna, P., Suganya, J., Malar, B. A., & Jothikumar, R. (2020). Social economic impact of COVID-19 outbreak in India. *International Journal of Pervasive Computing and Communications*, *16*(4), 309–319. doi:10.1108/IJPCC-06-2020-0053

Min, S., Zhang, X., & Li, G. (2020). A snapshot of food supply chain in Wuhan under the COVID-19 pandemic. *China Agricultural Economic Review*, *12*(4), 689–704. doi:10.1108/CAER-04-2020-0056

Nicola, M., Alsafi, Z., Sohrabi, C., Kerwan, A., Al-Jabir, A., Iosifidis, C., Agha, M., & Agha, R. (2020). The socio-economic implications of the coronavirus pandemic (COVID-19): A review. *International Journal of Surgery*, *78*, 185–193. doi:10.1016/j.ijsu.2020.04.018 PMID:32305533

Qiu, W., Rutherford, S., Mao, A., & Chu, C. (2017). The pandemic and its impacts. *Health, Culture and Society (Pittsburgh, Pa.)*, *9*, 1–11. doi:10.5195/HCS.2017.221

Sahoo, P., & Ashwani. (2020). COVID-19 and Indian economy: Impact on growth, manufacturing, trade and MSME sector. *Global Business Review*, *21*(5), 1159–1183. doi:10.1177/0972150920945687

Salleh, F. H. M. (2020). BE-1201 MACROECONOMICS:PRINCIPLES AND ISSUES: The contrast in economic impacts during SARS and COVID-19 pandemic. doi:10.13140/RG.2.2.31037.00480

Sultan, S., & Sultan, W. I. M. (2020). Women MSMEs in times of crisis: Challenges and opportunities. *Journal of Small Business and Enterprise Development*, *27*(7), 1069–1083. doi:10.1108/JSBED-06-2020-0226

Tashanova, D., Sekerbay, A., Chen, D., Luo, Y., Zhao, S., & Zhang, Q. (2020). Investment opportunities and strategies in an era of Coronavirus pandemic. SSRN *Electronic Journal*. doi:10.2139/ssrn.3567445

APPENDIX

White Paper

1. Impact of COVID-19 on Micro Small and Medium Scale Enterprises Published by: **North Orissa Chamber of Commerce & Industry** Compiled by:Swayam Chayanika Rath & Priyanka DasR

Reports

1. Micro Small and Medium Scale Enterprises Annual Reports 2019-2020
2. Micro Small and Medium Scale Enterprises Annual Reports 2018-2019
3. Micro Small and Medium Scale Enterprises Annual Reports 2017-2018
4. MSME (Micro Small and Medium Scale Enterprises) Pulse Outlook October 2020
5. MSME (Micro Small and Medium Scale Enterprises) Pulse Outlook April 2020

Websites

1. https://www.who.int/india/emergencies/coronavirus-disease-(covid-19)
2. https://www.mohfw.gov.in/pdf/ GuidelinesonpreventivemeasurestocontainspreadofCOVID19inworkplacesettings.pdf.
3. https://www.worldbank.org/en/news/press-release/2020/06/08/covid-19-to-plunge-global-economy-into-worst-recession-since-world-war-ii#:~:text=According%20to%20World%20Bank%20 forecasts,June%202020%20Global%20Economic%20Prospects.
4. https://www.business-standard.com/
5. https://www.statista.com/
6. https://www.mospi.gov.in/central-statistics-office
7. https://pib.gov.in/PressReleseDetailm.aspx?PRID=1628345
8. http://rbi.org/
9. https://udyamregistration.gov.in/
10. https://Micro Small and Medium Scale Enterprises.gov.in/know-about-Micro Small and Medium Scale Enterprises

Chapter 15
Weavers' Livelihoods and the COVID-19 Pandemic:
An Analysis of Sambalpuri Handloom, Odisha, India

Tushar Kanti Das
https://orcid.org/0000-0002-9039-3236
Sambalpur University, India

ABSTRACT

Sambalpuri Handloom weavers of Western Odisha are known for their rich skill, creativity, and innovative designs. Steady decline in the earnings has resulted in the migration of weavers both professionally and geographically. Economic crisis is forcing these weavers to face livelihood crisis. The weavers who have created history and brought glory by their rich artistry are being forced to change their livelihood. The present study has been undertaken in sixteen clusters of four districts of Western Odisha. It has been observed that the role played by the businessman (middleman) is quite important. Though the price of the product is quite high, the weavers are not satisfied with the emoluments amounts that they receive. The actual benefits from marketing of this handloom are accruing to the middlemen rather than the weavers. The COVID -19 pandemic and economic shutdown has broken the supply chain of both the backward and forward linkage of the Sambalpuri handloom industry. Necessary policy should be made both by the central and state governments to rescue these handloom weavers.

INTRODUCTION

After agriculture, handloom weaving is the largest economic activity, and this sector provides employment to more than 35 lakh weavers and allied workers[1] in India. 95% of the handloom product of the world are being produced in India. By exporting the handloom products, the sector is contributing to export earnings for India. Out of the total cloth production handloom contributes almost 15%. Handloom is identified as a cottage industry in Odisha which helps in rural development. Skill of weaving

DOI: 10.4018/978-1-7998-6896-5.ch015

in handloom industry, is transferred from generation to generation. In Odisha, handloom is a traditional cottage industry. This provides about 1.17 lakh handloom workers in the State to earn their livelihood. In Odisha, there are 63,223 weaver households according to the 4th Handloom Census (2019). Out of these, total number of handloom weavers and allied workers are respectively 53,472 and 64,364.

Handloom woven by weavers of Sambalpur are unique for its rich skill, innovative design, and creativity. Livelihood crisis is faced by the weavers which is very difficult for them to manage. The weavers who earlier brought glory in weaving are now forced to change their livelihood. Most often the weavers prefer to work as labourer because of the snag economic conditions. Migration of weavers both geographically and professionally resulted due to the steady decline in the income of the weavers. Poverty reduction strategies were introduced by Government to provide a coherent framework within which different stakeholders can work together towards the eradication of poverty. Livelihood is defined as 'the activities, the assets and the access that jointly determine the living gained by an individual or household'[2]. Large amount of money is being invested by both Central and State Government, but the benefit is not reaching the handloom weavers. Lack of social protection program has jeopardised weaving livelihood. Weaving encourages rural employment and women empowerment. It also creates employment opportunity for many persons.

The COVID -19 pandemic and economic shutdown have disrupted billions of lives and livelihoods. Economies are suffering from a devastating blow in the development progress. Countries are now with the objectives of handling the negative economic spill overs resulting from deep recession. To cope with situation, economies are trying to i) restrict the domestic outbreak of the pandemic and ii) start the economic process after the shutdown. In many developing and emerging economies large share of employment are in the informal sector, operative mitigation measures and financial support are hard to accomplish (World Bank, 2020)[3]. Now the concern is moving rapidly towards the economic dimensions – given the fall in output and its social effects. Humanity is already under heavy stress as shown by economic insecurity. Economies are shaping a new generation of inequalities (UNDP, 2020)[4]. Forward and backward linkage of the handloom weaving has devastated with the shut down and lockdown of different institutions associated with handloom. On the one hand they are unable to purchase the thread, colour, and dye and on the other they are unable to supply the earlier order taken by them and sell their products in the market. In view of these, the livelihood of the weavers of Sambalpuri handloom needs special attention.

Objective of the Study

Sambalpuri handloom is well known for its delicate weaving design and dying of fabrics. Bhulia Meher community started the Sambalpuri handloom weaving in 1726 AD. Two different communities of weavers namely Coasta Mehers (these weavers weave *tussar* sarees) and Kuli Mehers followed the Bhulia Mehers in weaving the Sambalpuri handlooms (UNIDO, 2008). Delicate design and rich artistry are the main architect of the handloom are gradually losing their importance. The family members of Sambalpuri weavers work as a family business. The weaving technique in most cases, they learn from their ancestors. Besides the weavers, most of the family members spend in preparing and colouring the yarn. In most of the cases the male members prepare the weaving loom and prefer to weave cloths. Female members usually take up ancillary activities associated with weaving.

For most of the handloom weavers weaving and preparing handloom is the only source of livelihood. They do not have any other means of livelihood. In view of all these, the aim here is to find out how the livelihood of the weavers and their family members can be improved and how it can be sustainable. To know about the livelihood of the weavers, the availability of finance, indebtedness of the labour force and sources of inputs for this sector must be analysed. The role of institutions in the development of a sector is important. The role played by the middlemen and co-operatives are important in the selling of the handloom products of Sambalpuri Handlooms. The weavers are many times exploited by them and are unable to get the appropriate price for their products. So, considering the factors affecting indebtedness; appropriate marketing strategies should be identified for this sector.

Review of Literature

The main objectives of the Sustainable Development Goals (SGDs) are to eradicate poverty in different economies. The General Conference of UNIDO in its fifteenth session held in Lime Peru[5] recognized poverty eradication as the central issue in different economies. Promotion and acceleration of inclusive and sustainable development (ISID) to achieve shared prosperity and environmental sustainability is the main objective here.

Changing market demand for Sambalpuri handloom are not met by the handloom weavers. The problems the weavers face is lack of working capital, proper training and almost non-existence of the market facilities. Factors like poor infrastructure such as quality control, water, electricity, roads, dye houses and low level of technologies restrict the competitiveness of these handlooms. As the productivity of the Sambalpuri handloom is very low, weavers prefer to move out of weaving. They prefer to leave weaving business and move out of villages. They move to different cities in search of jobs. Here other caste people come to or are brought to weaving business when the demand for handloom is high (Brenning, 1986).

The handloom in its production requires different types of labour in different stages. Also, the requirement of labour is more if the product is differentiated (Roy, 2002). Keeping this in view Government of India initiated support policies to the weavers through cooperatives and organisation relating to marketing of the handloom at the state level. However, in most of the cases the cooperatives are ineffective and marketing organisations are inefficient. Increase in the price of cotton and yarn resulted in a crisis this resulted in low profit for the weavers. Hence, the weavers prefer to move to some other trade in place of weaving. This is because weaving is no longer competitive in nature.

The share of weaver households decreased significantly pointing to considerable occupational diversification. The diversification is either inter sector or intra sector mobility. This is due to the changing market conditions and market demand (Bhattacharya and Sen, 2018). Handloom industry realized decline in the 2nd and 3rd handloom census (Libel and Roy, 2003). Challenges and competition from textile mills, outdated techniques of production and fall of demand of handloom products are some of the reasons of this fall (Menon, 1999; Solanki, 2008; Subhramanya, 2011).

Technological changes and innovations are continuous in the handloom industry. However, it is very limited with reference to the scale of the handloom industry (Libel and Roy, 2003). Continuous innovations in knowledge and improving the skill of the artisans it is possible to alleviate poverty. This can be done through investment in specific vulnerable spot by which the artisans can sustain themselves (Mamidipudi et.al., 2012).

Government of India has taken various promotional schemes for the handloom sector. One of the major schemes is Cluster System. The aim here is to develop the cluster of villages which are in identifiable geographical location having specialization in specific products. There are interdependence and close linkages among the different stakeholders in the cluster. The main purpose is to improve the infrastructure facilities, technological upgradation in post loom/ on loom / pre loom operations, better storage facilities, design raw materials, upgradation of skill and social protection like providing health insurance facilities and education facilities. These will in fact help the handloom weavers in the changing market demand both at domestic and international level. Side by side the standard of living of the handloom weavers will increase substantially[6].

Sambalpuri Handloom

Sambalpuri handloom can be categorised as one of the oldest handloom industries. It has excellent craftmanship which present and preserve the vibrant culture. Sambalpuri handloom weavers practising Ikat weaving are residing in different districts of Western Odisha namely Sambalpur, Sonepur, Bolangir and Bargarh. Weavers here prepare a special quality of handloom which is known as Ikat weaving, it is popularly known as 'Bandha Kala' in local language. The process is time consuming and labour intensive in nature. The design adopted by the weavers are preconceived and before weaving the yarn is tied and dyed (Mohapatra, 2014). If we look at the geographical environment of the Sambalpuri handloom weavers' village, most of the handloom weaving villages are near the bank of river Mahanadi or its canals or any other river. This is because preparing yarn and making it suitable for weaving requires more water. Primary source of income of the weavers here are handloom weaving after agriculture. Weaving is a caste-based family business of the Bhulia communities (Pradhan and Khandual, 2020). Intricacies of the design dictates the completion of the handloom weaving. If the saree design is simple, it may take seven to eight days and delicate sarees takes more time to complete weaving. The entire family are associated with the preparation of the handloom.

The weaving community such as Bhulia and Koshta are engaged primarily in Sambalpuri Handloom weaving (Ghosh and Ghosh, 2000). Another community namely, Kuli meher community are also involved in weaving Sambalpuri handloom. However, their weaving is not intricate as the earlier communities. Besides, after taking training on weaving some persons from the scheduled caste (SC) and scheduled tribe (ST) community are also adopting weaving as their livelihood.

These weavers can broadly be classified into three categories[7]. First, Independent weavers (entrepreneur weaver). These weavers purchase the inputs from the market. They work on their own designs and weave the handloom. They market their product independently through local bazars, traders, and various local markets. Second, labourer weavers. these Sambalpuri handloom weavers are broadly associated with the master weavers or traders or businessmen. These weavers get the inputs of weaving (such as dye, colour and yarn) from the master weavers or businessmen. The weavers return the handloom output for which they receive wages in return which is mutually decided by them. Third, Weavers associated with cooperative societies. The cooperative societies purchase the raw materials, give them to the weavers for weaving and collect the final product for selling after paying the wages. Boyanika and Sambalpuri Bastralaya are the renowned cooperative societies working in Western Odisha. These cooperative societies market the handloom product of the third category of weavers.

Most of the Sambalpuri handloom weaving are influenced by mythology, tradition, and local culture. Generally, village women particularly in Western Odisha prefer to wear Sambalpuri saree even if the families are poor. Weaving household women love to wear love to wear self-woven Sambalpuri saree. Various educational institutions in Western Odisha are using Sambalpuri handloom as their uniform. The most dependable market of Sambalpuri handloom in Western Odisha is the Balijhuri weekly market. Independent weavers, master weavers and allied workers such as businessman, traders and middleman visit this market to sell their handloom. Besides they also purchase the various accessories used in weaving besides the raw materials like yarn, colour, and dye. Independent traders of raw materials and accessories used for weaving also visit the market for their business. Buyers from inside and outside the state visit Balijhuri market to purchase Sambalpuri handloom. The weavers after selling their output, purchase the inputs and accessories required for weaving the handloom.

Handloom weavers whose financial condition are better generally work independently. Independent handloom enterprises owned by master weavers employ weavers to work in these enterprises. Many weavers are also associated with weavers' cooperative societies (WCSs) and self-help groups (SHGs) (Pradhan and Khandual, 2020). Existing handloom clusters or villages are developed with constant effort of the Government. In the process, need based interventions were initiated keeping in view the production bases. Self-help groups (SHGs) and weavers' cooperative societies (WCSs) were given the charge of developing common facility centres (CFCs), modernisation of the production process, credit linkage, developing designs and raw material banks. This will lead to collective participation and capacity building of the weavers in the region. In the cluster development a catalytic role is assigned to the master weaver. Under various activities Government is facilitating various skill development training.

Besides Government has floated various projects and policies to ensure production of fabrics with better market demand. There are various insurance schemes floated by Government for the handloom weavers. However, many of the schemes are now defunct particularly in Western Odisha.

Small and medium entrepreneurs, non-governmental organisations, and viable societies if actively associated cluster approach of development can be successfully adopted in handloom sector. Handloom weaving is classified as an unorganized sector. Most of the weavers are having lack of proper education, lack of professional skills and their standard of living is poor. They fail to avail the minimum health services. These are some of the reasons for the downfall of their livelihood. The weaving community particularly in Sambalpuri handloom weaving, is facing livelihood crisis because of the changing socio-economic conditions and lack of implementation of the governmental policies (Mohapatra, 2014; Sahu, 2009 and Pradhan, 2014). Closure of cooperatives and non-implementation of various governmental policies have forced many weavers to change their livelihood.

Data Source

Handloom weaving in Western Odisha is a community-based profession. Bhulias, Kosthas and Kuli community weavers weave the Sambalpuri handloom. They reside in different districts of western Odisha such as Bolangir, Sonepur, Bargarh, and Sambalpur. These weavers learn weaving technique from their ancestors. This weaving technique is passed from generation to generation. Besides some scheduled caste (SC), scheduled tribe (ST) and other caste people are now-a-days are also weaving Sambalpuri handloom after taking training from master weavers or cooperatives. Primary survey has been conducted to collect the data keeping in view the objective of the study. Both quantitative & qualitative research methods are applied as appropriate.

Categorisation of districts into A, B, and C type clusters are done basing on the number of handloom looms present in that district. If number of looms are more than 1000 it is termed as 'A' category, if number of looms are more than 500 but less than 1000 it is termed as 'B' category and in number of looms are more than 100 but less than 500 it is called 'C' category cluster district[8]. Total number of clusters in the four districts are eighteen. The number of clusters present in Bargarh, Sonepur, Bolangir, and Sambalpur are respectively 8,4,3, and 1. In the present analysis these sixteen clusters are selected for analysis and primary data are collected. Clusters according to their importance are categorized as cluster A or cluster B. Clusters in Bargarh and Sonepur are classified as category A and clusters in Bolangir and Sambalpur are classified as category B clusters[9]. The districts, clusters and villages taken for analysis are presented in Table -1. From each cluster two villages are selected keeping in view the household comprising the weavers' family.

Table 1. Clusters, villages, and sample

District	Name of the Cluster	Villages	No. of Samples	District	Name of the Cluster	Villages	No. of Samples
Bargarh (Cluster A)	Attabira	Jhilminda	50	Sonepur (Cluster A)	Birmaharajpur	Kendupali	49
		Singhpali	50			Kamalpur	47
	Bargarh	Kantapali	50		Sonepur	Sagarpali	49
		Bargaon	50			Hardakhol	50
	Bheden	Remunda	50		Ulunda	Nimna	50
		Jamdol	50			Dasrajpur	50
	Barpali	Dhangiripali	49		Binka	Nuapada	45
		Ambamuda	49			Meherpada	50
	Bijepur	Meher Srigida	50	Bolangir (Cluster B)	Patnagarh	Ulba	50
		Pada	50			Belpada	50
	Padampur	Khairpali	50		Agalpur	Raj Agalpur	50
		Jamala	50			Munupali	46
	Sohela	Sarkanda	50		Bongamunda	Garihapadar	50
		Jatala	50			Kansil	50
	Bhatli	Tarajunga	50	Sambalpur (Cluster B)	Rengali	Ramchandra Nagar	45
		Keseipali	50			Pondulai	45

The weavers start their weaving from early morning. They take their lunch early and go to sleep for around one hour after lunch. The weavers generally prefer that time to give response to the questionnaire i.e., after they get up. Keeping in view their suitability data are collected from the weavers using the questionnaire. From each cluster, two villages are taken for analysis keeping in view the number of weavers present. The sample of villages (32) and weaver households taken from each village are presented in table 1.

Research Methodology

The weavers for weaving of handloom collect or purchase thread, dye, and colour, prepare the colour and thread before weaving the handloom. The weaver of their own can purchase the thread and colour either from the cooperative or from the private sources. After preparing the handloom, they sell the product in the market. Another option is that businessman provides thread and colour to the weavers and the weavers are bound to sell the product to him. The third option is that the weavers are employed particularly by the master weavers on daily wage basis. The designs are pre-crafted by the master weavers. In view of these sample data were collected from the identified villages. The type of Government help, heterogeneity of the product, government training on the weaving etc. are also collected from the weaver households. Keeping in view the different attributes, classification and tabulation of the data are done.

Theoretical Framework and Estimation

Income of the weavers depend on the selling of the handloom products. This indicates that selling of the handloom affects the livelihood of the weaver. As the weaving household weave as a family business, the education of the household and age of family members lead crucial role. Time spent in preparing the loom, preparing the thread and time spent in weaving are other factors determining the livelihood.

Following McFadden (1973), logit model is applied in the present analysis. Here the weaver two choices namely, either he will sell the handloom in the market or give it in a cooperative. If we take it as a reference category that is Yi = 0.

$$L_i = ln\left[\frac{P_i(Y_i = 1)}{P_i(Y_i = 0)}\right] = B_i X_j$$

Three different types of weavers are identified in Sambalpuri handloom weaving. They are a) independent entrepreneur weavers; b) weavers associated with master weavers/ traders / businessmen; and c) cooperative fold weavers. Entrepreneur weavers act as entrepreneurs. They sell the handloom independently. Marketing risk is with these independent weavers, but the profit accrues solely to the weavers. Similar is the case for cooperative fold weavers. Weavers associated with master weavers, however, get only wage rate. All the profits are taken away by the traders / master weavers / businessmen who act as middlemen in the weaving process.

Therefore, the effect of different variables on the selling of the final product is analysed basing on the following binary choice model.

$$Y_i = \beta_0 + \beta_1 \text{ age}_i + \beta_2 \text{ edu}_i + \beta_3 \text{ fmem}_i + \beta_4 \text{ loan}_i + \beta_5 \text{ income}_{i+} \beta_6 \text{ time}_i + \varepsilon_i$$

Where, Y_i is the variable where 'i' take value either 0 or 1.

Y_i (=0) if weaver is selling the product independently or selling it to the cooperative and Y_i (=1) if the weaver is giving back to master weaver or businessman or money lender. Besides, age_i – 'i' th respondent's age; edu_i – 'i' th respondent's education. $fmem_i$ – number of members of 'i' th respondent associated with weaving; $loan_i$ - 'i' th weaver household's loan; $income_i$ - 'i' th respondent's income; $time_i$ - 'i' th respondent's time spent and ε_i - random error.

The collected primary data is applied to the model as outlined and the result is presented below. Here, z-statistic is used to test the significance of the estimated coefficients.

Findings of the Study

The collected data are tabulated, and the different tables are generated and are presented for the four districts namely Sambalpur, Bolangir, Bargarh and Sonepur. Government facilitates weaving community by providing the essentials of weaving like handloom machine (called *monga* in local language), yarn, dye, and colour. These are also provided to the weavers through the cooperatives. The buying of handloom instrument by the weavers are represented in table 2.

Table 2. Artisans' buying of handloom instrument (in percentage)

District	Respondent himself	Government	Cooperative
Bargarh	98.30	0.43	1.26
Sonepur	99.01	0.61	0.38
Bolangir	98.98	0.67	0.33
Sambalpur	97.00	0.92	2.08

Source: Author's own calculation from primary data.

Pit loom is generally used by the weavers for weaving in this region. From the table it is evident that only negligible quantity of handloom machine is supplied by both Government and cooperatives. On the other hand, more than 97% of the handloom machines are purchased by the weavers themselves in all the four districts under analysis. Weavers hence cannot rely on either Government or cooperatives for the supply of the machine. Table 3 present the supply of inputs (dye, colour, and thread) to the weavers in all the four districts. 91.09% of the colour, dye and thread are supplied by the businessmen in Sonepur. After weaving the handloom are given back to the person who provided it after receiving wage payments. Only 8.9% of the inputs are purchased by the artisans themselves from the market. In districts like Sambalpur, Bolangir and Bargarh, respectively 85.71%, 51.35% and 62.32% of the inputs are purchased by the weavers themselves. After weaving they sell the same in the market.

The design of the handloom to be prepared are finalised by the master weavers or businessmen. After finalising, they provide the inputs to the weavers to weave. Time taken to finish the weaving depends on the type of handloom. Usually, it takes one to two weeks to finish the weaving. If the thread is delicate also time consumption will be more. If the handloom is of '*tussar*' or '*bapta*' it will again take more time. The weavers weave the same with a self-negotiated wage rate among them. The problem of marketing the handloom arises for the weavers who sell the handloom in the market. But this is not an issue for the weavers who work as wage earners.

Proper marketing fetches good price for the marketed product. Same is also the the case for handloom products. If marketing is not proper, then the artisans do not get good price for the products. Similarly, the weavers who work as wage earners only earn wages. The weaving household work in weaving as family business. Starting from school and college going son and daughter almost everybody in the family work for weaving. The price they get for weaving in return are very less as compared to the work they provide. Hence it is very difficult to sustain the whole family with only weaving business.

Table 3. Supply of inputs to the artisans (in percentage)

District	Own purchase	Someone else
Bargarh	62.32	37.67
Sonepur	8.90	91.09
Bolangir	51.35	48.64
Sambalpur	85.71	14.28

Source: Author's own calculation from primary data.

After weaving the handloom, they are sold in the market or are given to the cooperatives, or businessmen providing thread or to someone given loans to the weavers. supply and sell of these handloom products in weaving districts by the weavers are presented in table 4.

Table 4. Selling of the handlooms by the weaving artisans (in percentage)

District	Market	Cooperative	Businessman providing inputs	Other (Someone else who has given loan)
Bargarh	66.16	2.85	27.66	3.30
Sonepur	9.41	0.25	90.07	0.25
Bolangir	50.33	2.70	46.95	0.02
Sambalpur	85.71	0.00	14.28	0.00

Source: Author's own calculation from primary data.

In Bargarh district, 66.16% of the weavers sell the finished handloom product in the market. In Bolangir, 50.33% of the weavers prefer to sell the finished weaving products in the market directly. Similarly, 85.71% of the handloom product is sold in the market by the weaving household in Sambalpur. In Sonepur, only 9.41% of the artisans sell the products directly in the market. Most of the artisans here give the weaving products back to the businessmen who have provided the inputs. These weavers do not face any marketing problem of the product. These weavers are however exploited for getting less wage as compared to their work. Proper marketing of the handloom products can fetch proper price for the handloom product. This problem is faced by the entrepreneur weavers. Weavers giving the handloom products to cooperatives and person providing loans to them is almost negligible in all the districts.

On an average the weavers take a week or two to weave a saree. The emoluments they receive generally varies from saree to saree. Delicacy of the handloom determines the wage paid for the handloom. The lowest range of wage paid for weaving a saree is from Rs 500 to Rs.700/-. If the handloom is more delicate the price of the weaver will be more. Also, the time consumed for weaving a sophisticated handloom is more. This is the case for the weavers where the inputs for weaving are received by the weaver from someone else. If the weaver himself is purchasing the inputs and weaving, then they sell the same in the market. The problem here is selling the handloom with proper marketing. Marketing is not possible on the part of the weaver who also weaves the clothes. Now the issue is whether the weaver is satisfied with their emoluments or not. This is presented in table 5.

Table 5. Weaver households happy / unhappy with the return (in percentage)

District	Happy	Unhappy
Bargarh	63.39	36.60
Sonepur	38.85	61.14
Bolangir	62.16	37.83
Sambalpur	60.71	39.28

Source: Author's own calculation from primary data.

It is observed that in Bargarh district 63.39% of the handloom weavers are happy with the emoluments they get. Similarly, weavers of Bolangir and Sambalpur are also satisfied with the returns. The 62.16% and 60.71% weavers in these two districts are satisfied with the amount of return they get from weaving. However, in Sonepur only 38.95% of the handloom artisans are satisfied with the return from business. On the other hand, 61.14% weavers are dissatisfied with the wages they get for weaving in Sonepur district. This is because as per the data most of the weavers in Sonepur get inputs from the businessmen or master weavers and they prefer to work as wage earners. They are dissatisfied as the emoluments they get for weaving is less as compared to their service. Weavers from Bargarh, Bolangir and Sambalpur are relatively satisfied as they prefer to work as independent entrepreneur weavers.

Generally, the handloom products are costly. Similar is the case for Sambalpuri handloom. Textile mills and power looms copy the design and sell duplicates of the handloom in the market. The price of these duplicate products is very less as compared to the original saree. Sambalpuri handloom got its GI tag in the year 2018. This led to reduction of the threat of copying the design to some extent. Although the handloom products are costly it is more durable as compared to its competitors. The handloom households are asked about the price of the handloom and their responses are presented in table 6.

*Table 6. Weavers view on Pricing of Sambalpuri Handloom (Costly or Not) (***in percentage***)*

District	Yes	No
Bargarh	97.97	2.02
Sonepur	98.85	1.85
Bolangir	95.03	4.97
Sambalpur	95.00	4.99

Source: Author's own calculation from primary data.

Almost more than 90% of the artisans are of the view that Sambalpuri handloom is costly.

The role of middleman who are providing thread, colour and dye are significant in marketing of Sambalpuri handloom. As the social conditions of the weavers are extremely poor, they sell the product to these persons. They cannot market the product and prefer to work as wage earners. On the other hand, independent entrepreneur artisans purchase resources from the market. After weaving they independently market the handloom. However, selling risk of the handloom is with the weavers. Thus, we have located two categories of weavers: First, Weavers weaving the handloom themselves and selling it in the market; and second, working as wage earners and selling the same to Businessmen or to the persons providing loan.

The livelihood of the weavers is affected by the determinant variables. This is computed by estimating a choice model. It is seen that the artisan is selling the handloom independently in the market or giving the finished product to the person who is providing the inputs. If they are giving it to the cooperatives also, they are getting good price for it. Both these categories are taken as the reference group (=0). All other artisans selling this handloom taken as 1. Logit model as stated above is applied and the result presented in table 7.

It is seen that age has significant effect on the determination of livelihood of the weaver. Similarly, no. of family members has significant effect on the livelihood of these artisan households. On the other hand, time spent in weaving, informal loans, and education have adverse effect on the livelihood. The effect of the independent variable on the livelihood is judged from the estimated p-value.

Table 7. Logit model for artisans in all four districts

Variable	All Districts (Bargarh, Sonepur, Bolangir & Sambalpur)		
	Co-efficients	z- statistics	p- value
Constant	0.729701*	2.0217	0.0432
Age	0.000766	0.1474	0.8828
Education	-0.044599*	-2.6738	0.0075
Family Members Engaged in Weaving	0.231854*	3.8032	0.0001
Monthly Income	-0.000055*	-2.1970	0.0280
Informal Loan	-0.000002	-0.8363	0.4030
Time Spent	-0.039468*	-2.8318	0.0046

Note: Y_i=0 if the artisans are selling the handloom and Y_i=1 otherwise.
*: Indicates the significance of the z-statistic at 1% level of significance.

Bargarh and Sonepur are included in the cluster A type. To check the outcomes of the variables on artisans, the model is applied for the individual districts. The results of the logit model are presented in table 8. In Bargarh district, age, time devoted for weaving, family members associated with handloom have positive effect on livelihood. Informal loan, and education have adverse effect on the choice of the livelihood. In Sonepur district, family members engaged have positive effect on the choice of livelihood of the weavers. Variables like, education, age, monthly income, informal loan, and household spending time in weaving have adverse effect. Education has significant effect on the choice of livelihood of the weaving household. If more persons are engaged in weaving in a particular household, they work with the person who have provided loan in Sonepur. Education of the household, amount of informal loan, and monthly income of artisans help the household to work as entrepreneur artisan in Sonepur district.

In B type of cluster Bolangir and Sambalpur are taken. The effect of the independent variables on the occupation of the artisans in the two districts are estimated and represented in table 9. In Bolangir, factors like age, number of persons in a family engaged in weaving, and informal loans have adverse effect. Monthly income and time have substantial effect on determining the livelihood of the weavers. It indicates if the household is more educated and informal loan incurred by the household is more, they prefer to work as entrepreneur artisans. On the other hand, the artisans prefer to work as wage earners with businesspersons when the households' time spent, and monthly income is more.

Table 8. Determination of weavers' livelihood in cluster A districts

Variable	Bargarh			Sonepur		
	Co-efficients	z- statistics	p- value	Co-efficients	z- statistics	p- value
Constant	-0.240363	-0.4606	0.6450	2.405384*	2.5322	0.0113
Age	0.008125	1.1364	0.2558	-0.018996	-1.3774	0.1684
Education	-0.067728*	-2.8477	0.0044	-0.090006*	-1.9264	0.0450
Family Members Engaged in Weaving	0.090905	0.9246	0.3552	0.150515	1.0827	0.2789
Monthly Income	-0.000070*	-1.9725	0.0485	-0.000006	-0.1466	0.8834
Informal Loan	-0.000001	-0.3288	0.7423	-0.000004	-0.6904	0.4899
Time Spent	0.010944	0.5640	0.5727	-0.019757	-0.5097	0.6102

Note: Y_i=0 if the artisans are selling the product and Y_i=1 otherwise.
*: Indicates the significance of the z-statistic at 1% level of significance.

In Sambalpur, no. of family members associated with weaving have substantial effect on the determination of occupation. Here, none of the estimated coefficients are positive except the time spent in weaving business. In Sambalpur, age, monthly income, education, and informal loan have adverse effect on livelihood. This indicates that the weavers prefer to work as independent weavers. They collect the inputs of weaving from the market weave the handloom and sell the same also in the market. Weavers work here with the master weaver if the time spent in weaving is more.

Table 9. Determination of weavers' livelihood in cluster B districts

Variable	Bolangir			Sambalpur		
	Co-efficients	z- statistics	p- value	Co efficients	z- statistics	p- value
Constant	0.337295	0.4647	0.6421	8.813103	1.1345	0.2566
Age	-0.007013	-0.6241	0.5326	-0.137983	-1.0228	0.3064
Education	-0.016410	-0.4755	0.6344	-0.260324	-0.6364	0.5245
Family Members Engaged in Weaving	-0.031274	-0.2526	0.8005	-1.107426*	-1.7955	0.0438
Monthly Income	0.000043	0.6964	0.4861	-0.000258	-1.1340	0.2568
Informal Loan	-0.000012*	-1.9657	0.0462	-0.000044	-1.0685	0.2853
Time Spent	0.005197	0.1446	0.8850	0.253129	1.5150	0.1298

Note: Y_i=0 if the artisans are selling the product and Y_i=1 otherwise.
*: Indicates the significance of the z-statistic at 1% level of significance.

Entrepreneur artisans of Sambalpuri handloom, if selling the product in the market after weaving the handloom, they generally get more return. On the other hand, if they are associated with weaving with master weaver or businessman who provide them loan then, a large part of the profit is taken by them.

CONCLUSION

Many months of lockdown due to the COVID –19 pandemic has left many weavers with loss of livelihood. This is serious for an unorganised sector like handloom where there is no social security. The orders which the weavers received before the start of the lockdown is not collected in most of the cases. Also, it is difficult for the weavers to get the inputs such as yarn, colour, and dye during this period. Hence the livelihood of the weavers is in a standstill. A day without work for the weavers would lead to no wage for them. With this lockdown, the supply chains of both forward and backward supply to handloom weavers have broken. In this crucial time, it is difficult for the whole household to earn their livelihood. More than 5.5 lakh migrant labourers have returned to Odisha. The government has sanctioned an additional amount of money to the Mahatma Gandhi National Rural Employment Guarantee Act (MGNREGA) scheme. Now the question is after the monsoon came to Odisha, what type of work the workers will do in MGNREGA for their livelihood. From 20th June the PM Garib Kalyan Yojana has started. However, this scheme is launched in four districts of Odisha. Bolangir district of Western Odisha is the only district coming under the Sambalpuri handloom cluster where this scheme is launched. These schemes will not solve the problems of the Sambalpuri handloom weavers. Given these, central and state governments should launch some special schemes especially for the handloom weavers keeping in view the loss of their livelihood.

Limitations

The present study is based on the samples drawn from different villages of the clusters of Western Odisha. If a greater number of villages will be taken in the sample the results will change.

ACKNOWLEDGMENT

The author would like to acknowledge Indian Council of Social Science Research (ICSSR), New Delhi for financial support to undertake the project 'Sustainable Livelihood of Sambalpuri Handloom Weavers: A Study in Western Odisha'. The present chapter is part of the study.

REFERENCES

Alwang, J., Siegel, P. B., & Jorgensen, S. L. (2001). *Vulnerability: A View from Different Disciplines, Social Protection Discussion Papers, No.: SP 0115.* World Bank.

Ashley, C., & Carney, D. (1999). *Sustainable livelihoods: lessons from early experiences.* Department for International Development.

Bortamuly, A. B., Goswami, K., & Hazarika, B. (2013). Determinants of Occupational Choice of Workers in the Handloom Industry in Assam. *International Journal of Social Economics*, *40*(12), 1041–1057. doi:10.1108/IJSE-03-2012-0042

Breman, J. (2001). An Informalised Labour System: End of Labour Market Dualism. *Economic and Political Weekly*, *36*(52), 4804–4821.

Brennig, J. J. (1986). Textile Producers and Production in Late 17th Century Coromandel. *The Indian Economic and Social History Review*, *23*(4), 333–355. doi:10.1177/001946468602300401

Carney, D. (1999). Approaches to Sustainable Livelihoods for the Rural Poor. *ODI Poverty Briefing. No. 2*. ODI.

Chamber, R. (1989). Editorial Introduction: Vulnerability, Coping and Policy, in Chambers R. (Ed.) Vulnerability, Coping and Policy, IDS Bulletin, 2(2), 1-7.

Chambers, R., & Conway, G. (1992). *Sustainable Rural Livelihoods: Practical Concepts for 21st Century, Discussion Paper 296*. IDS Sussex.

Creswell, J. W. (2003). *Research Design: Qualitative, Quantitative and Mixed Methods Approaches*. Sage Publication Inc.

Crill, R. (1998). *Indian Ikat Textiles*. Victoria and Albert Museum.

Das, T. K. (2021). Sambalpuri Handloom Weavers' Livelihood: An Analysis of Western Odisha Clusters, India. *The International Journal of Community and Social Development*, *3*(3), 215–235. doi:10.1177/25166026211038348

De Haan, A. (1999). Livelihoods and Poverty: The Role of Migration - A Critical Review of the Migration Literature. *The Journal of Development Studies*, *36*(2), 1–47. doi:10.1080/00220389908422619

De Haan, A. (2011). *Inclusive Growth? Labour Migration and Poverty in India, Working Paper No. 513*. The Hague.

De Neve, G. (2003). Expectations and Rewards of Modernity: Commitment and Mobility among Rural Migrants in Tirupur, Tamil Nadu. *Contributions to Indian Sociology, New Series*, *37*(1-2), 251–280. doi:10.1177/006996670303700111

Desai, C. (1989). *Ikat Textiles of India*. Thames, and Hudson Ltd.

Development Commissioner for Handlooms. (2019). *Fourth All India Handloom Census 2019-20, Ministry of Textiles, Government of India*. CDH.

Elkington, J. (1998). Partnership from Cannibals with Forks: The triple Bottom Line of 21st Century Business. *Environmental Quality Management*, *8*(1), 37–51. doi:10.1002/tqem.3310080106

Ellis, F. (2000). *Rural Livelihoods and Diversity in Developing Countries*. Oxford University Press.

Garderner, K., & Osella, F. (2003). Migration, Modernity and Social Transformation in South Asia: An Overview. *Contributions to Indian Sociology*, *37*, 1–2.

Ghosh, G. K., & Ghosh, S. (2000). *Ikat Textiles of India*. APH Publishing Corporation.

Gittinger, M. (1982). *Master Dyers to the World: Technique and Trade in early Indian Dyed Cotton Textiles*. Textile Museum.

Government of India (2012). Sambalpuri Bandha Saree and Fabrics, *Geographical Indications Journal, 44*.

Government of Odisha (2017). Handloom Policy - 2016. Department of Handlooms. *Textiles and Handicrafts*.

Graham, C. (2002). Mobility, Opportunity, and Vulnerability: The Dynamics of Poverty and Inequality in a Global Economy. *Journal of Human Development, 3*(1), 57–94. doi:10.1080/14649880120105380

Haynes, D. E., & Roy, T. (1999). Conceiving Mobility: Weavers' Migration in Pre-colonial and Colonial India. *The Indian Economic and Social History Review, 36*(1), 35–67. doi:10.1177/001946469903600102

Libel, M., & Roy, T. (2004). Handmade in India: Traditional Craft Skills in a Changing World. In J. M. Finger & P. Schuler (Eds.), *Poor People's Knowledge: Promoting Intellectual Property in Developing Countries*. World Bank.

Liu, W., Li, J., Ren, L., Xu, J., Li, C., & Li, S. (2020). Exploring Livelihood Resilience and its Impact on Livelihood Strategy in Rural China. *Social Indicators Research, 150*(3), 977–998. doi:10.100711205-020-02347-2

Mamidipudi, A., Syamasundari, B., & Bijker, W. (2012, June). Mobilising Discourses: Handloom as Sustainable Socio-Technology. *Economic and Political Weekly, XLVII*(25), 23, 41–51.

McFadden, D. (1973). Conditional Logit Analysis of Qualitative Choice Behaviour in Zarembka. P. (Ed.) Frontiers in Econometrics. Academic Press.

Mines, M. (1984). *The Warrior Merchants: Textiles, Trade and Territory in South India*. Cambridge University Press.

Ministry of Textiles. (2016). *Annual Report 2015-16*. Government of India.

Ministry of Textiles (2017). *Comprehensive Handloom Cluster Development Schemes (CHCDS) – Mega Handloom Cluster*. Development Commissioner.

Mohanty, B.C. (2003). Ikat Fabrics of Odisha and Andhra Pradesh. *Indian Culture.*

Mohapatra, N. (2014). A Management Approach to Sambalpuri Sari with a Sign of Cultural Facets. *Odisha Review, Bhubaneswar.*, (February - March), 130–135.

Narasaiah, M. L., & Krishna, C. H. T. (1999). *Crisis of Handloom Industry*. Discovery Publishing House.

Narayan, D., Patel, R., Schafft, K., Rademacher, A. and Koch-Schulte, S. (2000). *Voices of the Poor: Can Anyone Hear us?* World Bank.

Niehof, A., & Price, L. L. (2001). *Rural Livelihood Systems: A Conceptual Framework, Wageningen – UPWARD Series on Rural Livelihood No. 1*. WU-UPWARD.

Niranjana, S., & Vinayan, S. (2001). *Growth Prospects of the Handloom Industry*. Planning Commission, Government of India.

Parvin, M. T. (2020). Factors Determining the Credit Accessibility by the Small-Scale Entrepreneurs: A Case of Handloom Weaving in Bangladesh. *International Journal of Business and Management, 15*(8), 93–100. doi:10.5539/ijbm.v15n8p93

Planning Commission. (2002). *Orissa Development Report*. Government of India.

Planning Commission. (2008). Inclusive Growth; Eleventh Five Year Plan 2007-2012. Oxford University Press.

Post, O. (2018). National handloom day observed in the city. *Orissa Post*. https://www.orissapost.com/national-handloom-day-observed-in-city/

Pradhan, A. (2014). Sambalpuri Handloom fails to find place in Poll Plans. *The Times of India*.

Pradhan, S., & Khandual, A. (2020). Community, Local Practices and Cultural Sustainability: A Case Study of Sambalpuri Ikat Handloom. In S. S. Muthu & M. A. Gadetti (Eds.), *Sustainability in the Textile and Apparel Industries: Consumerism and Fashion Sustainability* (pp. 121–139). Springer Nature Switzerland A.G. doi:10.1007/978-3-030-38532-3_7

Rao, P. S. (2012). *Connecting the Dots: A Design Approach to Services for the Poor*. [Doctoral Thesis, Northumbria University].

Robinson, R. V., David, E. J. R., & Hill, M. (2016). Participatory Mixed Methods Research Across Cultures. In L. J. Jason & D. S. Glenwick (Eds.), *Handbook of Methodological Approaches to Community based Research* (pp. 273–282). Oxford University Press.

Roy, T. (1988). Size and Structure of Handloom Weaving in the Mid-Thirties. *The Indian Economic and Social History Review*, *25*(1), 1–24. doi:10.1177/001946468802500101

Roy, T. (2005). *Rethinking Economic Change in India: Labour and Livelihood*. Routledge. doi:10.4324/9780203023105

Sahu, D. (2020). Silence of the Looms: Sambalpuri Ikat Sarees Lie in Large Pile Amidst Empty Sacks of Yarn. *The New Indian Express*.

Sahu, I. (2017). Sambalpuri Textile Weaving Process. *Sahapedia*. https://www.sahapedia.org/the-sambalburi-textile-weaving-process

Scoones, I. (1998). *Sustainable Rural Livelihoods: A Framework for Analysis, Working Paper, No. 72*. University of Sussex, Brighton.

Scoones, I. (2009). Livelihoods Perspectives and Rural Development. *The Journal of Peasant Studies*, *36*(1), 171–196. doi:10.1080/03066150902820503

Sen, A. (1988). The Concept of Development, in H. Chenery and T.N. Srinivasan, (Eds.) Handbook of Development Economics. Elsevier Science Publishers, I. 9-26.

Sumner, A. (2007). Meaning Versus Measurement: Why Do Economic Indicators of Poverty Still Predominate? *Development in Practice*, *17*(1), 4–13. doi:10.1080/09614520601092485

Syamasundari, B., & Niranjana, S. (2006). Valuing the Non-Market. *Economic and Political Weekly*, *41*(31), 3394–3398.

UNIDO (2008). IKAT Handloom Weaving Cluster, Special Issue on Rural Livelihood and Poverty Alleviation. *UNIDO South Asia, 2*(2).

UNIDO. (2013). *Lima Declaration: Towards inclusive and sustainable industrial Development*. Fifteenth session of the UNIDO General Conference, Lima, Peru.

Business World. (2020). Vidya Balan Dons Saree with Mathematical Equations For 'Shakuntala Devi' E-Promotions. *Business World.*

Young, H., Jaspars, S., Brown, R., Frize, J., & Khogali, H. (2001). *Food Security Assessments in Emergencies: A Livelihoods Approach, Humanitarian Practice Network (HPN)*. Overseas Development Institute.

ENDNOTES

1 Development Commissioner for Handlooms (2019). Fourth All India Handloom Census 2019-20. Ministry of Textiles. Government of India. New Delhi. August.

2 Carney, D. (1999). Approaches to Sustainable Livelihoods for the Rural Poor. ODI Poverty Briefing. No. 2.

3 World Bank (2020). Global Economic Prospects: A World Bank Group Flagship Report. Washington DC.

4 UNDP (2020). COVID – 19 and Human Development: Assessing the Crisis, Envisioning the Recovery, Human Development Perspective. New York.

5 UNIDO (2013). Lima Declaration: Towards inclusive and sustainable industrial Development. Fifteenth session of the UNIDO General Conference. Lima. Peru. December 2.

6 Ministry of Textiles (2017). Comprehensive Handloom Cluster Development Schemes (CHCDS) – Mega Handloom Cluster. Development Commissioner, May.

7 UNIDO (n.d.) Barpali IKAT Weaving Cluster: Diagnostic Study, Cluster Development Programme. United Nations Industrial Development Program.

8 Department of Handloom, Textiles and Handicrafts (2018-19): Disaster Management Plan, Government of Odisha.

9 Handloom clusters in Odisha can be found in the Handlooms, Textiles and Handicrafts Department, Government of Odisha, webpage https://handloom.odisha.gov.in/handloomtab/important-handloom-clusters .

Compilation of References

Abi-Habib, M., & Yasir, S. (2020). For India's Laborers, Coronavirus Lockdown Is an Order to Starve. *The New York Times.* https://www.nytimes.com/2020/03/31/world/coronavirus-live-news-updates.html

Aboagye, E., Ansong, M., & Dagadu, J. (2016). E-Banking Preferences and Middle Class Values in Ghana. *Journal of Computing*, *4*(2), 35–46. doi:10.12691/jcsa-4-2-2

Açikgöz, Ö., & Günay, A. (2020). The early impact of the Covid-19 pandemic on the global and Turkish economy. *Turkish Journal of Medical Sciences*, *50*(SI-1), 520–526. doi:10.3906ag-2004-6 PMID:32283904

Adhikari, B., Devkota, N., Parajuli, S., Paudel, U. R., Upretee, S., Mahato, S., . . . Dhakal, K. (2023). Teachers' Perceptions on Adoption of Education 4.0 in Schools in Nepal: Evidence From Structural Equation Modelling. In Handbook of Research on Education Institutions, Skills, and Jobs in the Digital Era (pp. 341-358). IGI Global.

Adhikari, K. P. (2019). Determinants of E-Banking in Nepal. *Management Dynamics*, *22*(2), 89–94. doi:10.3126/md.v22i2.30241

Adoption of the Paris Agreement. (n.d.). Retrieved November 28, 2020, from https://unfccc.int/files/essential_background/convention/application/pdf/english_paris_agreement.pdf

Agarwal, B. (2021). Livelihoods in COVID times: Gendered perils and new pathways in India. *World Development*, *139*, 105312. doi:10.1016/j.worlddev.2020.105312

Agbola, F. W., Damoense, M. Y., & Saini, Y. K. (2004). South Africa. *International Journal of Social Economics*, *31*(7), 721–731. doi:10.1108/03068290410540909

Agri Exchange, A. P. E. D. A. (2020). *India export Statistics*. Retrieved from APEDA Agri Exchange: https://agriexchange.apeda.gov.in/IndExp/PortNew.aspx

Ahasanul Haque, A. (2009). *Issues of E-Banking Transaction: An Empirical Investigation on Malaysian Customers Perception*. Academic Press.

Ahmad, M. (2018). *Review of The Technology Acceptance Model (TAM) in Internet banking and Mobile banking*. Academic Press.

Aitken, A. (n.d.). *Measuring Welfare Beyond GDP*. Retrieved November 28, 2020, from https://journals.sagepub.com/doi/full/10.1177/002795011924900110

Al Jazeera. (2020, September 29). *'Agonising milestone': One million people dead from COVID-19*. Retrieved November 28, 2020, from https://www.aljazeera.com/news/2020/9/29/global-death-toll-from-covid-19-exceeds-one-million-people

Alfred, R. B., & Simeon, S. (2020, April 13). *Google scholar*. Retrieved November 10, 2020, from Google scholar: https://ssrn.com/abstract=3586622

Ali, J., & Khan, W. (2020, August 15). Impact of COVID-19 pandemic on agricultural wholesale prices in India: A comparative analysis across the phases of thelockdown. *Waley*, 1-6. doi:10.1002/pa.2402

Alshurideh, M. T., Al Kurdi, B., & Salloum, S. A. (2021). The moderation effect of gender on accepting electronic payment technology: a study on United Arab Emirates consumers. *Review of International Business and Strategy.*

Alvaro, M., de Assisand, G., & Fernando, L. (2011). Lessons Learned from September 11th: Telework As an Organizational Resource to the Business Continuity Planning. *The Japanese Journal of Telework*, *9*(1), 46–51.

Alwang, J., Siegel, P. B., & Jorgensen, S. L. (2001). *Vulnerability: A View from Different Disciplines, Social Protection Discussion Papers, No.: SP 0115*. World Bank.

Aman, K. S., Krushna, R., & Thejesh, G. N. (2020). *India Non-Virus Deaths During lockdown (Version 20200730)* [Data set]. Zenodo., doi:10.5281/zenodo.4630198

Andrade, M. S., Westover, J. H., & Kupka, B. A. (2019). The Role of Work-Life Balance and Worker Scheduling Flexibility in Predicting Global Comparative Job Satisfaction. *International Journal of Human Resource Studies*, *9*(2), 80. doi:10.5296/ijhrs.v9i2.14375

Andrew, M., & Anthony, M. (2020). *The impact of the COVID-19 crisison trade: Recent evidence from East Africa;* https://www.brookings.edu/wp-content/uploads/2020/07/EAC_COVID_Mold_Mveyange.pdf

Angelucci, M., Kapteyn, A., Angrissani, M., & Schaner, G. (2020). *Remote Work and the Heterogeneous Impact of COVID-19 on Employment and Health.* NBER Working Paper Series-27749. Available from https://ideas.repec.org/p/nbr/nberwo/27749.html

Apulu, I., & Latham, A. (2011). Drivers for Information and Communication Technology Adoption: A Case Study of Nigerian Small and Medium Sized Enterprises. *International Journal of Business and Management*, *6*(5). Advance online publication. doi:10.5539/ijbm.v6n5p51

Arso, S. S., Sfenrianto, S., & Wahyudi, M. (2018). Employee Performance Measurement in Teleworking Using Balanced Scorecard. *Iranian Journal of Electrical and Computer Engineering*, *8*(6), 5178. doi:10.11591/ijece.v8i6.pp5178-5184

Arumugam, U., Kanagavalli, G., & Manida, M. (2020). COVID-19: Impact of agriculture in India. *Aegaeum Journal*, *8*(5), 480–488.

Asgary, A., Ozdemir, A. I., & Özyürek, H. (2020). Small and medium enterprises and global risks: Evidence from manufacturing SMEs in Turkey. *International Journal of Disaster Risk Science*, *11*(1), 59–73. doi:10.100713753-020-00247-0

Ashe, D. (2020, June 15). *A Crucial Step Toward Preventing Wildlife-Related Pandemics*. Retrieved November 28, 2020, from https://www.scientificamerican.com/article/a-crucial-step-toward-preventing-wildlife-related-pandemics/

Ashley, C., & Carney, D. (1999). *Sustainable livelihoods: lessons from early experiences*. Department for International Development.

Athnere, S., Greeshma, K., Reddy, A. A., & Ashwini, P. (2020). Impact of COVID-19 on agriculture and food security in India: A review. *JPP, 9*(5), 263-270.

Bailey, D. E., & Kurland, N. B. (2002). A Review of Telework Research: Findings, New Directions, and Lessons for the Study of Modern Work. *Journal of Organizational Behavior*, *23*(4), 383–400. doi:10.1002/job.144

Baker, T., & Judge, K. (2020). How to help small businesses survive COVID-19. SSRN *Electronic Journal*. doi:10.2139/ssrn.3571460

Baldwin, R., & Tomiura, E. (2020). Thinking ahead about the trade impact of COVID-19. In R. Baldwin & B. Weder di Mauro (Eds.), *Economics in the Time of COVID-19*. Centre for Economic Policy Research Press.

Baldwin, R., & Weder di Mauro, B. (2020). *Economics in the Time of COVID-19*. Centre for Economic Policy Research Press.

Banerjee, A., & Duflo, E. (2007). The Economic Lives of the Poor. *The Journal of Economic Perspectives*, *21*(1), 141–167. doi:10.1257/jep.21.1.141 PMID:19212450

Banerjee, O., Darbas, T., Brown, P. R., & Roth, C. H. (2014). Historical Divergence in Public Management of food grain Systems in India and Bangladesh: Opportunities to Enhance Food Security. *Global Food Security*, *3*(3-4), 159–166. doi:10.1016/j.gfs.2014.06.002

Bank, W. (2020, June 21). *Employment in services*. Retrieved from The World Bank: https://data.worldbank.org/indicator/SL.SRV.EMPL.ZS?locations=IN

Barik, S. (2020), Bed shortage in COVID-19 hospitals forces Odisha to change strategy. *The Hindu*. https://www.thehindu.com/news/national/other-states/bed-shortage-in-covid-19-hospitals-forces-odisha-to-change-strategy/article32599863.ece on 26/09/2020

Battaile, W. F., Leonardo, H., & Vivian, N. (2015). *Debt Sustainability in Sub-Saharan Africa: Unraveling Country-Specific Risk. World Bank*. doi:10.1596/1813-9450-7523

Beck, T. (2020). Finance in the times of coronavirus. In R. Baldwin & B. Weder di Mauro (Eds.), *Economics in the Time of COVID-19*. Centre for Economic Policy Research Press.

Belch, G. E., & Belch, M. A. (2002). *Advertising and Promotion: An Integrated Marketing Communications Perspective*. McGraw Hill/Irwin.

Ben, D. (2019, December 23). *Who invaded Rwanda from the North starting the Rwandan civil war?* Retrieved November 23, 2020, from Mvorganizing.org: https://www.mvorganizing.org/who-invaded-rwanda-from-the-north-starting-the-rwandan-civil-war/

Béné, C. (2020). Resilience of local food systems and links to food security–A review of some important concepts in the context of COVID-19 and other shocks. *Food Security*, 1–18. PMID:32837646

Bentley, T., Teo, S., Mcleod, L., Tan, F., Bosua, R., & Gloet, M. (2016). The role of organisational support in teleworker wellbeing: A socio-technical systems approach. *Applied Ergonomics*, *52*, 207–215. doi:10.1016/j.apergo.2015.07.019 PMID:26360212

Bhatia, A. (2020), Here's What Odisha Is Doing To Fight COVID-19 Battle Successfully. *SwCH India*. swachhindia.ndtv.com/heres-what-odisha-is-doing-to-fight-covid-19-battle-successfully-4423/

Bhattarai, M. (2020). Working from Home and Job Satisfaction During the Pandemic Times. doi:10.13140/RG.2.2.21515.11046

Blanca, M. J., Arnau, J., López-Montiel, D., Bono, R., & Bendayan, R. (2013). Skewness and kurtosis in real data samples. *Methodology: European Journal of Research Methods for the Behavioral and Social Sciences*, *9*(2), 78–84. doi:10.1027/1614-2241/a000057

Bloom, N., Liang, J., Roberts, J., & Ying, Z. J. (2015). Does Working from Home Work? Evidence from a Chinese Experiment. *The Quarterly Journal of Economics*, *130*(1), 165–218. doi:10.1093/qje/qju032

Bochtis, D., Benos, L., Lampridi, M., Marinoudi, V., Pearson, S., & Sørensen, C. G. (2020, October 05). AgriculturalWorkforce Crisis in Light of the COVID-19 Pandemic. *Sustainability (Basel)*, *12*(12), 1–13. doi:10.3390u12198212

Bortamuly, A. B., Goswami, K., & Hazarika, B. (2013). Determinants of Occupational Choice of Workers in the Handloom Industry in Assam. *International Journal of Social Economics*, *40*(12), 1041–1057. doi:10.1108/IJSE-03-2012-0042

Boswell, W. R., Shipp, A. J., Payne, S. C., & Culbertson, S. S. (2009). Changes in newcomer job satisfaction over time: Examining the pattern of honeymoons and hangovers. *The Journal of Applied Psychology*, *94*(4), 844–858. doi:10.1037/a0014975 PMID:19594229

Brahmane, M. P., Gaikwad, B. B., Kochewad, S. A., Kumar, M., Kurade, N. P., & Meena, K. K. (2020). *National Lockdown and Agriculture: Impacts and Remedies*. ICAR-National Institute for Abiotic Stress Management Baramati.

Breman, J. (1996). *Footloose Labour: Working in India's Informal Economy*. Cambridge University Press. doi:10.1017/CBO9781139171076

Breman, J. (2001). An Informalised Labour System: End of Labour Market Dualism. *Economic and Political Weekly*, *36*(52), 4804–4821.

Brennig, J. J. (1986). Textile Producers and Production in Late 17th Century Coromandel. *The Indian Economic and Social History Review*, *23*(4), 333–355. doi:10.1177/001946468602300401

Brizi, A., & Biraglia, A. (2020). "Do I have enough food?" How need for cognitive closure and gender impact stockpiling and food waste during the COVID-19 pandemic: A cross-national study in India and the United States of America. *Personality and Individual Differences*, *168*, 110396. doi:10.1016/j.paid.2020.110396 PMID:32982000

Brodeur, A., Gray, D., Islam, A., & Bhuiyan, S. J. (2020). *A Literature Review of the Economics of COVID-19*. Discussion Paper Series, No. 13411. IZA Institute of Labour Economics.

Brough, P., Holt, J., Bauld, R., & Biggs, A. (2008). The Ability of Work-Life Balance Policies to Inñuence Key Social/Organizational Issues. *Asia Pacific Journal of Human Resources*, *46*(3), 261–274.

Buckler, A., Chamberlain, L., Stutchbury, K., & Hedge, C. (2020). *Minimising 'distance' in distance learning programmes during a global health crisis: Framing an international education response to COVID-19*. UKFIET. https://www.ukfiet.org/2020/minimising-distance-in-distance-learning-programmes-during-a-global-health-crisis-framing-an-international-education-response-to-COVID-19/

Buheji, M., da Costa Cunha, K., Beka, G., Mavrić, B., Leandro do Carmo de Souza, Y., Souza da Costa Silva, S., Hanafi, M., & Chetia Yein, T. (2020). The extent of COVID-19 pandemic Socio-economic impact on global poverty. A global integrative multidisciplinary review. *American Journal of Economics*, *10*(4), 213–224. doi:10.5923/j.economics.20201004.02

Burgess, S., & Sievertsen, H. H. (2020). *Schools, Skills and Learning: The Impact of COVID-19 on Education*. https://voxeu.org/article/impact-covid-19-education

Business World. (2020). Vidya Balan Dons Saree with Mathematical Equations For 'Shakuntala Devi' E-Promotions. *Business World.*

Bytes, O. (2020). Odisha Govt Caps treatment costs for Covid-19 patients in Private hospitals. Retrieve from https://odishabytes.com/odisha-govt-sets-norms-for-private-hospitals-to-treat-covid-19-patients/on 28/11/2020

Caba. (2020). *What financial wellbeing*. Retrieved at https://www.caba.org.uk/help-and-guides/information/what-financial-wellbeing

Calisir, F., & Gumussoy, C. A. (2008). Internet banking versus other banking channels: Young consumers' view. *International Journal of Information Management, 28*(3), 215–221. doi:10.1016/j.ijinfomgt.2008.02.009

Camarinha-Matos, L. M., Afsarmanesh, H., Galeano, N., & Molina, A. (2009). Collaborative networked organizations - Concepts and practice in manufacturing enterprises. *Computers & Industrial Engineering, 57*(1), 46–60. doi:10.1016/j.cie.2008.11.024

Caramela, S. (2020). *Working from Home Increases Productivity.* https://www.businessnewsdaily.com/15259-working-from-home-more-productive.html

Carbon Pricing. (n.d.a). *CDP Disclosure Best Practice*. Retrieved November 28, 2020, from http://b8f65cb373b1b7b15feb-c70d8ead6ced550b4d987d7c03fcdd1d.r81.cf3.rackcdn.com/cms/guidance_docs/pdfs/000/001/567/original/CDP-technical-note-carbon-pricing.pdf?1523952114

Carbon Pricing. (n.d.b). Retrieved November 28, 2020, from https://www.cdp.net/en/climate/carbon-pricing

Cariappa, A. G., Acharya, K. K., Adhav, C., & Ramasundaram, P. (2020). *Pandemic Led Food Price Anomalies and Supply Chain Disruption: Evidence from COVID-19 Incidence in India.* Academic Press.

Carlsson, M., Dahl, G. B., Öckert, B., & Rooth, D. (2015). The effect of schooling on cognitive skills. *The Review of Economics and Statistics, 97*(3), 533–547. doi:10.1162/REST_a_00501

Carmen, V. R., Georgiana, R. L., Sorin, B., Florentina, C., Corina, I., & Ionut, L. P. (2021). Impact of the COVID-19 Pandemic on the Romanian LaborMArket. *Sustainability*, 1–23.

Carney, D. (1999). Approaches to Sustainable Livelihoods for the Rural Poor. *ODI Poverty Briefing. No. 2.* ODI.

Ceballos, F., Kannan, S., & Kramer, B. (2020). Impacts of a national lockdown on smallholder farmers' income and food security: Empirical evidence from two states in India. *World Development, 136*, 105069. doi:10.1016/j.worlddev.2020.105069

Cecchetti, S. G., & Schoenholtz, K. L. (2020). Contagion: Bank runs and COVID-19. In R. Baldwin & B. Weder di Mauro (Eds.), *Economics in the Time of COVID-19.* Centre for Economic Policy Research Press.

CGIAR. (2020). https://www.cgiar.org/newsevents/news/covid-19-and-food-security-india-and-itsjobs-crisis/

Chakraborty & Thomas. (2020). COVID-19 and Macroeconomic Uncertainty: Fiscal and Monetary Policy Response. *Economic and Political Weekly, 40*(15), 10-12.

Chakraborty, L., & Harikrishnan, S. (2022). COVID-19 and Fiscal- Monetary Policy Co-ordination: Empirical Evidence from India. *Economic and Political Weekly, 57*(4), 18-21.

Chamber, R. (1989). Editorial Introduction: Vulnerability, Coping and Policy, in Chambers R. (Ed.) Vulnerability, Coping and Policy, IDS Bulletin, 2(2), 1-7.

Chambers, R., & Conway, G. (1992). *Sustainable Rural Livelihoods: Practical Concepts for 21st Century, Discussion Paper 296.* IDS Sussex.

Chao, C. M. (2019). Factors determining the behavioral intention to use mobile learning: An application and extension of the UTAUT model. *Frontiers in Psychology, 10*(1), 1–14. doi:10.3389/fpsyg.2019.01652 PMID:31379679

Charlene, M., & Sabrina, W. (2020, July). *Repec.* Retrieved November 29, 2020, from Repec Website: https://ideas.repec.org/p/iza/izadps/dp13443.html

Chatterjee, R. (n.d.). Indian agriculture and role of agricultural extension system to cope up with COVID-19 crisis. *Food and Scientific Reports, 1*(6).

Chatterji, S., McDougal, L., Johns, N., Ghule, M., Rao, N., & Raj, A. (2021). COVID-19-Related financial hardship, job loss, and mental health symptoms: Findings from a cross-sectional study in a rural agrarian community in India. *International Journal of Environmental Research and Public Health, 18*(16), 8647. doi:10.3390/ijerph18168647 PMID:34444394

Chaturvedi, K. (2020). COVID-19 and its impact on education, social life and mental health of students: A survey. *Children and Youth Services Review*. Advance online publication. doi:10.1016/j.childyouth.2020.105866 PMID:33390636

Chaudhary, M., Sodani, P. R., & Das, S. (2020). Effect of COVID-19 on Economy in India: Some Reflections for Policy and Programme. *Journal of Health Management, 22*(2), 169–180. doi:10.1177/0972063420935541

Chauhan, B. S., Mahajan, G., Sardana, V., Timsina, J., & Jat, M. L. (2012). Productivity and sustainability of the rice–wheat cropping system in the Indo-Gangetic Plains of the Indian subcontinent: Problems, opportunities, and strategies. *Advances in Agronomy, 117*, 315–369. doi:10.1016/B978-0-12-394278-4.00006-4

Chauhan, V., Yadav, R., & Choudhary, V. (2019). Analyzing the impact of consumer innovativeness and perceived risk in internet banking adoption: A study of Indian consumers. *International Journal of Bank Marketing, 37*(1), 323–339. doi:10.1108/IJBM-02-2018-0028

Cheng, T. C. E., Lam, D. Y. C., & Yeung, A. C. L. (2006). Adoption of internet banking: An empirical study in Hong Kong. *Decision Support Systems, 42*(3), 1558–1572. doi:10.1016/j.dss.2006.01.002

Climate damages and adaptation potential across. (n.d.). *Nature*. Retrieved November 28, 2020, from https://www.nature.com/articles/s41558-019-0444-6.epdf?no_publisher_access=1&r3_referer=nature

Climate Restoration. (n.d.). Retrieved November 28, 2020, from https://foundationforclimaterestoration.org/wp-content/uploads/2020/03/20200306c_f4cr4_white-paper.pdf

Climatechange 27 07 03. (n.d.). WHO. Retrieved November 28, 2020, from https://www.who.int/globalchange/climate/en/chapter6.pdf

CNBC. (2020, May 31). *CNBC*. Retrieved November 07, 2020, from CNBC: https://www.cnbc.com/2020/05/31/new-jobs-created-as-a-result-of-the-coronavirus-pandemic.html

Cochrane, J. H. (2020). Coronavirus monetary policy. In Economics in the Time of COVID-19. Centre for Economic Policy Research Press.

Congressional Research Service. (2020). *Global Economic Effects of COVID-19*. CRS Report prepared for members and committees of congress, R46270. https://crsreports.congress.gov

Coronavirus and Climate Change. (2020, July 6). Retrieved November 28, 2020, from https://www.hsph.harvard.edu/c-change/subtopics/coronavirus-and-climate-change/

Coronavirus cases: Worldometer. (2023, February 7). Retrieved February 7, 2023, from https://www.worldometers.info/coronavirus/

Coronavirus disease (COVID-19). (n.d.). Retrieved November 28, 2020, from https://www.who.int/emergencies/diseases/novel-coronavirus-2019

COVID-19 to slash global economic output by $8.5 trillion over next two years. (n.d.). UN DESA Department of Economic and Social Affairs. Retrieved November 28, 2020, from https://www.un.org/development/desa/en/news/policy/wesp-mid-2020-report.html

COVID-19. Implications for business. (2020, November 25). Retrieved November 28, 2020, from https://www.mckinsey.com/business-functions/risk/our-insights/covid-19-implications-for-business

Creswell, J. W. (2003). *Research Design: Qualitative, Quantitative and Mixed Methods Approaches*. Sage Publication Inc.

Crill, R. (1998). *Indian Ikat Textiles*. Victoria and Albert Museum.

Cronin, Doran, & Rough. (2020). *Geopolitical Implications of the Coronavirus*. Hudson Institute.

Crosbie & Moore. (2004). Work–life Balance and Working from Home. *Social Policy & Society, 3*(3), 223–233 doi:10.1017/S1474746404001733

Csath, M. (2020). Crisis situations: How should micro, small and medium enterprises handle them with a long term view? *Development and Learning in Organizations*, *35*(3), 10–12. doi:10.1108/DLO-04-2020-0086

Da Vanzo, J. (1983). Repeat Migration in the United States: Who Moves Back and Who Moves on. *The Review of Economics and Statistics*, *65*(4), 552–559. doi:10.2307/1935923

Da'ar, O. B., Haji, M., & Jradi, H. (2020). Potential implications for weak health systems and conflict zones in the Middle East and North Africa region. *The International Journal of Health Planning and Management.*

Dale, T., & Christopher, A. (1994). Review of Economic Studies: Job Creation and Job Destruction in the Theory of Unemployment. Academic Press.

Damghanian, H., Zarei, A., & Siahsarani Kojuri, M. A. (2016). Impact of Perceived Security on Trust, Perceived Risk, and Acceptance of Online Banking in Iran. *Journal of Internet Commerce*, *15*(3), 214–238. doi:10.1080/15332861.2016.1191052

Danie, G., & Alexandre, O. (2021, April 1). *Labour market responses to the Covid-19 crisis in the United States and Europe.* Retrieved May 21, 2021, from https://www.ceps.eu/: https://www.ceps.eu/wp-content/uploads/2021/04/WD2021-01_Labour-market-responses-to-Covid.pdf

Danurdoro, K., & Wulandari, D. (2016). The Impact of Perceived Usefulness, Perceived Ease of Use, Subjective Norm, and Experience Toward Student's Intention to Use Internet Banking. *Jurnal Ekonomi Dan Ekonomi Studi Pembangunan*, *8*(1), 17–22. doi:10.17977/um002v8i12016p017

Das, A. (2020), How Odisha and Kerala are leading from the front in war against Covid. https://www.livemint.com/opinion/columns/opinion-how-odisha-and-kerala-are-leading-from-the-front-in-war-against-covid-11587810374135.html on 26/09/2020.

Dasgupta, S., Paul, R., & Fuloria, S. (2011). An Empirical Study to Understand the Different Antecedents of Relationship Quality in the Indian Context with Reference to the Mobile Telecommunication Sector. *Romanian Journal of Marketing*, *6*(1), 1–117.

Das, T. K. (2021). Sambalpuri Handloom Weavers' Livelihood: An Analysis of Western Odisha Clusters, India. *The International Journal of Community and Social Development*, *3*(3), 215–235. doi:10.1177/25166026211038348

Day, B., Burnice Mckay, R., Ishman, M., & Chung, E. (2004). The new normal: Lessons learned from SARS for corporations operating in emerging markets. *Management Decision*, *42*(6), 794–806. doi:10.1108/00251740410542357

De Haan, A. (2011). *Inclusive Growth? Labour Migration and Poverty in India, Working Paper No. 513.* The Hague.

De Haan, A. (1999). Livelihoods and Poverty: The Role of Migration - A Critical Review of the Migration Literature. *The Journal of Development Studies*, *36*(2), 1–47. doi:10.1080/00220389908422619

De Neve, G. (2003). Expectations and Rewards of Modernity: Commitment and Mobility among Rural Migrants in Tirupur, Tamil Nadu. *Contributions to Indian Sociology, New Series*, *37*(1-2), 251–280. doi:10.1177/006996670303700111

De Onis, M., Borghi, E., Arimond, M., Webb, P., Croft, T., Saha, K., ... Hayashi, C. (2019). Prevalence thresholds for wasting, overweight and stunting in children under 5 years. *Public Health Nutrition*, *22*(1), 175–179. doi:10.1017/S1368980018002434 PMID:30296964

Deloitte. (2016). Global manufacturing competitiveness index: report. London: *Deloitte Touche Tohmatsu Limited*. https://www2.deloitte.com/global/en/pages/manufacturing/articles/global-manufacturing-competitiveness-index.html

Deloitte. (2020). *Economic impact of the COVID-19 pandemic on East African Economies*. Nairobi: Deloitte Insights.

Desai, C. (1989). *Ikat Textiles of India*. Thames, and Hudson Ltd.

Deshingkar, P. (2003). Improved Livelihoods in Improved Watersheds: Can Migration be Mitigated. In *Watershed Management Challenges: Improving Productivity, Resources and Livelihoods*. International Water Management Institute.

Deshmukh, S. G., & Haleem, A. (2020). Framework for Manufacturing in Post-Covid-19 World Order: An Indian Perspective. *International Journal of Global Business and Competitiveness*.

Deshmukh, S. G. (2016). Manufacturing Competitiveness: Research Opportunities. *International Journal of Global Business and Competitiveness*, *11*(1), 1–6.

Deshpande, T. (2017). *State of Agriculture in India*. PRS Legislative Research.

Dev, Mahendra, & Sengupta. (2020). *Covid-19: Impact on the Indian Economy*. Working Paper, No. 13. Indira Gandhi Institute of Development Research.

Dev, S. M., & Sengupta, R. (2020). *Covid-19: Impact on the Indian economy*. Indira Gandhi Institute of Development Research.

Devakumar, D., & Sunil, S. (2020). Racism and discrimination in COVID-19 responses. *Lancet*.

Development Commissioner for Handlooms. (2019). *Fourth All India Handloom Census 2019-20, Ministry of Textiles, Government of India*. CDH.

Devereux, S., Béné, C., & Hoddinott, J. (2020). Conceptualising COVID-19's impacts on household food security. *Food Security*, *12*(4), 769–772. doi:10.100712571-020-01085-0 PMID:32837651

Deyshappriya, N. P. R. (2020). Economic impacts of COVID-19 macro and microeconomics evidences from Sri Lanka. SSRN *Electronic Journal*. doi:10.2139/ssrn.3597494

Dhoot, P. (2020). Impact of COVID-19 on Higher Education in India. *International Journal of Creative Research Thoughts*, *8*(6), 1263-1273. https://www.ijcrt.org/papers/IJCRT2006171.pdf

Diala, A. M., Valentina, F., Frederik, G. T., & Hoon, L. (2021, March 5). *The Short-Term Impact of COVID-19 on Labor Markets, Poverty and Inequality in Brazil*. Retrieved April 22, 2021, from IMF elibrary: https://www.elibrary.imf.org/view/journals/001/2021/066/article-A001-en.xml

Diary, O. (2020). AMRI introduces Covid-19 Virtual home service facility. Retrieve from https://orissadiary.com/amri-introduces-covid-19-virtual-home-service-facilities/?utm_source=nyoooz&utm_medium=post

Documents & Reports - All Documents. (n.d.). The World Bank. Retrieved November 28, 2020, from https://documents.worldbank.org/curated/en/156521468767069279/pdf/multi-page.pdf

Donnelly, N., & Proctor-Thomson, S. B. (2015). Disrupted work: Home-based teleworking (HbTW) in the aftermath of a natural disaster. *New Technology, Work and Employment*, *30*(1), 47–61. doi:10.1111/ntwe.12040

Dossier. (2020). Pandemic and the Crisis of Capitalism. *Rethinking Marxism.*

DPFP. (2020). https://dfpd.gov.in/food-grain-bulletin.html

Drabek, T. E., & McEntire, D. A. (2003). Emergent Phenomena and the Sociology of Disaster: Lessons, Trends and Opportunities from the Research Literature. *Disaster Prevention and Management*, *12*(2), 97–112. doi:10.1108/09653560310474214

du Bruyn, R. (2008). A proposed reporting framework for HIV/Aids disclosure by listed South African companies. *Meditari Accountancy Research*, *16*(1), 59–78. doi:10.1108/10222529200800004

Dunn, C. G., Kenney, E., Fleischhacker, S. E., & Bleich, S. N. (2020). Feeding low-income children during the Covid-19 pandemic. *The New England Journal of Medicine*, *382*(18), e40. doi:10.1056/NEJMp2005638 PMID:32227759

Dupor, B. (2020). *Possible Fiscal Policies for Rare, Unanticipated, and Severe Viral Outbreaks. Economic Synopses, 1-2(6).* doi:10.20955/es.2020.6

Dynan, K., & Powell, W., III. (2022, April 1). *US employment and wages are rising briskly amid strong labor demand.* Peterson Institute for International Economics. Retrieved May 21, 2022, from https://www.piie.com/blogs/realtime-economic-issues-watch/us-employment-and-wages-are-rising-briskly-amid-strong-labor

Dzigbede, K. D., & Pathak, R. (2020). COVID-19 economic shocks and fiscal policy options for Ghana. *Journal of Public Budgeting, Accounting & Financial Management*, *32*(5), 903–917. doi:10.1108/JPBAFM-07-2020-0127

Economic consequences of Covid-19: A multi-country analysis. (n.d.). Retrieved November 28, 2020, from https://voxeu.org/article/economic-consequences-covid-19-multi-country-analysis

Economic Policy Institute. (2020, March). *Google scholar.* Retrieved January 23, 2021, from www.google.com: https://www.epi.org/newsroom/useful_definitions/

Economic Survey of Odisha-2017-18. (n.d.). Planning and Co-ordination Department. Directorate of Economics and Statistics, Government of Odisha.

Economic Times. (2020). *Odisha announces Covid-19-dedicated hospitals with 1,000 beds.* https://economictimes.indiatimes.com/industry/healthcare/biotech/healthcare/odisha-announces-countrys-first-covid-19-dedicated-hospitals-with-1000-beds/articleshow/74832053.cms?from=mdr

Economically Sustainable Carbon Capture. (n.d.). Retrieved November 28, 2020, from https://www.blueplanet-ltd.com/

Elkington, J. (1998). Partnership from Cannibals with Forks: The triple Bottom Line of 21st Century Business. *Environmental Quality Management*, *8*(1), 37–51. doi:10.1002/tqem.3310080106

Ellen, J. S., David, C., & Donald, K. (2020, June 16). *UNDP.* Retrieved November 10, 2020, from UNDP Website: http://www.UNDP-rba-COVID-assessment-Sierraleone.pdf

Ellis, F. (2000). *Rural Livelihoods and Diversity in Developing Countries.* Oxford University Press.

Emmanuel. (2018, April 10). *Academia.edu.* Retrieved October 09, 2020, from Academia.edu: https://www.academia.edu/35421416

Engage, E. P. W. (2020). Controlling the Corona Virus: Examining Nation States and their Approach towards Fighting Viral Diseases? *Economic and Political Weekly.* Available at https://www.epw.in/engage/article/controlling-coronavirus--nation-states-viral-diseases

EPRN. (2018). *Policy Dialogue: NST 1- Creating 1,500,000 Decent and Productive Jobs: challenges and policy actions*. EPRN.

Equity, B. (2020). Quality or Variety: Brands thriving with a health kick Retrieve from https://brandequity.economictimes.indiatimes.com/news/marketing/opinion-quality-or-variety-brands-thriving-with-a-health-kick/77903060 on

Erokhin, V., & Gao, T. (2020). Impacts of COVID-19 on trade and economic aspects of food security: Evidence from 45 developing countries. *International Journal of Environmental Research and Public Health*, *17*(16), 5775. doi:10.3390/ijerph17165775 PMID:32785155

ESG in the Mainstream: The Role for Companies and. (n.d.). BSR. Retrieved November 28, 2020, from https://www.bsr.org/reports/BSR_ESG_Integration_Report__Sept_2009_final.pdf

ESG. Do you or Don't you? (n.d.). UBS Global - Asset Management. Retrieved November 28, 2020, from https://www.ubs.com/global/en/asset-management/insights/sustainable-and-impact-investing/2019/esg-do-you-or-don-t-you.html

Etikan, I. (2016). Comparison of Convenience Sampling and Purposive Sampling. *American Journal of Theoretical and Applied Statistics*, *5*(1), 1. doi:10.11648/j.ajtas.20160501.11

Falk, G. (2020, November 9). *Congressional Research Service*. Retrieved March 20, 2021, from crsreports.congress.gov: https://crsreports.congress.gov/product/pdf/IN/IN11457

FAO. (2020a). *Covid-19 Pandemic: Impact on Food and Agriculture*. Food and Agricultural Organisation. https://www.fao.org/2019-ncov/q-and-a/en/

FAO. (2020b). https://www.fao.org/2019-ncov/q-anda/impact-on-food-and-agriculture/en/

FAO. (2021). *The state of food insecurity in the world 2001*. Available: http://www. fao.org/3/y1500e/y1500e00.htm

Faria e Castro. (2020). *Fiscal Policy during a Pandemic*. Working Paper 2020-006D. Research Division Working Paper Series, Federal Reserve Bank of St. Louis. doi:10.20955/wp.2020.006

Fauk, N. K., Mwakinyali, S. E., Putra, S., & Mwanri, L. (2017). The socio-economic impacts of AIDS on families caring for AIDS-orphaned children in Mbeya rural district, Tanzania. *International Journal of Human Rights in Healthcare*, *10*(2), 132–145. doi:10.1108/IJHRH-01-2017-0002

FCI. (2020). *Movements - Food Corporation of India*. Food Corporation of India. https://fci.gov.in/movements.php

Featherman, M. S., Miyazaki, A. D., & Sprott, D. E. (2010). Reducing online privacy risk to facilitate e-service adoption: The influence of perceived ease of use and corporate credibility. *Journal of Services Marketing*, *24*(3), 219–229. doi:10.1108/08876041011040622

Fedorko, I., & Bačik, R. (2021). *Performance expectancy using electronic banking: Effort expectancy and social influence factors as main determinants of performance expectancy using electronic banking*. doi:10.21511/bbs.16(2).2021.03

Felstead, A., & Henseke, G. (2017). Assessing the growth of remote working and its consequences for effort, well-being and work-life balance. *New Technology, Work and Employment*, *32*(3), 195–212. doi:10.1111/ntwe.12097

Felstead, A., Jewson, N., & Walters, S. (2003). Managerial Control of Employees Working at Home. *British Journal of Industrial Relations*, *41*(2), 241–264. doi:10.1111/1467-8543.00271

Ferinia, R. (2015). Contribution of Knowledge Leader and Communication toward Employee Productivity at West Java Conference Office. *International Journal of Basic and Applied Sciences*, *4*(2), 193. doi:10.14419/ijbas.v4i2.4176

FGV IIU International Intelligence Unit Rio. (2020). *FGV IIU Flash Notes the World Corona Changed: Preliminary Thoughts on the Coming World Order*. Author.

Financial Express. (2020). Coronavirus brings business competitors on one table. *Financial Express*. https://www.financialexpress.com/industry/ coronavirus-brings-business-competitors-on-one-table-cci-allows-firms-to-work-together/1933729/

First Covid-19 case happened in November, China government records show - report. (2020, March 13). Retrieved November 28, 2020, from https://www.theguardian.com/world/2020/mar/13/first-covid-19-case-happened-in-november-china-government-records-show-report

Fode, N. (2020, June). The Socio-Economic Impact of COVID-19 in Rwanda. *COVID-19 in Rwanda*.

Food & Agriculture Organization UN. (2020). https://www.fao.org/documents/card/en/c/ca8497en

Forest and Nature Policy Group. (n.d.). Retrieved November 28, 2020, from https://www.wur.nl/upload_mm/6/e/6/998c6e88-c6e2-4a38-92e3-c883ea847cee_20181010_Environmental_impacts_forest_certifications.pdf

Fornaro, L., & Wolf, M. (2020). *Covid-19 Coronavirus and Macroeconomic Policy: Some Analytical Notes*. CREI/UPF and University of Vienna. http://www.crei.cat/wp-content/uploads/2016/07/CMP.pdf

Fred, D., & Davis, J. (1980). *A technology acceptance model for empirically testing new end-user information systems: theory and results*. doi:10.1126/science.146.3652.1648

Garderner, K., & Osella, F. (2003). Migration, Modernity and Social Transformation in South Asia: An Overview. *Contributions to Indian Sociology*, *37*, 1–2.

Garikipati, N. (2020). Odisha's quiet success in war on Covid-19 pandemic. Policy Circle, Retrieve from https://www.policycircle.org/life/odishas-quiet-success-in-war-on-covid-19-pandemic/ on 28/11/2020

Gettleman, J., & Raj, S. (2020). Powered by Fear, Indians Embrace Coronavirus Lockdown. *New York Times*.

GHI. (2019). *2019 Global hunger index results by severity. Global hunger index – Peer-reviewed annual publication designed to comprehensively measure and track hunger at the global, regional, and country levels*. https:// www.globalhungerindex.org/results.html

Ghosh, J. (2020). A critique of the Indian government's response to the COVID-19 pandemic. *Economia e Politica Industriale*, *47*(3), 519–530. doi:10.100740812-020-00170-x

Giovanis, A. N., Binioris, S., & Polychronopoulos, G. (2012). An extension of TAM model with IDT and security/privacy risk in the adoption of internet banking services in Greece. *EuroMed Journal of Business*, *7*(1), 24–53. doi:10.1108/14502191211225365

Gittinger, M. (1982). *Master Dyers to the World: Technique and Trade in early Indian Dyed Cotton Textiles*. Textile Museum.

Global Climate Restoration for. (n.d.). Retrieved November 28, 2020, from https://thunderbird.asu.edu/sites/default/files/global_climate_restoration_report_2020.pdf

Global Migration Group (GMG). (2010). *Statement of Global Migration Group on the Human Rights of Migrants in Irregular Situation*. Statement Adopted by the Principles of Global Migration Group in Geneva on 30th September.

Global warming: Severe consequences for Africa. (n.d.). Africa Renewal. Retrieved November 28, 2020, from https://www.un.org/africarenewal/magazine/december-2018-march-2019/global-warming-severe-consequences-africa

Golden, T. (2009). Applying Technology to Work: Toward a Better Understanding of Telework. *Organizational Management Journal*, *6*(4), 241–250. doi:10.1057/omj.2009.33

Goldin, I., & Muggah, R. (2020). End of International Cooperation? How Corona virus Has Changed the World Permanently. *The National Interest*. https://nationalinterest.org/blog/buzz/end-international-cooperation-how-coronavirus-has-changed-world-permanently-139092

Gonzales, M. (2022, February 17). *Nearly 2 Million Fewer Women in the Labor Force*. SHRM. Retrieved May 21, 2022, from https://www.shrm.org/resourcesandtools/hr-topics/behavioral-competencies/global-and-cultural-effectiveness/pages/over-1-million-fewer-women-in-labor-force.aspx

González, M. E., Mueller, R. D., & Mack, R. W. (2008). An Alternative Approach in Service Quality: An e-Banking Case Study. *The Quality Management Journal*, *15*(1), 41–58. doi:10.1080/10686967.2008.11918055

Google Scholar. (2020, April 1). Retrieved June 2020, 2020, from CMI Website: https://www.managers.org.uk/

Google Scholar. (n.d.). Retrieved October 20, 2020, from Google scholar: https://en.wikipedia.org

Gopalakrishnan, S., Wischnevsky, J. D., & Damanpour, F. (2003). A multilevel analysis of factors influencing the adoption of internet banking. *IEEE Transactions on Engineering Management*, *50*(4), 413–426. doi:10.1109/TEM.2003.819648

Gopalan, H. S., & Misra, A. (2020). COVID-19 Pandemic and Challenges for Socioeconomic Issues, Healthcare and National Programs in India. *Diabetes & Metabolic Syndrome: Clinical Research & Reviews.*

Gope, P. C., Gope, D., & Gope, A. (2021). Higher Education in India: Challenges and Opportunities of the COVID-19 Pandemic. *Asian Journal of Distance Education*, *16*(1), 54–73. doi:10.5281/zenodo.4643552

Gopinath, C. (n.d.). *IMF: New predictions suggest a deeper recession and a slower recovery*. Retrieved November 28, 2020, from https://www.weforum.org/agenda/2020/06/imf-lockdown-recession-covid19-coronavirus-economics-recession/

Government of India (2012). Sambalpuri Bandha Saree and Fabrics, *Geographical Indications Journal*, *44*.

Government of Odisha (2017). Handloom Policy - 2016. Department of Handlooms. *Textiles and Handicrafts*.

Government of Odisha. (2020). *Odisha Economic Survey 2019-20*. Planning and Convergence Department. Directorate of Economics and Statistics. https://pc.odisha.gov.in/Download/Economic_Survey_2019-20.pdf

Government of Odisha. (2020a). *Odisha Economic Survey 2019-20*. Planning and Convergence Department, Directorate of Economics and Statistics.

Government of Odisha. (2020b). *Odisha Economic Survey 2020-21*. Planning and Convergence Department, Directorate of Economics and Statistics.

Government of Odisha. (2020c). *The number of Confirmed Cases and deaths of corona disease*. Available at https://statedashboard.odisha.gov.in/

Government of Odisha. (2022), *Covid Dashboard*. State Dashboard. https://statedashboard.odisha.gov.in

Goyal, S. (2020). *Impact of Coronavirus on Education in India*. https://www.jagranjosh.com/general-knowledge/impact-of-coronavirus-on-education-in-india-1587642880-1

Graham, C. (2002). Mobility, Opportunity, and Vulnerability: The Dynamics of Poverty and Inequality in a Global Economy. *Journal of Human Development*, *3*(1), 57–94. doi:10.1080/14649880120105380

Greenberg, J. (2011). *Behavior in Organizations* (8th ed.). Pearson Education.

Gummadi, S., Jyotishi, A., & Prashanth, D. (2021). Malnutrition and Inequality among the Vulnerable Social Groups: A Study of Two Villages. *Journal of Development Policy Review, 1*(4).

Gupta, A., & Goplani, M. (2020). Impact Of COVID-19 On Educational Institution In India. *Purakala (UGC Care Journal), 31*(21), 661-671. https://papers.ssrn.com/sol3/papers.cfm?abstract_id=3679284

Gupta, S. (2020). *The Impact of the Coronavirus SARS-CoV-2 on the Education Sector in India*. http://confluence.ias.ac.in/the-impact-of-the-coronavirus-sars-cov-2-on-the-education-sector-in-india/

Gupta, S., Seth, P., Abraham, M., & Pingali, P. (2021). COVID-19 and women's nutrition security: Panel data evidence from rural India. *Economics and Politics*, 1–28. PMID:35422584

Guriting, P., & Oly Ndubisi, N. (2006). Borneo online banking: Evaluating customer perceptions and behavioural intention. *Management Research News*, *29*(January), 6–15. doi:10.1108/01409170610645402

Haass, R. (2020). Foreword. In *The End of World Order and American Foreign Policy*. Council Special Report No. 86. https://cdn.cfr.org/sites/default/files/report_pdf/the-end-of-world-order-and-american-foreign-policy-csr.pdf

Hameiri, S. (2020). Covid-19: Why did global health governance fail? *The Interpreter Lowy Institute*. https://www.lowyinstitute.org/the-interpreter/covid-19-why-did-global-health-governance-fail

Harker Martin, B., & MacDonnell, R. (2012). Is Telework Effective for Organizations? A Meta-Analysis of Empirical Research on Perceptions of Telework and Organizational Outcomes. *Management Research Review*, *35*(7), 602–616. doi:10.1108/01409171211238820

Harris, J., Depenbusch, L., Pal, A. A., Nair, R. M., & Ramasamy, S. (2020). Food system disruption: Initial livelihood and dietary effects of COVID-19 on vegetable producers in India. *Food Security*, *12*(4), 841–851. doi:10.100712571-020-01064-5 PMID:32837650

Harris, J., & Todaro, M. P. (1970). Migration, Unemployment and Development: A Two-Sector Analysis. *The American Economic Review*, *60*, 126–142.

Hartog, M., & Frame, P. (2003). *From Rhetoric to Reality into The Swap of Ethical Practice: Implementing Work-Life Balance*. Blackwell Publishing Ltd.

Hassan, H. E., & Wood, V. R. (2020). Does country culture influence consumers' perceptions toward mobile banking? A comparison between Egypt and the United States. *Telematics and Informatics*, *46*, 101312. doi:10.1016/j.tele.2019.101312

Haynes, D. E., & Roy, T. (1999). Conceiving Mobility: Weavers' Migration in Pre-colonial and Colonial India. *The Indian Economic and Social History Review*, *36*(1), 35–67. doi:10.1177/001946469903600102

Hicks, J. R. (1932). *The Theory of Wages*. Macmillan.

Hoeven, C. L. T., & Zoonen, W. V. (2020). Helping Others and Feeling Engaged in the Context of Workplace Flexibility: The Importance of Communication Control. *International Journal of Business Communication*. Advance online publication. doi:10.1177/2329488419898799

Hofman, B. (2020). Final, long-term risk is that the pandemic will feed protectionism around the world, The COVID-19 Pandemic. *EAI, 14*.

Housen, T., Hopkins, S., & Earnest, J. (2013). A Systematic Review on the Impact of Internal Remittances on Poverty and Consumption in Developing Countries: Implications for Policy. *Population Space and Place*, *19*(5), 610–632. doi:10.1002/psp.1743

How Africa will be affected by climate change. (2019, December 15). Retrieved November 28, 2020, from https://www.bbc.com/news/world-africa-50726701

Ibrahim, I. B. (2020). *Research gate*. Retrieved November 10, 2020, from Research gate: https://www.researchgate.net/publication/344581589

Ibrahim, M., Abdullah, Z., Md Syed, M., & Yatim, M. (2018). *Supervisory Communication and Employees' Job Satisfaction in the Small and Medium-Sized Enterprises (SMEs).* Jurnal Komunikasi. *Malaysian Journal of Communication, 34*(4), 285–302. doi:10.17576/JKMJC-2018-3404-17

Igoe, K. J. (2020). *Developing Public Health Communication Strategies—And Combating Misinformation—During COVID-19.* Harvard Press. https://www.hsph.harvard.edu/ecpe/public-health-communication-strategies-covid-19/

ILO. (2005). *Global Report on Forced Labour in Asia: Debt Bondage, Trafficking and State-imposed Forced Labour.* ILO.

ILO. (2020a, April). *ILO Monitor: COVID-19 and the World of Work.* ILO.

ILO. (2020b). *Impact of the COVID-19 Pandemic onthe Labour Market in the Occupied Palestinian Territory.* International Labour Organization.

ILO. (2020c). *COVID-19 and the world of work. Second edition: Updated estimates and analysis.* https://www.ilo.org/wcmsp5/groups/public/---dgreports/---dcomm/documents/briefingnote/wcms_740877.pdf

ILO. (2022, January 17). *ILO downgrades labor market recovery forecast for 2022.* ILO. Retrieved May 15, 2022, from https://www.ilo.org/global/about-the-ilo/newsroom/news/WCMS_834117/lang--en/index.htm

Implications of the 1.5°C limit in the Paris Agreement for. (n.d.). Retrieved November 28, 2020, from https://climateanalytics.org/media/1p5_australia_report_ci.pdf

Imran, R., Majeed, M., & Ayub, A. (2015). Impact of Organizational Justice, Job Security and Job satisfaction on Organizational Productivity. *Journal of Economics, Business and Management, 3*(9). doi: .2015.v3.295 doi:10.7763/joebm

India Today Web Desk. (2020). *Covid-19: 4 negative impacts and 4 opportunities created for education.* https://www.indiatoday.in/education-today/featurephilia/story/covid-19-4-negative-impacts-and-4-opportunities-created-for-education-1677206-2020-05-12

India, N. S. E. (2020). *Macro Reports.* National Stock Exchange. https://www.nseindia.com/resources/publications-macro-reports

Industry, M. o. (2020). *Directorate General of Commercial Intelligence and Statistics.* Retrieved from Ministry of Commerce and Industry: http://www.dgciskol.gov.in/

Insights: System Positive. (n.d.). Retrieved November 28, 2020, from https://www.generationim.com/research-centre/insights/system-positive/

International Monetary Fund. (2020). *COVID-19-Impact and Policy Considerations.* G-20 Finance Ministers and Central Bank Governors' Virtual Meeting.

International Monetary Fund. (2020). *Policy Responses to Covid-19.* IMF. https://www.imf.org/en/Topics/imf-and-covid19/Policy-Responses-to-COVID-19

Iriani, S. S., & Andjarwati, A. L. (2020). Analysis of perceived usefulness, perceived ease of use, and perceived risk toward online shopping in the era of Covid-19 pandemic. *Systematic Reviews in Pharmacy, 11*(12), 313–320. doi:10.31838rp.2020.12.50

Is Europe's far-right using coronavirus as a new avenue of agitation? (2020, November 26). Retrieved November 28, 2020, from https://www.euronews.com/2020/11/26/is-europe-s-far-right-using-covid-restrictions-as-a-new-avenue-of-agitation

Is Sustainable Investing Moving Into the Mainstream? (2019, December 2). Sponsor Content From UBS. Retrieved November 28, 2020, from https://hbr.org/sponsored/2019/11/is-sustainable-investing-moving-into-the-mainstream

Ivanov, D., & Dolgui, A. (2020). Viability of intertwined supply networks: Extending the supply chain resilience angles towards survivability. A position paper motivated by COVID-19 outbreak. *International Journal of Production Research, 58*(10), 2904–2915. doi:10.1080/00207543.2020.1750727

Jackson, J. K., Weiss, M. A., Schwarzenberg, A. B., Nelson, R. M., Sutter, K. M., & Sutherland, M. D. (2021). *Global Economic Effects of COVID-19.* Congressional Research Service, No. R46270. Available at https://crsreports.congress.gov

Jackson, K., & Kallaste, E. (2010). Beyond Flexibility: Reallocation of Responsibilities in the Case of Telework. *New Technology, Work and Employment, 25*(3), 196–209. doi:10.1111/j.1468-005X.2010.00248.x

Jackson, L. T., & Fransman, E. I. (2018). Flexi work, financial well-being, work–life balance and their effects on subjective experiences of productivity and job satisfaction of females in an institution of higher learning. *Suid-Afrikaanse Tydskrif vir Ekonomiese en Bestuurswetenskappe, 21*(1). Advance online publication. doi:10.4102ajems.v21i1.1487

Jacobs, M., Yu, W., & Chavez, R. (2016). The effect of internal communication and employee satisfaction on supply chain integration. *International Journal of Production Economics, 171*, 60–70. doi:10.1016/j.ijpe.2015.10.015

Jain, P., Baghla, K., & A, R. (2020). Effect of corona / COVID19 on the agricultural sector in India. *The Pharma Innovation Journal, 9*(5), 41-45. Retrieved 04 03, 2020, from www.thepharmajournal.com

Janahi, Y. (2021). *The Impact of Internet Banking Adoption in The Kingdom of Bahrain - Overcoming Barriers to Adoption Through the Use of Biometrics.* Academic Press.

Jarrod, M. (2014, December). Outcomes of work–life balance on job satisfaction, life satisfaction and mental health: A study across seven cultures. *Journal of Vocational Behavior, 85*(3), 361–363. doi:10.1016/j.jvb.2014.08.010

Jeanne, C. (2004). Social Work in a Multicultural Society. *Social Work, 49*(1), 5–6. doi:10.1093w/49.1.5 PMID:14964513

Jena, P. R. (2019). *Living under Fiscal Rules: Fiscal Management Response and Resource Allocation Choices for State of Odisha.* Working Paper, No. 264. National Institute of Public Finance and Policy.

Jena, P. K. (2020). Impact of Covid-19 on higher education in India. *International Journal of Advanced Education and Research., 5*(3), 77–81. https://papers.ssrn.com/sol3/papers.cfm?abstract_id=3691541

Jena, P. K. (2020). Impact of Pandemic COVID-19 on Education in India. [IJCR]. *International Journal of Current Research, 12*(7), 12582–12586. http://journalcra.com/article/impact-pandemic-covid-19-education-india

Jena, P. R. (2011). Public Expenditures Management at Sub National Level: A Perspective from the State of Orissa. *Orissa. Economic Journal (London), 43*(1&2), 237–262.

Jha, M. (2020). The Un Role in times of Corona Virus. *The Business Line.*

Jhajhria, A., Ankita, K., Balaji, S. J., Jaya, J., Kingsly, I., & Kiran, K. (2020). *Covid-19, Lockdown and Indian Agriculture: Options to reduce the Impact.* ICAR-National Institute of Agricultural Economics and Policy Research New Delhi.

Jha, R. (2020). Challenges of adoption of internet banking service in cooperative banks in India. *UGC Care Group I Journal, 10*(7), 178–194. doi:10.1108/IJBM-01-2013-0001

Jiyaul Hak Ansari, H. A. A. K. (2019). Course code : BE309E Name / Candidate no.: Jiyaul Hak Ansari Hafiz Abrar Anwar Khan Total number of pages. Academic Press.

John, T. (2020). How Prepared Is India to Control the COVID-19 Pandemic? *Economic and Political Weekly, 55*(11), 13-15.

Jose, J., Mishra, P., & Pathak, R. (2021). Fiscal and monetary response to the COVID-19 pandemic in India. *Journal of Public Budgeting, Accounting & Financial Management, 33*(1), 56–68. doi:10.1108/JPBAFM-07-2020-0119

Joshi, P. K. (2016). Pathways to Improve Food Security and Reduce Poverty in Emerging India. *Agricultural Economics Research Review, 29*(2), 171–182. doi:10.5958/0974-0279.2016.00045.8

Julius, E., Nuugulu, S., & Julius, L. H. (2020). Estimating the economic impact of COVID-19: A case study of Namibia. Unpublished. https://doi.org/doi:10.13140/RG.2.2.30419.32806

Jyotishi, A., & Sridevi, G. (2021). A hunger-free nation: How India can leverage existing institutions. *The News Minute.*

Kaduk, A., Genadek, K., Kelly, E. L., & Moen, P. E. (2019). Involuntary vs. voluntary flexible work: Insights for scholars and stakeholders. *Community Work & Family, 22*(4), 412–442. doi:10.1080/13668803.2019.1616532 PMID:36090310

Kang, M., & Sung, M. (2017). How symmetrical employee communication leads to employee engagement and positive employee communication behaviors. *Journal of Communication Management (London), 21*(1), 82–102. doi:10.1108/JCOM-04-2016-0026

Kapasia, N., Paul, P., Roy, A., Saha, J., Zaveri, A., Mallick, R., Barman, B., Das, P., & Chouhan, P. (2020). Impact of Lockdown on Learning Status of Undergraduate and Post graduate Students During COVID-19 Pandemic in West Bengal, India. *Children and Youth Services Review, 116*, 105194. Advance online publication. doi:10.1016/j.childyouth.2020.105194 PMID:32834270

Kar, S. (2020). Low testing, poor health services – how scrambling to fight Covid after good start.

Karanges, E., Johnston, K., Beatson, A., & Lings, I. (2015). The influence of internal communication on employee engagement: A pilot study. *Public Relations Review, 41*(1), 129–131. doi:10.1016/j.pubrev.2014.12.003

Karlsson, M., & Nilsson, T. (2014, July). The impact of the 1918 Spanish flu epidemic on economic performance in Sweden: An investigation into the consequences of an extraordinary mortality shock. *Journal of Health Economics, 36*, 1-19. Available at https://www.sciencedirect.com/science/article/abs/pii/S0167629614000344

Karmen, N. (2020, June 10). *Africa Portal.* Retrieved July 09, 2020, from https://www.africaportal.org/features/labour-market-challenges-covid-19-pandemic-sub-saharan-africa/

Kassarjian, H. (1977). Content analysis in consumer research. *The Journal of Consumer Research, 4*(3), 19–27.

Kazekami, S. (2019). Mechanisms to improve labor productivity by performing telework. *Telecommunications Policy, 101868.* Advance online publication. doi:10.1016/j.telpol.2019.101868

Kesar, S., Abraham, R., Lahoti, R., Nath, P., & Basole, A. (2021). Pandemic, informality, and vulnerability: Impact of COVID-19 on livelihoods in India. *Canadian Journal of Development Studies. Canadian Journal of Development Studies, 42*(1-2), 145–164. doi:10.1080/02255189.2021.1890003

Khaled, A. B. (2019). Impact of Work-Life Balance, Happiness at Work, on Employee Performance. *International Business Research, 12*(2). doi:10.5539/ibr.v12n2p99

Khan, M. I. (n.d.). *COVID-19 lockdown: 50 Public Distribution System shops sealed in Bihar for illegal trade.* Available at: https://www.downtoearth.org.in/news/governance/covid-19-lockdown-50-PublicDistributionSystem-shops-sealed-in-bihar

Khan, M. A., Naqvi, H. A., Hakeem, M. M., Din, G. M., & Iqbal, N. (2022). Economic and financial impact of the COVID-19 pandemic in South Asia. *Environmental Science and Pollution Research International*, *29*(11), 15703–15712. doi:10.100711356-021-16894-9 PMID:34636009

Kharbikar, H. L., Radhika, C., Naitam, R. K., Daripa, A., Malav, L., & Raghuvanshi, M. S. (2020). Consequences of COVID-19 pandemic and lockdown on food and agribusiness sector in India. *Food and Scientific Reports, 1*(6), 13-18.

Khatri, J. R., & Upadhyaya-Dhungel, K. (2013). Internet Banking in Nepal: Use and Challenges. *Banking Journal*, *3*(2), 57–77. doi:10.3126/bj.v3i2.8544

Khemani, S. (2007). Does delegation of fiscal policy to an independent agency make a difference? Evidence from intergovernmental transfers in India. *Journal of Development Economics*, *82*(2), 464–484. doi:10.1016/j.jdeveco.2006.04.001

Kishore, A., & Chakrabarti, S. (2015). Is more inclusive more effective? The 'New Style' Public Distribution System in India. *Food Policy*, *55*, 117–130. doi:10.1016/j.foodpol.2015.06.006

Kissinger, H. A. (2020). The Corona Virus Pandemic will forever alter the World Order. *The Wall Street Journal*. https://www.wsj.com/articles/the-coronavirus-pandemic-will-forever-alter-the-world-order-11585953005

Kolbe, R. H., & Burnett, M. S. (1991). Content analysis research: An examination of applications for improving research reliability. *The Journal of Consumer Research*, *18*(3), 243–264. doi:10.1086/209256

Kolodko, G. W. (2020a). After the Calamity: Economics and Politics in the Post-Pandemic World. *Sociological Review*, *2*(210), 20. https://www.pte.pl/pliki/2/36/Kolodko.pdf

Kracauer, S. (1952). The challenge of qualitative content analysis. *Public Opinion Quarterly*, *16*(Winter), 631–642. doi:10.1086/266427

Kristensen, P. M. (2017). After Abdication: America Debates the Future of Global Leadership. *Chin. Polit. Sci. Rev*, *2*(4), 550–566. doi:10.100741111-017-0078-7

Kumar, D. N. S. (2020). *Impact of Covid-19 on Higher Education*. Higher Education Digest. https://www.highereducationdigest.com/impact-of-covid-19-on-higher-education/

Kumar, A. (2020). Impact of COVID-19 and What Needs to Be Done. *Economic and Political Weekly*, *LV*(14), 10–12.

Kumar, A., Padhee, A. K., & Kumar, S. (2020). How Indian agriculture should change after COVID-19. *Food Security*, *12*(4), 837–840. doi:10.100712571-020-01063-6 PMID:32837635

Kumar, S., Maheshwari, P, Prasanna, P., Suganya, J., Malar, B. A., & Jothikumar, R. (2020). Social economic impact of COVID-19 outbreak in India. *International Journal of Pervasive Computing and Communications*, *16*(4), 309–319. doi:10.1108/IJPCC-06-2020-0053

Kurmann, A., Lalé, E., & Ta, L. (2020). *The impact of COVID-19 on U.S. Employment and Hours: Real-Time Estimates with Homebase Data*. Available from https://www.lebow.drexel.edu/sites/default/files/1588687497-hbdraft0504.pdf

Kutu, S., Devkota, N., Upretee, S., Paudel, U. R., & Dhakal, K. (2023). Commercial Bank Readiness for Adoption of Marketing 4.0: Evidence From Nepal. In Marketing and Advertising in the Online-to-Offline (O2O) World (pp. 247-266). IGI Global.

Laborde, D., Martin, W., Swinnen, J., & Vos, R. (2020). COVID-19 risks to global food security. *Science*, *369*(6503), 500–502. doi:10.1126cience.abc4765 PMID:32732407

Lahiri, A. K. (2000). Budget Deficits and Reforms. *Economic and Political Weekly, 35*(46), 4048-4054.

Lai, V. S., & Li, H. (2005). *Technology acceptance model for internet banking : An invariance analysis.* doi:10.1016/j.im.2004.01.007

Larson, B. Z. (2019). It Time to Let Employees Work from Anywhere? *Harvard Business Review*. Retrieved at https://hbr.org/2019/08/is-it-time-to-let-employees-work-from-anywhere

Larson, B. (2020). *Companies Can Help Employees Working Remotely During the Covid-19 Pandemic*. Northeastern University Boston.

Lauterbach, W. (1987). Psychological Impacts of Unemployment: Theory, Research Methodology, Assessment and Help. *Health Systems Research*, 23.

Lee, M. C. (2009). Factors influencing the adoption of internet banking: An integration of TAM and TPB with perceived risk and perceived benefit. *Electronic Commerce Research and Applications*, *8*(3), 130–141. doi:10.1016/j.elerap.2008.11.006

Leitão, J., Pereira, D., & Gonçalves, Â. (2019). Quality of Work Life and Organizational Performance: Workers' Feelings of Contributing, or Not, to the Organization's Productivity. *International Journal of Environmental Research and Public Health*, *16*(20), 3803. doi:10.3390/ijerph16203803 PMID:31658595

Lewis, W. A. (1954). Economic Development with Unlimited Supplies of Labor. *Manchester School*, *22*(2), 139–191. doi:10.1111/j.1467-9957.1954.tb00021.x

Libel, M., & Roy, T. (2004). Handmade in India: Traditional Craft Skills in a Changing World. In J. M. Finger & P. Schuler (Eds.), *Poor People's Knowledge: Promoting Intellectual Property in Developing Countries*. World Bank.

Listings of WHO's response to COVID-19. (n.d.). Retrieved November 28, 2020, from https://www.who.int/news/item/29-06-2020-covidtimeline

Liu, W., Li, J., Ren, L., Xu, J., Li, C., & Li, S. (2020). Exploring Livelihood Resilience and its Impact on Livelihood Strategy in Rural China. *Social Indicators Research*, *150*(3), 977–998. doi:10.100711205-020-02347-2

Lokshin, M., Bontch-Osmolovski, M., & Glinskaya, E. (2010). Work Related Migration and Poverty Reduction in Nepal. *Review of Development Economics*, *14*(2), 323–332. doi:10.1111/j.1467-9361.2010.00555.x

Lrfan Bashir, C. M. (2015). *Trust, Social Influence, Self-Efficacy, Perceived Risk and Internet Banking Acceptance: An Extension of Technology Acceptance Model in Indian Context*. Academic Press.

Lu-Hai, L. (2020). *How Covid-19 led to a nationwide work-from-home experiment.* Retrieved at https://www.bbc.com/worklife/article/20200309-coronavirus-covid-19-advice-chinas-work-at-home-experiment

Lukovic, V. (2021). *Online Banking and Information Technology During the Covid-19 Pandemic: Between the Need and the Ability*. Academic Press.

Machado, L. S. (2019). Parent in science: The impact of parenthood on the scientific career in Brazil. In *2019 IEEE/ACM 2nd international workshop on gender equality in software engineering (GE)* (pp. 37–40). IEEE

Mahajan, K., & Tomar, S. (2020). COVID-19 and Supply Chain Disruption: Evidence from Food Markets in India. *American Journal of Agricultural Economics*. PMID:33230345

Mahamallik, M., & Sahu, P. (2015). Paradox of Fiscal Imbalances: Recommendations of Fourteenth Finance Commission. *Artha Vijnana*, *57*(4), 301–320. doi:10.21648/arthavij/2015/v57/i4/111493

Mahapatra, A. Sharma, P (2020). Education in times of COVID-19 pandemic: Academic stress and its psychosocial impact on children and adolescents in India. *International Journal of Social Psychiatry, 67*(4), 397–399. doi:10.1177/0020764020961801

Maharjan, P., Devkota, N., Mahapatra, S., Padda, I. U. H., Dhakal, K., & Mahato, S., ... Bhattarai, U. (2022, Summer). FinTech Adoption among Online Grocery Buyers during COVID-19 Lockdowns in Nepal. *Journal of Private Enterprise*, *37*, 57–89.

Mahbob, M., & Wan Sulaiman, W. (2015). Kepentingan Kecerdasan Emosi dalam Komunikasi Keorganisasian dan Pengaruhnya Terhadap Kepuasan Kerja [The Importance of Emotional Intelligence in Organizational Communication and Its Influence on Job Satisfaction]. *Journal of Communication*, *31*(2), 533–546. doi:10.17576/JKMJC-2015-3102-30

Mahler, J. (2012). The Telework Divide: Managerial and Personnel Challenges of Telework. *Review of Public Personnel Administration*, *32*(4), 407–418. doi:10.1177/0734371X12458127

Mamidipudi, A., Syamasundari, B., & Bijker, W. (2012, June). Mobilising Discourses: Handloom as Sustainable Socio-Technology. *Economic and Political Weekly*, *XLVII*(25), 23, 41–51.

Mandle & Sahu. (2021). Fiscal Compression, Jeopardised Recovery, the Humanitarian Crisis and Reforms. *Economic and Political Weekly*, *56*(21), 39-46.

Mann, C. L. (2020). Real and financial lenses to assess the economic consequences of COVID-19. In R. Baldwin & B. Weder di Mauro (Eds.), *Economics in the Time of COVID-19*. Centre for Economic Policy Research Press.

Manzoor, A. (2020). *Online Teaching and Challenges of COVID-19 for Inclusion of PWD in Higher Education*. https://dailytimes.com.pk/595888/online-teaching-and-challenges-of-covid-19-for-inclusion-of-pwds-in-highereducation/

Maqbool, A. (2018). Review of the technology acceptance model (TAM) in internet banking and mobile banking. *International Journal of Information Communication Technology and Digital Convergence*, *3*(1), 23–41.

Maruyama, T., & Tietze, S. (2012). From Anxiety to Assurance: Concerns and Outcomes of Telework. *Personnel Review*, *41*(4), 450–469. doi:10.1108/00483481211229375

Mas-Machuca, M., Berbegal-Mirabent, J., & Alegre, I. (2016). Work-life balance and its relationship with organizational pride and job satisfaction. *Journal of Managerial Psychology*, *31*(2), 586–602. doi:10.1108/JMP-09-2014-0272

Mastran, S. (2021). Opportunities and Challenges of Online Banking in Nepal. *The Batuk*, *7*(2), 37–51. doi:10.3126/batuk.v7i2.39498

Matsuo, M., Minami, C., & Matsuyama, T. (2018). Social influence on innovation resistance in internet banking services. *Journal of Retailing and Consumer Services*, *45*(August), 42–51. doi:10.1016/j.jretconser.2018.08.005

Mazmanian, M. (2013). *Avoiding the Trap of Constant Connectivity: When Congruent Frames Allow for Heterogeneous* Practices. *Academy of Management Journal*, *56*(5), 1225–1250. doi:10.5465/amj.2010.0787

McFadden, D. (1973). Conditional Logit Analysis of Qualitative Choice Behaviour in Zarembka. P. (Ed.) Frontiers in Econometrics. Academic Press.

McKibbin, W., & Fernando, R. (2020). The economic impact of COVID-19. In R. Baldwin & B. Weder di Mauro (Eds.), *Economics in the Time of COVID-19*. Centre for Economic Policy Research Press.

McLean, G., Osei-Frimpong, K., Al-Nabhani, K., & Marriott, H. (2020). Examining consumer attitudes towards retailers' m-commerce mobile applications–An initial adoption vs. continuous use perspective. *Journal of Business Research*, *106*, 139–157. doi:10.1016/j.jbusres.2019.08.032

Medscape. (2021, June 25). *What is COVID-19?* Retrieved June 12, 2021, from Medscape Website: https://www.medscape.com/answers/2500114-197401/what-is-covid-19

Meltzer, M. I., Cox, N. J., & Fukuda, K. (1999, September-October). The Economic Impact of Pandemic Influenza in the United States: Priorities for Intervention. *Emerging Infectious Diseases*, *V*(5), 659–671. doi:10.3201/eid0505.990507 PMID:10511522

Mendola, M. (2012). Rural Out-migration and Economic Development at Origin: A Review of the Evidence. *Journal of International Development*, *24*(1), 102–122. doi:10.1002/jid.1684

Mheidly, N. and Fares, J. (2020). Leveraging media and health communication strategies to overcome the COVID-19 infodemic. *Journal of Public Health Policy*. DoIhttps://doi.org/ doi:10.1057/s41271-020-00247-w

MHRD Notice. (2020). *COVID-19 Stay Safe: Digital Initiatives*. https://www.mohfw.gov.in/pdf/Covid19.pdf

Mincer, J. (1978). Family Migration Decision. *Journal of Political Economy*, *86*(5), 749–743. doi:10.1086/260710

Mines, M. (1984). *The Warrior Merchants: Textiles, Trade and Territory in South India*. Cambridge University Press.

Ministry of Finance. (2013). *Report of the Committee for Evolving a Composite Development Index of States*. Working Papers id:6728, e Social Sciences. https://finmin.nic.in/sites/default/files/Report_CompDevState.pdf

Ministry of Human Resource Development. (2019). *All India Survey of Higher Education 2018-19*. Department of Higher Education, Government of India. http://aishe.nic.in/aishe/viewDocument.action?documentId=262

Ministry of Human Resource Development. Department of Women and Development. (n.d.). *Annual Report 2019-2020*. Government of India Press.

Ministry of Textiles (2017). *Comprehensive Handloom Cluster Development Schemes (CHCDS) – Mega Handloom Cluster*. Development Commissioner.

Ministry of Textiles. (2016). *Annual Report 2015-16*. Government of India.

Min, S., Zhang, X., & Li, G. (2020). A snapshot of food supply chain in Wuhan under the COVID-19 pandemic. *China Agricultural Economic Review*, *12*(4), 689–704. doi:10.1108/CAER-04-2020-0056

Mishra, A. K., Rath, B. N., & Dash, A. K. (2020). *Does Indian Financial Market Nosedive by COVID-19 Outbreak in Comparison to Post-Implementation of Demonetisation and GST?* Asia Pacific Applied Economics Association Working Paper Series, WP/AP/2020-01.

Mishra, K. (2020). *Covid-19: 4 negative impacts and 4 opportunities created for education*. https://www.indiatoday.in/education-today/featurephilia/story/covid-19-4-negative-impacts-and-4-opportunities-created-for-education-1677206-2020-05-12

Mishra, K., & Rampal, J. (2020). The COVID-19 pandemic and food insecurity: A viewpoint on India. *World Development*, *135*, 105068. doi:10.1016/j.worlddev.2020.105068

Mishra, S., & Mishra, S. (2013). Impact of E-Education on School Going Children. *International Journal of Humanities and Social Science Invention.*, *2*(7), 58–61.

Mohammed, A. H., & Ward, T. (2006). The effect of automated service quality on Australian banks' financial performance and the mediating role of customer satisfaction. *Marketing Intelligence & Planning*, *24*(2), 127–147. doi:10.1108/02634500610653991

Mohanty, B.C. (2003). Ikat Fabrics of Odisha and Andhra Pradesh. *Indian Culture.*

Mohapatra, N. (2014). A Management Approach to Sambalpuri Sari with a Sign of Cultural Facets. *Odisha Review, Bhubaneswar.*, (February - March), 130–135.

Moher, D., Liberati, A., Tetzlaff, J., & Altman, D. G.Prisma Group. (2009). Reprint—preferred reporting items for systematic reviews and meta-analyses: The PRISMA statement. *Physical Therapy*, *89*(9), 873–880. doi:10.1093/ptj/89.9.873 PMID:19723669

Mols, N. P. (1999). The Internet and the banks' strategic distribution channel decisions. *International Journal of Bank Marketing*, *17*(6), 295–300. doi:10.1108/02652329910300341

Monica, T., & Edwards-Levy, A. (2020). *Many Workers Would Prefer to Keep Working from Home at Least Some of the Time-Most People Working from Home Due to The Coronavirus Wouldn't Be Disappointed If the Change Were Permanent, A New HuffPost/YouGov Survey Finds.* You Gov & Huffing Post. Retrieved at https://www.huffpost.com/entry/work-from-home-permanent-survey_l_5ecd34d6c5b67f9b9befbc86

Mor, N. (2020). *Resources for NGOs During the COVID-19 Epidemic.* Available at: https://www.researchgate.net/publication/340246895_Resources_for_NGOs_During_the_COVID-19_Epidemic

Moslehpour, M., Pham, V. K., Wong, W. K., & Bilgiçli, I. (2018). e-purchase intention of Taiwanese consumers: Sustainable mediation of perceived usefulness and perceived ease of use. *Sustainability (Basel)*, *10*(1), 234. Advance online publication. doi:10.3390u10010234

Motkuri, V. (2020). COVID19 Cases and Testing: A Cross Country Analysis. Nabakrishna Chaudhary Center for Development Studies, Bhubaneswar.

Mukherjee, S., & Badola, S. (2021). *Public Finance Management in India in the Time of COVID-19 Pandemic.* Working Paper, No. 337. National Institute of Public Finance and Policy.

Mutahar, A. M., Daud, N. M., Thurasamy, R., Isaac, O., & Abdulsalam, R. (2018). The Mediating of Perceived Usefulness and Perceived Ease of Use. *International Journal of Technology Diffusion*, *9*(2), 21–40. doi:10.4018/IJTD.2018040102

Mwai, C. (2020). *COVID-19: How recovery funding will be disbursed.* Available from https://www.newtimes.co.rw/news/covid-19-recovery-funding-disbursed

Naeem, M., & Ozuem, W. (2021). The role of social media in internet banking transition during COVID-19 pandemic: Using multiple methods and sources in qualitative research. *Journal of Retailing and Consumer Services, 60*(October), 102483. doi:10.1016/j.jretconser.2021.102483

Naing, N. N. (2003). Determination of sample size. *The Malaysian Journal of Medical Sciences : MJMS*, *10*(2), 84–86. PMID:23386802

Naja, F., & Hamadeh, R. (2020). Nutrition amid the COVID-19 pandemic: A multi-level framework for action. *European Journal of Clinical Nutrition*, *74*(8), 1–5. doi:10.103841430-020-0634-3 PMID:32313188

Namahoot, K. S., & Laohavichien, T. (2018). Assessing the intentions to use internet banking: The role of perceived risk and trust as mediating factors. *International Journal of Bank Marketing*, *36*(2), 256–276. doi:10.1108/IJBM-11-2016-0159

Nanda, P. K., & Khanna, P. (2020). *Every House a School, Every Parent a Teacher as Covid-19 Impacts Education of 300mn Students.* https://www.livemint.com/news/india/every-house-a-school-every-parent-a-teacher-as-covid-19-impacts-education-11585140662556.html

Narasaiah, M. L., & Krishna, C. H. T. (1999). *Crisis of Handloom Industry.* Discovery Publishing House.

Narayan, D., Patel, R., Schafft, K., Rademacher, A. and Koch-Schulte, S. (2000). *Voices of the Poor: Can Anyone Hear us?* World Bank.

National Planning Commission, University of Namibia. (2020). *Estimating the Economic Impact of COVID-19: A case study of Namibia.* Windhoek: University of Namibia.

Nepal Rastra Bank. (2021). Financial Access in Nepal. Academic Press.

Nguyen, O. T. (2020). Factors affecting the intention to use digital banking in Vietnam. *Journal of Asian Finance. Economics and Business*, *7*(3), 303–310. doi:10.13106/jafeb.2020.vol7.no3.303

Nguyen, P. H., Kachwaha, S., Pant, A., Tran, L. M., Ghosh, S., Sharma, P. K., & Menon, P. (2021). Impact of COVID-19 on household food insecurity and interlinkages with child feeding practices and coping strategies in Uttar Pradesh, India: A longitudinal community-based study. *BMJ Open*, *11*(4), e048738. doi:10.1136/bmjopen-2021-048738 PMID:33883156

Nicola, M., Alsafi, Z., Sohrabi, C., Kerwan, A., Al-Jabir, A., Iosifidis, C., Agha, M., & Agha, R. (2020). The Socio-economic Impact of Coronavirus Pandemic (COVID-19):A Review. *International Journal of Surgery*, *78*, 185–193. doi:10.1016/j.ijsu.2020.04.018 PMID:32305533

Niehof, A., & Price, L. L. (2001). *Rural Livelihood Systems: A Conceptual Framework, Wageningen – UPWARD Series on Rural Livelihood No. 1*. WU-UPWARD.

Nilles, J. M. (1998). *Managing Telework: Strategies for Managing the Virtual Workforce*. John Wiley & Sons.

Nilles, J. M., Carlson, F. R., Gray, P., & Hanneman, G. (1976). *The Telecommunications— Transportation Tradeoff, Options for Tomorrow*. John Wiley & Sons.

Niranjana, S., & Vinayan, S. (2001). *Growth Prospects of the Handloom Industry*. Planning Commission, Government of India.

NRB. (2020). *Payment System Oversight report*. NRB.

NSIR. (2020). *Labor Force Survey Trends-February 2020(Q1)*. https://www.statistics.gov.rw/publication/labour-force-survey-trends-february-2020q1

Oates, W. E. (1972). The Fiscal Federalism, Harcourt Brace Jovanovich Inc.

Oberoi, S., & Kansra, P. (2019). Factors influencing medical tourism in India: A critical review. *SAMVAD*, *17*, 9–16.

Oberoi, S., & Kansra, P. (2020). Economic menace of diabetes in India: A systematic review. *International Journal of Diabetes in Developing Countries*, *40*(4), 1–12. doi:10.100713410-020-00838-z PMID:32837090

Odisha, G. o. (2020). *Covid-19: Impact on Agriculture & Allied Sectors in Odisha (Odisha Economic Survey 2019-20)*. Government of Odisha.

OECD. (2020, September). *OECD Policy Responses to Coronavirus (COVID-19)*. Retrieved October 15, 2020, from https://www.oecd.org/coronavirus/policy-responses/what-have-platforms-done-to-protect-workers-during-the-coronavirus-covid-19-crisis-9d1c7aa2/#section-d1e187

O'Guinn, Thomas, Allen, Chris Semenik, Richard J. (2003). *Advertising and Integrated Brand Promotion*, 3e. South-Western College Publishing.

Olivero, J., Real, R., & FA, J. E. (n.d.). *Recent loss of closed forests is associated with ebola virus disease outbreaks*. Scientific reports. https://pubmed.ncbi.nlm.nih.gov/29085050/

Oneyma. (2020). Impact of Coronavirus Pandemic on Education. *Journal of Education and Practice*, *11*(13), 108–121. https://genbase.iiep.unesco.org/workspace/applis/epidoc/fichiers/EPIDOC/38698_52821_56584_1_PB.pdf

OPEPA. (2017). *Status of Elementary Education & Secondary Education in Odisha 2017-18*. Dept. of School and Mass Education, Government of Odisha. http://osepa.odisha.gov.in/webadmin/pdf_link/udise%20booklet%20 2017_11_29_24am8046c2c2aa57e4cc68d42dc129f0b444.pdf

Organization, W. T. (2020). *COVID-19 and agriculture: A story of resilience*. Geneva: World Trade Organization. Retrieved from https://www.wto.org/

OrgI. F. P. R. I. (2020). https://www.ifpri.org/blog/how-indias-food-based-safety-net-responding-covid-19-lockdown

Orissa Economic Association. (2020). *Covid-19 and the economy of Odisha-Challenges and the way forward*. OEA. http://www.orissaea.in/COVID-19/COVID_19%20and_The%20Economy_of_Odisha_OEA.pdfon 26/09/2020

ParasharB. K. (2018). https://www.hindustantimes.com/lucknow/uttar-pradesh-among-states-with-lowest-quality-of-life-says-study/story-goJLFpONnWKCr2YwZuz3CJ.html

Paripurna, D., & Gede, I. (2013). Pengaruh Kepemimpinan, Lingkungan Kerja dan Komunikasi terhadap Kepuasan Kerja Karyawan. *E-Jurnal Manajemen-Universitas Udayana*, *2*(5), 58–67.

Parvin, M. T. (2020). Factors Determining the Credit Accessibility by the Small-Scale Entrepreneurs: A Case of Handloom Weaving in Bangladesh. *International Journal of Business and Management*, *15*(8), 93–100. doi:10.5539/ijbm.v15n8p93

Patel, K. J., & Patel, H. J. (2018). Adoption of internet banking services in Gujarat. *International Journal of Bank Marketing*, *36*(1), 147–169. doi:10.1108/IJBM-08-2016-0104

Pathak, A. (2019). Work Life Balance & Job Satisfaction: A Literature Review. *International Journal of Computer Sciences and Engineering*. Retrieved at https://www.researchgate.net/publication/332112828_Work_Life_Balance_Job_Satisfaction_A_Literature_Review

Pathak, P., Gope, T., & Bader, N. (2020). Effect of COVID-19 on Public Distribution System in India. *International Journal of Community Medicine and Public Health*, *7*(6), 2411. doi:10.18203/2394-6040.ijcmph20202508

Paweenawat, S. W. (2021). *The Impact of COVID-19 on the labour markets in Thailand*. ERIA Discussion Paper Series, No.378. Bangkok: University of the Thai Chamber of Commerce, Thailand.

Pegram, T. (2020). Coronavirus is a failure of global governance – now the world needs a radical transformation. *Conversation*.

People's Health Movement. (2022). *Hunger Watch Press Handouts*. https://phmovement.org/wp-content/uploads/2022/09/Feb-23-Hunger-Watch-Press-Handouts-1.pdf

Pérez-Escamilla, R., Cunningham, K., & Moran, V. H. (2020). *COVID-19 and maternal and child food and nutrition insecurity: a complex syndemic*. Academic Press.

Pirbasti, M. F., Bashar, H. P., Ramezani, A., Moradi, M., & Tabatabai, S. (2014). The relationship between job satisfaction and organizational commitment. *Advances in Environmental Biology*, *8*(10), 318–323.

Piszczek, M. M. (2016). Boundary control and controlled boundaries: Organizational expectations for technology use at the work-family interface. *Journal of Organizational Behavior*, *38*(4), 592–611. doi:10.1002/job.2153

Planning Commission. (2002). *Orissa Development Report*. Government of India.

Planning Commission. (2008). Inclusive Growth; Eleventh Five Year Plan 2007-2012. Oxford University Press.

Pneumonia of unknown cause – China. (2020, January 30). Retrieved November 28, 2020, from https://www.who.int/csr/don/05-january-2020-pneumonia-of-unkown-cause-china/en/

Post, O. (2018). National handloom day observed in the city. *Orissa Post*. https://www.orissapost.com/national-handloom-day-observed-in-city/

Pradhan, A. (2014). Sambalpuri Handloom fails to find place in Poll Plans. *The Times of India*.

Pradhan, S., & Khandual, A. (2020). Community, Local Practices and Cultural Sustainability: A Case Study of Sambalpuri Ikat Handloom. In S. S. Muthu & M. A. Gadetti (Eds.), *Sustainability in the Textile and Apparel Industries: Consumerism and Fashion Sustainability* (pp. 121–139). Springer Nature Switzerland A.G. doi:10.1007/978-3-030-38532-3_7

Prassl, Boniva, Golin, & Rauh. (2020). *Inequality in the Impact of the Coronavirus Shock: Evidence from Real Time Surveys*. IZA institute of Labour Economics.

Pratheeesh, J. T., & Arumugasamy, G. (2020). Impact of Coronavirus in Indian economy and banking sector-an overview. *Studies in Indian Place Names*, *40*(18), 2090–2101.

PRS Legislative Research. (2020). *Economic Survey 2019-20*. New Delhi: PRS Legislative Research. Retrieved from https://www.prsindia.org/sites/default/files/parliament_or_policy_pdfs/Economic%20Survey%202019-20%20Summary.pdf

Pyöriä, P. (2011). Managing Telework: Risks, Fears and Rules. *Management Research Review*, *34*(4), 386–399. doi:10.1108/01409171111117843

Qiu, W., Rutherford, S., Mao, A., & Chu, C. (2017). The pandemic and its impacts. *Health, Culture and Society (Pittsburgh, Pa.)*, *9*, 1–11. doi:10.5195/HCS.2017.221

Rado. (2021). The Impact of the COVID-19 Pandemic on the Quality of Educational Process: A Student Survey. *International Journal of Environmental Research and Public Health*, *18*(11), 6177. https://www.mdpi.com/867768 PMID:34200515

Rahi, S., & Ngah, A. H. (2018). *A structural equation model for evaluating user's intention to adopt internet banking and intention to recommend technology*. https://doi.org/ doi:10.5267/j.ac.2018.03.002

Rahi, S., & Abd. Ghani, M. (2018). The role of UTAUT, DOI, perceived technology security and game elements in internet banking adoption. *World Journal of Science. Technology and Sustainable Development*, *15*(4), 338–356. doi:10.1108/WJSTSD-05-2018-0040

Rai, R. K., Kumar, S., Sekher, M., Pritchard, B., & Rammohan, A. (2015). A Life-Cycle Approach to Food and Nutrition Security in India. *Public Health Nutrition*, *18*(5), 944–949. doi:10.1017/S1368980014001037 PMID:24866692

Rajaraman & Majumdar. (2005). Equity and Consistency Properties of Twelfth Finance Commission Recommendations. *Economic and Political Weekly, 40*(31), 3413-3420.

Ramdoo, I. (2020, June). *IGF.* Retrieved September 15, 2020, from https://www.igfmining.org/: https://www.iisd.org/system/files/publications/covid-19-employment-mining-key-points-en.pdf

Ranganath, V. G. (2015). Food Security: Issues and Concerns. *IUP Law Review*, *5*(4), 7–13.

Rangarajan & Srivastava. (2004a). Fiscal Transfers in Australia: Review and Relevance to India. *Economic and Political Weekly, 40*(27), 3709-3722.

Rangarajan & Srivastava. (2004b). Fiscal Transfers in Canada: Drawing Comparisons and Lessons. *Economic and Political Weekly, 39*(19), 1897-1909.

Rangarajan & Srivastava. (2005). Fiscal Deficit and Government Debt: Implications for Growth and Stabilization. *Economic and Political Weekly, 40*(27), 2919-2934.

Rao, M. G. (2002). State Finances in India: Issues and Challenges. *Economic and Political Weekly, 37*(31), 3261-3271.

Rao, M. G. (2004). Linking Central Transfers to Fiscal Performance of States. *Economic and Political Weekly, 39*(18), 1820-1825.

Rao, M. G. (2020). The Key Strategy is Fiscal Empowerment of States. *The Hindu.*

Rao, P. S. (2012). *Connecting the Dots: A Design Approach to Services for the Poor.* [Doctoral Thesis, Northumbria University].

Rao, M. G., & Sen Tapas, K. (1996). *Fiscal Federalism in Theory and Practice in India.* Indian Council of Social Science Research.

Rawal, V., Kumar, M., Verma, A., & Pais, J. (2020). COVID-19 Lockdown: Impact on Agriculture and Rural Economy. New Delhi: Society for Social and Economic Research. doi:978-81-937148-7-4

Ray, A. (2020, May 22). *India's GDP growth in 2020-21 to remain in negative territory: RBI.* https://www.livemint.com/industry/banking/india-s-gdp-growth-in-2020-21-to-remain-in-negative-category-rbi-11590122207688.html

Ray, P., Acharya, K. K., & Thakur, A. (2020). COVID-19 Impact and implication to Agriculture and Food security. *Food and Scientific Reports, 1*(7).

Ray, Subramanian, & Vandewalle. (2020). India's Lockdown. Policy Insight, No. 102. Centre for Economic Policy Research.

Reardon, T., Mishra, A., Nuthalapati, C. S., Bellemare, M. F., & Zilberman, D. (2020). Covid-19's disruption of India's transformed food supply chains. *Economic and Political Weekly*, *55*(18), 18–22.

Reddy, S. (2020). A roadmap to tackle Covid-19. *The Hindu.*

Rele, S. (2020). Emerging outbreaks and epidemic threats: The practicality and limitations in the development and manufacturing of treatments for Coronavirus (COVID-19). *Polymorphism*, *4*, 45–52.

Renard, T. (2009). The Coming Order: Strategic and Geopolitical Impacts of the Economic Crisis. *World Politics Review.*

Report, S. A. (2020). *Tourism sector recovery plan COVID-19 Response.* https://www.tralac.org/documents/resources/covid-19/countries/3992-south-africa-tourism-sector-recovery-plan-covid-19-response-august-2020-request-for-comments/file.html

Riadi, M. (2019). *Produktivitas Kerja - Pengertian, Aspek dan Pengukuran.* Retrieved at https://www.kajianpustaka.com/2019/11/produktivitas-kerja-pengertian-aspek-pengukuran-dan-faktor-yang-mempengaruhi.html

Roberts, M., & Pettigrew, S. (2007). A thematic content analysis of children's food advertising. *International Journal of Advertising*, *26*(3), 357–367. doi:10.1080/02650487.2007.11073018

Robinson, R. V., David, E. J. R., & Hill, M. (2016). Participatory Mixed Methods Research Across Cultures. In L. J. Jason & D. S. Glenwick (Eds.), *Handbook of Methodological Approaches to Community based Research* (pp. 273–282). Oxford University Press.

Rogaly, B., & Rafique, A. (2003). Struggling to Save Cash: Seasonal Migration and Vulnerability in West Bengal, India. *Development and Change*, *34*(4), 659–681. doi:10.1111/1467-7660.00323

Rout, S. K. (2020). How Odisha is managing COVID-19 in framework of Universal Health Coverage. News Click. https://www.newsclick.in/Odisha-Managing-COVID-19-Framework-Universal-Health-Coverage on 28/11/2020

Roy, T. (1988). Size and Structure of Handloom Weaving in the Mid-Thirties. *The Indian Economic and Social History Review*, *25*(1), 1–24. doi:10.1177/001946468802500101

Roy, T. (2005). *Rethinking Economic Change in India: Labour and Livelihood.* Routledge. doi:10.4324/9780203023105

Rupietta, K., & Beckmann, M. (2017). Working from Home – What is the Effect on Employees' Effort? *Schmalenbach Business Review*, *70*(1), 25–55. doi:10.100741464-017-0043-x

Sahoo, J., & Samal, K. (2020, July 26). Impact of COVID-19 on Indian Agriculture. *Agriculture Letters, 1*(3), 45-46. Retrieved from https://agletters.in/

Sahoo, Pravakar, & Ashwani. (2020). *Covid 19 and The Indian Economy: Impact on Growth, Manufacturing, Trade and MSME sector.* IEG Working Paper, 390.

Sahoo, P., & Ashwani. (2020). COVID-19 and Indian economy: Impact on growth, manufacturing, trade and MSME sector. *Global Business Review*, *21*(5), 1159–1183. doi:10.1177/0972150920945687

Sahu, D. (2020). Silence of the Looms: Sambalpuri Ikat Sarees Lie in Large Pile Amidst Empty Sacks of Yarn. *The New Indian Express.*

Sahu, I. (2017). Sambalpuri Textile Weaving Process. *Sahapedia.* https://www.sahapedia.org/the-sambalburi-textile-weaving-process

Sahu, P., & Mahamallik, M. (2019, December). Centre-State Relation in India: Issue of Cooperative Federalism. *Madhya Pradesh Journal of Social Sciences*, *24*(2), 94–106.

Sahu, P., & Mahamallik, M. (2020, December). The Rhetoric of Fiscal Performance: A Study of Odisha, India. *Artha Vijnana*, *62*(4), 336–355.

Sain & Saha. (2020). E-class, an alternative of classroom teaching. *International Journal of Creative Research Thoughts, 8*(5), 2902-2910. https://www.ijcrt.org/papers/IJCRT2005381.pdf

Salleh, F. H. M. (2020). BE-1201 MACROECONOMICS:PRINCIPLES AND ISSUES: The contrast in economic impacts during SARS and COVID-19 pandemic. doi:10.13140/RG.2.2.31037.00480

Sandell Steven, H. (1977). Women and the Economics of Family Migration. *The Review of Economics and Statistics*, *59*(4), 406–414. doi:10.2307/1928705

Sandhu, S., & Arora, S. (2020). Customers' usage behaviour of e-banking services: Interplay of electronic banking and traditional banking. *International Journal of Finance and Economics,* 1–13. doi:10.1002/ijfe.2266

Sangita, S. (2017). *Poverty and Migration: Evidence of Distress Migration in India.* Paper prepared for IARIW-ICIER Conference, New Delhi, India.

Sanni, Y., Otu, A., & Labonté, R. (2020). Globalisation in the time of COVID-19: Repositioning Africa to meet the immediate and remote challenges. *Globalization and Health*, *16*(1), 51. doi:10.118612992-020-00581-4 PMID:32580728

Sanyal, R., & Economist, C. R. (2020, July). *COVID-19 Impact: Brazil's Labor Market Puzzle.* Retrieved September 20, 2020, from https://info.ceicdata.com/covid-19-brazils-labour-market-puzzle: https://info.ceicdata.com/covid-19-brazils-labour-market-puzzle

Saraswati, D. (2020). *Impact of COVID-19 on the Education Sector in Nepal: Challenges and Coping Strategies.* https://eric.ed.gov/?id=ED609894

Schilling, J. (2006). On the pragmatics of qualitative assessment: Designing the process for content analysis. *European Journal of Psychological Assessment*, *22*(1), 28–37. doi:10.1027/1015-5759.22.1.28

Scoones, I. (1998). *Sustainable Rural Livelihoods: A Framework for Analysis, Working Paper, No. 72*. University of Sussex, Brighton.

Scoones, I. (2009). Livelihoods Perspectives and Rural Development. *The Journal of Peasant Studies*, *36*(1), 171–196. doi:10.1080/03066150902820503

SeemaC. (2020). https://indianexpress.com/article/explained/howcoronavirus-lockdown-has-impacted-indian-farmer-stheir-yields-6421569/

Sen, A. (1988). The Concept of Development, in H. Chenery and T.N. Srinivasan, (Eds.) Handbook of Development Economics. Elsevier Science Publishers, I. 9-26.

Shah, A. (2006). The Labour of Love: Seasonal Migration from Jharkhand to the Brick Kilns of other States in India. *Contributions to Indian Sociology, New Series*, *40*(1), 91–118. doi:10.1177/006996670504000104

Shahid Iqbal, M., Ul Hassan, M., & Habibah, U. (2018). Impact of self-service technology (SST) service quality on customer loyalty and behavioral intention: The mediating role of customer satisfaction. *Cogent Business and Management*, *5*(1), 1. Advance online publication. doi:10.1080/23311975.2018.1423770

Shanti, K. (2005). *Gender Dimensions in Rural –Urban Migration in India: Policy Imperative*. Paper delivered at 25th population Conference, Tours, France.

Shirsath, P. B., Jat, M. L., McDonald, A. J., Srivastava, A. K., Craufurd, P., Rana, D. S., ... Jat, H. S. (2020). Agricultural labor, COVID-19, and potential implications for food security and air quality in the breadbasket of India. *Agricultural Systems*, *185*, 102954. doi:10.1016/j.agsy.2020.102954 PMID:32982021

Shmailan, A. (2015). The relationship between job satisfaction, job performance and employee engagement: An explorative study. *Issues in Business Management and Economics*, *4*(1), 1–8. doi:10.15739/IBME.16.001

Siagian, S. P. (2014). *Manajemen Sumber Daya Manusia*. Bumi Aksara.

Simon, K. (1955). Economic Growth and Income Inequality. *The American Economic Review*, (45), 1–28.

Singh, K. S., & Rosmann, M. (2020). Government of India Issues Three Ordinances Ushering in Major Agricultural Market Reforms. USDA.

Singh, P., & Khanna, P. (2011). Work-Life Balance a Tool for Increased Employee Productivity and Retention. *Lachoo Management Journal*.

Singhal, D., & Padhmanabhan, V. (2009). A Study on Customer Perception Towards Internet Banking: Identifying Major Contributing Factors. *Journal of Nepalese Business Studies*, *5*(1), 101–111. doi:10.3126/jnbs.v5i1.2088

Singh, D. R., Sunuwar, D. R., Adhikari, B., Szabo, S., & Padmadas, S. S. (2020). The perils of COVID-19 in Nepal: Implications for population health and nutritional status. *Journal of Global Health*, *10*(1), 010378. doi:10.7189/jogh.10.010378 PMID:32582440

Singh, R. (2018). The cause of unemployment in current market scenario. *Vivechan International Journal of Research*, *9*(1), 81–86.

Singh, S., Kumar, R., Panchal, R., & Tiwari, M. K. (2020). Impact of COVID-19 on logistics systems and disruptions in food supply chain. *International Journal of Production Research*, 1–16.

Sjaastad Larry, A. (1962). The Costs and Returns of Human Migration. *Journal of Political Economy*, *70*(5), 80–93. doi:10.1086/258726

Smith, S. A., Patmos, A., & Pitts, M. J. (2015). Communication and Teleworking: A Study of Communication Channel Satisfaction, Personality, and Job Satisfaction for Teleworking Employees. *International Journal of Business Communication*, *55*(1), 44–68. doi:10.1177/2329488415589101

Sogani, A. (2020, July). *The Great Lockdown vs The Great Depression and the 2008 Global Financial Crisis.* Retrieved September 11, 2021, from E-internationals Relations: https://www.e-ir.info/2020/07/02/the-great-lockdown-vs-the-great-depression-and-the-2008-global-financial-crisis/

Sood, R. (2020). The trends shaping the post-COVID-19 world. *The Hindu.*

Srinivasan, N., Tagat, V., & Sriniva, G. (2020). *Indian agriculture during and after the pandemic.* MSC.

Standard, B. (2020). Apollo Hospital plans 5000 isolation rooms, Covid-19 treatment on anvil. *Business Standard.* https://www.business-standard.com/article/current-affairs/apollo-hospitals-plans-5-000-isolation-rooms-covid-19-treatment-on-anvil-120032601351_1.html on 28/11/2020

Strielkowski, W. (2020). *COVID-19 Pandemic and the Digital Revolution in Academia and Higher Education.* https://www.researchgate.net/publication/340684703_COVID-19_Pandemic_and_the_Digital_Revolution_in_Academia_and_Higher_Education

Stückelberger, C. (2020). *Post-Corona World: Balancing International Cooperation ad National Sovereignty.* MGIMO University. https://repository.globethics.net/bitstream/handle/20.500.12424/3958494/St%C3%BCckelberger%20%20Post_Corona_Virus_National_Sovereignty.pdf?sequence=1&isAllowed=y

Sue Enfield Institute of Development Studies. (2021, February). *Covid-19 impact on employment and skills for the labor market.* Retrieved March 11, 2021, from google.com: https://opendocs.ids.ac.uk/

Sukhwani, V., Deshkar, S., & Shaw, R. (2020). Covid-19 lockdown, food systems and urban-rural partnership: Case of Nagpur, India. *International Journal of Environmental Research and Public Health, 17*(16), 5710. doi:10.3390/ijerph17165710 PMID:32784648

Sultan, S., & Sultan, W. I. M. (2020). Women MSMEs in times of crisis: Challenges and opportunities. *Journal of Small Business and Enterprise Development, 27*(7), 1069–1083. doi:10.1108/JSBED-06-2020-0226

Sumner, A. (2007). Meaning Versus Measurement: Why Do Economic Indicators of Poverty Still Predominate? *Development in Practice, 17*(1), 4–13. doi:10.1080/09614520601092485

Syamasundari, B., & Niranjana, S. (2006). Valuing the Non-Market. *Economic and Political Weekly, 41*(31), 3394–3398.

Tan, W., Rajkarnikar, N., Jeong, S. R., Shrestha, D., & Wenan, T. (2020). *Consumers attitude towards Internet banking services in an underdeveloped country: A case of Pokhara. Journal of Internet Services and Applications, 21*(5), 75–85

Tashanova, D., Sekerbay, A., Chen, D., Luo, Y., Zhao, S., & Zhang, Q. (2020). Investment opportunities and strategies in an era of Coronavirus pandemic. SSRN *Electronic Journal.* doi:10.2139/ssrn.3567445

The Asia Foundation. (2021). *A rapid assessment on the impact of the COVID-19 pandemic on employment in Middle-order cities of Nepal.* The Asian Foundation.

The Economics Times. (2020). Odisha trains 1.72 lakh health personnel to combat Covid-19 in state. *The Economic Times.* https://economictimes.indiatimes.com/news/politics-and-nation/odisha-trains-1-72-lakh-health-personnel-to-combat-covid-19-in-state/articleshow/75643447.cms on 28/11/2020

The Future of ESG Data. (n.d.). Retrieved November 28, 2020, from https://www.generationim.com/research-centre/insights/the-future-of-esg-data/

The Hindu. (2020). *Coronavirus | Odisha says cost of treatment will be borne by the State.* https://www.thehindu.com/news/national/other-states/coronavirus-odisha-says-cost-of-treatment-will-be-borne-by-the-state/article31211494.ece

The New Indian Express. (2020). In addition to COVID-19, hospital mismanagement stress for patients in Odisha. *The New Indian Times.* https://www.newindianexpress.com/states/odisha/2020/aug/04/in-addition-to-covid-19-hospital-mismanagement-stress-for-patients-in-odisha-2178869.html on 28/11/2020

The New Indian Express. (2020). *Rural Odisha: No state for online education.* https://www.newindianexpress.com/cities/bhubaneswar/2020/may/17/rural-odisha-no-state-for-online-education-2144400.html

The Paris Agreement. (n.d.). Retrieved November 28, 2020, from https://www.un.org/en/climatechange/paris-agreement

This paper does not represent US Government views. (n.d.). dni.gov. Retrieved November 28, 2020, from https://www.dni.gov/files/documents/climate2030_india.pdf

Today, I. (2020). *Odisha Govt to defer salaries of CM, ministers to counter economic impact of Covid-19.* https://www.indiatoday.in/india/story/odisha-govt-to-defer-salaries-of-cm-ministers-to-counter-economic-impact-of-covid-19-1661946-2020-04-01

Tripathi, A. (2020). *Positive Sides of Lockdown-Digital Inclusion.* https://timesofindia.indiatimes.com/blogs/agyeya/positive-sides-of-lockdown-digital-inclusion/

Tsai, M.-T., Chuang, S.-S., & Hsieh, W.-P. (2009). An integrated process model of communication satisfaction and organizational outcomes. *Social Behavior and Personality*, *37*(6), 825–834. doi:10.2224bp.2009.37.6.825

Udmale, P., Pal, I., Szabo, S., Pramanik, M., & Large, A. (2020). Global food security in the context of COVID-19: A scenario-based exploratory analysis. *Progress in Disaster Science*, *7*, 100120. doi:10.1016/j.pdisas.2020.100120 PMID:34173442

UN. (2020). Available at: https://www.un.org/en/un-coronavirus-communications-team/un-working-avert-dual-crises-covid-19-hits-hunger

UNDP. (2020a). *A UN framework for the immediate socio-economic response to COVID-19.* https://unsdg.un.org/sites/default/files/2020-04/UN-Framework-for-the-immediate-socio-economic-response-to-COVID-19.pdf

UNDP. (2020b). *A Strategic Framework for a immediate socio-economic response to Covid-19 in Yemen 2020-21.* https://www.arabstates.undp.org/content/rbas/en/home/library/crisis-response0/a-strategic-framework-for-and-immediate-socio-economic-response-.html

UNECA. (2020, April 9). *Tralac.* Retrieved October 15, 2020, from Tralac: https://www.tralac.org/docments/resources/COVID-19/3293-COVID-19-protecting-african-lives-andeconomies-uneca-april-2020/file.html

UNESCO. (2020). *Education: From disruption to recovery.* Retrieved from https://en.unesco.org/covid19/educationresponse

UNIDO (2008). IKAT Handloom Weaving Cluster, Special Issue on Rural Livelihood and Poverty Alleviation. *UNIDO South Asia, 2*(2).

UNIDO. (2013). *Lima Declaration: Towards inclusive and sustainable industrial Development.* Fifteenth session of the UNIDO General Conference, Lima, Peru.

UNSDG. (2020). https://reliefweb.int/report/world/policybrief-impact-covid-19-food-security-and-nutrition-june2020

Upadhyay, M. K., Patra, S., & Khan, A. M. (2020). Ensuring availability of food for child nutrition amidst the COVID—19 pandemic: Challenges and Way forward. *Indian Journal of Community Health*, *32*(2), 251–254. doi:10.47203/IJCH.2020.v32i02SUPP.015

Upadhyay, R. P., & Palanivel, C. (2011). Challenges in achieving food security in India. *Iranian Journal of Public Health*, *40*(4), 31–36. PMID:23113100

USDA. (2019). *Definitions of Food Security.* United States Department of Agriculture (USDA). Available: https://www.ers.usda.gov/topics/food-nutrition-assistance/foodsecurity-in-the-us/definitions-of-food-security.aspx

Viner. (2020). *School closure and management practices during coronavirus outbreaks including COVID-19: A rapid systematic review*. doi:10.1016/S2352-4642(20)30095-X

Viotti, S., Sottimano, I., Converso, D., & Guidetti, G. (2020). The relationship between psychosocial characteristics of the work environment and job satisfaction in an Italian public ECE service: A cross-lagged study. *Early Childhood Research Quarterly*, *53*, 464–475. doi:10.1016/j.ecresq.2020.06.002

von Grebmeret, K. (2022). *Global Hunger Index Food Systems Transformation And Local Governance.* Concern World-wide and Welthungerhilfe. https://www.globalhungerindex.org/pdf/en/2022.pdf

Wandschneider & Mishra. (2003). *The role of small rural towns in Bolangir District, India: A village-level perspective.* NRI Report No: 2750, DFID-World Bank.

Wani, A. (2020). Impact of COVID-19 Lockdown on Agriculture in India: A Review. *International Journal of Scientific Research*, *09*(06), 1727–1728. doi:10.21275/SR20627172107

WB. (2015). *An analysis of issues shaping Africa's economic future.* https://www.worldbank.org/content/dam/Worldbank/document/Africa/Report/Africas-Pulse-brochure_Vol12.pdf

WEF. (2020). *An overwhelming majority of people want real change after COVID-19.* Available from https://www.weforum.org/agenda/2020/09/sustainable-equitable-change-post-coronavirus-survey?utm_source=facebook&utm_medium=social_scheduler&utm_term=COVID-19&u

WFP. (2019). *2019—The state of food security and nutrition in the world (SOFI): Safeguarding against economic slow-downs and downturns.* https://www.wfp.org/publications/2019-state-food-security-and-nutrition-world-sofi-safeguarding-against-economic

What are the impacts of climate change? (n.d.). Retrieved November 28, 2020, from https://www.science.org.au/learning/general-audience/science-climate-change/7-what-are-impacts-of-climate-change

What is CITES? (n.d.). Retrieved November 28, 2020, from https://cites.org/eng/disc/what.php

WHO. (2020). *From governance to community resilience: Odisha's response to Covid-19.* WHO. https://www.who.int/india/news/feature-stories/detail/from-governance-to-community-resilience-odisha-s-response-to-covid-19 on 28/11/2020

WHO. (2020). *Weekly Operational Update on COVID.* Geneva: Health Emergencies Programme. Retrieved from https://www.who.int/emergencies/diseases/novel-coronavirus-2019

WHO. (2022). *Covid 19.* WHO. https://covid19.who.int/table on 04-06-2022 on 04/06/2022

William Lewis, R. A. (2003). Sources of influence on beliefs about information technology use: An empirical study of knowledge workers1 By. *Management Information Systems Quarterly*, *27*(4), 657–678. doi:10.2307/30036552

Wilson, N., Alvita, M., & Wibisono, J. (2021). the Effect of Perceived Ease of Use and Perceived Security Toward Satisfaction and Repurchase Intention. *Jurnal Muara Ilmu Ekonomi Dan Bisnis*, *5*(1), 145. doi:10.24912/jmieb.v5i1.10489

Winarso, W. (2018). Organizational communication; a conceptual framework. INA-Rxiv. Retrieved at doi:10.31227/osf.io/g9ubc

Workie, E., Mackolil, J., Nyika, J., & Ramadas, S. (2020). Deciphering the Impact of COVID-19 pandemic on food security, agriculture, and livelihoods: A review of the evidence from developing countries. *Current Research in Environmental Sustainability*, *2*, 100014. doi:10.1016/j.crsust.2020.100014 PMID:34977605

World Bank. (2020a). *GDP per capita (constant 2010 US$).* World Bank Group. https://data.worldbank.org/indicator/NY.GDP.PCAP.KD

World Bank. (2020b). *Unemployment, total (% of the total labor force) (national estimate)—India.* https://data.worldbank.org/indicator/SL.UEM.TOTL.NE.ZS

World Bank. (2020c). https://www.worldbank.org/en/news/feature/2020/04/27/covid19-coronavirus-india-response-health-undernutrition-anganwadi-workers-healthcare

World Economic Forum. (2020, October). https://www.weforum.org/agenda/2020/10/

World Economic Outlook Update. June 2020: A Crisis Like No Other, An Uncertain Recovery. (2020, June 1). Retrieved November 28, 2020, from https://www.imf.org/en/Publications/WEO/Issues/2020/06/24/WEOUpdateJune2020

World Health Organisation. (2020). *A UN framework for the immediate socio-economic response to COVID-19.* https://unsdg.un.org/resources/un-framework-immediate-socio-economic-response-covid-19

World Health Organization. (2020). *The Number of Cases of Corona Disease.* Available from https://covid19.who.int/?gclid=Cj0KCQiAh4j-BRCsARIsAGeV12B-WrtLBICk1963VqpTEMlXEurjro8sjB39Y24yGpEgdmyFjyt-f58aAqwnEALw_wc

Worldometer (2022), *Covid-19 Coronavirus Pandemic.* Meters. https://www.worldometers.info/coronavirus/?utm_campaign=homeAdUOA?Si

World's biggest companies face $1 trillion in climate change risks. (n.d.). Retrieved November 28, 2020, from https://www.cdp.net/en/articles/media/worlds-biggest-companies-face-1-trillion-in-climate-change-risks

WTO. (2020). *WHO Coronavirus Disease (COVID-19) Dashboard.* Retrieved from World Health Organization: https://covid19.who.int/?gclid=Cj0KCQiA7qP9BRCLARIsABDaZzhiVe7ydEgHNhDWQTYF9k5tNnVmOYnx7J70fI-gy7CyCWdZzMy9JLIaAq8LEALw_wcB

YacoubA. R.ZomorM. E. (2020). Would COVID-19 be the turning point in history for the globalization era? The short-term and long-term impact of COVID-19 on Globalization. https://ssrn.com/abstract=3570142 orhttp://dx.doi.org/10.2139/ssrn.3570142 doi:10.2139/ssrn.3570142

Yannick, F. D. (2021). The adverse impact of the Covid-19 pandemic on the labor market in Cameroon. *African Development Review*, 31–44. PMID:33821111

Yhome, K. (2020). *Regional dimensions of global response to COVID-19.* Observer Research Foundation.

Young, H., Jaspars, S., Brown, R., Frize, J., & Khogali, H. (2001). *Food Security Assessments in Emergencies: A Livelihoods Approach, Humanitarian Practice Network (HPN).* Overseas Development Institute.

Zahid, H. (2020). *What about public sector wage bill cuts to finance coronavirus response?* https://blogs.worldbank.org/governance/should-public-sector-wages-be-cut-finance-coronavirus-response

Zhu, Y., Bell, M., Henry, S., & White, M. (2013). Rural-urban Linkages and the Impact of Internal Migration in Asian Developing Countries. *Asian Population Studies*, *9*(2), 119–123. doi:10.1080/17441730.2013.797296

Zimmermann, K. F., Karabulut, G., Bilgin, M. H., & Doker, A. C. (2020). Inter-country distancing, globalisation and the coronavirus pandemic. *World Economy*, *43*(6), 1484–1498. doi:10.1111/twec.12969 PMID:32836720

About the Contributors

Sushanta Kumar Mahapatra, is currently working at Department of Economics, ICFAI School of Social Sciences, The ICFAI Foundation for Higher Education (IFHE) Deemed University, Hyderabad, India. His research areas are applied development economics, agricultural economics, trade and environment, water governance, institutions and policies, climate change and sustainable development, microfinance and livelihood. He has collaborated in research projects supported by organisations like International Rice Research Institute (IRRI), ILO Geneva, Harvard School of Public Health, Sir Ratan Tata Trust, Ministry of Rural Development, Ministry of Education, Govt of India, ICSSR, SBI and NABARD. He has worked as a Consultant to World Bank, Japan International Cooperation Agency (JICA) and Inter State Water Issue (ISWI), Department of Water Resources, Govt of Odisha for Mahanadi Water Disputes Tribunal (MWDT), Constituted by Central Government of India. He has published his research ideas in books, Scopus, ABS, ABDC, UGC-CARE indexed journals, working papers and acted as reviewer for several journals. He is the recipient of Malcolm Elizabeth Adiseshiah Doctoral Merit Fellowship from Madras Institute of Development Studies (MIDS), under University of Madras, Chennai, India and European Commission Erasmus Mundus Post-Doctoral Fellowship (PDF), from the Department of Science Economics (DSE), University of Bologna, Italy.

Vishal Sarin has obtained PhD degree in Economics (Thesis title: Trade relations between India and ASEAN Countries 1991) from Punjabi University, Patiala, Punjab, India. Currently working as Professor in the Department of Economics at Mittal School of Business (ACBSP accreditation by the USA, and the 2nd ranked in the Management field in India) with Lovely Professional University (LPU) since September 2007. His Area of Research included International Trade, Trade Specialization and Competitiveness, Trade Analytics, Trade and Financial Integration, Digital Currency, Financial Inclusion. In academic career spanning over 16 years he has published more than 30 research papers in coveted journals including ABDC Ranking and SCOPUS listed journals, presented papers in 22 conferences, published 4 books, resource person in 12 FDPs on data analysis and research methodology. Prof. Sarin also supervised eight Ph.D. scholars successfully. His area of research includes competitiveness, trade analytics, digital currency and financial inclusion. He is also a member of the Doctoral Board for Economics and evaluated many research scholars at various platforms. Holder of two copyrights on (i) 'Talent Management Index' and (ii) Academic Leadership Competency Assessment Tool (ALCAT) and Academic Leadership Competency Scorecard (ALCS).

* * *

Roshan Adhikari is an MBA graduate from Quest International College. He aspires to be a researcher, and is working hard to improve his knowledge and research abilities. His research interests is in the realm of general management (finance).

Muskaan Arora is working as an Assistant Professor in TSLAS Department of Thapar University. She has 10+ years of working experience in various areas of industry, academics and research. Before joining the current job she worked as financial advisor for 2 years in finance industry and 8 years in top universities and colleges (Chitkara University, Chandigarh University and others) in Punjab. She also worked as Research associate in ICSSR Project at Thapar University. She has attended international conference and her paper is also awarded as best paper in one of the international conferences held in Australia She is also an editor of two derivative books related to Covid 19. Her current job position includes various teaching and administrative related responsibilities in the university. Her keen interest area is doing research and career counselling for the students.

Sugandh Arora is an Assistant Professor at Sharda School of Business Studies, Sharda University, Uttar Pradesh (India). Her work mainly focuses on the effectiveness of household food security in Punjab and on the various PDS reforms. Her recent publications are under Int. J. Economic Policy in Emerging Economies (Inderscience); Emerging Trends in Business Economic, Vol 1. (2020); International Journal of Research and Analytical Reviews (IJRAR) Vol 6. (2019) and Management in Practice Challenges and Strategies (2019). Her research interest areas are Agriculture economics, International Trade, and global food security.

Ida Nyoman Basmantra, was born on October 7 th 1986 in Karangasem-Bali. In 2009, the author was graduated his academic degree of Bachelor of Education from Ganesha University of Education in Singaraja-Bali. He is interested of academic research for business education, assessment and evaluation. Now, he is living in Gianyar Regency of Bali Province and working as international academic staff at Universitas Pendidikan Nasional. Since 2014, he starts his career at international office which responsible for some divisions such as international partnership, international student recruitment, and international service and administration. Then in December 2021, the author graduated from the graduate program of Binus Business School, Bina Nusantara University, Jakarta majoring in Business Management. Now he is active as researcher and assistant professor in Faculty of Economics and Business of Universitas Pendidikan Nasional, Bali, Indonesia. During his career as academic staff, he is continuing his PhD in Istanbul Medipol University, Türkiye.

Shilpa Vasant Bhide is Associate Professor Department of Management Sciences Savitribai Phule Pune University.

Shreyansh Budhia is a George Washington University Economics alumnus. He is an Analyst with Mongabay, worked with TechnoServe Inc. as an associate, an Advisor with the GW School of Business Customer Experience Certificate program, and an Executive Committee Member at the Healthy Climate Initiative. Shreyansh has been published previously by Stanford Economic Review, a Stanford University Economics Journal, and Open Americas, a magazine about current affairs in the Americas. He has completed courses on Environmental law and policy, data analytics, and sustainability, and is an

FMVA candidate set to graduate in August 2022. In his free time, Shreyansh can be found hiking the mountains, watching amazing wildlife, or just reading a good book!

Sevenpri Candra is presently an associate professor at BINUS University. He also serves as a Reviewer for several prominent journals and conferences. Prior to joining BINUS, he has more than 7 years professional career in IT & Consulting Business that give a credence as a Manager. Throughout the time working in different industry and roles, he put his knowledge to focus as a Faculty Member at BINUS. My research interest area is in Business & Technology as well as my specialties as a professional.

Tushar Kanti Das is currently working as Professor in the Department of Business Administration, Sambalpur University, Odisha, India. His research areas are social safety net, social development, centre state financial relations, livelihood study, convergence theory, micro-finance and sustainable development. He has published his research papers in edited books, scopus, UGC-CARE indexed national and international journals. He also acted as reviewer for several journals. He presented his research papers in many national and international conferences.

Niranjan Devkota is an economist with the special focus on cross border activities and climate change related issues focusing adaptation. He has over 10 years of experience in the field of economics related research with varietal dynamics. His recent research focuses ranges from development economics especially in cross-border activities and agriculture. He received his PhD degree from Tribhuvan University Nepal. He has experience in impact analysis and model building. He has worked in terms to prepare strategic and implementation plans of several economic issues as a research associates. He has received high level training and capacity building workshop on international co-operation, natural resource management and trade related activities from several international agencies like SANDEE (ICIMOD), NDRC (China), Hi-Aware (ICIMOD), SANEM (Bangladesh) and from esteemed organizations and universities (online mode). He has command over STATA and basic knowledge of R.

Krishna Dhakal is an MBA graduate from Quest International College. He is currently working as a research associate in Quest Research Management Cell. He has published articles in different journals and attended different national and international conferences. He has brief knowledge on SPSS, AMOS, Kobo Toolbox, Arc GIS and basic knowledge of STATA.

Ruyuna Eric holds PhD degree in economics with specialization of agricultural production economics and Master's degree in applied economics obtained from Annamalai University, India and Bachelor degree in economics and management sciences with economy as option received from Kigali Independent University, Rwanda. He has more than 3 years of experience in teaching at university level where he taught modules including Agriculture, Agricultural Economics II, agricultural production economics, Farm management and Labour economics at Kibogora Polytechnic, Kigali Independent University (Master's Program) and KIM University. He was appointed to be a team supervisor in the consultancy of World Vision Rwanda on the evaluation of community empowerment through economic development "Inzozi nziza project" and participate in the writing of the final report and a consultant at International Union for Conservation of Nature on the business case of payments for ecosystems Services (PES). His interest areas are agricultural production economics, agri business of organically, inorganically and both combined produced commodities through which he seeks to provide significative solutions toward to the reduction of poverty and achieve food security. Moreover, He applies research methodology, Statistics and econometrics to deriving scientific results.

Durafshan Fetrat is currently lecturer at Department of Business and Administration, Economics Faculty, Takhar University, Takhar- Afghanistan. Master of Science (Economics) from Mittal school of business, Lovely Professional University, Phagwara, Punjab India and B.Sc (Economics) from Balkh University-Balkh- Afghanistan. She has worked as lecturer in Department of Business and Administration, Economics faculty at Takhar University since 2015, attended 15 field relevant training and courses, participated in 10 national and international conferences and guided 100 BSc students monographs. Address: District 4- Taloqan city- Takhar province- Afghanistan

Mochammad Firmansyah is a Hospital IT Expert with more than 17 years of experiences in Hospital IT Management, Database Management, Software Analyst and Programming, and also strong knowledge and concept in IT Infrastructure Server, network design, implementation using VMware virtualization. Now Firmansyah handles several hospitals, university and agribusiness at Pundi Raya Group. On 2019 take Postgraduate Magister Management Program at Binus University.

Innocent Gahamanyi recently worked as Accountant at Dream Centre (Africa New Life Ministries) Handling Africa college of Theology accounts (ACT) and six different communities accounts from 2018 August - to date. Gahamanyi is part-time at UNIK (University of Kibungo) Rulindo campus in Areas of Accounts, Finance, and also works partly as Assistant Lecturer at Peace Integrated Polytechnic of Rwanda Kigali Campus in Area of Logistics and Procurement. Gahamanyi used to train Cambridge students about accounting and Finance linked by word link.

Archana Goel is an assistant professor in Chitkara Business School. She has done M.Com, B.Ed.,P.h D and has 12 years of corporate and academic experience. Her P.hd is in corporate governance. Her research areas include corporate governance, mergers and acquisitions, financial reporting etc. She is specialised in teaching accounts, statistics, research methodology and finance courses. She has around 20 papers published in national and international journals of repute and has attended lot of conferences at national and international level. Currently she is guiding one P.hD scholar as well.

Sridevi Gummadi is a Ph.D student. Sridevi is working as a professor at School of Economics, University of Hyderabad. She is currently working on a collaborative UoH-IoE major research project on "Food and Nutrition Security" and has completed research projects on climate change, education and commons. Her research areas cover a wide range of issues relating to food security, health, gender, climate change and economics of discrimination. She has published articles in various journals and edited volumes. She has been teaching courses such as economics of discrimination, commons and livelihoods, international trade and payments, microeconomics and mathematical economics and her research areas interests include food and nutrition security, health care, gender and poverty, economics of discrimination and climate change.

Sourav Gupta is PhD and specializes in Communication for Development, Media Aesthetics and Gender & Cultural Studies. He has a teaching experience of over a decade. He has the rare distinction of teaching in three states. Between 2008-11, he taught at Gurudas College, Kolkata, Central University of

Bihar, Patna and from 2012 onwards he is teaching at the Central University of Odisha, Koraput, where he is presently serving as a Senior Assistant Professor in the Department of Journalism & Mass Communication. He has published 35 research papers in reputed academic journals and as book chapters, presented papers in 20 seminars and delivered 25 invited lectures as Resource Person in prestigious institutions. He is a member of editorial board of several academic journals and has guest edited issues like 'Thetre & Communication' Issue of the Global Media Journal-Indian Edition in 2014.

Aprilia Kusumaningtyas was born on 25 April 1995 in Denpasar, Bali. In 2013 the author continued her undergraduate education at President University, Bekasi, West Java until graduating in 2017 as a Bachelor of Arts in International Relations, with Diplomacy as the concentration. After graduating from college, the author worked at a Public Relations (PR) Agency company in Jakarta as a PR Consultant since 2018. Then in 2019, the author was registered as a student at Binus Business School, Bina Nusantara University, Jakarta majoring in Business Management, and graduated in December 2021.

Surendra Mahato is an assistant professor in the faculty of Management at the Nepal Commerce Campus, New-Baneshwor, Kathmandu, Nepal. Dr. Mahato teaches undergraduate students and conducts research in the area of social science and management. (OrcID 0000-0002-1065-0010)

Lopamudra Mishra is currently working as Assistant Professor in the Department of Economics, Sambalpur University, Odisha, India. She teaches Growth and Development, Econometrics, Macroeconomic Theory and Research Methodology to Post Graduate Students. Her area of research includes ecological economics, social development, public finance and utility regulation. She has published her research articles in edited books, Scopus indexed, UGC-CARE indexed national and international journals. She presented her research papers in many national and international conferences.

Shila Mishra is a well-traveled and published author with a Ph.D. in Economics from RUDN University in Moscow, Russia. Before moving back to Nepal in 2021, she also taught economics and business management to graduate and undergraduate students at her alma mater. Dr. Mishra published work has been primarily focused on international economics and management. She has also collaborated with researchers from multiple reputed universities in economic powerhouses such as the USA and Russia. Dr. Mishra completed her doctoral thesis on the impact of foreign direct investment on the economic growth of Nepal. After coming back to her home country, she worked at National Planning Commission for about two years as a Research Associate and help improve the regional and national economic situation in Nepal.

Fidele Mweruli is Assistant Lecturer at Kibogora Polytechnic.

Tawheed Nabi is currently Assistant Professor at Mittal School of Business ACBSP USA, Accredited, Lovely Professional University, Punjab (India). Dr. Nabi received his Ph.D. degree from DOS in Economics, Karnatak University, Dharwad, and has been a UGC-UPE research fellow. His expertise entails areas like International Trade, Agriculture Economics, and Business Models. He has published his research ideas in journals, edited volumes, conference proceedings in the areas of International Economics, Agricultural Economics, and Business Models. He has presented several papers in International and National level seminars and participated in various workshops and FDP's.

Azatullah Nazari is from Afghanistan and he received the school Diploma (2012) and B.Sc (2015) in economics from Jowzjan University, Jowzjan, Afghanistan and currently, he is a student of M.Sc. economics at Mittal School of Business, Lovely Professional University, and Punjab, India. He has been worked with different universities as a lecturer in Afghanistan, and he looking forward to working as an analyst or a researcher in the field of economics.

Balaji Patturi is working as a UoH-IoE project associate at School of Economics in University of Hyderabad. He pursued M. Phil. from Centre for Development Studies, Trivandrum, Kerala (affiliated to Jawaharlal Nehru University, New Delhi). He worked as a Research Associate at Centre for Economic and Social Studies (CESS) in Hyderabad. He has publications in academic journals and news articles.

Udaya Raj Poudel is a lecturer in the director and faculty of Management at the Quest International College, Kathmandu, Nepal. Mr. Paudel teaches undergraduate students and conducts research in the area of social science and general management.

Karishma Rana is a PhD research scholar of the Department of Economics, Central University of Odisha. She is also working as a Lecture in the Department of Economics in Betnoti College, Mayurbhanj. She is also a motivated, adaptable and responsible fellow with more than five research publications.

Keshab Chandra Ratha is currently working as an Assistant Professor in the School of Political Science, Gangadhar Meher University, Sambalpur, India. He has published his research ideas in various peer-reviewed, Scopus and CARE listed journals and also in working papers, edited volumes, and conference proceedings both national and international. He has participated in a number of orientation and refreshers courses organized and sponsored by University Grants Commissions, Indian Council of Social Science Research, etc. His research areas cover Gender studies, Chinese studies, International Politics, and Governance issues.

Pierre Rutavisire received the following: 2006-2009; Bachelor's degree in Social Work and Social Administration from Kabale University 2011-2013; Master of Arts in Development Studies from Kabale University 5th July-20th Sep 2014; Certificate of teaching in Higher Education institutions from Kabale University 2015-upto data: PhD research scholar at Volgograd state University in the Russian federation

Minati Sahoo is working as an Assistant Professor in the Department of Economics since May, 2013. Prior to joining Central University of Odisha, she has worked as a Lecturer in Economics in Ravenshaw University. She did her MA in Economics from Ravenshaw Autonomous College, Cuttack; M Phil in Economics from Utkal University and Ph.D. in Economics from Ravenshaw University. She has also qualified UGC-NET in Economics. She has published various research papers in leading peer-reviewed national and international journals and edited books. She has also presented several research papers in national and international conferences/seminars. Her research pursuits include Economics of Natural Resources, Gender Economics, Tribal Economics and Agricultural Economics. She is currently teaching Macroeconomic Analysis, Agricultural Economics, Environmental Economics, International Trade, Industrial Economics, and Indian Economic Analysis.

Pareswar Sahu currently serves as Lecturers of Economics at, Barpali College, Barpali, Odisha, India. He received his MA, MPhil and Ph.D from Sambalpur University, Odisha, India. He has participated in number of training, orientation, research methodology and refreshers courses. He has published his research ideas in various journals, edited volumes and working paper series in the areas of Public Finance, Development Studies. Besides, he has presented several papers in International and National level seminars.

Priya Shanmugam is working as an Associate Professor and also Head, Department of Economics, Mount Carmel College Autonomous, Bengaluru. Her area of specialisation includes Industrial Economics, Public Economics, and Macro Economics. She has teaching experience of nearly two decades. She teaches Research Methodology, Environmental Economics, Public Economics and Macro Economics to the graduate and post graduate levels. The utmost that is cherished is the learning experience as a teacher and the bondage shared with the student community.

Rajender Singh is currently working as Associate Professor, Economics at Mittal School of Business (MHRD NIRF India Rank 52; ACBSP USA, Accredited), Lovely Professional University, Phagwara, Punjab (India). In academic career spanning over 15 years, he has served at Assistant Professor Economics, JCDM College of Engineering, Sirsa (Hry), at Assistant Professor, Department of Economics, CDLU Sirsa (Hry), Associate Professor Economics, Mizan Tepi University, Mizan, Ethiopia (Africa). He has attended 15+ relevant training and courses for continuous learning; attended 30 conferences, and published 18 research papers. He has guided 14 M. A. Projects.

Index

A

Accessibility 86-89, 92, 96, 150, 161, 262
Advertisement 201, 206, 210-213, 215
Agriculture Sector 132, 183, 243
APEDA Products 183, 189, 191
Artisans 250, 255-259

B

Banks 18-20, 22, 24, 26, 28, 33, 36-37, 118, 136, 208, 240, 242, 252
Binary choice model 117, 248, 254

C

campaign 80, 201, 203, 219
Carbon Tariff 1, 8
Carbon tax 1, 7-8
CITES 1, 12-13, 16, 204
Climate Change 1, 3-5, 8-11, 13-14, 16-17, 77-78, 111
Cluster 2, 56, 248, 250, 252-253, 258-260, 262-264
Colour 248-249, 251-253, 255, 257, 260
Communication Function 39, 41, 44, 46-50, 53-57
content analysis 201, 206, 218
Coronavirus 2, 14, 16-17, 60, 64-65, 67-69, 71, 73-76, 92, 101, 103, 128, 131, 141-142, 162-164, 178-179, 181, 184-186, 193, 196, 198, 200, 202, 209, 219-222, 231-232, 246
COVID-19 1, 14-16, 18, 20, 28-29, 32-33, 36-37, 39-42, 50, 56, 60, 63-72, 74-78, 80, 89-92, 96, 98-107, 119, 121, 124-130, 132-133, 135-142, 144-149, 151-152, 157-158, 161-167, 174, 178-181, 183-185, 191, 193, 196, 199-204, 206-212, 214-221, 225, 227-229, 231-232, 240, 243, 245-248
Curricular 147
Customers 18-23, 25-28, 32-34, 38, 96, 100, 127, 136, 228

D

Debt Bondage 107, 110, 115, 122
Development 5-7, 15, 19, 37, 56, 64, 69-73, 88-90, 92, 98, 101-102, 104, 108-109, 121-123, 125-126, 128, 130, 142, 147-148, 151-153, 159-161, 163, 165, 168-170, 173, 179-181, 184-186, 196, 198, 203, 217, 220-221, 232-234, 244-246, 248-250, 252, 260-264
Digital Education 147, 149-153, 155-158, 160, 165
Dye 248-253, 255, 257, 260

E

Economic 2-6, 8, 10, 12-13, 15-16, 63-65, 68-73, 75, 77-79, 82, 87, 90-91, 96-97, 99, 101, 103, 105-111, 116-117, 121-123, 125-131, 136-137, 140-142, 148, 150-151, 162, 166-171, 173-175, 178-181, 183-186, 194, 196-200, 202, 206, 217-218, 228, 230-231, 233, 235, 239-241, 243-249, 261-264
Educational Expenses 150, 165
Educational Institutions 39-40, 42, 50, 56, 72, 147-148, 150-152, 156-157, 161, 251
Educationally Disadvantaged 165
ESG 1, 8-9, 13, 15-16

F

Fiscal Policy 166, 168, 174, 179-180, 245
Food Assistance Programmes 89, 91
Food Security 3-4, 67, 72, 78-79, 84, 87-93, 96-106, 168, 183-184, 186, 192-193, 196, 198, 264

G

Global Economy 2, 5, 63-66, 69-70, 74, 89, 125, 127, 132, 196, 244, 262
Globalisation 63, 67, 69, 75-76
Government 4, 6-7, 9, 15-18, 28, 33, 40, 46, 50, 53,

56, 65, 70, 72, 74, 78, 82, 87, 89, 91, 96-101, 103-104, 107, 109-110, 119, 121, 124, 131-132, 136, 138, 148-149, 154-158, 160-164, 166-171, 174-175, 179-182, 184-185, 194, 196, 198, 200-203, 205-213, 215-217, 220-222, 224-225, 228-230, 234, 238, 240-243, 245, 249-250, 252, 254-255, 260-264
Green GDP 1, 7, 13, 17

H

Handloom 119, 121, 249-264
Health 2, 5, 12-13, 40-41, 55, 57, 59-60, 63-66, 68-69, 71-75, 77-79, 84-90, 96, 98-100, 102-103, 105-106, 125-126, 129-130, 132, 136, 139, 141, 147-148, 150, 157, 162, 164, 166-171, 173-175, 178-179, 181, 184, 192, 196, 198, 200-218, 220, 230, 235, 238, 246, 251-252

I

Ikat 248, 251, 261-264
Impact 2-3, 5, 8, 10-13, 20-23, 26, 31-33, 35-36, 38, 40-45, 47-49, 53-57, 59-60, 64-67, 69-70, 72, 74-76, 78, 89-90, 96, 99, 101-106, 119, 122-126, 129-133, 139-142, 149, 156-157, 162-169, 174, 178-181, 183, 185, 187, 192-193, 196, 199-200, 208, 215-216, 220-222, 232-233, 235, 239-247, 262
India 1-4, 7, 16, 36, 63, 67, 70-71, 77-80, 82-92, 96-97, 99-110, 119, 121-123, 148-155, 158-163, 165-168, 170, 174, 177-186, 191-193, 197-202, 205, 210, 212, 217, 219-222, 224-225, 227-231, 233, 235-239, 241, 243-244, 246-248, 250, 261-264
Indian Economy 75, 79, 102, 167, 169, 176, 179, 183-185, 225, 232, 235, 246
International Bodies 63-64
Internet Banking 18-29, 32-38
Involuntary Work From Home 39-43, 46-50, 53-54, 56-57

J

Job Satisfaction 39, 41-42, 44, 46-50, 53-62

K

Kathmandu Valley 18, 20, 25, 33

L

Labor Force 106, 124-125, 127-131, 133-135, 137-141, 239
Labour 70, 75, 78, 108-111, 114-116, 118, 121-123, 140-141, 178, 208, 222, 225-226, 228, 230, 248, 250-251, 261, 263
Learning 16, 34, 40, 42, 50, 59, 125, 147-151, 153, 156-163, 165, 227-228, 244-245
Livelihood 3, 65, 72, 99, 103, 107, 109-110, 114, 117, 119, 122, 130, 184-185, 196-197, 199, 248, 250-252, 254, 258-263
Lockdown 68, 71-72, 78-79, 84, 87-88, 90, 96-98, 101-106, 127-130, 136, 142, 148-150, 156-158, 161, 163, 165-168, 171, 173-175, 181, 183, 196-197, 200, 202, 206-207, 217, 221-222, 226, 233, 235-236, 238-243, 245, 249, 260
Loom 248-249, 251, 254-255

M

Manufacturing Industry 220-222, 225, 227-230
Marginalised Group 77
Media 16-17, 37, 41, 49, 51, 70, 79, 165, 201, 203-207, 210, 213-214, 218
Micro Small and Medium Scale Enterprises 233-245, 247
Migration 44, 63, 67, 73, 82, 96, 107-111, 114, 116-123, 208, 248-249, 261-262
MoHFW 163, 201, 247

N

New Normal 8, 67, 149, 161, 220, 222, 226, 228-229, 243, 245
Nutritional Security 77, 84, 92

O

Odisha 101, 107-114, 116, 121-123, 147, 149-158, 160-162, 164, 166-173, 175, 178-179, 181-182, 184, 200-203, 205-210, 216-219, 248-249, 251-252, 260-262, 264
Online 19-22, 25-27, 32-38, 40, 44, 50-51, 56-57, 59-60, 126, 130-132, 138, 147-150, 152-153, 155-165, 201-202, 204, 214, 234, 240, 244
Online Platform 165

P

Pandemic 2-3, 12-13, 32, 36-37, 39-42, 44, 46-48, 50, 54-58, 60, 62-72, 74-79, 82, 84, 87, 89-92, 96-100, 102-104, 106-107, 119, 121, 124-142, 144-149, 152, 156-158, 160-168, 171, 174-175, 179-180, 184, 196, 199-203, 205-206, 209-211, 213-217, 219-223, 225-229, 231, 233-236, 239-246, 249, 260
Pedagogy 149, 165
performance 8-9, 22, 35, 37, 41-46, 48-49, 58, 60-61, 84, 101, 126, 130, 150, 167-168, 170-173, 179-181, 184, 201, 203, 205-206, 208, 240
Post Pandemic 2020 220, 228
Private 1, 7, 13, 36, 40, 91, 127, 129, 132, 136-138, 156, 159, 169, 176, 186, 202-210, 213-217, 242, 253
Public Policy 107, 121-122

R

Regional Institutions 63-64, 67
Restoring 73, 124, 128, 138
Rwanda 124, 126-128, 130-131, 133-140

S

Sector 7, 12, 19-20, 35, 63, 65, 69, 75, 78, 87, 90, 100, 104, 109, 125-127, 129-133, 136-139, 141-142, 147, 149, 157, 160-162, 164, 174-175, 182-187, 191, 193-194, 196-203, 205-208, 220-224, 226-231, 233-246, 248-250, 252, 260
Self-Paced Learning 149, 165
Socially Disadvantaged 107, 111, 114, 119, 122
Socio 233
Stability 43, 49, 72, 79, 84, 86-89, 101, 171, 196, 198, 221
Strategies 8, 61, 73, 102, 104, 124-125, 127-129, 133-135, 138-139, 160-161, 164-166, 174, 194, 202, 209, 218, 222, 226, 244, 246, 249-250
Sustainability 1, 7-10, 13, 37, 91-92, 102, 106, 139, 161, 165, 171, 194, 198-199, 250, 263

T

Technological Illiteracy 149, 165
Telecommuting 41, 43, 47
Teleworking 41, 47, 58, 61

U

Unemployment 6, 77, 82-84, 87-89, 106, 121-122, 124, 128, 131-133, 135-141, 143, 145-146, 148, 150, 169, 240
Utilization 84, 89, 92, 96, 169

W

Weavers 121, 249-252, 254-262
WHO 2, 8, 14, 16, 22, 25-26, 28, 32, 40-42, 45, 49-50, 55, 57, 64-67, 69, 72-74, 78-79, 84-88, 90, 98-99, 107, 111, 114-116, 119, 122, 126, 128, 136, 139, 148-150, 157, 165, 167, 169, 181, 184, 200, 202-203, 205, 208-209, 213, 217, 219-220, 222, 230, 240-241, 244, 247-249, 254-259
Work From Home 39-51, 53-57, 150
Work Life Balance 39, 41-45, 47-50, 55-57, 61
Work Productivity 39, 42-50, 53-57

Y

Yarn 121, 249-252, 255, 260, 263